THE GENIUS OF SPIRIT
Using Dreams, Meditation, and Self-Awareness
To Stop Insanity and Help Humanity

BY
DR. MARINA QUATTROCCHI

"The Genius of Spirit," by Dr. Marina Quattrocchi. ISBN 978-1-62137-388-9 (Softcover) 978-1-62137-389-6 (eBook)

Library of Congress Control Number: 2014903646

Published 2014 by Virtualbookworm.com Publishing Inc., P.O. Box 9949, College Station, TX 77842, US. ©2014, Dr. Marina Quattrocchi. All rights reserved. No part of this publication may be reproduced, stored in a retrieval system, or transmitted in any form or by any means, electronic, mechanical, recording or otherwise, without the prior written permission of Dr. Marina Quattrocchi.

Manufactured in the United States of America.

DEDICATED

*In loving memory of my parents Mary and Murray Quattrocchi,
who always encouraged me to write and to dream.*

CONTENTS

FINDING PEACE

We're brought up in this restless world of money, stress, and greed,
Believing that prestige and power, are really what we need.
We spend a lot of money, but it never seems enough,
Needing countless things, makes life forever tough.
Houses are expensive, clothes, cars, all this stuff.
To keep up with this spending, for anyone is rough.
We need degrees or training, in order to succeed,
To earn a lot of money, to match these endless needs.
We're trained to live so fast, we hardly stop to think,
That we can live a different way, that's not just swim or sink.

With all this frenzy and flurry, how can peace or insight grow?
In a world that moves so fast, there is wisdom in moving slow.
Our minds listen to countless trends, telling us how we must be,
But the mind has little common sense, because only the spirit can see.
Spirit understands this folly of jumping from trend to trend,
Your spirit is there for solace; it's always been a true friend.
Spirit flows like a graceful river, with a purpose and power that's true,
While the mind careens like a roller coaster, losing sight of you.

The things on earth most precious, can never be bought or sold,
Peace, tranquility, compassion, love, are the soul's dealings in gold.
We could own five Mercedes, and a castle in England and France,
But if we have poverty of spirit, the soul never learns how to dance.
We cultivate peace and compassion, by connecting to our hearts,
Praying for guidance and insight each day, is the best way to start.
Then our soul will whisper to us, conveying the wisdom of spirit,
But we must rest and be quiet each day, before we can actually hear it.

We don't have to give up all pleasures, live in a convent, or stop drinking wine,
We don't have to sit cross legged for hours, meditating on something divine.
Simply gaze at a tree or the water, watch a candle, or go for a walk,
Slowly we lose the insanity, as we listen, rather than talk.
Over time our life changes, as spirit makes us wise.
We drop the layers of ego, that have been a clever disguise.
We begin to see the seductions, that have always kept us trapped,
A bigger TV, or a gadget that's free, illusions so nicely wrapped.

Instead, we cherish memories of a sunset, a trip, or a friend,
We stop buying endless stuff in a life that's all pretend.
Slowly the dramas fade away while a peace and rhythm ensue,
Life falls into a natural order that is the authentic you.
We understand it's more important to live ethically each day,
Treating everyone with respect has been the only way.
When we go for walks we marvel in the beauty all around,
We sing, play music, paint, or dance, and savor every sound.

Until one day we realize, that spirit soars above the mind,
Crossing into dimensions that do not imprison or bind.
What we really needed to discover these wings and soar,
Was patience, faith, and quiet, to find that elusive door.

May you find your way out of sadness, discontent, and despair,
To a place of greater purpose; fulfillment that's always been there.
May you soar with the greatest purpose, tranquility, and relief,
As you rise above the craziness, that causes us so much grief.

May the warmth and wisdom of spirit, bring you a purpose that's true,
With grace and a heightened awareness, a calming support for you.
May you carry these gifts of spirit, bringing peace to our troubled Earth,
May you light the way for others, knowing this light gives birth.
For peace and love are precious, they're the fuel we need to live,
And like all gifts of spirit; they are free for us to give.

Marina

INTRODUCTION

FOR MOST OF MY LIFE I've been trying to operate with limited brain capacity, which I'm sure is why genius fascinates me. Since childhood, I've experienced chronic migraines, struggling to simply get through a day. When a migraine strikes, I'm literally a zombie: it feels as if my brain cells have been sucked through a vacuum or migrated offline. Nothing is easy or automatic as I struggle with simple tasks like dialing a telephone or cooking a meal. I'm literally a space cadet. Everything is slow, tedious, and takes inordinate amounts of energy. If I do something ambitious like make my bed, I need to rest. Talking becomes a gargantuan task because you can't retrieve words–it's difficult and draining to follow a conversation if someone phones. I stride into rooms, then have absolutely no idea why I'm there; open kitchen cupboards and discover frozen chicken that should be in the freezer. I can't remember anything; names, faces, what appointments I might have, or what day it is. I stumble, lose my balance, fall, drop things, and break coffee cups, as my world becomes a precarious place that spins, gyrates, darkens, or projects a dazzling display of colors, clouds, and spiraling lines. If a migraine hits while I'm driving, I can't remember where I am, where to turn, or where I'm going! When I was still desperately trying to lead a normal life as a teacher, I often had no memory of what I taught the day before, or what I just said in a lecture. Thoughts, words, actions evaporated into elusive ethers. Fortunately, I must have been a great actress. One day when I was teaching a senior English class a student asked me to explain something in an assignment I'd given out the day before, but I had no memory of writing it, or what the assignment was about, so I couldn't answer his question. I knew at that instant, I was losing it totally and couldn't keep up the charade of being a teacher any longer. I was severely burned out. My brain was beyond fried–it was almost disintegrated and desperately needed repair. But on days when I didn't have migraines it's as if all my brain cells have suddenly jettisoned back online. I can tackle complex theories in books, read for hours, write, and remember how to dial the phone. I've spent most of my life in a crazed world where I flip back and forth from brain dead to fully functioning. Since I'm so seriously brain impaired during these migraines that often last weeks or months, when my brain does kick in again, I actually feel like a genius. So I know firsthand it's possible to switch from a life of seething insanity, to one of graceful genius. I'm also aware I don't have to be a genius myself to activate wisdom and genius in others.

A second reason stems from what I observed from my students while teaching. When you teach a compulsory subject like English, there will be students who are brilliant, while others struggle to form a simple sentence, with one clear exception—whenever we did dreamwork, miraculously all their brain cells fired in perfect harmony. They had clear insights and heightened awareness—they were overnight sages, seasoned scholars when they discussed or wrote about their dreams. Grammar and sentence structure altered dramatically and they waxed eloquent. The first time this happened, I actually thought this student had cheated; someone else must have penned that sage-like assignment. Except, they were all just as clear and insightful when they did their oral presentations. Their speech matched their writing. I am eternally grateful to these students who taught me the mystery of genius that resides in spirit.

In addition to being mentally impaired most of the time, I've also spent much of my life residing in the world of dreams where fortunately I've never had a migraine. For as long as I can remember, my dream recall was vivid and very real, so I've gone through life straddling both dimensions, the physical world, and the endlessly fascinating dimensions of dreams. I've journaled and studied my dreams for over 30 years now, and spent about the same amount of time as a serious meditator, activities which change your life indelibly. Without the guidance from my dreams and the peace and tranquility that ensues from meditation, I'm sure I would have jumped off a bridge way before now. The spirit worlds have always been my place of sanity and solace and they are real, viable, and vital to me. However, I am very aware that this is not the case with everyone. For most readers much of this information will be new, unfamiliar terrain; and that's fantastic. I compared my first book *Dreamwork Uncovered*, to a fourteen course meal and told readers it was fine if they didn't digest all fourteen courses. I knew there would be concepts and theories many people would be uncomfortable with. I also said no teacher or writer is God on a mountaintop and we certainly don't have all the answers. No book could be one hundred percent accurate unless the writer was fully enlightened, and if I was fully enlightened I wouldn't be putting frozen chicken in my cupboards. So early on I feel a need to repeat the same message. There will be concepts here that completely challenge your linear left-brained way of thinking. There will be times you may be shaking your head and thinking I've taken way too many pain meds. But, there may also be times, when something you've read resonates inside you completely, like finding that last piece of a puzzle you needed so desperately. It's not my intent to convince anyone they need to agree with everything they read here. Later in the book we're going to examine the principals of karma and dharma, and I believe it's exceedingly karmic to expect anyone to accept all of your beliefs. There are universal truths, but there are also individual truths, and each of us is here to hone our gifts of discernment—to know deep inside if something we read or hear is *our* truth. How boring our world would be if we all robotically believed the same things. Much of the information you will read is an attempt to activate the right brain, and grasping this type of information can be tough. I remember feeling like it was giving me headaches from the mental gymnastics of it all, so be gentle with yourself. Assimilating new concepts takes time. After meditation or yoga, we're advised not to jump up immediately, to allow the information and insights time to settle into the psyche. We all need time to allow information to filter through the complex structure of our brains until it settles as understanding. I hope you will digest only those thoughts and ideas that nourish you and feel right, but that the entire book will be food for thought.

We desperately need this genius of spirit in our insane, yet beautiful world. I believe the mind is simply not capable of the wisdom needed to end wars, poverty, pollution, and global unrest. Genius lies waiting to be discovered within all of us. It has always been the only way out of darkness and despair—the transition from a hell or god-awful earth, to a heaven on earth. Genius of spirit is the portal we're all destined to pass through to transition from mere mortals, mediocre, mechanical, often depressed and despairing, to alert, awake, aware–gracious gods operating with heightened awareness, wisdom, compassion, love, and superpowers our mortal minds could never have imagined. Consider that reading these pages is akin to entering that portal, making the discoveries and connections that challenge and coax your mind to new levels of understanding, awareness, and most certainly peace. As you journey through these pages I hope you will savor and enjoy each time you feel more of those brain cells waking up and activating your personal genius.

PART ONE
ACTIVATING A COMPASSIONATE MIND

There is more to life than simply increasing its speed.
Mohatma Ghandi

CHAPTER ONE
WAKING UP TO THE DREAM OF LIFE

*Reading books about anything and everything does not
necessarily lead to wisdom.
It's just as easy to be an educated fool as it is to be an untaught genius
What you need more than information is insight.*
Phil Booth-astrologer

*Wisdom is not to be obtained from textbooks,
but must be coined out of human experience in the flame of life.*
Morris Raphael Cohen

A donkey with a load of holy books is still a donkey.
Sufi saying

Genius of the Heart versus Insanity of the Mind

LIKE MANY PEOPLE I WANTED to be rich, smart, and successful. So my ego tricked me into believing the only way to achieve this was through the mind. I listened to those relentless voices that said, "You're really stupid, you'll never be good enough, she's way smarter," or, "You have to make something of yourself." As a child, I felt different, like the ugly duckling born into an alien world. Needing an escape, I turned to reading, devouring books like candy; they became my refuge and solace. In school, even though I managed to get good marks, things didn't come easily; I felt like a caterpillar crawling through life. Since I struggled for every mark, it was no simple task cramming my head with all these facts. As a teenager, I studied to become smart and successful, until my brain just about exploded. I tried desperately to fit in or be accepted, even though I was never sure I wanted to be part of a world that seemed insane at its best, and cruel at its worst. My mind told me there were no alternatives—you just needed to fit in.

Early in life, I began getting excruciating migraines. I tried to push away the pain like last night's nightmare, but it always resurfaced. The pain was relentless, an ominous cloud that seemed to suck any joy and purpose from my life. It felt like living inside a dark, heavy, oppressive, storm system with no way out. I took courses to become smarter, trying to forget about the pain, believing if I could shift my focus away from the pain, in time it would go away, except it never did. So I took more courses, and read about migraines and pain because I was sure the answers had to lie in books. I studied and read so much, I was no longer aware that truth and insight were waiting to be discovered in spirit.

Life became robotic—I went through the motions, going to work each day to become successful. With all these headaches, courses, degrees, and qualifications I didn't have the time, inclination, or energy for love. I rarely dated, never married, and didn't have children. I became an automaton—controlled by a mind linked to this insatiable ego. Acquiring knowledge, like money, drugs, alcohol, possessions, or sex, can be an addiction. I never felt I had enough—always wanted more. So I took more courses, eventually completing five degrees and a myriad of qualifications. This continued into my forties until I became so burned out and pain ridden I couldn't work. Ironically, after spending a lifetime building up credentials, I couldn't use any of them, and my mind felt like soggy porridge. Then all those emotions I had buried for decades broke through. For years I cried and felt sorry for myself. It felt like I needed buckets around my neck to contain this tsunami of pain and despair. Secretly, I wished I could drown my sorrows in drugs or alcohol like the rest of the world, except they only made the migraines worse. My mind convinced me I was a dismal failure, too pathetic to even bury my angst in the escapist world of drugs or alcohol.

Around this time, a friend, Deborah, suggested I write a book on dreams, but she said I must write from my heart, not my head. My porridge-like mind thought, "Don't you have to write *everything* from your mind? Doesn't wisdom, genius, facts, common sense, all come from the mind? How could it be any other way? My mind wasn't able to figure this out, because the mind has absolutely no wisdom; facts maybe, information, knowledge, statistics, but not insight, clarity, or true genius. I had devoured every book, magazine, website, and journal article written on migraines, but that didn't make me one iota smarter when it came to eliminating the pain. You can read books until your brain just about explodes, but not really be that clever. You can be a Ph.D. with little common sense. You can study world religions, philosophy, self-help and spirituality, but never feel peace or contentment. You can be a psychiatrist, analyst or psychologist, who is dismal and depressed, leading a totally dysfunctional life. You can be the president of a country with no ethics, vision, and a heart of stone. You can be a prime minister, politician or priest, who has never felt or expressed empathy or compassion.

My case was one of extreme lopsidedness—pushing away soul or spirit, the only thing that truly heals and informs, but I've observed I'm not that different from most of the world. We're working longer hours, never have enough time, reading about wars daily in the papers, then dying of cancer or heart attacks, before we've had time to enjoy our retirement. We're so desperately out of balance, living in a world of great physical and emotional pain, living from crisis to crisis, until we become so robotic, so entrained, we believe this is the only way to exist.

Somehow in this muddle, I realized there is a different road if we learn to operate more from our hearts, not solely from our minds—soul or spirit informing the mind, not the other way around. When we live in a world out of balance, a world dominated by ego or mind, we experience the whole gamut of mind-based lunacy—despair, depression, hopelessness, doubt, fear, guilt, and physical pain. The key to ending this insanity is embedded deep within our hearts or spirit, the place of meditation and dreams.

Peace versus Power

Most of us spend our energy seeking the highs in an effort to avoid the lows.
Unfortunately these false highs are not really nourishing.
Niro Asistent

Nature is full of genius, full of the divinity.
Ralph Waldo Emerson

How far to heaven? Just open your eyes and look. You are in heaven.
Sri Ravi Shankar

We're indoctrinated into a world that tells us money, success, and personal power are the elixirs of life, and when we achieve them, we'll be happy. Since working long hours, having lots of degrees, and being constantly exhausted is also equated with success, I had been tremendously successful, but it felt horrible and unfulfilling. Finally, I realized all I'd ever been searching for was the peace and tranquility that's found from connecting to your spirit. Rather than trying to find peace I was seeking happiness in the highs of life. I wanted to be at the top of the roller coaster all the time, because I didn't understand it's impossible to maintain this state; it's even a scientific law—what goes up must come down. However, it is possible to find and maintain the wisdom and serenity of balance, or the middle road that Buddhists speak of. Peace and tranquility does have the power to sustain us—we can't coast forever on the energy of artificial highs. Like most people on the planet, I was under the illusion that happiness was equated with these highs. This doesn't mean we have to give up any of these things; instead we keep these activities in balance. A glass of wine with our meals is healthy, but alcoholism is a life out of balance. Karen Casey, a recovered alcoholic, explains this universal dilemma well. She says for her serenity didn't feel like happiness because, "It was too quiet, too mellow and too calm. It didn't make our hearts race. Our addictions had sent us soaring and we defined that high as happiness." She says true happiness feels more like contentment, and it takes time to build the discernment needed "to appreciate this quieter, longer-lasting happiness." This epidemic of seeking highs isn't a chronic situation only with young people, extreme sports enthusiasts, alcoholics, and drug addicts—it has plagued much of the world, zapping us of equanimity or balance. Part of the problem is that spirit doesn't shout to get our attention. It waits, with the patience of eternity, never intruding when it's not wanted; working instead while we dream, meditate, or simply go with the flow.

When we do find peace, it's like walking temporarily in heaven, and there are many fringe benefits: we gain the ability to love unselfishly, the clarity and insight to see through illusions and to know what is truth, we have the focus to carry out our destiny, and unending joy in experiencing little things in life, like the song of a bird, the beauty of a sunset, or the caress of a loved one. When we truly feel peace, we lose that incessant desire for more external things and replace it with gratitude for all we have, allowing simplicity and harmony. The desire for great amounts of money, prestige, or power, fall away naturally like a snake shedding its skin. We realize we have the ability to earn what we need to live comfortably, creating balance, rather than accruing massive amounts of money creating great "abundance" or imbalance. If it's our destiny to earn millions, we use this money to give back, helping those in need, and ironing out the imbalances.

When I understood that peace and balance was this golden elixir I needed to survive, I couldn't go to my corner variety store to buy it. I wasn't really acquainted with peace because for a lifetime I'd been led by my mind, and peace can only be felt through connection to spirit. I tried desperately to acquire peace by reading books. I had an impressive library of books on religion and spirituality, but this was all mind stuff. My friend Deborah was right; this was not operating from the heart. I don't think I began feeling my first true moments of peace, or natural highs, until I stopped working full time, put all these academic books aside for a long time, started reading what my mind told me was fluffy stuff like novels, and spent years going for very long walks and bike rides alone. When I felt these first fleeting moments of peace I finally understood the phrase, "heaven on earth." I seemed transported to a place that felt either like heaven, or the best drug or alcohol money could buy. It was like being transported to a parallel dimension, a movie set, dream world, lala land, maybe the place where angels or fairies reside, but it definitely felt different from the artificial or superficial highs of earth. When you begin experiencing this place even for a few seconds, you hooked—never want to return to those ups and downs or harsh realities of life—except you must, until you've done the hard emotional work of cleaning up karma and living in dharma, which we'll talk about later in this book.

Reaching this blissful feeling of heaven is simple, yet so complex. With peace, we also feel clarity rather than confusion, faith rather than fear, joy rather than despair, and a deeper love, since we feel a dynamic connection to everything in the universe. We can't conceive of hurting anyone, because we understand how we're all inextricably linked; it's akin to harming yourself. Love and peace are intrinsically related like the Chinese yin yang symbol; part of something simple, beautiful, and whole.

It was easiest to feel this peace surrounded by nature, jumping into a lake on a summer day and feeling my whole body tingle, or going for long walks in the country. The first twenty minutes was just clearing my head, then I would observe and listen to the beauty that surrounded me, and I'd start feeling I didn't need all my material possessions, because I could be completely happy forever in a T-shirt and shorts. The trappings of life began to feel artificial, unnecessary. I've felt peace going for long bike rides, only after I'd cleared my head of everything I had to do and when I got to a place I could just immerse myself in nature, listen to the birds singing and watch the sunlight playing on the creek beside me. I've felt peace sitting alone at night meditating, watched the slow warm burn of a candle, or when my cat sat on my chest purring as I stroked him. The same feelings emerged in the middle of a yoga class, when my mind was suspended, my body just began to flow effortlessly, and time slipped away. But these moments were elusive, like fireflies illuminating the night. After that momentary feeling of bliss, you realize you don't have the jar, bottle, or skill to contain these highs for more than a few seconds.

As I've gotten older, I'm starting to have more of these experiences that feel like I've been momentarily transported to another dimension. I'm convinced we establish doorways or portals into these experiences through service to others, meditation, connection to nature, prayer, and dream work, and as the earth's changes continue, I believe we're moving into a golden time in history—an age when the doors to these dimensions will be opened for true seekers, often when we least expect. One summer evening I was driving north on the Don Valley Parkway in Toronto, after having dinner with my cousin Joanne. It was around 8:30 p.m., and the sun was beginning to set. I hadn't been on this particular highway for years and was marveling at how lush and green it had become. Then, in a seamless instant, it felt like I had been transported to another dimension—my mind knew I was in the middle of Toronto, but I was in a parallel place of indescribable beauty, a meandering highway in another place where the colors were breathtakingly vibrant and beautiful—rich purples and pinks like nothing on earth. It filled me with awe, wonder, and incredible peace lasting about 10 minutes, then faded slowly as I merged onto the 401, another major highway.

Another time I was in bed with a horrible migraine. I had awoken at 5 a.m. with pounding pain, then finally drifted asleep and slept until 11 a.m. When I opened my eyes, it felt like I was in a parallel place of unequaled beauty. My cat Small Fry came and sat on my chest, and as I stroked him I felt intense peace, love, and comfort. The sun was bright and as it came into the window everything sparkled like thousands of diamonds—it felt like I was in another enchanted land. This feeling was a warm, magical comfort, and I felt calm, surrounded by stunning beauty beyond words.

I believe these places and experiences of peace, bliss, and harmony are available to everyone, except that most of us are just too busy and caught up in life to find them. Imagine being told you were royalty, and that your birth place was a kingdom of great beauty and balance. You'd never really tried to go "home" before, because you really weren't aware this was your place of origin. We're all like this, lost souls, not realizing it's our birthright to feel contentment, fulfillment, peace, and unconditional love on a regular basis. This is our true state—not the plastic insanity we're used to. It's not impossible to gradually enter an awareness, to live in a place that feels much different from the heaviness and insanity of earth. That's what this book is about—learning to hold onto those moments, until they become woven into the fabric of who we are. It takes focus, determination, and faith. It's not easy, but not impossible. In fact, living any other way is incredibly harder. There will always be great hardships and heartbreaks in life—loved ones will die, we may lose our jobs, or our health. There will be earthquakes, storms, floods, hurricanes, poverty, disease, and disappointment. This is why it's important to connect to something greater, bigger, more expansive, wise, and comforting, to buffer us through the turbulent times. It is possible to leave the madness temporarily, to be nurtured and restored, then to calmly return, strong and grounded, like an oak tree, unscathed by countless storms.

Dimensional Travel—Finding Heaven on Earth

I would rather live in a world where my life is surrounded by mystery, than live in a world so small that my mind could comprehend it.
Henry Emerson Fosdick

If at first, the idea is not absurd, then there is no hope for it.
Albert Einstein

Many of us grew up believing that heaven was some mystical pie in the sky, an ethereal, non-physical domain, with streets of gold, angels playing harps, and wispy clouds concealing endless joys. But what if heaven really resembles the most beautiful places on earth? What if it's not really up? What if we don't have to die to visit heaven because it's more than just a place; it could be an experience, a heightened awareness, a gift, a connection to spirit that elevates and alters.

If crossing into other dimensions seems totally ludicrous, the first step is probably to begin journaling your dreams. When we become serious students of dreamwork, it's much like travelling to distant countries for the first time—suddenly all those once imaged destinations become real, vibrant, and meaningful. But for a more immediate understanding visualize a block of ice—something solid that can be compared to our human body. If the temperature rises that block of ice will turn into water. Now it has greater mobility and is not confined to one spot, flowing and moving outwards and even merging with its surroundings. If the water is heated again, it becomes steam, rising up into an invisible state. If we're watching water being boiled, we know it still exists somehow, only now it's in a more energetic, gaseous form with its greatest capacity for movement. In our lowest form we're all like those blocks of ice, with limited mobility, but in our spirit or soul form we're like the water vapor possessing greater metaphysical energy and unlimited ability to move and explore.

Like that invisible water vapor, heaven exists right here on earth. It is a parallel dimension, only we can't see it with our physical eyes because it vibrates at a much higher frequency. We're not really separated from heaven, even though we can't buy an airline ticket to travel there. Visualize several places or dimensions overlapping, while still being part of a larger system; like the shades of Venetian blinds, the pleats in a skirt, a string of beads, or floors in an apartment building—all are inextricably linked. There are doors, portals, and passageways into heaven, just as there are many doors, exits, elevators, and levels in large buildings. We've all had pure, simple, joyful, or unadulterated moments, when we've found these portals and crossed into temporary peace or bliss. When we have these experiences, if only for a few seconds, we come back changed, lighter, transformed; we vibrate at a slightly different level, and the more awakened our vibrational level, the easier the next crossing becomes. It's like taking spiritual medicine in small doses that eventually rids us of all germs and infections. At some level, we all know we have much loftier purposes for coming to earth than simply retiring comfortably, or buying a dream home. In fact, we will never feel completely at peace, we will always be restless, wondering, stressed and obsessed, until we find the way to the true home of our soul—heaven on earth. We live in an auspicious time, because this partnering of heaven and earth has never been closer; it's been prophesied for centuries in all the great mystical teachings, and is available for every faith, religion, or atheist, since God or spirit excludes no one. Astrologer Phil Booth tells us, "Other dimensions or planes of existence surely exist out there, but we won't find them through space travel. Access to them will come through a journey into our inner universe. Socrates, Buddha and Christ taught to look within to find enlightenment." In the Bible, (Ephesians 1:10) St. Paul tells us that when the times have reached their fulfillment, all things in heaven and earth will be brought together under one head. In Revelations, Chapter 21, John tells us, "I saw a new heaven and a new earth. The first heaven and the first earth disappeared, and the sea vanished. And I saw the Holy City, the new Jerusalem, coming down out of heaven...I heard a loud voice speaking from the throne: 'Now God's home is with mankind! He will live with them, and they shall be his people. God himself will be with them, and he will be their God. He will wipe away all tears from their eyes. There will be no more death, no more grief or crying or pain. The old things have disappeared." Jesus tells us, "Let not your heart be troubled....In my Father's house are many mansions: If it were not so, I would have told you. I go to prepare a place for you." (John 14:1-3) Isn't it possible that these mansions are actually dimensions, and that Jesus needed to use a language that people could understand two thousand years ago? Jesus ushered in the age of Pisces. Before his coming brutality, hatred, inhumanity were rampant; people flocked to stadiums to watch gladiators fight to the death, women suspected of adultery were stoned to death, thieves were crucified, races were enslaved and treated like animals. His simple yet profound messages of love, faith, tolerance, and compassion began to transform the world. Now we're entering a new era, the sign of Aquarius, and astrologers explain this transition won't happen overnight—it takes a few hundred years and earth's events are rapidly unfolding, ushering in possibilities that until now were the stuff of our wildest imaginations. This is a time of greater compassion, possibility, and hope; when darkness will be forced to claw back its illusions, seductions, and infections, to make way for an earth that is much like a satellite of heaven. Marianne Williamson talks about this in *Everyday Grace,*

"I have always had a sense that something is missing in this world—that at the very least there is something important we're not discussing. I believe that hunger for a 'lost dimension' of experience is a natural yearning in all of us, and it doesn't go away just because we ignore it. It is evidenced among other places in the millions of children and adults who obsessively read the Harry Potter books. It is said that fiction is where someone gets to tell the truth. We *are* a bunch of silly Muggles, and really *do* miss out on the magic of existence. There's a collective knowing that a dimension of reality exists beyond the material plane, and that sense of knowing is causing a mystical resurgence on the planet today. It's not just children who are looking for a missing piece. It's a very mature outlook to question the nature of our reality."

In *The Faith Club*, a compelling book bridging the three major faiths of a Muslim, Christian and Jew, Craig Townsend says, "…Maybe we are living with one foot in this world and one foot in the other, but because we are stuck in our bodies, in this space and time, we can't perceive it…Heaven is not a reward for faith. But rather, our faith allows us to see that we're in God's kingdom already…" Kathleen McGowan tells us in *The Poet Prince,* that we're all really here for one thing, "creating heaven on earth …The pure and perfect truth of life is that we are here to create heaven on earth, to bring the perfection of what is above down to us, and in doing so to become transformed as human beings into something great and beautiful." She says we accomplish this through "the utter appreciation of Beauty in all its forms" and "through the veil of love."

We can begin the work of dimensional travel with the same methodical preparation it takes to plan any trip. We begin simply with the desire for heightened awareness, consciously working to release our dark side or karmic patterns, by journaling and being attentive to our dreams, and by spending time in nature, with animals, or in quiet meditative activities. As these pages unfold, we're not going to talk only about dreams, although dreams play a huge part; we're going to examine life. Dreams were never meant to be separate from our lives. They're meant to inform and instruct, just as our lives inform our dreams. The mind or left brain likes to put everything in boxes. It categorizes and sees boundaries and divisions. When we're left brain or mind dominated we have a separate category for dreams, then we deal with the *real* stuff in our physical life. Hopefully you will begin breaking down those boundaries. Meditation and dreams prepare us for that subtle shift of consciousness into heaven while still living on earth. Perhaps you've had a decadent banana split, chocolate cheesecake, great sex, walked in a lush garden, listened to uplifting music, gazed in awe at a sunset, or had a vacation on a tropical paradise, and said, "That was heaven." You were absolutely right. Heaven is a shift in vibration and awareness and it can be a heartbeat away. Beginning to reach heaven on earth is often shifting our awareness to one singular event—single pointed focus. As we'll learn—that's all meditation really is—single pointed focus into a timeless, soothing place. To reach heaven on earth we need to learn how to stop or suspend the mind and its incessant worrying and chatter. We all know how to do this; the trouble is we don't do it often enough. We're all out of practice, and we don't value it in our chaotic society. To prove this, whenever you've felt transported by that banana split or decadent pizza, concert, symphony, romantic encounter, garden, wildlife reserve, or sunset, you probably weren't thinking; "I've got to set my alarm for 6:30 tomorrow morning, I've got to make sure I iron my pants before I go to bed, or I need to buy milk on the way home." When you experienced bits of heaven, you weren't thinking at all, which was why you were able to be transported—you temporarily suspended the barriers of your ego, mind, or left brain. When these boundaries break down, subtle doors open, and we drift into heaven.

The novel, *The Celestine Prophecy,* describes a time when humans learn to raise their vibrations so high, they become invisible to those around them, like an airplane propeller revolving so fast we can't see it. The book says this future time "will signal that we are crossing the barrier between this life and the other world from which we came and which we go after death...At some point everyone will vibrate highly enough so that we can walk into heaven, in our same form...." It also says that reaching heaven on earth is why we're here in the first place, which makes more sense than dying in wars, bombings, and car crashes, or hell and purgatory or limbo. Isn't it possible that our bodies don't *always* need to experience a physical death? Ever wonder why people in the Bible were still fathering children and giving birth when they were 150? Wouldn't God, a loving Creator, be more likely to design a child who lived forever? Or would He create a less efficient version—one whose body broke down after eighty or ninety years? Wouldn't a wise, compassionate God allow us to travel and work in other dimensions, rather than dying a slow painful death from heart disease, cancer, or AIDS? Wouldn't He weep, just as we do, when someone we love dearly dies, seemingly gone forever, or is the finality of death just another clever illusion? Renowned physic Edgar Cayce, was able to restore the health of thousands of clients, often bringing people back from the brink of death. Because of this, he is often considered the father of holistic medicine since his cures involved natural remedies. Cayce believed if one maintained a healthy diet, lifestyle and attitude, there was no reason to believe we could not live as long as we wanted. In a reading he said there is no death, except in our minds. We only believe we must die because we have watched it happen to so many before us. Unfortunately, Cayce did not follow his own advice—his diet was deplorable and he worked himself to exhaustion, but he certainly left us with something to consider. We're going to examine longevity and how we definitely are going in this direction later in the book.

My favorite activity is definitely sleeping and dreaming, probably because after over 30 years of recording dreams, it's became apparent I was traveling into other dimensions; worlds where colors were more vibrant, where you can jump into the air and fly, or climb onto a horse's back and soar over stunning landscapes. I'd go to places of incredible peace, but sometimes dimensions where the customs, laws, and ways of living were completely different, sometimes unsettling, verging on cruel. Often these parallel dimensions were so similar I believed I was on earth, but familiar buildings or streets that should have been there were missing, so I'd walk around in circles. My body was on earth, but my soul had travelled to other dimensions, helping me become more aware, and to gain an understanding of parallel places or the astral plane. Over the years I've realized that I've traveled to or experienced five separate dimensions. Most of our dreams take place right here on earth and those dreams are unmistakable because we might dream we visit a friend in England, return to the place we work, or ride our bike down a familiar street. Dimension two is one of time, we frequently go forward in time while dreaming to observe, test things out, and experiment with possibilities. Since we can't change the past, we frequently time travel into the future. Dimension three is the astral plane, a place that looks similar to earth, but is quite different—it's here where we often get lost. Dreams in dimension four are rare, but unmistakable because of the vibrant colors and intensity—here you may see flowers that are huge—hybrids of what we have on earth with pulsing energy. The architecture of buildings is futuristic and more advanced with warmer, richer colors. Sunsets and the sky are glorious beyond words; in one of these dreams I recorded that the sky was like huge panes of stained glass windows constantly changing color. And finally there was once a fifth dimension—perhaps the closest to heaven—here everything is a dazzling pure white, and rather than seeing physical bodies there are beings that are translucent moving forms of energy.

If you've never worked with your dreams, this concept of parallel or overlapping dimensions is like the stuff of science fiction or fantasy, but once you become a serious student of dreamwork, it's impossible not to begin accepting these worlds as viable and real. We can't see these dimensions with our physical eyes, but they're definitely there, vibrating in different frequencies. It's like tuning into different radio or television frequencies; while we hear only one station on our dial, this doesn't mean that hundreds of other stations don't exist simultaneously. We just need a radio or television set to capture them. Consider that you may be able to capture heaven on earth, with your eyes shut, and spiritual eyes open; we can travel to other dimensions, which is why people love daydreaming.

For hundreds of years, planes, boats, and people have been disappearing into the Bermuda Triangle, an ocean area bounded by Bermuda, Florida, and Puerto Rico. Despite extensive investigations, these phenomena can't be explained. Thousands of people have vanished, possibly crossing to a different dimension, frequency, vibration. Historically, we've been intrigued by civilizations that seemed to vanish with no logical explanation of where they went or why: the Mayans, Incas, Atlanteans, and inhabitants of mystical Avalon and Shangri-La. Maybe they were advanced enough to raise their vibration and cross to a safer place. Perhaps there has always been this option of a more peaceful crossing over, but our minds convinced us otherwise. Possibly, in this century, a few enlightened individuals will show us the way.

One hundred years ago, the concept of flying an airplane was considered science fiction or fantasy. People thought Orville and Wilbur Wright were out of their minds, crazy, hopelessly delusional, for thinking they could fly. Scientists believed a heavier than air flying machine was a physical impossibility, and it had been proven mathematically by the leading experts in physics in their time. The very idea was a gross violation of the laws of nature. But Orville and Wilbur Wright were creative geniuses who had dreamed, observed birds in flight, experimented, compiled databases, analyzed, tested, and retested—they didn't listen to the naysayers. Their first flight in 1903, at Kitty Hawk, North Carolina, lasted only 12 seconds and covered a distance of 120 feet. But five years later, at Fort Meyer, Florida, Orville Wright took off, circled the field one-and-a-half times, and landed after one minute and eleven seconds. President Roosevelt, who witnessed the event, said the crowd went crazy with excitement. "When the plane first rose, the crowd's gasp of astonishment was not alone at the wonder of it, but because it was so unexpected. I'll never forget the impression that sound from the crowd made on me. It was a sound of complete surprise." By 1911, the Wright's first airplane crossed the United States. The flight took 84 days, stopping 70 times, and it crash landed so many times that little of the original materials were intact when it arrived in California. A hundred years later, thousands of planes take off and land every second, and we can't conceive a world without air travel. Isn't it possible that one hundred years from now, people won't be able to fathom a world without dimensional travel? Certainly cheaper and less cumbersome than commercial flying!

Preparing to Fly

Fantasies are more than substitutes for unpleasant reality; they are also dress rehearsals, plans. All acts performed in the world begin in the imagination.
Barbara Grizzuti Harrison

Despite realizing that all wisdom can't be found in books, I've never stopped a lifelong love affair with them, because the best books *are* inspired by spirit. An ever increasing number of books and movies are exploring parallel worlds, other dimensions, and being transported or teleported through worm holes. A hundred years ago, few books dealt with these topics—perhaps we weren't ready for this one giant leap. Dimensional travel might have begun in 1865 with Lewis Carroll's *Alice's Adventures in Wonderland*. In the novel Alice falls down a rabbit hole, what we would describe today as a dimensional tunnel, until she feels she must be "getting somewhere near the center of the earth." Alice encounters strange customs and other worldly beings like the White Rabbit, Cheshire Cat, Caterpillar, Tweedledum and Tweedledee, Mad Hatter, and Queen of Hearts. She leaves only after waking up from her dream. The original Mary Poppins books, penned between 1934 and 1988, described the magical powers of English nanny Mary Poppins, including her ability to fly. In *The Chronicles of Narnia*, written by C.S Lewis, between 1949 and 1954, four English children, Lucy, Susan,

Peter and Edmund, walk through a wardrobe, the portal or dimensional door into another kingdom, Narnia, where they return many times to courageously break the spell of an evil witch. Lewis was a close friend to J.R.R Tolkien, whose 1950s *Lord of the Rings* series takes place in another dimension, Middle Earth, a land of hobbits, elves, dwarves, and wizards. His books are so detailed and carefully crafted, one wonders if they are not real. In J.K. Rowling's fictional series, Harry Potter and his friends cross dimensions by walking through a wall or gate at a train station, gate 9 3/4, into their true home, or magical kingdom. Here everyone has the ability to use powers that would astound mere mortals, like us, or Muggles, who are completely unaware that a whole universe lies right beside them. In Neil Gaiman's novel *Stardust,* the hero, teenager Tristan Thorn, ventures across a forbidden wall at the edge of his English countryside town, and walks into a parallel world. Although these worlds are just footsteps away, no one in Tristan's dimension, (except his father) has ventured into this separate reality, or is aware it's even there. In Guy Gavriel Kay's trilogy, *The Fionavar Tapestry,* five University of Toronto students are transported into another world of kings, seers, princes, shamans, unicorns, magis, dwarves, and dark gods. The students make several journeys into this kingdom, despite a catastrophic war being fought in this parallel land. Why? They realize if darkness has been unleashed in Fionavar, it will spread like a virus to other dimensions, eventually trickling down to earth.

Phillip Pullman's Dark Materials trilogy, beginning with *The Golden Compass*, is an intriguing series to get our minds around the concept of multiple dimensions that are separate, yet joined. The heroine, Lyra, lives in a dimension much like England, except everyone has a strong emotional link to their dæmon, (pronounced demon, which is a muse, guide, or guardian spirit) an animal believed to be part of their soul. Lyra, like Harry Potter, is a Messiah figure; her birth was prophesied, and she has an enormous role to play in fighting darkness. In the second novel, *The Subtle Knife,* we meet twelve-year-old Will Perry who resides in a parallel universe. Will stumbles upon a small window or dimensional door that has been left open, and crosses into a third reality, Cittagazze. It looks much like earth, except soul-eating Specters have infiltrated, killing off many humans and turning it into a huge ghost town. If these energy zapping Specters are not stopped, they will completely devastate this world. In Cittagazze, Will meets Lyra, and he becomes the guardian of this subtle knife which allows him to cut doorways into other dimensions. In the final novel, *The Amber Spyglass,* the children go back and forth between three dimensions, Lyra's, Will's and Cittagazze, but we're introduced to a fourth dimension—a dark underworld, where the dead are rescued or released by the heroine Lyra.

A fascinating movie *Jumper*, directed by Doug Liman, uses teleporting or jumping to other places to examine the human condition. Liman's question behind this movie was, what if we really had the ability to teleport to other places, what would we do with these super powers? He believes these abilities would act like an amplifier and whatever vices or karma you had would just get stronger. The movie illustrates that saying, "Absolute power corrupts, absolute power corrupts absolutely." David Rice, played by Hayden Christensen, realizes at age fifteen, that he has the power to jump or transport himself through wormholes to any place on earth. With all this power, David's life might have followed two paths. He could have taken the high road or dharmic path, becoming a superhero like Batman, or Superman, rescuing victims in car accidents, flood, fires, or robberies. Or he could choose a karmic, hedonistic, egocentric route. Unfortunately, David chooses the low road, and the movie explores how karmic choices always turn our lives into a living hell. David was deserted by his mother when he was five, his father is an alcoholic, and he's had no real role models. Once David masters these powers, one of his first jumps is inside a bank vault. He begins teleporting back and forth, stealing enough money so that he'll never need to work or worry about money again. It never occurs to David that he could help himself or others with these powers; he's under the illusion that money, status, and power bring happiness—a deadly trap.

Eventually he becomes a playboy, living in a luxurious New York apartment, spending the day surfing in Australia, having lunch atop the Spinx in Egypt, or strolling in Rome's Coliseum. This self-indulgent lifestyle lasts about eight years until David is pursued by Roland, played by Samuel L. Jackson, a "palain", whose mission in life is to kill every "jumper" he can find. Palains have been hunting and killing "jumpers" for centuries and Roland believes, "no one except God should have that kind of power." He tells David, "You think you can go on like this forever—living like this with no consequences. There are always consequences." With Roland in pursuit, David's life becomes a frantic quest just to stay alive.

In television, our fascination with dimensional travel began in the 1960s with *Star Trek*. In the series, the star ship Enterprise had a mission to seek out new civilizations and "boldly go where no man had gone before." We watched as Captain Kirk and his crew went to the transporter room, their bodies dematerialized, and they were sent around the galaxy by Scotty, the ship's teleporter. It looked as easy as taking a shower, and this tricky business of beaming down to other galaxies and star ships, usually went off without a hitch.

Thirty years later, another television series *Stargate SG1*, became one of the longest-running shows in history. It gave birth to a sister series, *Stargate Atlantis,* where a group of scientists has discovered the lost city of Atlantis. In a third series, *Stargate Universe*, a present day exploration team is unable to return to earth after traveling to a distant corner of the universe. In *Stargate SG1*, a more sophisticated system of space travel has been discovered. Scholar Daniel Jackson decodes ancient Egyptian artifacts revealing an intergalactic gateway, or Stargates, wormholes linking earth to distant planets and galaxies, allowing space teams to dial the co-ordinates of where they wish to go, step through the gate, and arrive in seconds, far less time than the hundreds of millions of years it would take in a spaceship. These Stargates or mini airports, which exist around the galaxy, are huge rings or gates, like airport terminals. Several Stargate teams, operated by the United States Air Force, travel around the universe fighting darkness and engaging in interstellar peace-keeping missions.

We are indeed endeavoring to go where no human has gone before, because teleporting through space has taken quantum leaps into the world of physics. Michio Kaku, a theoretical physicist at the City College of New York, is a respected leader in this interstellar universe. He's written several books, hosts a nationally syndicated radio science program, and has appeared on television shows such as *Nightline, 60 Minutes, Good Morning America,* and *Larry King Live.* Kaku is the co-creator of string field theory, and his research pursues Einstein's dream of a "theory of everything" a unifying theory of all the forces in nature. His 2005 book, *Parallel Worlds: A Journey Through Creation, Higher Dimensions, and the Future of the Cosmos* became a bestseller. He tells readers another universe or dimension could be floating a millimeter away on a "brane" or membrane parallel to earth. If earth was ever doomed or threatened in the future, we could escape to other universes or build a "time warp" and travel back to our past; an entire civilization might inject its seed or genetic code through a dimensional gateway, and re-establish itself completely! In 2008, he published *Physics of the Impossible: A Scientific Exploration of the World of Phasers, Force Fields, Teleportation, and Time Travel,* where he explores force fields, psychokinesis, telepathy, time travel, teleportation, faster-than-light travel, parallel universes, and precognition. Kaku says, "Any science fiction aficionado has seen it all before; beaming through walls, riding in starships that move faster than light, or traveling instantly to distant places in space and time. These ideas aren't just creative fantasies, though; they emerge from theoretical physics, especially the work of Albert Einstein, whose vision included a universe that curves back on itself in three dimensions of space, and a fourth, invisible dimension of time. If Einstein's version of the universe is correct and experiments done over the last century suggest that essentially it is, then the fictionalized feats based on his theories might be possible as well." Kaku envisions a future where humans are able to teleport to other places and dimensions. He says, "Physicists hope to teleport complex molecules in the coming years. After that, perhaps a DNA molecule or even a virus could be teleported within decades."

String theory, or this unifying "theory of everything" is relatively new, originally developed in the early 1970s, but immensely important, because for the first time scientists began realizing that several unobservable dimensions must exist. It's an attempt to link quantum physics which studies the smallest objects in nature, things like atoms, particles, quarks and electrons, with relativity, which studies the big things, planets, galaxies and the universe. Anything attempting to unite these two, are theories of quantum gravity, and string field theory may be our most promising hope because it has the potential to unravel the biggest mysteries of the universe, how gravity (the big picture) and quantum physics (the little picture) fit together. It was this "unified theory" or "theory of everything" that challenged Einstein and remained unsolved until the end of his life. In 1951 he wrote, "The unified field theory has been put into retirement. It is so difficult to employ mathematically that I have not been able to verify it somehow, in spite of my efforts. This state of affairs will no doubt last many more years, mostly because physicists have little understanding of logical-philosophical arguments." String theory only makes sense when we have more than three dimensions, and we do have three dimensions in space, left/right, up/down, and front/back, *but* it's believed the extra dimensions of space are curled up or *compactified* to such small sizes the human eye can't see them. It's also believed that every object in the universe is composed of vibrating filaments or strings and membranes or *branes* of energy. One may visualize this by thinking of strings on a violin, with the membranes or branes of energy as the wooden base, making our universe a vast harmonic symphony of celestial energy or as Einstein once said, "the music of the spheres."

Kip Stephen Thorne is a professor of theoretical physics at the California Institute of Technology, and an expert on the astrophysical implications of Einstein's general theory of relativity. Thorne's research deals with stars, black holes, and gravitational waves, but he's best known for his controversial theory that worm holes could be used for time travel. He's written, "Time travel was once solely the province of science fiction writers. How times have changed! One now finds scholarly analysis of time travel in serious scientific journals, written by eminent theoretical physicists...Why the change? Because we physicists have realized that the nature of time is too important an issue to be left solely in the hands of science fiction writers."

There is already evidence that our DNA can be electromagnetically teleported with the work of biologist Luc Montagnier who won the Nobel prize in 2008 for establishing the link between HIV and AIDS. Montagnier published a paper in 2010, "DNA waves and water," explaining the reasons for his research were to "develop highly sensitive detection systems for chronic bacterial and viral infections." His dream is to eradicate HIV, so that patients in the future will no longer need to be treated for life with toxic and expensive drugs. His research suggests that DNA can teleport itself with the use of electromagnetic signals. In the experiment two test tubes were used, one containing a fragment of DNA, and the other contained pure water. The two test tubes were isolated in a special chamber. Several hours later DNA was recovered from both tubes even though the second should have only contained water. Montagnier believes that DNA emits its own electromagnetic signals that imprints on the DNA's structure on other molecules, in this case water. This means DNA can project itself where copies could be made or quantum teleportation of genetic material. Since this paper was released, other research teams around the world have reported their own versions of teleportation, notably a research team at the University of Science and Technology of China. They successfully entangled two photons and sent the higher energy one through a ten-mile tunnel–a giant leap from previous experiments!

And dimensional travel is not just the stuff of novels, movies, and television shows. Every night while we sleep, our soul transports us to other dimensions as we dream. Back in 1958, a successful New York businessman, Robert A. Monroe, began floating out of his physical body, without any apparent cause. He had full conscious awareness of these events, which took place when he was napping or sleeping. It was Monroe who first coined the phrase "out of body experiences" or OBEs. When these OBEs first took place he was forty-two, married with two children, taking no medication, using no drugs, drank very little alcohol, and wasn't involved in any religion, nor was he an advocate of Eastern philosophies. Monroe chronicled his multi-dimensional experiences for over 40 years, publishing three books, *Journeys Out of the Body, (1971) Far Journeys (1985)* and *Ultimate Journey (1994)*. In the beginning Monroe said it was "impossible to describe the fear and loneliness that took over these episodes." He even consulted and was tested by a psychiatrist and psychologist, who assured him he wasn't psychotic! Reassured he was of sound mind, Monroe documented each journey out of his body like a rigorous scientific experiment. In the first few years he described blunders such as getting stuck by huge walls he had no idea how to penetrate, and learning how to deal with demonic little entities that would wrap themselves around his back! As he gained experience, his fears receded and were replaced with intense curiosity, which we'll discover is the trademark of all geniuses or wisdom seekers. Much like a veteran pilot, he became a master in dimensional travel, recognizing and naming multiple layers of reality, routinely visiting friends he had made in distant universes, and even discovering how to assist ghosts or lost souls who had no idea they had died. Monroe tells us in *Ultimate Journey* this separation from our physical bodies can be two inches or thousands of miles; in the out-of-body state we're no longer bound by time and space, and our nonphysical self is comfortable in other energy systems. We have a great sense of freedom, but in fact we're not totally free because like a balloon or kite on a tether, at the other end an invisible cord is connected to our human body. In *Far Journeys* he explains that during out-of- body experiences, "you find yourself outside of your physical body, fully conscious and able to perceive and act as if you were fully functioning physically—with several exceptions. You can move through space...slowly or apparently somewhere beyond the speed of light. You can observe, participate in events, make willful decisions based upon what you perceive and do. You can move through physical matter such as walls, steel plates, concrete, earth, oceans, air, even atomic radiation without effort or effect...You can visit a friend three thousand miles away. You can explore the moon, the solar system, and the galaxy." During these explorations Monroe was taught by higher or enlightened beings, who helped him realize the importance of service to humanity and the power of love. He realized the goal of humanity was to reach this state of enlightenment, or as he says, "to grow and evolve somehow into the awe-inspiring yet warm being that I happily called my "INSPEC" (short for intelligent species). Fueled by these discoveries, in the early 1960s, he funded and opened The Monroe Institute, initially to study his own OBE experiences. He assembled a team of hundreds of specialists in psychology, psychiatry, medicine, biochemistry, electrical engineering, physics and education, along with computer programmers, corporate executives, artists and musicians, and it has grown into a research and educational organization recognized worldwide for its work in understanding human consciousness. Thousands of students travel to Virginia each year to take part in their programs on how to have

OBE experiences, emotional and spiritual growth, tapping into our healing powers, developing psychokinetic abilities (using the mind to manipulate matter, time, space or energy), remote viewing, losing fears of dying, strengthening the immune system, and support for pregnancy and childbirth.

Every night while dreaming, like Monroe, we become our own interstellar travelers, without needing Scotty to beam us up. Because our souls are already master navigators, the best place to begin experiencing dimensional travel and teleporting is through meditation and dreams. In *The Promise of Sleep,* Dr. William Dement, a sleep and dream pioneer tells us, "Every night nearly every person on the planet undergoes an astounding metamorphosis. As the sun sets, a delicate timing device at the base of our brain sends a chemical signal throughout our body, and the gradual slide toward sleep begins. Our body becomes inert, and our lidded eyes roll slowly from side to side. Later the eyes begin the rapid eye movements that accompany dreams, and our mind enters a highly active state where vivid dreams trace our deepest emotions. Throughout the night we traverse a broad landscape of dreaming and non-dreaming realms, wholly unaware of the world outside. Hours later, as the sun rises, we are transported back to our bodies and to waking consciousness. And we remember almost nothing."

Power Training—Choosing Earth over Heaven

In childhood we learned to compete with our classmates, and this taught us to be critical of one another. No teacher tested us on how we expressed love; rather, we worked on spelling and multiplication tables, and we were pitted against the students for the gold stars.
Karen Casey in *A Woman's Spirit*

If we are disconnected from our spirit, and rarely experience the innate joys of heaven on earth, the ego or mind takes the helm and we invariably follow two routes. First we turn to all things external; drugs, alcohol, work, affairs, shopping, books, movies, television, entertainment, or holidays, all in an attempt to capture those fleeting highs. But often, we try to use any form of power or money as a substitute just as David Rice does in the movie *Jumper*. This quest for power has become an insidious virus, deeply ingrained, and mindlessly carried out. Power has become the universal drug of choice since it gives a tremendous high, but ironically, we can achieve greater natural highs when really linking into spirit, our authentic or real power.

Power training begins in childhood where we're encouraged to get the highest marks, score the most goals, come first in the music competition, dance your way to number one, or finish college or university to "make something of yourself." But we are already "something" since our spirit has tremendous natural powers that lay largely untapped. Making something of yourself is usually mind based and external, often equated with making lots of money; we're encouraged to do a lot, and spend a lot, putting our soul or spirit on the back burner, never discovering why we're here in the first place, and what our true purpose and power really is.

Most children's games are competitive, and just about every movie, game, magazine, and television show carries the insidious message that to be successful you need to somehow make a lot of money, achieve power or recognition, or buy a lot of stuff, to become happy. As children we're groomed to believe in Santa Claus, the giver of gifts and happiness. We're brainwashed to believe that we can make children happy at Christmas by buying them a lot of toys, feeding the monster of consumerism. But Santa is an illusion, along with the fact that Jesus was born in December. What was originally a winter Solstice Festival celebrating increased days of light, has morphed into Santa, a time when we power shop. For some, this is a time of light, warmth and family; for others a time of deep depression, suicide, and despair. Isn't it interesting that not long ago, Santa Claus in a red suit didn't exist at all? Our ancestors didn't buy into the madness that is now Christmas. Instead, Christmas was either a celebration of light, or the birth of Jesus, the bringer of light and peace, and more people understood and revered their dreams rather than Santa and shopping.

This quest for things and personal power has infiltrated our world like a virus. We grow up in the belly of a monster, vicariously wanting success and power even in our sports and hobbies. Our language reflects this obsession; we have power shopping, power walking, power cardio, power bars, power drinks, heroes with super powers, even power yoga, a meditative activity initially intended as a path to enlightenment and peace. We idolize sports celebrities, creating pseudo gods who are paid millions to throw a football, kick a soccer ball, or put a puck in a net. There is absolutely nothing wrong with playing a sport for a living. It's incredibly hard work and some of these superstars are inspiring role models; the problem lies in balance—in the last hundred years we've created a society where we pay people more money to play games than we pay doctors, nurses, firefighters, or paramedics to save lives. Those who want power in their jobs intimidate, boss and bully in an attempt to reach the top, or work incessantly long hours to make more money. Religions claim to be all-knowing, corporations attempt to be number one, and countries vie to be superpowers, killing and destroying each other in the name of false gods to keep this power, while we desperately try to achieve world peace. We idolize the rich and famous, making them our false gods and goddesses, unconsciously giving them the same status once reserved for mythical Greek heroes. Somehow we've forgotten our real goal is not physical power and money, rather the authentic and lasting power that comes from richness of spirit.

In 2004, the CBC television ran a campaign to determine who had been the greatest Canadian of all time—in other words who had most powerfully captured our hearts and minds? The competition was fierce; Wayne Gretsky, Don Cherry, Terry Fox, Pierre Trudeau, and David Suzuki were some of the candidates. The winner was probably the greatest humanitarian Canada has ever known, Tommy Douglas, the Father of Medicare. Thanks to Douglas, every Canadian has access to free universal health care. This came about when Tommy was a young boy living in Scotland, where he had fallen, injuring his right knee. Osteomyelitis an infection in the bone marrow set in, and he underwent several operations. After immigrating to Winnipeg, the osteomyelitis flared up again and doctors informed his parents that Tommy's leg needed to be amputated. Fortunately, a well-known surgeon intervened and agreed to operate for free, as long as his parents would allow medical students to observe the surgical procedures. Several operations followed, and his leg was saved, a life-altering experience, convincing him that health care should be free for everyone. "I made up my mind that if ever I had the power I would, if it were humanly possible, see that the financial barrier between those who needed health services and those who gave health services was forever removed." To pursue that goal he transitioned from Baptist preacher to premier of Saskatchewan, never compromising his spiritual beliefs. Indeed it was his years as a preacher that made him such a dynamic speaker. Douglas believed, "Politics is rooted in spirituality and the desire for a better world." He also believed that politics was all about service and not ideology. He once said, "I'm not interested in power, except for how it can help other people." Douglas understood what true power was all about. In 1973 he said, "To accept the principal that all power proceeds from the barrel of a gun, is to accept a society which will be dominated by those with the biggest guns." Even though he was never elected as prime minister, it's said he pursued his ideals so relentlessly, they became so mainstream that other political parties claimed them as their own. In additional to being a political star, the Douglas family contained its share of movie stars. Tommy's daughter Shirley Douglas followed in her father's footsteps becoming a social activist, then an accomplished actress. She married actor Donald Sutherland, and their son, Kiefer Sutherland is Tommy's grandson. However, the Douglas family never lost sight of what true power was all about. The only power that passes the test of time, comes from the heart, and always lies in service to others.

Reality Television—The Social Mirror

The true measure of a human being is determined primarily by the measure and the sense in which he has attained liberation from the self.
Albert Einstein

With all this adulation of the rich and famous, it's no surprise that reality television has gone viral, quite a phenomenon since reality television didn't really take off until 1999-2000. Reality television presents a fascinating mirror reflecting back the consciousness of our times, the good, the bad, and the all too often ugly. We've become captivated by these programs, despite the fact that they often portray humanity at its worst, with all our thorns, issues, and dysfunctions. Perhaps they are a huge social experiment designed to wake us up, because ironically dreams work *exactly* the same way. We rarely have blissful or pleasant experiences in dreams, because their purpose is to hold up a huge mirror to our lives, reflecting back all our issues, fears, insecurities and karmic patterns.

Here are just a few of the most popular reality shows that have transformed our air waves;

America's Got Talent, American Idol, America's Next Top Model, Average Joe, Amazing Adventures of a Nobody, Beauty and the Geek, Big Brother, Canadian Idol, Celebrity Rehab with Dr. Drew, Dancing with the Stars, Dating in the Dark, Deal or no Deal, Extreme Makeover: Home Edition, Fake-A-Date, Farmer Wants a Wife, FearFactor, For Love or Money, Gene Simmons Family Jewels, Hell's Kitchen, Here Comes Honey Boo, Boo, Househusbands of Hollywood, How to Look Good Naked, I Didn't Know I Was Pregnant, I Love Money, I'm a Celebrity Get me Out of Here, I Want to be a Hilton, Jersey Shore, Joe Millionaire, Jon & Kate Plus 8, Kate Plus 8, Keeping Up With the Kardashians, Kitchen Nightmares, Kourtney and Kloé Take Miami,

Make me a Supermodel, Megan Wants a Millionaire, My Big Redneck Wedding, My Dad is Better Than Your Dad, My Big Fat Obnoxious Fiancé, Outback Jack, Pussycat Dolls Present, Sister Wives, So You Think You Can Dance, Sexy Cam, Survivor, Trading Spouses, The Apprentice, The Apprentice: Martha Stewart, The Amazing Race, The Bachelor, The Bachelorette, The Biggest Loser, The Celebrity Apprentice, The Osbournes, The Restaurant, The Search for the Next Doll, The Simple Life, The Swan, Train Wrecks, Paris Hilton's My New BFF, Race to the Alter, Real Housewives, Second Chance: America's Most Talented Senior, So You Think You Can Dance, Village on a Diet, Virgin Diaries, Wife Swap, Who Wants to Marry my Dad?

Ironically, most of these shows reflect a created reality; they are elaborate, costly constructions, fabrications, often with the sole motivation of making money, and since they're not real, they perpetuate sophisticated illusions of the mind. The mind, like the "Me" or "I" generation, competes, eliminates, manipulates, tricks, deceives, lies, judges, gloats, and excludes, all in its quest for domination and power. It's a lone wolf, never a team player. Reality shows are even more insidious because many thrive on creating losers who experience all the negative emotions of the mind: depression, rejection, low self-esteem, anger, humiliation, jealousy, and contempt. In contrast, soul or spirit never wants to be number one, the best, richest, and most glamorous. Competition is not the way of spirit, but these shows have become so insidious, that many young people growing up on a steady diet of reality TV are socialized to believe one of the best ways to achieve success is through competition. Spirit in its wisdom does exactly the opposite; it co-operates, welcomes, honors, respects, accepts, nurtures, encourages, inspires, builds alliances, and includes. When we believe we must compete to claw our way to the top or even survive, we lose that vital connection with spirit—that tiny voice inside that guides us in the right direction helping us use our God-given talents to achieve our destiny or dharma. We lose faith in the natural order of things and replace it with artificial reality. The only way out of this reality insanity is to rely on or seek the wisdom and solace of spirit.

The hilarious thing about human beings is that we never want to admit we're less than perfect, which is why we dream every night reflecting a truer reality. Even members of the Mafia idolize their dons, believing they are clever heroes. Reality television does exactly the same thing as many of our dreams. When we watch these shows we sometimes see humanity at its greediest worst. But all of these people, clamoring to get on the shows, believe their behavior is perfectly normal, and they're right, it is perfectly normal for the mind to behave this way—but never spirit. We watch as the minds of these participants delight in confusing, lying to, and manipulating their opponents. Perhaps in twenty or thirty years if these contestants watched themselves, they would be shocked at their behavior, but while appearing on the show, they're immersed in a complete ego-based culture. These participants are focused, which is a good thing, but their focus is all in a karmic direction—fame, money, success, winning, being number one, often completely at odds with their soul or spirit. Competition is not the way of spirit. Often these participants, like Faustus, are selling their souls to the false gods of television, who promise fame, money and success.

Real power or success is not a million dollars or the accolades of being the best celebrity dancer, survivor, or next Pussy Cat Doll, because real or genuine success is not physical or external in nature—it's spiritual. The type of power touted on reality television is elusive—you can lose a million dollars in a heartbeat with one bad investment, and even if voted the best dancer or singer, that fame only lasts until the next series declares a new winner. Nothing physical lasts forever.

We're all familiar with the phase, "more power to you," and how it's synonymous with achieving worldly power as an ultimate goal. Hey, you're vice president now, more power to you! You've bought a bigger home, more power to you! You ran the marathon, more power to you! But on a deep level this desire for physical power comes from a sense of lack, or feeling powerless. In *The Book of Awakening,* Mark Nepo reminds us of that childhood game, King of the Hill, and how it becomes power training for life. If one clamors their way to the top he says, "You're completely alone and paranoid, never able to trust anyone, constantly forced to spin and guard in every direction…those on top can be so enslaved by guarding their position that they rarely enjoy the view." He says worldly power is really controlling power—power over things, people and situations, what most of us strive for our entire lives, rather than working towards *inner power*, the authentic "power that comes from being a part of something larger–connective power."

Real power is moving closer to the awareness and grace of enlightenment, where you are truly free of the viral need for money, wealth, or fame. In an advanced state of enlightenment, you have no need for millions because you can manifest whatever you need. You can't lose your voice or break your leg because you're no longer completely physical. If humanity was more awake, more evolved, this is the success we would all be clamoring to achieve. This success is the real deal—you earn it through lifetimes of hard work, patience, faith, and perseverance, and once you're there, no one can take it away from you, except elements of darkness, but in this enlightened state, you have far too much genius to throw it away. It's more precious than the finest gold—it's the authentic you.

Think back one hundred years ago, another era, when our great-grandparents' homes didn't have televisions, radios, telephones, or even light bulbs and the main method of transportation was horse and buggy. Can you imagine your great-grandfather wanting to compete on a reality television show like *Survivor, The Apprentice,* or *The Biggest Loser*? Back then, life was more focused on survival, only it wasn't a game, and people's lives focused around making ends meet and community. Competition wasn't part of the game because it didn't foster survival. Farmers built barns and homes; women had cooking and quilting bees, everyone gathered at the general store, and danced together on Saturday nights. They had far less materially, but weren't as greedy, selfish, or self-absorbed. Reality television is only popular because we keep succumbing to the illusion that a million dollars is the key to happiness and success, despite the fact that ninety-five percent of all lottery winners claim it ruined their lives. For all our sophisticated gadgets, we've taken enormous steps backwards when it comes to wisdom, spiritual genius, and how to genuinely be at peace.

If you love reality television, there is certainly a reason, so I'm not advocating anyone giving it up. Perhaps watch it more consciously, as a giant screen for all that is distorted, greedy, dysfunctional, and desperate in our world. It is a fascinating social and psychological drama that never ceases to amaze. Like everything else in life, it can be viewed positively or negatively—it has brought people with tremendous talent to the forefront and launched their careers. But it has caused immeasurable tears and heartbreak. Why would you need to be the best celebrity dancer, when you are already a celebrity worth millions? How much celebrity status is enough? Reality television is indeed viral, but the real virus is the insatiable need for money, recognition, fame, and power and this type of virus can only be healed by connecting to our spirits.

Having money is fine, in fact, it's necessary to function on earth, as long as we balance money with spiritual wealth, or head with heart. When we achieve this balance, we may just find that elusive success the whole world is chasing after in reality television. We all want sanity, balance, fairness, and peace, it's just that our conscious mind or ego leads us astray. If you could finish your high school diploma by writing a five-hour exam, or spending five hours helping a starving family, what would it be? If you could earn the same amount of money working a 60-hour week, as you could a 40-hour week, what would you choose? How about choosing between fighting in a war for three years where your best friend is killed, or working for three years to promote no war at all? Most of us have been brainwashed since childhood to believe we need success and power, so reality television shows flourish, and we live in a world of insanity and poverty of spirit.

Power Training and Hoarding to Insanity

The bird of paradise alights only upon the hand that does not grasp.
John Berry

It is preoccupation with possessions, more than anything else, that prevents us from living freely and nobly.
Bertrand Russell

Most of us have more stuff than we know what to do with—yet we're never happy, always wanting more. We're a generation of stuffaholics, shopping until we've filled our basement, garage, storage locker, and closets. Ever buy a present, stuff it away, forget we bought it, then buy the same thing? If you've ever done this you are a bonafide stuffaholic. Or if you have to hire a professional organizer to help you get rid of stuff, just to have adequate living space. We have garage sales, to get rid of our stuff, so we'll have room to buy more stuff, because acquiring stuff has become an addiction. Comedian George Carlin satirized this incessant need to keep buying when he said, "That's the whole meaning of life isn't it, trying to find a place for your stuff... your house is a place for your stuff. If you didn't have so much...stuff you wouldn't need a house....That's all your house is, a pile of stuff with a cover on it....it's a place to keep your stuff while you go out and get more stuff."

In Annie Leonard's book, *The Story of Stuff*, she explains how this addiction is laying waste to the earth, polluting our soil and water, and depleting irreplaceable resources. Psychologists Randy O. Frost and Gail Steketee take a different approach in *Stuff: Compulsive Hoarding and the Meaning of Things*. They shed light on compulsive hoarders; people so attached to stuff, it destroys their lives. One of the most notorious early cases occurred in 1947 when New York police were called to the three-story mansion of wealthy recluses Langley and Homer Collyer. They found a house packed from floor to ceiling with 120 tons of rotting stuff, including 14 grand pianos, an x-ray machine, a Model T Ford, and a two-headed fetus! It took police three weeks to find

Langley Collyer's body, which was crushed between fallen piles of newspapers in a tunnel he used to navigate through his home. His brother Homer, an invalid, who depended on Langley for food, was found in his room, starved to death.

In the 1940s, stories like this were rare, but after the world recovered from the Great Depression, and the Second World War, we entered into a period of economic prosperity. In the sixties, we started building shopping malls, and big box outlets, ushering in an era of increased spending. Since then, we've been creating more stores, more gadgets and goods at lower prices, often produced in Asian countries where laborers are overworked, underpaid, and exploited in inhumane conditions, allowing Westerners to buy cheap stuff. With this advent of rampart consumerism hoarding is no longer a rarity; it gone mainstream, an epidemic excluding no one: rich, poor, educated, and non-educated. Now we have reality television shows presenting graphic views of the inside of hoarders homes, conditions that are a living nightmare, or hell on earth. They've shrunk their personal space with junk, creating health hazards hovels. These homes are no longer functional; there is no counter or sink space to cook a meal, a table to eat on, or a bed to sleep in. Since it's a condition of the mind, hoarders believe they can't exist without this stuff to cushion their private hells. Without the wisdom of spirit, insanity ensues, because our minds rarely inform us that we really don't need to pile old newspapers to the ceiling. Wisdom, caring, and common sense have been shoved aside; parents subject children to cruel lives of sleeping in cramped, stuffy, smelly, inhumane places, and never cooking a meal. Seniors surround themselves with so much stuff, they ostracize family and friends—children can't visit because there isn't a place to sit down. When attempts are made to help clean up, they're met with anger, insults, hostility, and rage, all products of the insanity of an unbalanced mind—spirit has left the house for lack of room or space to expand or grow.

But the reality is, although we can peer into the lives of extreme hoarders, they serve as mirrors to society at large where our basements, closets, garages, and storage lockers are filled to the brim. Our ancestors never needed storage lockers. When our entire life revolves around gaining and maintaining stuff, we become mentally overcrowded, boxed into a world controlled by faulty or fuzzy belief systems. Our minds convince us we will need those rusty golf clubs we haven't used in ten years, or if we bring those bags of clothes to the Salvation Army, someone might buy them who is rich! Many become like perpetual children, afraid to let go of their security blankets, when letting go of all this stuff opens up the mind to the wisdom and possibilities of spirit.

Clearing away stuff literally makes us lighter—physically and spiritually. It's a choice—do we choose to live in the physical wastelands of our minds, or do we unclutter our personal spaces, open up to balanced order and greater simplicity, possibly creating a personal oasis, or more sacred space, a private heaven on earth. Hoarding in any fashion, is clinging to the physical, the external, at the expense of our heart and souls. Stuff stagnates spirit. It complicates, confuses, and requires enormous amounts of energy and time to maintain—really just an elaborate guise to ignore our spirits. In the west we equate simplicity with poverty, emptiness, or a boring existence. But simplicity adds quality to life, because you identify what is truly important and meaningful, and in the end you are richer in spirit. Leonardo da Vinci once said, "Simplicity is the ultimate sophistication." Taoist writer Derek Lin explains, "The less cluttered your life becomes, the more you will be able to let the natural flow of life move freely through you. This gives rise to an authentic power within, and as this power radiates outward, everything falls into place so that the impossible becomes easy and the miraculous becomes commonplace."

Most of us are so accustomed to buying things we really don't need that we operate under the illusion that this is normal and healthy. We do it because it's cheap and we can. Except we have all this stuff at the expense of the other half of the unbalanced and exploited world who are not able to afford enough to survive on—yet we rarely consider this unbalance when we buy that plastic singing flower. Social activists Craig and Marc Kielburger work tirelessly to help us become more aware of spending patterns. They've explained that in China's southern Guangdong province, children never receive toys at Christmas because they make them."Guangdog is the epicenter of China's multi-billion dollar toy industry, with upwards of 1.5 million workers in 5,000 factories. They make everything from stuffed animals to video games, most of which are exported to places like Canada and the U.S. in time for Christmas. Many of those workers are children from impoverished rural areas. Their desperate parents are often tricked by factory owners into signing contracts they cannot read, unknowingly committing their children to work in the country's burgeoning industrial cities...In many of them, rows and rows of children, some younger than 10, sit at tiny desks assembling toys. They are usually housed in giant warehouse-like buildings with poor ventilation, meaning chemicals and toxins never escape. There is a bitter taste in the air. Most of the workers are girls—second-class citizens under China's one child policy. The children work 80-hour weeks and earn as little as a dollar a day...If they don't work fast enough, they are beaten. During the holiday rush, when orders from the West increase dramatically, it's not uncommon for factory employees to work seven days a week, with overtime, for months at a time. That kind of workload can be fatal." China produces 75 percent of the world's toys, and although fewer than 4 percent of the world's children are American, they consume 40 percent of the toys. We're often not aware that owning and consuming is indeed a luxury, and we are the privileged few. Here are some facts illustrating this global unbalance.

- Almost *half* the world's population or *three billion people* live on less than $2.00 a day
- *1.3 billion people get by on less than $1 a day.*
- 70 percent of those living on less than $1 a day are women.
- At least 80 percent of humanity lives on less than $10 a day.
- If we don't address this issue, *in 30 years we will have 5 billion people living on less than $2 a day* according to World Bank.
- This disparity does not affect only developing nations; Fort York Food Bank in wealthy Toronto, Canada, reports that clients feed their families on $4 a day.
- The United States, the wealthiest country in the world, has the widest gap between rich and poor of any industrialized nation. This trend is the same in China, the world's second richest country.
- 2.5 billion people, roughly 40 percent of the world's population, do not have toilets or electricity.
- 2 billion people have no clean water, resulting in diseases killing 33,000 children daily.
- Every 15 seconds a child dies because of lack of clean water.
- According to UNICEF, 22,000 children die daily of poverty—a death almost every 3.6 seconds.
- Every day 25,000 people die of hunger.
- 121 million children don't attend school because they work to support their families.
- 158 million children aged 5-14 work as child laborers (one in six children in the world).
- Less than 1 percent of the world's annual weapons budget could have put every child in school.
- One out of four adults in the world is illiterate—nearly a billion people entered the 21st century unable to read a book or sign their name.
- African women walk six miles a day to get water; the average American walks 6 miles a month.

- Americans spend 1 billion a day eating out, while each night 799 million people go to sleep hungry.
- American teens spend $101 a week. This would send two African children to school for a year.
- Average life expectancy in America is 77–in Zambia 35.
- 20 percent of the world's population lives in developed countries–they consume 48.7 percent of the world output of energy, eat 44 percent of the meat, and own 80 percent of the world's motor vehicles.

If the World Was a Village of 100

In greed, humans lose their 'souls', their freedom, their composure, their inner peace, and thus that which makes them human.
Declaration Toward A Global Ethic

The Lorax said, 'Sir you are crazy with greed, There is no one on earth who would buy that fool Theed...I laughed at the Lorax, 'You poor stupid guy! You can never tell what some people will buy.'
The Lorax Dr. Seuss

Imagine we could reduce the world's growing population of 7 billion people to a community of just 100. This formed the basis for the Miniature Earth Project, or State of the Village Report, published in 1990 by American environmental scientist Dr. Donella Meadows, entitled *Who Lives in the Global Village?* Although Dr. Meadows passed away in 2000, her work is carried on by the Sustainability Institute which she founded, and other organizations. The data varies, depending on the source, and when it was collected, but each list provides a telling picture of our global community. Imagine the world as a village of 100 people:

- There would be 18 cars in the village.
- One villager would have AIDS, 26 would smoke, and 14 would be obese.
- 50 would be malnourished and 1 would be dying of starvation.
- 63 live without proper sanitation.
- 14 can't read, 7 have only a grade two education, and one has a college or university education.
- 12 have a computer and 3 have an Internet connection.

- Total spending on defense is $1.12 trillion dollars, with only $100 billion on development aid.
- 18 people live on just $1.00 a day, and 53 people live on just $2.00 a day.
- 6 people own 59 percent of the entire wealth of the community, 74 people own 39 percent, and 20 share the remaining 2 percent.
- Of the energy of this village, 20 people consume 80 percent, and 80 people share the remaining 20 percent.
- If you do not live in fear of death by bombardment, armed attacks or land mines, rape or kidnapping by armed groups, then you are more fortunate than 20 that do.
- If you can speak and act according to your faith and your conscience without harassment, imprisonment, torture or death, then you are more fortunate than 48 who can't.
- If you have a bed to sleep in, a fridge to store food, a closet to keep clothes, and a roof over your head, you are richer than 75 percent of the world. If you have a bank account you are richer than 35 percent.

Despite these facts, we're more focused on an American dream based on how much stuff we can own. Where is the genius, wisdom, or heart in this mindset? Many believe happiness is buying a home, having two cars, going on vacations, and watching a 60 inch high definition TV. We've been duped into believing if we don't achieve and maintain this goal, we've missed the boat, or something has gone terribly wrong in this game of life. And game it is, where the stakes are debt, greed, and the right to keep buying more stuff. Except it's not our unquestionable right to value money and stuff over humanity and compassion. Our *real* goal is cleaning up our karma, and living in a dharmic fashion that creates freedom from all that stuff that is like a ball and chain around our necks. *Real freedom and the ultimate success is achieving the genius of the enlightened state. Real freedom, the real American dream, is the ability to love, to create, to act on our beliefs, and walk freely into a heaven on earth.* If everyone let go of the illusionary American dream, we'd realize we're all inter-connected, and while Joe Rich is a billionaire with three homes and five cars, hundreds of people are starving and homeless. All we need is enough to live comfortably; the rest is greed, and this greed has created cruel imbalances. We've been socialized into believing that owning all this stuff brings happiness, a huge illusion. For many years the wealthiest man in Canada was Ken Thomson, who built a newspaper empire, while notorious for being a penny-pincher. Thomson seemed to possess a soul—he loved art and animals, but he rose to the top completely possessed by greed. He once said, "For enough money I'd work in hell," and on another occasion advised his sales reps, "The difference between rapture and rape is salesmanship." But true wisdom from the ages came from philosopher Marcus Aurelius who said, "Very little is needed to make a happy life; it is all within yourself, in your way of thinking." Trappist monk Thomas Merton considered one of the world's most brilliant men writes, "Any fool knows that you don't need money to get enjoyment in life." He also counsels, "If you have money, consider that perhaps the only reason God allowed it to fall into your hands was in order that you might find joy and perfection by giving it all away." And this doesn't mean that we live in poverty or do without the pleasures of life; instead, that we live in responsible balance. Rather than being obsessed with money, it's our responsibility to maintain what God has given us—air, water, rivers, oceans, earth, plants, animals, and natural resources, but we are polluting, dishonoring, exploiting, genetically modifying, cloning, wasting, and over consuming.

The false American dream is a controlling, illusionary, ego-based, physical desire—our shadow side, devoid of love or compassion. But the real dream happens each night when we sleep, and these nocturnal dreams exist to guide us back to our true spiritual homes, not homes of bricks and boards that can be obliterated in a heartbeat. Our spiritual homes in other dimensions are places of great harmony, beauty, and balance. There are no millionaires and billionaires, but we are rich beyond earthly measure, and we have everything we want or need.

Here's just one example of the insanity the American dream has created. In the United States, the Friday after the American Thanksgiving, called Black Friday, ushers in the beginning of Christmas shopping, and is the most lucrative day of the year for American retailers. The name is from the theory that retailers operate in the red or at a loss for most of the year, but profits skyrocket into the black during the holiday season starting in late November. During this time, big box stores open at 5 a.m. and people line up all night to get 50 percent discounts and advertised bargains. During the Black Friday of 2008, the United States was in a major recession, so middle class America was hungry for deals, making shopping a high octane spectator sport, on par with bull fights. Peter Goodman, in the *New York Times* explained, "For decades, Americans had been effectively programmed to shop... after 9/11, President Bush dispatched Americans to the malls as a patriotic act." The line ups on Black Friday are "early-morning shopping as contact sport. American business has long excelled at creating a sense of shortage amid abundance, an anxiety that one must act now or miss out...In a sense, the American economy has become a kind of piñata—lots of treats in there, but no guarantee that you will get any, making people prone to frenzy and sending some home bruised."

But this frenzy causes more than mere bruises. On November 27, shoppers started lining up on Thursday night, filling sidewalks, and stretching across a huge parking lot at the Green Acres Mall Wal-Mart, not far from the Queens border in New York. By 3:30 a.m. extra police were called for crowd control and an officer on a bullhorn was pleading for order. By 4:55 a.m. with no officers in sight, the crowd of 2,000 reached a frenzy; fists banged, and shoulders pressed against the sliding-glass double doors, eventually crashing it under the pressure. The crowd poured through in a mad rush, and security guard Jdimytai Damour was thrown onto the floor, and trampled in the stampede. Damour, 34, was pronounced dead an hour later in hospital. Four other people, including a 28-year-old woman, who was eight months pregnant, were treated for injuries. Jdimytai Damour, weighing 270 pounds, was no weakling. He had been hired as a temporary worker by a company known for low wages and weak benefits. And for what? A worker from the electronics department said, "It was crazy. The deals weren't even that good." Det. Lt. Michael Fleming, in charge of the investigation, referred to the mob scene as "utter chaos." He explained, "I've heard other people call this an accident, but it is not. Certainly it was a foreseeable act." And the reaction from the mob? When told they had to leave because an employee had been killed, they were angry and some yelled, "I've been in line since yesterday morning!" Most just kept shopping. Sadly, it was back to business within a few hours. Wal-Mart officials and police cleared the store, swept the shattered glass, and then re-opened at 1 p.m.—anxious to appease their programmed shoppers.

Every year since, Black Friday insanity increases. By 2012, Black Friday actually began on Thursday as stores decided it was easier to open at midnight rather than 3 a.m. or 5 a.m. Comedian Ron James refers to this day as Black Magic or Black Death telling us, "Soccer riots are less violent." Three years later, although most stores were relatively calm, one California woman pepper-sprayed Wal-Mart shoppers to prevent them from grabbing the Xbox she wanted. In California and South Carolina, two Wal-Mart shoppers were shot in the stores' parking lots, and in three states, police arrested angry shoppers who were fighting over merchandise. Five years later Black Friday sales in the United States painted a picture of humanity at its worst with numerous brawls and shootings. A shopper holding a big-screen TV at a Target in Las Vegas was shot. While struggling with the gunman he was shot a second time in the leg when he tried to load the TV into his vehicle. At a Virginia Wal-Mart, a man's arm was "sliced to the bone," according to police in an argument over a parking space. And the insanity spread across the ocean to Belfast where a women was injured and taken to hospital over discounted TVs at an Asda supermarket which is owned by Wal-Mart. Of course with its close proximity to the United States, the viral insanity of Black Friday is now firmly entrenched in the Canadian psyche, with Black Friday sales everywhere robotically culling millions to another mindless shopping extravaganza.

The Insanity of Maintaining Poverty

We appeal as human beings to human beings; remember your humanity...
If you can do so, the way lies open to a new Paradise: if you cannot, there
lies before you the risk of universal death.
Albert Einstein & Bertrand Russell

One must be poor to know the luxury of giving!
George Eliot (Mary Ann Evans)

Before Europeans came to America most native cultures took only from the land what they needed. Concepts like over-fishing, over-farming, and deforestation would have been considered ludicrous. For many of these native cultures, gross materialism was equated with insanity. Greed is a social disease and its infectious germs create poverty. We've lived in a world awash in poverty for so long, that many have become complacent, believing such is life—unbalanced and unequal. The rich will always get richer, while the poor slip further into poverty. Except every disease has a cure, and I believe with greater awareness we will stop worshipping these false gods of greed and demand a more humane way of life. In 1845 Friedrich Engels wrote, "Social and economic inequality do not abstractly exist, they are actively maintained." He said allowing these conditions to exist "is murder just as surely." It's insane, murderous, and expensive to maintain poverty, and it is possible to eliminate it in our lifetime. In truth, the real unbalances exist within the hearts of the greedy—just as the ancient Egyptians believed, with heavy hearts like stone it is impossible to enter heaven, yet those who are humble yet unjustly treated may possess a lightness of spirit that qualifies for passage into the higher realms. And so it serves everyone, rich and poor to eliminate these unbalances because poverty is not just an issue in third world countries. Wealthy countries like Canada and the United States have hit new lows not seen since the Great Depression of the '30s. Let's examine some of the facts taken from the Canadian documentary *Poor No More*, *Toronto Star*, National Council of Welfare Report entitled The Dollars and Sense of Poverty, and Falling Behind, A Report of the Ontario Common Front.

- It would cost approximately $12.6 billion to bring the 3.5 million Canadians living in poverty to an income above the poverty level—yet Canadians spend **double** that amount treating the consequences of poverty every year over $24.4 billion.
- Poverty costs every Ontario household (the richest province in Canada) approximately $2,229 every year, about 5 percent of our GDP or gross domestic product.
- Most adults living in poverty have a job—many have two or three jobs—the problem is these jobs pay so poorly they are forced into an endless cycle of poverty.
- A low minimum wage contributes to poverty. Although both the United States and Canada have raised the minimum wage over the years, anyone earning minimum wage still lives below the poverty level.
- In the United States most of the new jobs that are being created are so low paying that median incomes continue to decline.
- In the United States, cash grants to every low-income household bringing their stand up living to a minimum income level would cost $397 billion a year—but would save almost **four** times that amount.
- Childhood poverty costs the US approximately $500 billion annually, or nearly 4 percent of the GDP.
- In the United Kingdom the costs of child poverty each year are approximately 20 billion, and the costs of below average employment rates are approximately $41 billion.
- More than half or 52 percent of low wage workers employed by the 10 largest U.S. fast food restaurants earn so little they must rely on public assistance to pay for basic necessities. This ends up costing U.S. taxpayers $3.8 billion dollars each year.
- The U.S fast-food industry generates sales of $200 billion a year. These companies maintain that entry level jobs like flipping burgers are stepping stones to higher paying jobs, but, the median age of a fast food worker is 28 and the medium wage is $8.94.
- Contrary to the stereotypes of low-income Canadians, they contribute large proportions of time and money to help others. The latest survey showed that people with incomes less than $20,000 donated on average 1.6 percent of pre-tax incomes to

charities and non-profit organizations, compared to those making over $100,000 who contributed 0.5 percent. The lowest income group also volunteered the most with a 31 percent rate of formal volunteer hours or 200 hours.

- 80 percent of incarcerated Canadian women are there for poverty related crimes and 39 percent are there for failing to pay a fine. It costs $1,400 to incarcerate a women who fails to pay a $150 fine. Seventy percent are single mothers.

- Solid data shows that stress causes the rates of mental illness to rise considerably for those living in poverty. In Canada and the United Kingdom rates of mental illness are at 20 percent, while those rates are 26 percent in the United States.

- Illegal drug use, obesity, and infant mortality are highest in poor neighborhoods.

- In Canada poor neighborhoods have a 28 percent higher death rate and double the suicide rate. Type-2 diabetes, arthritis, and cancer are also higher. The rate of heart attacks is 37 percent higher. The infant mortality rate is 60 percent higher in the lowest income neighborhoods.

- It Calgary it costs the Canadian government $40 a day in some shelters to give a homeless person a mat on the floor and meal, for a total of $1,200 a month. That homeless person could live in an apartment for $600 to $800 a month.

- Failure to recognize the qualifications and experience of immigrants costs the Canadian economy $3.42 billion to $4.97 billion every year.

- In Canada education is expensive and tuition rates are constantly rising, yet someone with a bachelor's degree earns a total of $769,720 more over 40 years than someone with only a high school education. Norway where education is free has the highest standard of living in the world. Other countries now offering free education are; Estonia, Argentina, Finland, Sweden, Greece and Brazil.

- As of 2009 Canada takes more in university tuition fees than it does corporate taxes

- Cuts to corporate and private income tax in Canada have had an enormous effect on the poor and disadvantaged since much of that money funded social services. Ontario one of the most aggressive tax cutters has roughly $15 billion less each year to spend on helping the poor and needy, while benefits have gone disproportionally to the wealthy who don't rely on social services.

- Studies by Harvard University, the Center for American Progress, Economic Policy Institute , and Pew Research Center have shown a direct correlation between union membership and wealth held by the middle class. In the U.S. 28 percent of workers belonged to a union in 1968; by 2010 the number had dropped to 12 percent.
- When unions became strong during the first 70 years of the last century the gap between rich and poor narrowed. When unions were weakened by free trade, globalization and anti-labor legislation beginning in the 80s, the gap between rich and poor went off the charts.
- Over 70 percent of McDonald's restaurants in Sweden are unionized.
- In 1968 in the United States, 28 percent of workers were unionized, and the middle class had 53.2 percent of the national income. By 2010 union membership had plummeted to 12 percent, with the middle class income dropping to 46.6 percent.
- In Canada union membership was 37.6 percent in 1981, dropping to 31.5 percent in 2010.
- Canada's 4.5 million organized workers earn $5.11 more per hour than non-union workers, or about $793 million per week. The Canadian Labour Congress contends that all this goes right back into the economy.
- In Canada 7 million people live under the poverty level of $20,000 per year. Most work for large corporations who exploit employees by only allowing casual or part time work with no benefits, sick days, or holiday pay. Meanwhile many of these companies avoid paying taxes on billions of dollars of earnings.

Feeding the Monster

If you were a jerk before, you'll be a bigger jerk with a billion dollars.
Warren Buffet

Average sex is better than being a billionaire.
Ted Turner founder of CNN

Accruing a million dollars used to be a big deal. But by the twenty-first century millionaires had become as ubiquitous as air. There are so many, it's virtually impossible to count them, and there are different rating systems around the planet as to how much wealth one needs to actually become a millionaire. There are also numerous categories of millionaires: multimillionaires who have a net worth of more than 2 million, decamillionaires with over 10 million, and hectomillionaires with over 100 million. In 2011, Capegemini and Merrill Lynch reported there were 24.2 million millionaires on the planet, and in 2013 Wealth Insight reported there were 16 million millionaires worldwide. Now the new buzz world is billionaires. That old adage *the rich get richer while the poor get poorer* has been around for decades, but what's changed is the warp speed at which the wealthy are accumulating massive sums of money, while an increasing number of people are homeless and desperate. The U.S. Congressional Budget office reported that since the 80s, the rich or top 1 percent saw their incomes grow by 275 percent, while the poorest 20 percent experienced only 18 percent growth. A billion dollars is an enormous sum of money; one thousand million—that's nine zeros. To understand how much money we're talking about consider this. Astronomer Terence Dickinson explains a million sheets of paper of average thickness would form a tower as high as a 30-story building. A billion-page pile of papers, would be 10 times higher than Mount Everest. A trillion pages, (a million million, or 1,000 billion) would reach more than a quarter of the way to the moon—we're talking about sums of money literally out of this world.

In 1916, American industrialist John D. Rockefeller became the world's first billionaire. By 1913 he had so much money his biggest worry was what to do with it, so he founded the Rockefeller Foundation with a mandate "to promote the wellbeing of mankind throughout the world." It's been estimated he gave away over $500 million, worth about $5 billion today. Rockefeller came from humble beginnings, and understood the greatest fulfillment in amassing a fortune lies in giving it away.

Although many millionaires and billionaires achieve success through hard work, Scott Klinger, associate fellow at the Institute for Policy Studies and policy director for Wealth for the Common Good, explains it's often government that creates such disparity. "Tax rates have fallen on upper income citizens and corporations worldwide. Fifty years ago in the United States, the highest marginal income tax rate was 91 percent; today it is 34 percent." He says the fortunes of many billionaires "rest upon paying their employees poverty wages. Such is the case for the Walton family... Wal-Mart is the largest private employer in the world. Many of its workers in the United States are so poorly paid; they must rely on food stamps and other forms of public assistance to get by." Meanwhile, one family, the Waltons, owners of Wal-Mart, has amassed the same wealth as the bottom 30 percent of all

Americans. We know worldwide billions are gained in countries where people labour in sweatshop conditions. Klinger says, "The chasm between rich and poor is not a divide between who has intelligence and drive and who does not. Rather it results from a society whose rules allow some to amass wealth greater than could be enjoyed in a thousand lifetimes, while they deny others enough money to scrape through just one lifetime."

No one agrees more than billionaire investor Warren Buffet, worth over $50 billion, and consistently on *Forbes* list as one of the top richest men in the world. Buffet, known as the Oracle of Omaha, made his fortune through insurance and investment company Berkshire Hathaway. As a billionaire he's unique, still living in his original home in Omaha, Nebraska, which he purchased in 1958 for $31,500. He's written, "While the poor and middle class fight for us in Afghanistan, and while most Americans struggle to make ends meet, we mega-rich continue to get our extraordinary tax breaks…blessings are showered upon us by legislators in Washington who feel compelled to protect us, much as if we were spotted owls or some other endangered species. It's nice to have friends in high places." Buffet said the previous year he had paid only 17.4 percent of his taxable income, while the 20 people that work in his office had tax burdens ranging from 33 to 41 percent. "I know well many of the mega-rich and, by and large, they are very decent people. They love America and appreciate the opportunity this country has given them…Most wouldn't mind being told to pay more in taxes as well, particularly when so many of their fellow citizens are truly suffering… My friends and I have been coddled long enough by a billionaire-friendly Congress. It's time for our government to get serious about shared sacrifice."

To demonstrate the huge disparity that's developed between the rich and poor, let's explore the rise of billionaires over a 25 year period, from 1986 when *Forbes* magazine began its annual ranking of billionaires, until 2011 when the incomes of the richest 1 percent had sky rocketed so high, it was 225 times bigger than a typical household. Before 1986, the number of American billionaires was a trifling 13. By 1986, personal wealth was increasing at such a rapid pace that *Forbes* magazine began reporting and ranking the number of billionaires: there were 140 worldwide. By 2004, this number had exploded to a record 587 billionaires. The combined wealth of these super-rich reached staggering record levels–$1.9 trillion. In 2005, for the third consecutive year, the trend continued. *Forbes* reported the net worth of the nation's wealthiest climbed to $1.13 trillion, and only 26 people on their list were not billionaires. The wealth of these few hundred people exceeded the combined gross domestic product of the world's 179 poorest countries!

In 2006 *Forbes* reported, "Making a billion isn't what it used to be. In our inaugural ranking of the world's richest people 20 years ago, we uncovered some 140 billionaires. Just three years ago we found 476. This year the list is a record 793. They're worth a combined 2.6 trillion, up 18 percent since last March. Their average net worth: $3.3 billion." Half of the world's billionaires lived in the United States and in 2006, *Forbes* announced that for the first time that the 400 richest Americans were all billionaires. By 2008, another first; the number of billionaires *Forbes* identified reached four figures, 1,125, with 50 of these billionaires under the age of 40. Their total net worth was $4.36 trillion, up $892 billion from the year before. *Forbes* also reported there were probably billionaires they didn't even know about.

In 2009, with the world in a major recession, the number of billionaires declined for the first time since *Forbes* began keeping records. There was a drop from 1,125 in 2008, to 793 in 2009. During the recession the disparity between rich and poor was still huge and growing like a monster. Bill Gates had a loss of a staggering $18 billion, but managed to retain his position as richest man in the world, with a net worth of $40 billion. Many billionaires were dropped from the list, but despite massive stock declines, currency devaluations, and stories of doom and gloom, 38 new billionaires emerged from eleven countries. During these tough economic times, many businesses as diverse as hospitals to fertilizers actually prospered and thrived. And the rich we so idolized didn't always earn their money in an honorable fashion. One of Mexico's most wanted men, drug lord Joaquin Guzman, was tied at number 701 on *Forbes* list. His $1 billion was earned through the illegal shipment of drugs to the United States, perhaps shattering the illusion that billionaires belonged to a prestigious business elite.

Despite a global recession from 2008 to 2010 the number of billionaires experienced only a minor setback, then catapulted ahead. By 2010, the number of billionaires had climbed back up to 1, 011 from 793 the year before. Until 2010, Bill Gates, cofounder of Microsoft, held the title of world's richest man for fourteen years, accumulating more wealth than the bottom 45 percent of all American households. Gates who taught himself how to program computers at age thirteen, dropped out of Harvard to start Microsoft in 1975, a company he ran as a hard driving executive for thirty-one years. He slipped to the number two spot because he had given away billions to charity. The world's richest man was now a Mexican, Carlos Slim, with a net worth of $53.5 billion—the first man from a developing country to hold that title. Much of his money came from buying troubled government- owned companies, fixing them up, and reselling them for huge profits, until his holdings in retail, manufacturing, telecommunications, and construction dominated Mexico. Mexicans were talking on a Slim-operated cell phone, while they had a coffee from a Slim-owned restaurant, at a Slim-owned shopping center, waiting to pay their bill at a Slim-owned company, at a Slim-owned bank. The fact that Slim came from a developing country drew much criticism. In Mexico, a country of 107 million people, 50 million live in poverty, with not enough money to meet housing, education and other expenses, and 20 million live in extreme poverty, defined as not having enough money to buy food.

By 2011, the 25th year of *Forbes* annual report, much of the world was still reeling in recession. While millions had lost their homes, jobs, and were living in poverty, the number of billionaires was surging ahead. In its 25th year of tracking billionaires *Forbes* reported two records; the total number of billionaires had grown to 1,210, and their combined wealth totaled $4.5 trillion. Brazil, Russia, India and China produced 108 of the 214 new names, a new trend since before 2011 only the U.S. had ever produced more than 100 billionaires. China had 115 billionaires and Russia had 101. Carlos Slim remained the world's richest man for the second year in a row with a record $74 billion; in one year he had added an unbelievable $20.5 billion to his fortune, more than any other billionaire. *Forbes* also reported that Bill Gates, number two and worth $56 billion, was now investing in the Mexican stock market, and again he had slipped to the number two spot because he had donated $30 billion to his charity, the Bill & Melinda Gates Foundation. *Forbes* was philosophical in this report, asking, "Why do we spend so much time counting other people's money? Because these moguls have the power to shape our world. Telecom billionaire turned prime minister Najib Mikati is keeping Lebanon's government together. Ernesto Bertarelli...is now focusing on saving the oceans from mass extinction. Gates and Buffet have already traveled to three continents working to change giving practice among the ultra-rich. Where their inspiration leads, we will follow." Unfortunately, billionaires with a social conscience remain a minority, and research indicates this trend of the rich getting richer is barreling ahead like King Kong on a rampage.

In Michael Moore's film about corporate greed—*Capitalism: A Love Story,* he compares capitalism to a growing beast that's never satiated, "...no matter how many strings or ropes you try and tie it down with that beast just wants more and more money. And it will go anywhere. It will try to gobble up as much as it can. The word 'enough' is the dirtiest word in capitalism, 'cuz there's no such thing as enough with these guys." When he made this film in 2009, the richest 1 percent of America, had more financial wealth than the bottom 95 percent combined, making capitalism by his definition "legalized greed." He compared this to having a pie on the table with ten slices. One guy at the table says, "Nine of those slices are mine," while the other nine fight over that last slice.

When the Deloitte Center for Financial Services in New York teamed up with Oxford Economics, they discovered that in 25 countries wealth among millionaires will likely double during the next decade, growing from an estimated $92 trillion to $202 trillion in 2020—a growth of 119 percent . Their findings indicate that emerging markets, (Brazil, China, India, Malaysia, Mexico, Poland, Russia, South Korea, Taiwan and Turkey), may experience growth at a staggering 260 percent. India is likely to experience the greatest millionaire surge at 405 percent, followed by China at 394 percent , Brazil at 257 percent , and Russia at 241 percent . The United States and Europe will maintain their position as global wealth centers, and if their forecasts are accurate, by 2020, 43 percent of the world's millionaire households will still be centered in the United States.

In Canada, a report by the Canadian Centre for Policy Alternatives released in early 2014 showed that the average CEO salary was $7.9 million in 2012 which is 171 times higher than the average wage. This was up from their $7.7 million in 2011. Meanwhile Joe average Canadian was earning $46, 634 a year. Another way of looking at this, is that by 1:11 p.m. on January 2, the top 100 CEO's will already have earned as much as the average Canadian makes all year long! The report also looked at the U.S. and Britain where the same trend is taking place. It said, "Despite the growing outcry among shareholders, the general public and politicians over the widening income gap between rich and poor and soaring executive pay, very little has changed." Hugh Mackenzie an economist with the policy group said, "For me, the remarkable thing about the last two or three years is what's *not* happening. That's *not* happening is any moderation despite the focus on the 1 percent, despite the constant stories about excessive executive compensation in the U.S., here and in Britain. Despite all of that pressure these salaries have been remarkably resilient." More importantly he said, "There's no recognized measure of corporate performance that bears any relationship to executive pay. They're just getting what they can get." Indeed that was the report's conclusion, that there was no clear relationship between CEO's salaries and their job performance. They make outrageous sums of money because they can. Mackenzie believed this was largely due to "a sense of entitlement." If an individual takes over a job from someone earning $19 million a year, then why shouldn't they expect $20 million? All this just proving that old adage–the more things change, the more they stay the same. Unless of course, we all do something about it.

The New Breed of Gods and Goddesses

No matter how insignificant what you do may seem,
it is most important that you do it.

Ghandi

While some millionaires and billionaires are greedily lining their pockets, businesses, select individuals, movie stars, and rock stars are countering this through inspiring social activism. Once these celebrities achieve wealth and fame, they catapult their star power into humanitarian causes, donating millions, and often leaving glamorous careers to work among the sick, starving, and destitute. Celebrities or stars, often referred to as rock gods or screen goddesses, seem to garner the same reverence once reserved for ancient Greek gods and goddesses. However, our knowledge of these Greek heroes is not entirely myth; although the original stories have been changed or distorted, kernels of truth remain. In ancient Greece, enlightened beings, possessing what we would today consider super powers, did walk the earth. Spiritual enlightenment or self-realization brings amazing abilities: command of several languages, ability to cross dimensions, the ability to disappear, and to create from energy. Enlightened beings always serve and work to preserve humanity, and in ancient Greece they played vital roles; serving in government, building hospitals, setting up schools, libraries, art galleries, and acting as goodwill ambassadors. Although much of this history has been destroyed, we still have remnants; the city of Athens, Greece, was named after Athena, the Goddess of wisdom, technology, domestic skills, war, justice, and protection. The Parthenon's architecture still inspires us, because it was the sacred space or temple where Athena and her goddesses worked. Perhaps, our modern screen idols lived in these ancient times, and are doing what comes naturally, utilizing latent talents encoded in their DNA.

Decades ago, only a few stars were lauded for their charity work; Danny Kaye was an anomaly as UNICEF's first celebrity spokesperson, a position he held from 1954 until his death in 1987. He traveled tirelessly to raise money; most notable was a 1975 trip where he flew to 65 cities in five days. Kaye said, "I believe deeply that children are more powerful than oil, more beautiful than rivers, more precious than any other natural resource a country can have." Jerry Lewis was another pioneer in the sixties, with his annual Labor Day Telethon for muscular dystrophy.

But social philanthropy among stars wasn't popular until Diana, Princess of Wales, began shaking up the world in the 1980s and '90s, ushering in a new level of social awareness and activism. With cameras following her everywhere, Diana did immeasurable good. She shocked the world by touching AIDS patients in hospitals when many believed the disease was contagious, catapulting a disease that was taboo and grossly misunderstood, into one of global support. She did the same in hospices, and countries riddled with land mines. Now it seems, if you're a celebrity, you need a social cause. Reporter Leslie Scrivener wrote, "It's not enough to be an actor; the modern star needs some of Mother Teresa's DNA." Celebrity causes are now so prominent, in 2006, a husband-and-wife team, Steve and Myria Purcell, launched a website *Look to the Stars* chronicling celebrity philanthropy.

Among these super stars is Bono, lead singer for U2, who set up a group called DATA, lobbying Washington and European countries to provide aid to Africa's poorest countries. He's also launched "ethical clothing" labels promising fair working conditions in Africa's textile factories. Bono is committed, but he's also done his research, even attending classes at Massachusetts Institute of Technology (MIT) to learn how to direct aid most effectively. Oprah Winfrey has built and financed a girl's school in South Africa. When disaster strikes, Angelina Jolie and Brad Pitt are always there, and they're known for sticking around even when public interest has died, and listening to resident's needs. Together they visit refugee camps around the world as UN ambassadors, and in 2006 they launched the Jolie-Pitt Foundation donating millions to relief organizations when disasters strike. Brad Pitt heads Make It Right, his charity which pledged $5 million to build 150 homes for the victims of Hurricane Katrina. When Haiti was ravaged by an earthquake, Sean Penn spent months financing and managing a refugee camp. Madonna has adopted two children from an orphanage in Malawi, financed that orphanage, and raised awareness for African schools and charities. Colombian pop star Shakira formed the Barefoot Foundation, which has opened several schools, and provides nutrition to over 6,000 children in Columbia. In 2008, her Barefoot campaign was so successful, it spread to the United States where she works to encourage government spending on education programs in developing countries. In 2003, she became UNICEF's youngest Goodwill Ambassador. Matt Damon's greatest passion is the charitable foundation OneXOne which provides water, food, healthcare, education, and play and sport opportunities to children around the world. Although many celebrities are involved with One X, Damon serves as the public face of the organization, logging countless hours in countries such as Haiti, Rwanda, and Ethiopia. He's also a founding member of Not on Our Watch, raising awareness on humanitarian issues. Superstars George Clooney, Don Cheadle, and Mia Farrow, have raised money for Sudan's Darfur region, and spoken before the United States Congress. Mia Farrow, an ardent humanitarian and defender of children's rights, has 13 children, of which 11 are adopted. Clooney donates money and time to the UN World Food Program, helped found Not on Our Watch, and supports ONE campaign which fights poverty worldwide. Ben Affleck has visited war-torn Congo, and made a documentary to highlight its problems.

In 2006, the world's wealthiest man, Bill Gates, announced he was stepping down as chairman of Microsoft to devote his time to charity. That same year, The Bill & Melinda Gates Foundation accumulated $29 billion, teaming up with Warren Buffet who tossed in $37.4 billion, or 99 percent of his wealth, creating what seemed like a charity behemoth. The momentum continued in 2010, when Bill and Melinda Gates and Warren Buffet announced their Giving Pledge Program. They lobbied for a year to get the Giving Pledge started, holding dinners and talking to wealthy Americans, urging them to think about their wealth and how it could be used. The Giving Pledge is not a charity—it's a commitment. Participants promise to give at least 50 percent of their money to charitable causes during their lifetimes or after their death. The pledge is a moral commitment to give, not a legal contract, and each billionaire is encouraged to find unique ways to contribute. Donors are asked to publicly state their intention in a letter, hopefully drawing others into philanthropy. When the pledge was announced, it already had an impressive array of donors; George Lucas, media mogul Ted Turner, New York mayor Michael Bloomberg, and Jeff Skoll, creator of e-Bay. When the two twenty-six-year-old founders of Facebook, Mark Zuckerberg and Dustin Moskovitz, signed on four months later, it inspired youth activism. Zuckerberg who was worth $4 billion said, "People wait until late in their career to give back. But why wait when there is so much to be done?" A few months earlier, he donated $100 million to the public schools in Newark, New Jersey. Gates and Buffet hope this pledge continues for generations; they also plan to inspire billionaires around the world to join their cause.

Three years later many of these billionaires appeared on the television show *60 Minutes* in a segment entitled "The Giving Pledge: A New Club for Billionaires." In three years Buffet and Gates had convinced 115 billionaires to contribute over half a trillion dollars to the

Giving Pledge ushering in "a golden age of philanthropy." These billionaires ranged in age from 27 to 98, and although some had inherited their wealth, most were self-made, earning their money in businesses ranging from technology and social media to pizza and hair care. Gates had committed 95 percent of his wealth to the pledge, and Buffet who had pledged 99 percent, said "a significant percentage" of members were planning to give away over half of their wealth. Individual pledgers were contributing to causes that were close to their hearts; unemployment in South Africa, detecting and treating brain cancer, tax reform, failing schools, medical research, climate change, pandemics, nuclear proliferation and movies that promote philanthropic goals. It was felt they were bringing "the same brashness to their philanthropic ambition that helped them build their financial empires." Gates and Buffet had even started inviting pledgers once a year to exclusive resorts to learn how to give away their money more effectively. Member Jeffrey Skoll admitted there was always the danger of arrogance, "of feeling like we know the answers. And the reality is we don't." Together they were learning how to use their money to make the most needed impact. And there was great reason for optimism with Bill and Melinda's Gates work coming close to wiping out polio globally.

In the next chapter we'll see how Einstein, considered the greatest genius of the 20th century, spent the first half of his life promoting science, then the second half focused on humanitarian pursuits. Perhaps Bill Gates true genius is following that same altruistic route. After working full time as a philanthropist for five years, Gates was interviewed by CBS correspondent Charlie Rose who explained, "He is driven as much as any man we have ever met to make the world a better place." Gates' goal is to help what he terms is the 'bottom 2 billion,' or one third of the population, those people who live on less than $2 a day without electricity, clean water or toilets. His mission is to eradicate preventable diseases like polio, tuberculosis, and malaria which kill millions of children under five every year, or one child every 20 seconds. When Gates longtime friend Steve Jobs, creator of Apple, was still alive, he was asked by a reporter, "Do you envy Bill a bit, this second act that he has?" Jobs replied, "I think the world is a better place because Bill realized that his goal isn't to be the richest guy in the cemetery." Charlie Rose believes that Steve Jobs, "has not done, did not do in philanthropy, what Bill has done, and some will suggest that Bill will be long remembered for his philanthropy when people have perhaps forgotten about Microsoft."

With Bill Gates, it seems that Biblical phrase "give and you will receive," is absolutely true. After being knocked off the top of the mountain as the richest man in the world by Carlos Slim in 2010, by May 16, 2013 he had regained his position as the wealthiest man on the planet according to the Bloomberg Billionaires Index, a daily ranking of the world's 300 wealthiest individuals. By early 2014, Gates now worth 78.2 billion was back on top, closely followed by Carlos Slim with 72 billion. Gates accomplished this even though he had donated 28 billion to his charity the Bill & Melinda Gates Foundation.

With all this philanthropy by all these powerful people, one might ask why poverty still exists? Although this represents a staggering sum of money, it's only around 2.3 percent of the world's total wealth. Although more of our world's billionaires are setting stellar examples—they can't do it all. An interview entitled, "Shaking the Foundations of Charity" with Stephen Lewis, former United Nations special envoy for HIV and AIDS in Africa, puts everything in perspective. He explained that we need a global shift in awareness, by governments, financial institutions, business, industry, and individuals, before anything will change. Lewis said that Hollywood celebrities are actually moving in to fill the gaps that are left by governments. Bill Gates, worth 78.2 billion by 2014, one of the richest men in the world, can only offer 2½ percent of what's required every year to end poverty worldwide. Instead, if the leaders of the G7 countries devoted 0.7 percent of their gross national product to fighting world poverty, $200 billion could be raised and the world's poor would have the shelter, food, and water they need to live. Lewis says, "It is possible to overcome poverty, but it will never happen without a grand coalition of governments, non-government organizations, international financial institutions, and devoted community activists in country after country. Above, all the world needs political will. The poor have been waiting—and dying—for eternity."

In 1998, a United Nations report estimated the basic needs in all "developing" countries could be met if $13 billion was spent each year. This would represent less than one percent of the wealth of the world's billionaires. But we can't just blame the billionaires for not giving more, since insanity and imbalance have become global epidemics. While people are starving, in Western and industrialized countries we have an ever increasing problem—obesity. In the United States alone, 64 percent of Americans are overweight or obese, 1 in 5 children are obese, $75 billion is spent a year on weight related diseases, more than 325,000 people each year die from obesity-related illnesses, and, these numbers rise every year. The World Health Organization tells us that worldwide obesity has doubled since 1980. By 2008 more than 1.4 *billion adults* were overweight, and 65 percent of the world's population live in countries where being overweight and obesity kills more people than being underweight. Their projections indicate that by 2015, about 2.3 billion adults will be overweight, and more than 700 million will be obese. While over a billion of our world population is overweight, 25,000 people die every day of starvation, and half our population lives on less than $2 a day—that's insanity! Industrialized countries could also prevent starvation and malnourishment globally, if we watched or redirected the amount of food we throw away. In Canada, a study by the Value Chain Management Center in Guelph found the average Canadian throws away 40 percent of our food every year, an estimated $27 billion worth of perfectly good meat, and vegetables. (This is more than twice the amount the United Nations needs to wipe out poverty in all developing countries.) In *American Wasteland: How America Throws Away Nearly Half of Its Food*, Jonathan Bloom writes, "Depending on who you ask, we squander between a quarter and a half of all the food produced in the United States." It's the same in the United Kingdom where a government-funded agency discovered one-third of people's food is thrown away each year.

For more insanity let's examine a few spending patterns. In Canada, our heaviest shopping day occurs on December 23rd when 8 million Canadians spend nearly $12 billion in a last minute frenzy, averaging five to six hundred bank or credit card transactions a minute. The insanity intensifies on Boxing Day when people are restless after spending an entire day without shopping. Representatives from Visa predicted that Canadians alone would spend $1.9 billion, or an average of $414 per person, in one day, after we've already been indulged with presents the day before, and, this number increases each year. If Canada, the United States, and a few other countries kicked in what half their populations spend on December 23 and 26th, on presents that are often returned, forgotten or thrown away, we could wipe out mass poverty worldwide. We could also do this if for just one year all the developed countries redirected the amount of money they spent on Halloween candy, costumes, and decorations. If we look at Halloween spending in the United States the figures are astounding. According to the National Research Federation's 2010 Halloween Consumer Intentions and Actions Survey, on average Americans spend $66.28 on costumes, candy and decorations, with these figures rising every year. Total spending in America over Halloween is just under $6 billion! Americans alone could wipe out global poverty if they just redirected two years of Halloween money. The implications of this are enormous; if every person in every wealthy country didn't buy more food than they needed, or decided that instead of buying Christmas presents or Halloween candy for just *one* year, and redirected their money to fight poverty or homelessness, those basic needs of all developing countries could easily be met. Instead, we decorate our lawns with skeletons, witches, and goblins, glorifying darkness, and drive to shopping malls like programmed zombies, and no matter how much we spend it never seems to be enough, because we've been cleverly programmed since childhood.

In developing countries according to UNICEF, a child dies every 3.6 seconds from poverty. According to The Hunger Project, this translates to approximately 22,000 children who die every day. Every time you've read a sentence, a child has died. Try to imagine the newspaper headlines if this was happening in wealthy North America. Although we pride ourselves in the twenty-first century for being civilized, peace loving individuals, this is largely an illusion. Social activists Craig and Marc Kielburger highlight some amazing social statistics. Globally we spend more money on war than anything else, a staggering trillion dollars every year, $2 billion a day, or $90 million an hour. We spend ten times more on war than we do on international aid. Worldwide we spend $18 billion a year on makeup while it has been estimated that it would take $18 billion to end malnutrition for every child in the world. According to the United Nations, it would cost $15 billion to put every child in the world into school. Europeans alone spend $11 billion a year eating ice cream, while Stephen Lewis has pleaded that it would only cost $10 billion to completely stop of spread of HIV-AIDS in Africa. Worldwide we spend staggering amounts on things that don't help humanity one iota; $50 billion on cigarettes in Europe, $105 billion on alcohol in Europe, and $400 billion worldwide on narcotic drugs. Marc Kielburger contends we don't have a global money problem, rather "a values problem." There is little genius in the way we spend our money.

Nobel prize-winning economist Joseph Stiglitz has calculated that the United States' war on Iraq would cost America upwards of $2 trillion before it is finished. And this doesn't include any of the costs incurred by Iraq, or other countries who have sent troops. Economist Jeffrey Sachs, the Worldwatch Institute, and the United Nations, estimated if the United States used about one tenth of this $2 trillion, or $156.3 billion it could have singlehandedly eliminated extreme poverty around the world (cost $135 billion), achieved universal literacy, (cost $5 billion a year), immunized every child in the world against deadly diseases (cost $1.3 billion a year), and ensured developing countries had enough money to fight the AIDS epidemic ($15 billion).

Adding to this insanity is the rat race of many large countries to increase their arsenal of nuclear weapons, rather than providing for the basic health, safety, and educational needs of their people. There is no compassion in this race; it is relentless, forgetting that human life is both fragile and sacred. Instead, the new god is nuclear technology. We're no farther advanced than ancient civilizations who watched gladiators fight to the death, sacrificed virgins, and threw people into volcanoes to appease what they believed were angry gods causing these eruptions. Our minds have convinced us that we've made social progress, but have we really? Some countries have spent fortunes on the research, development and maintenance of their nuclear arsenals, *after* the Nuclear Non-Proliferation Treaty of July 1, 1968. Although this treaty to limit the spread of nuclear weapons was signed by 189 countries, four nations did not sign; India, Israel, Pakistan and North Korea. Despite signing this treaty, the United States spends $35 billion a year maintaining its nuclear weapons—money that could be spent on health care, education and social services. In total the United States spends staggering amounts on its military, $682 billion a year, while Canada, a much smaller country spends $22.5 billion. Military spending in Pakistan is about $4.5 billion, but less than $400 million is spent on education. This means families who can't afford private schools often turn to free madrassas, many of which teach radical ideology and oppose the education of girls. China could be extolled as the one country helping more people out of poverty than any nation in history. But this decline took place in the 1980s when the rural poverty rate fell from 76 percent in 1980 to 23 percent in 1985, and there has been little change since, with the gap between the rich and poor rising steadily. According to the World Bank, China's income inequality is on par with Latin American and African countries. Despite this, China's military spending has tripled since the 1990s to around $166 billion a year. In one month, February 2008, India's government allocated $26 billion for defense and weapons, while nearly 80 percent of its population lives on less than one dollar a day. The same day that I read these statistics, a newspaper story carried the headline *Suicide rate growing as debt cripples India's farms.* It provided a graphic account of farmer, Jasbir Singh, living in Sangrur, India, who doused his body with gasoline, lit a match, and died en route to the hospital. He could see no way out of the whopping 30 percent interest rate he was being charged by a private money lender to maintain his farm. The article estimated 150,000 farmers have committed suicide since 1997. David Krieger, president of the California-based Nuclear Age Peace Foundation, has said, "We've put this money down a black hole of so called security...In a more just and humane society, that money would be spent on health care, housing and the alleviation of poverty...We have a tremendous responsibility to do something. No other generation in the past has had to confront the possibility of human annihilation by means of its own cleverness."

Jeffrey Sach, special advisor to the United Nations, and author of *The End of Poverty,* is renowned for his work as economic advisor to governments around the world. He's been hailed as one of the world's most 100 influential people for his global inequality efforts. When Sachs developed a theory to eliminate world poverty, he was optimistic things would improve. In African villages where his plan and resources were put into action, people are no longer starving, there was a reduction in sickness and disease, and literacy rates increased. However, Sachs explains the real deterrents to his efforts lie with governments like the United States and Canada, who have gone on a military approach to the world's problems particularly in Iraq and Afghanistan, rather than a humanitarian one. He says, "If we bomb villages from the air, rather than helping them grow food and build roads on the ground, you don't win these battles. Instead of finding ways to promote global development, build bridges of understanding and allocating funds to alleviate poverty, these governments are focused on fueling the war machine...I am worried about our capacity to kill each other faster than we can understand each other." Traditionally, world leaders have spent money on war and nuclear stockpiles, instead of creating a just world where everyone has adequate shelter, enough food to eat, receives an education, and will not die of an infectious disease. All a matter of choice, priorities, and values.

Million Dollar Baby

The narrow notion of "every person for himself" does not belong in today's world, which demands that we learn to see beyond our wounds, beyond our differences for the good of all.
Canadian Governor General Michaelle Jean's installation speech

When we're led by the mind, it convinces us we need everything in reach. Anyone controlled solely by their mind is like an impetuous two-year-old. Mantras of the mind morph only slightly from childhood, "me want, I want, give me, that's mine, I want more, I can have more, I want money, marry for money, and the new age motto, "Everyone deserves abundance." Only the mind would desire abundance, knowing that 33,000 die every day of poverty. Today our left brain, mind, or ego has convinced us that abundance is desirable and actually a good thing, but this wasn't always so. It's always about balance, and a life without abundance can still be like having a balanced full cup of coffee. To the ancient sages abundance represented excess and waste; it was akin to a messy overflowing cup spilling everywhere, and eventually needing to be cleaned up.

The movie *Million Dollar Baby* is a perfect, yet tragic example of what happens when this quest for money supersedes the soul, spirit, or heart. It's the story of one women's struggle for self-esteem, power, recognition, and fame. Maggie, the protagonist, believed her heaven or ultimate goal was being good at boxing, so her mind relentlessly pursued this course. When the movie begins we're told, that boxing is all about getting respect for yourself, by taking it away from your opponent. At first, this left brain logic makes sense. However, spirit would wisely counsel us that high-fueled competition is about power—getting it for yourself, and taking it away from the other guy because you've never been taught there are other ways to feel good inside. True respect only comes from the heart or spirit—it's about increasing it for yourself and others. The mind takes away, because it has no real source of energy, believing it has to fight and steal for power. When the mind is disconnected from spirit, it knows no other options. But spirit comes from an infinite source of internal energy or em*power*ment—God. It doesn't need to take; instead it creates and gives freely.

In *Million Dollar Baby,* Maggie Fitzgerald, played by Hilary Swank, has never experienced peace, feelings of heaven on earth, or love. She tells her trainer Frankie Dunn (Clint Eastwood), on her 32nd birthday, that she's a failure because she's worked as a waitress since she was thirteen. Her brother is in prison, her sister cheats on welfare by pretending one of her babies is still alive, her father is dead, and her mom weighs 320 pounds. Maggie desperately wants love, recognition, and respect, but her mind has convinced her the *only* way to achieve this is to become a famous boxer. She tells Frankie boxing is the only thing that makes her feel good, and if she can't box, or is too old too box, she has nothing in life. But the real problem is her mindset that without a specific career we have nothing. Our soul or spirit is most certainly something. Maggie's real problem lies within the illusions of her mind. Maggie's mind wasn't capable of self-love, self-honor, or self-esteem, because these flow from connection to spirit. It's okay to love any sport and to feel good performing that sport, and healthy competition is fine, as long as it's kept in balance. It's never okay to restrict ourselves to one sport, game, or profession that elevates our egos so much it destroys us. In God or spirit's eyes, you can be enormously successful if it's your destiny to be a waitress and you do your job each day honorably, ethically, and convey enthusiasm and peace to each client. A waitress has the ability to make the day for a whole lot of people. The mind never sees other options or possibilities; that's the function of spirit. The mind has tunnel vision, repeating only what it knows from the past, or what it has been trained or socialized to believe, regardless of how unethical or harmful this may be. But spirit through meditative activities and dreams, shows us limitless options and potential. Maggie's problem was that she'd never been taught to use inner resources, learning self-honor and self-respect, journaling dreams and emotions, meditating, going with gut feelings, recognizing symbols and synchronicity. Using only her ego or mind, she believes becoming world champion is her *only* ultimate goal—the mind operates with tunnel vision.

Frankie Dunn, operating under the same mind-based illusion, agrees to become her trainer. We see Maggie winning fight after fight; winning becomes euphoric, a high, like a drug, and like all drugs, after a short time, she can't imagine living without it. Unfortunately, this high of winning or being on top, is followed by a low, making us crave the next high. So we seek constant highs in life, winning the trophy, taking the drug, getting the raise, making the deal, selling the most, buying a bigger house, all because we're never taught, except maybe in science class, that what goes up, must come down, and the higher the climb, the greater the fall.

At first Maggie and Frank are somewhat caring individuals, but over time their minds become increasingly infected with the power virus. Slowly, insidiously, the virus infiltrates and they become monsters without being aware of this transformation. When Maggie wins a major fight, she asks Frankie how the other boxer is doing. She's told her opponent suffered a concussion and broken eardrum. When Maggie asks about sending her something, Frankie sarcastically suggests she send her a check. By the time Maggie makes it to the world championship, a million dollar match, the virus has taken over. They've lost connection to their hearts, along with wisdom, or compassion; they're completely ruled by dark, infected minds.

In her final game, realizing she's losing, Maggie asks Frankie what to do. His advises her to hit her opponent right up the sciatic nerve, and to just keep digging away. Maggie's robotic mind obeys. But while her back is turned, she's hit so hard that her two cervical vertebrae in the neck, C1 and C2 are shattered beyond repair. Karma—we reap what we sow—the energy you give out comes back to you. After this fight, Maggie is paralyzed and her body remains in this helpless state for months. She can't breathe without a respirator. Eventually both her legs are amputated, enormous stakes for fame and money. Maggie tries repeatedly to kill herself but fails. Finally, Frankie slips unnoticed into her room, administers a lethal injection into her IV, then out of guilt and shame disappears.

Our minds might tell us Maggie was a success. Didn't she obtain her dream—fame, recognition and glory—and didn't she make so much money she could buy her poor mother a mortgage free home? This depends on whether mind or spirit is defining success. Just before her death Maggie's soul would have been in utter distress, knowing a life of enormous potential had been destroyed by infected thinking. Her soul might say, "If only Maggie had listened to me and spent time in meditation or self-reflection I could have shed some insight on her mind. She didn't have to suffer like this, or go through horrible physical and emotional pain. Maggie never had to be paralyzed or lose her legs; this was all her mind's foolish folly. She didn't need to die so young. That's not ultimate success, and it's certainly not being a hero. Heroes have vision that helps all humanity. Maggie's vision became self-serving and self-absorbed because she couldn't think with clarity; she couldn't imagine anything beyond her own ego-based glory. She could have learned to feel outside the ring. Boxing could have been a stepping stone, but she couldn't feel or intuit when it was time to shift direction. I tried to show her in dream after dream. I tried to warn her this last fight could be disastrous—but she ignored me. Her "training" never included dreams, recognizing gut feelings, or intuitive nudges. Her million dollar dreams were illusions of the mind, all in the pursuit of power. If she had allowed me to wake her up, I could have prevented her physical body from dying. Maggie became the victim of her own infected mind. She could have experienced genuine highs, but tragically she died without ever experiencing genuine love, fulfillment, peace, or those satisfying thrills of heaven on earth."

Head and Heart–Understanding Right and Left Brain

There is wisdom of the head, and wisdom of the heart.
Charles Dickens

The mind in its own place and in itself can make heaven
of hell or a hell of heaven.
Milton

So often, like Maggie, we take the hardest route when there are options our minds are not aware of. Learning to link our minds to spirit can provide a path out of emotional pain and insanity. There are two ways of knowing. We can use logic, reason, facts, or left brain, linear thinking, and there is absolutely nothing wrong with this. We definitely need logic, common sense, and practicality for survival. Left brain thinking is good, except for one critical thing—it's not the realm of spirit, heartfelt guidance, love, ethics, intuition, compassion, or balanced genius. If we relied solely on the left brain we would be logical, practical, and knowledgeable, but there would be no personal growth or movement forward, and life could become cruel and repetitious. We'd be like the original Mr. Spock on *Star Trek*, an intelligent robot, or walking encyclopedia, without the ability to love or feel emotion—effective at work perhaps, but terribly unbalanced. We'd have precious little music, art, dance, poetry, writing, ethics, or fun! There would be no insights, growth, or flashes of genius. Hitler, an example of left-brain to the extreme, was a very intelligent man, but he didn't make the world a better place. True progress comes via heart, intuition, inner nudges, and our ability to transcend the mind. It's the spirit, heart or soul, informing the brain and allowing it to be brilliant, creative, insightful, and compassionate. *It's as if our soul has an energy or brain of its own, that informs both the left and right hemispheres.* Genius or arriving at true wisdom and peace comes from using both sides of our brain as one harmonious unit. Let's get a clearer picture of the left and right brain, and how they work by using mnemonics or memory clues; left brain is logical, linear, language oriented, while right brain is roses, rock and roll, right here, and right now. The left brain is associated with head, ego, mind, thinking, and masculinity; while the right brain is associated with heart, being, accommodating, and femininity. Imagine fraternal twins; Leo the left brain logical sibling loves workbooks, worksheets, repetition and drill, demonstrations, copying, following directions, collecting data and facts, mathematical computations, record keeping, and making displays. Leo thinks he might be an accountant, bank manager, medical researcher or scientist. His twin sister Rebecca loves creative activities, painting, sculpture, dancing, singing, guided imagery, day dreaming, meditating, creative writing, poetry, using metaphors, designing, solving old problems in new ways, mythology, fairy tales, open-ended discussions, and self-expressive activities like journaling insights and dreams. She'd like to be an artist, dancer, or writer. As twins, Leo and Rebecca are inseparable, joined at the hip, but they're also polar opposites. Leo likes the tried, the true, the traditional, orthodox, while Rebecca loves to rock traditional and be creative. Leo prefers to follow his five senses; he's rooted in the physical, and doesn't believe in anything unless he can see it. He prefers things to be black and white, while Rebecca can distinguish the many shades of grey. Leo controls language so does all of the talking, while Rebecca is largely silent, is guided by her sixth sense and pictures, and is better at recognizing faces. She also has superior visual-spatial skills needed for finding her way around a new building or neighborhood, or driving a car. Rebecca is pure intuition; she pulls insights from the ethers and believes anything is possible. Left brain Leo is fixated, focused, and driven by time, often worried about missing his next appointment, while his right brained sister enjoys living in the moment. Leo thrives on detail, organization and problem solving. Life for Leo is linear, days, weeks, months, years, while Rebecca lives in a three dimensional world—she wonders about that mystical land she visited last night in her dreams. When they're visiting the woods Leo sees, observes and appreciates individual trees. Rebecca is awed by the overall beauty of the forest. Left brained Leo is rational and focused on what he should be doing, while Rebecca is more emotional and focuses on what she's feeling. Leo tends to be judgmental and thinks in right/wrong and good/bad, while Rebecca is more accepting, and sees her connected to everyone and everything.

Jill Bolte Taylor's book, *My Stroke of Insight*, is a fascinating account of the differences between the right and left brain. The author, a neuroanatomist, suffered a major stroke when a blood vessel exploded on the left side of her brain. This stroke literally wiped out her "rational, grounded, detail-and-time oriented" left brain, and left her swimming in the blissful "euphoric nirvana of the intuitive and kinesthetic right brain." Being a brain scientist, she was able to observe, understand, then record the unique functions of both sides of her brain. In her book she says, "Our right hemisphere is all about this present moment. It's all about right here right now." In February 2008, speaking in Monterey, California, at a TED conference (Technology, Entertainment, Design) she explained the right brain, "thinks in pictures and it learns kinesthetically through the movement of our bodies. Information in the form of energy streams in simultaneously through all of our sensory systems...I am an energy being connected to all the energy all around me through the consciousness of my right hemisphere. We are energy beings connected to one another through the consciousness of our right hemispheres as one human family. And right here, right now, all we are brothers and sisters on this planet, here to make the world a better place. And in this moment we are perfect. We are whole. And we are beautiful.

My left hemisphere is a very different place. Our left hemisphere thinks linearly and methodically. Our left hemisphere is all about the past, and it's all about the future. Our left hemisphere is designed to take that enormous collage of the present moment. And start picking details and more details and more details about those details. It then categorizes and organizes all that information. Associates it with everything in the past we've ever learned and projects into the future all our possibilities. And our left hemisphere thinks in language. It's that ongoing brain chatter that connects me and my internal world to my external world. It's that little voice that says to me, 'Hey, you gotta remember to pick up bananas on your way home, and eat 'em in the morning.' It's that calculating intelligence that reminds me when I have to do my laundry. But...most important, it's that little voice that says to me, 'I am, I am.' And as soon as my left hemisphere says to me 'I am,' I become separate. I become a single solid individual separate from the energy flow around me and separate from you." In her book she says, "My stroke of insight is that at the core of my right hemisphere consciousness is a character that is directly connected to my feeling of deep inner peace. It is completely committed to the expression of peace, love, joy, and compassion in the world...I believe the more time we spend running our inner peace/compassion circuitry, then the more peace/compassion we will project into the world, and ultimately the more peace/compassion we will have on the planet." She says that "peace is only a thought away" and that all we need do to access this peace is to learn how to "silence the voice of the dominating left mind." She often describes her experience of being right brain dominated as living in nirvana or bliss, heaven on earth, a marvelous mystical place. "Freed of all perception of boundaries, my right mind proclaims, 'I am a part of it all. We are brothers and sisters on this planet. We are here to help make this world a more peaceful and kinder place.' My right mind sees unity among all living entities, and I am hopeful that you are intimately aware of this character within yourself."

Although we may talk of left and right brain functions, none of us operates solely with our left brains, just as it's almost impossible to operate exclusively with our right brains. Our brains are not divided down the middle by a brick wall, so it's important not to think of left brain, right brain dynamics as black and white. There's always integration with the two sides of our brain inextricably linked. Neurologist Kevin Nelson explains that the cerebral cortex is like a cover or mantle overlying the brain, and the right and left hemispheres are connected by a dense band of 300 million nerve fibers, the corpus callosum. "The two hemispheres communicate information and knowledge from one side to the other, making our minds whole." Bolte Taylor explains, "Because our two hemispheres are so neuronally integrated via the corpus callosum, virtually every cognitive behavior we exhibit involves activity in both hemispheres, they simply do it differently." She describes these two co-existing entities as the "we" inside of me, and Nelson says, "In all of us the 'me' is distributed throughout our brains." Even in individuals who have had brain surgery where the two halves are split, there is still communication between the two hemispheres–the brain simply finds new channels or pathways. This is similar to being right- or left-handed. We may be left-handed, but still use our right hand frequently. Imagine how difficult it would be to get dressed, tie shoelaces, or play the flute, with just one hand. Similarly, in the brain there's always an integration of both hemispheres. For example, we use our left brain to read a technical manual, but if we're reading a folk or fairy tale, with symbolic content, both sides are needed. When listening to music, most people focus on the overall melody and employ their right brain, but professional musicians who have learned to be more analytical, may use the left brain by breaking the piece down into component parts.

This means that success, wisdom, or true genius doesn't mean we're logical, and rational all the time, neither does it mean we're always carefree, spontaneous, intuitive driven. Instead, we use both ways of knowing, allowing a synergy or partnership to take place. If we link left and right brain information to heart or soul, we're brilliant in a wise, just, creative, compassionate, ethical fashion, the opposite of Hitler's unbalanced self-serving intelligence. It's extremely important to nurture the right brain, because left to its own devices, the left brain can fabricate the grandest illusions, lies, excuses and rationalizations, since it is the center of language, and like Hitler, it can talk people into doing the most atrocious acts. In *The Spiritual Doorway to the Brain,* Nelson explains that the right hemisphere "maintains a veridical (objective straightforward, unembellished) record of experience...The left generates hypotheses, interprets patterns, and makes associations (even when none exist!). It creates stories, constructs theories, seeks explanations, and gives us the 'why' for our experiences. Accuracy is not a primary concern of the left hemisphere; rather, its priority is weaving experience into a comprehensible or at least explainable whole. In other words, the left hemisphere not only talks—it makes things up!" During the last hundred years left brained rational thought, logic, and technology, have dominated our world. There has been little heart and soul to provide equilibrium. We believed reason and intellect would give us all the answers. We deified and glorified materialism, war, technology, all left brain, pursuits. We have an excess of yang, but no yin; too much violence and aggression without the nurture and wisdom of spirit.

Imagine our mind discovers a way to inject cows with a new growth hormone enabling us to produce twice the amount of beef or milk. However, this process would shorten the cow's life span, create respiratory problems, and they would experience pain in their joints and limbs because they would grow too rapidly. Our mind might convince us this was an ingenious plan because it could double our profits, producing more beef in a shorter time. If we relied only on the mind, we'd go ahead with this scheme. But spirit understands this as cruel and unethical since these cows would suffer tremendously. Spirit would tell us this process was unnatural and we were tampering with an already perfect animal created by God. We've been given more than enough to eat by nature. Wanting more is greedy and controlling. Spirit would inform us that our motivation wasn't to improve the quality of life, but to make money or achieve fame.

A few months after writing this hypothetical example, a picture of a Holstein cow in the newspaper caught my eye with the headline, Madame Ovary of bovines. The subtitle read, "Buyers bet on her million dollar babies." This bodacious bovine, named Lila, at three-years-old is said to be "the most valuable cow in the world because of her pedigree, milk production and breeding potential. She's been given fertility drugs that cause her to 'super-ovulate.' The eggs are removed and implanted in other heifers. She's got 20 babies on the way...The eggs she produces—up to 100 over her lifetime—are being removed and implanted in other heifers to carry to term." Her former owner, Albert Cormier, earning $1.15 million from the sale, responded to the criticism, with his left brain by saying, "The fact that she can reproduce that many spread out around the world has a tremendous marketability...She's very much capable of living until she's 10, 12, or more...Whether she's capable of actually enjoying those years is another matter." Stephanie Brown, of the Canadian Coalition for Farm Animals responded from her right brain, "The very process of the super-ovulation is an invasive process. It's not natural." Whenever money, power or "marketability" is the sole objective, there may be a long period of success or glory, but eventually, like the Roman Empire, everything crumbles and self-destructs. The mind builds an illusionary, unreliable foundation, without the wisdom and insight provided by heart or spirit. Only with spirit can we begin building anything that stands the test of time.

Typically we build with bricks, boards, or steel. But did you ever consider what God might have used when He created human beings? How come despite all the wars, disease, plagues, and pestilence we've managed to survive? Among the energetic elements of lasting creation are most certainly wisdom and love. This is our essence or core—it's encoded in our DNA—it's our birthright. The opposite of this is building from a desire to make money, control, dominate, or forcing your ideas on someone. Cloning, despite its hype, in the long run will never really work. Dolly the sheep was a docile Frankenstein; in time playing God always results in disaster.

There is Genius in Spirit—Alpha

If the individual is to be happy, healthy and prosperous, he must change from the Law of the Mind (negative) to the Laws of the Soul. (positive)
Highland Beam Club

We'll never have world peace or peace in our neighborhoods, schools, and workplaces until we understand this insatiable quest for power has tipped the scales and left harmony and balance in the shadows. When we've been groomed our entire lives to chase after power, it's no easy task to see other options. Each chapter attempts to teach how this heart and mind connection unfolds through dreams, meditative experiences, focus, and heightened awareness. Poverty, chaos, and war will continue to plague us, unless we reach a critical mass of people operating from the wisdom of their hearts, rather than the insanity of the mind. But what do dreams and meditation have to do with genius? In the alpha state, that precarious realm of dreams and meditation, our brain waves are relaxed, between 8 and 12 cycles per second, our core or true state. Alpha is the *only* brain rhythm where we can be both awake and alert *or* asleep, so it is the only state where we can consciously work to enhance our lives. In the other rhythms, beta, theta and delta we're either completely awake or asleep. Our brain waves operate at different oscillating electrical voltages or frequencies, and alpha was discovered first by German neurologist Hans Berger, the man who also invented the EEG machine or electroencephalogram which measures these frequencies. They're called alpha because they were the frequency discovered first, and Alpha is the first letter of the Greek alphabet—they're also known as "Berger's wave." As a young man when Berger was enrolled in the cavalry, his horse reared during a training exercise and he landed in the path of a horse-drawn carriage. Berger didn't receive serious injuries, but was shaken and never forgot this brush with death. His sister who lived several miles away had a sudden premonition he was in danger and insisted their father telegraph him. Berger believed this was a case of "spontaneous telepathy" and while he was in danger, somehow he transmitted these thoughts to his sister. He entered medicine with the goal of investigating this psychic energy in the brain. Like many important discoveries, his findings were met with skepticism, and colleagues considered him a crank. He successfully recorded the first alpha brain waves in 1924, but filled with doubt, didn't publish his findings until 1929. It took another 14 years before EEG machines gained global recognition. Thanks to Berger, in the twenty-first century researchers around the world are better able to understand the genius of the alpha state. Neurofeedback allows researchers to watch the brain in action, and train participants through brainwave biofeedback to become aware of and maintain the alpha state for longer periods of time. Corydon Hammond, at the University of Utah School of Medicine, a leader in this field, writes that neurofeedback training has the potential to quiet the mind and "It can also be used to improve concentration and focus, to improve cognitive function and emotional control following concussions and mild head injuries, and it has untapped potential to increase physical balance in gymnastics, ice skating, skiing, and other areas of performance." Hammond believes neurofeedback training can enhance sports performance without the use of drugs. He feels it holds great promise for "enhancement of concentration and attention, reduction of anxiety, improving control over emotions (e.g., anger), for overcoming effects from mild head injuries and concussions..." Studies have shown that alpha brain waves increase just before peak performances, while novices or inexperienced athletes do not exhibit these same alpha spikes. Before their best free throws elite basketball players show a burst of alpha brain waves. Elite golfers produce a burst of alpha waves before their best shots. Elite marksmen and archers display this same increased alpha pattern, and this extends into other areas where focus and concentration are needed. Greater alpha brain wave spindles have also been found in highly skilled musicians.

Alpha is the place of genius where our soul or spirit is free from the clutter of the mind–free to achieve individual greatness. When we dream, meditate, focus, or relax we're able to activate spiritual genius, and this is available to everyone. If we become overly reliant on technology we lose that ability to truly be present and focus—we're plugged into external devices rather than tapping into our own brilliant electrical devices—alpha brain waves. I'm not advocating giving up our gadgets, rather reaching a place of balance, where we're not enslaved by them. If we really master the alpha state, our minds have the potential to go beyond these gadgets—imagine having the ability to communicate telepathically with your best friend rather than using your cell phone! In the alpha state we can tap into a universal consciousness and akashic records of all that has transpired in history. In this alpha state we're at our most perfect or peak level of insight and awareness, and so it is the place that all humanity may strive for in the future. When enough people understand its potential the world will change. When we dream, meditate, or relax in alpha, we remember who we truly are. We're not just a body, or a mind. In our true or core state of alpha, we release all confusion, forgetfulness, disorientation, ego, judgment, fears and anxieties; we strive towards our greatness and we're ingenious. We glimpse the future with its unlimited possibilities.

Dreams which occur in alpha help us recognize the hold ego has on us. In dreams we face, recognize, and work through fears. We can never feel balanced or genuine peace if we're afraid. We'll see how we get caught in those seductions, traps, or karmic loops, experiencing heartache and disappointment. We'll look at visions and miracles as the work of spirit, guiding and providing hope and faith. Finally we'll delve into meditation, and how it works with dreams to balance our lives. Hopefully, by the end of this book, a shift will occur and you'll see that genius has never resided in the mind, that individual and world peace can only be achieved by activating spirit and allowing it to shed much needed light on our restless, tormented minds. To understand this further, let's begin by examining two geniuses of the twentieth century, no doubt masters of the alpha state, since they were humanitarians and visionaries.

CHAPTER TWO
Saving Humanity by Activating True Genius

Whatever you can do or dream, begin it. Boldness has genius power and magic.

Goethe

SOMETIMES YOU READ A FEW words, hear a song, or catch something on television, and it's etched in your memory like indelible ink. Years ago I read an article explaining the differences between a genius and someone of average intelligence. It said when faced with a problem most people keep doing the same thing repeatedly, believing their method will eventually work, like being a rat in a maze, trying that same route, but never finding the cheese. But a true genius tries different approaches, never wasting time repeating the same things; they're innovative and think outside the box. Hence, Albert Einstein's words, "We can't solve problems by using the same kind of thinking we used when we created them." With this bit of wisdom ingrained in my brain, it became obvious I wasn't the spawn of Einstein, since I did keep doing the same things over and over, expecting them to work, like every time I tried to assemble a piece of IKEA furniture. Each time, it never occurred to me there could be a different way. I would usually give up in frustration, or, if it required assembly, phone my neighbor Dean or brother Frank for help. Then I would watch in utter fascination, as my brother put together that IKEA desk in 45 minutes without reading the manual that I had spent four weeks trying to assemble. It's like your mind only runs on certain tracks and you have no idea how to switch gears. But a genius is never limited to one track, and every genius shares this trait, like the crew of *Star Trek*, they boldly go where no one has gone before. Many believe a genius creates a change that lasts forever, giving us something that endures the test of time, altering our perceptions, daily life, or the way we view reality—individuals like Bach, Mozart, Socrates, Newton and Einstein.

But what exactly is a genius? The original meaning of genius was *attendant spirit* and everyone had one. In antiquity, genius was not equated with brilliance of mind; rather, it was a force or spirit, guiding spirit, inexplicable mystery, or the indwelling nature of a person, place or thing. Individual places had a genius, what we might describe today as energy, and so did everything in society. It was the genius within an acorn enabling it to become an oak tree, the genius within a seed urging it to become a sunflower, the genius of a tadpole that develops into a frog, or the genius within a piece of music that made it successful. Genius could also be a family spirit (*gens*) influencing the individual toward good or bad. So, this genius or force could be dharmic, a blessing or grace, it could have enormous force like a volcano, or it could be karmic in nature associated with a devil or darkness. In ancient Rome the term genius applied to gods, there was father god, *Jupiter,* and mother god, *Juno,* but it was also used to describe virtually everything in society; houses, doors, gates, streets, neighborhoods, and tribes each had their own distinct genius. It also represented an individual's natural optimism, something that guided one towards happiness, since it was believed life was meant to be enjoyed. Birthdays were seen as occasions for honoring this innate genius or spiritual nature, and were accompanied by gifts of incense, wine, garlands and cakes. Romans believed that genius was the generator and preserver of human society and spirits or *gens* guarded their cities and homes. Stories of genies in a bottle come from the ancient Roman word *genii*—the concept that every person and place had a guiding spirit or deity. The Romans believed this genius or guardian spirit protected everyone throughout their lives, helped with difficulties, and offered inspiration.

But, around the time of the Renaissance, roughly 500 years ago, people began speaking of genius in a different fashion; there are historical accounts referring to the genius of Michelangelo and other great Italian artists. The term genius started losing its meaning as a guiding force, spirit, or the protection that everyone possessed, and it now referred to a select group of individuals possessing extraordinary talents and skills. When psychologists began developing IQ or intelligence tests at the turn of the 20th century the transition became complete. Genius was no longer an integral part of every human being; instead it was something possessed by only a privileged few. The first person to seriously measure intelligence in the late 1890s was Francis Galton, a half cousin to Charles Darwin. In 1859, after reading Darwin's *Origin of Species*, Galton became fascinated with his cousin's theories that only the strongest survived. Historians believe this book changed his life, because after reading it, he became convinced that success in life was due to superior qualities that were largely heredity. In 1899, he published *Hereditary Genius,* the first scientific study of genius and greatness. Today, we talk about "nature versus nurture," or whether we're more influenced by our nature or heredity, or by nurture, upbringing, and environment. Galton who first coined that phrase believed intelligence was the number one factor determining success in life.

In 1883, Galton's left brain came up with *eugenics*, a movement for improving the biology of human beings through selective breeding. He believed there should be restrictions on having children to limit the birth of what he termed "feeble-minded." He felt there should be monetary incentives for families of high social rank to marry early, followed by offers of money to produce superior children. Galton's work influenced Alfred Binet in France, who developed the first IQ test at the turn of the 20th century. Both men were interested in sifting out "the idiots and imbeciles," and encouraging only those "born to be kings." Over a century later, the nature versus nurture controversy still rages, and there has been vehement criticism of eugenics and IQ tests. Binet's original IQ test has been changed, revamped, and reinvented by numerous psychologists, and that force, mystery, or spirit of genius our ancestors believed in seems forever lost. Genius has devolved into scores on intelligence tests, (a high IQ or Intelligence Quotient), a combination of verbal ability, numerical ability, logical reasoning, and memory. For example, on one widely used IQ test, the WISC-R, a score 69 or below means you are mentally challenged or mentally deficient, 70-79 indicates borderline intelligence, 80-89 is low average, 90-109 is average intelligence, 110-119 high average, 120-129 superior intelligence, and anyone producing a score above 130 is considered a genius. But the definition of genius varies depending on which IQ test you take. Two psychologists considered experts in intelligence were Lewis Terman and Leta Hollingworth. Terman believed anyone with an IQ over 140 was a genius, but Hollingworth believed you must score 180. (We'll revisit Terman in chapter three with his work on gifted students and longevity.) I've administered a few IQ tests while working on my doctoral degree in psychology, and discovered they deal primarily with English and Math. The whole process of administering tests was disheartening. I'd assumed IQ tests had to be brilliant and had considered becoming an educational psychologist, going to different schools testing children. But you didn't have to be a genius to quickly discover the serious flaws in these tests. They left out so many essentials to life, and were culturally biased. I watched many of my young students, whom I believed had great energy, creativity, social skills, and potential, take the test, only to be forever labeled learning disabled. Each time it felt like a kick in the stomach.

In his essay *"The Power of Genius"* Shel Kimen tell us "history has proven a number of times that great heroes don't necessarily have high IQs." He says IQ tests serve a capitalist agenda—to bring more players with high IQs into a competitive system. Through IQ tests scientists limit the number of geniuses in society with standardized testing, college entrance exams, and funding of special programs to cultivate "gifted" children, when we clearly have no proof being gifted means you will go on to better humanity. He concludes, "The word genius has evolved from the spirit world into a manipulative social agent...And in the last century it's been used to both limit and broaden our educational system to advance political and possibly economic agendas."

There is an international society of geniuses, Mensa, (meaning table in Latin because of their round table approach), that accepts any candidate regardless of race, color, creed, nationality, age, political affiliations, or education. The society was founded in England in 1946, by two lawyers who met on a train. They wanted to provide "a stimulating intellectual and social environment" for members, and to gather great minds together to solve the many problems of a post-war world. Today Mensa has three primary goals, to foster intelligence for the benefit of humanity, to encourage research into the uses of intelligence, and to provide a stimulating social opportunities for its members. The Mensa Canada brochure explains, "We party, discuss, invent, learn, teach, play music, fall in love, climb mountains, cry on each others' shoulders, laugh a lot and invent the most appalling puns." To become a member of Mensa you need to score in the top 2 percent on one of over 200 standard IQ tests. Currently there are about 115,000 Mensas in more than 100 countries. Who are these geniuses? There's really no common denominator; members have been high school dropouts, and PH.Ds. The Mensa website tells us, "There are Mensas on welfare and Mensas who are millionaires. As far as occupations, the range is staggering. Mensa has professionals and truck drivers, scientists and firefighters, computer programmers and farmers, artists, military people, musicians, laborers, police officers, glassblowers..." The list of famous Mensas includes actress Geena Davis, Donald Peterson, former chairman of Ford Motor Company, Bobby Czyz, boxing champion, and Dr. Julie Peterson, a former Playboy Playmate.

One of my long-time friends, Don Speller, has been a member of Mensa for over 25 years. Mensa can definitely be an ego trip—one can walk around wearing their Mensa baseball cap, but Don actually kept this hidden for many years. When he told me about Mensa everything made sense because Don was decidedly different, but in a good way, our conversations were never superficial or frivolous. Don and I have been friends now for over thirty years and I'm always impressed by his array of abilities. Shortly after graduating from university, he founded Tarandus, an environmental consulting company specializing in biological and ecological service. Don is accomplished in biology, marine life, scuba diving, running a business, environmental issues, computers, fitness, squash, cross country skiing, snowshoeing, woodworking, reading, solving puzzles, fine wine, gourmet cooking, even making his own maple syrup. I get a headache just attempting to answer Mensa's sample quizzes, but Don finds these puzzles, "challenging, interesting, and fun." I would have been a nervous wreck even thinking about taking their IQ test, while Don was intensely *curious* about how he would do, and was pretty sure he had passed. In the beginning he was an active member, enjoying many of their activities: lunches, movie nights, dinners, puzzle events, theater, concerts, book night, brunches, coffee and conversation, but now says he mainly reads their monthly journals and news bulletins. Don assured me, "Mensans are just like everyone else. You'll find some with lots of interests and hobbies and some who are couch potatoes. You'll find professionals, blue-collar workers, a relatively even gender distribution. Some are boring, some interesting, some are jerks, some are truly nice and kind. I suppose the only things that I've noticed is that most Mensans have interesting opinions, are good problem solvers, can look at something from a different or even unique perspective. But then, lots of non-Mensans do those sorts of things too." When I told Don I was writing a book on spiritual genius he was adamant that I "keep in mind there are several different types of intelligence or genius. The smarts that are measured during the Mensa exam and other IQ tests are only one kind of intelligence." He wanted to ensure that I'd talked about emotional intelligence and artistic intelligence. His most brilliant piece of advice was this; "Genius can have a capacity for good or evil, and I'm sure the term 'evil genius' is one you've heard before. There are a lot of people who are smart, but f___ing evil!" And that, I assured Don, is exactly what this book is trying to discourage.

The smartest person in the world is a Mensa, Marilyn vos Savant, with an IQ of 228. She lives in New York with her husband Robert Jarvik, the inventor of the Jarvik artificial heart. Perhaps the perfect head and heart combination! Marilyn is an executive at Jarvik Heart, Inc., but is also an author, lecturer, playwright and magazine columnist. In 1986, she started writing *Ask Marilyn* for *Parade*, the Sunday magazine that's distributed to 379 newspapers worldwide. She answers questions on topics from the philosophical to personal, mathematical to "just plain nuts." When the 1986 *Guinness Book of World Records* listed her as the smartest person in the world, this led to testing, retesting, and examining her past IQ records. We learned measuring high IQs is questionable because each test produced different results, and scores varied every year; her scores were 167, 186, 218, 228 and 230. *The Guinness Book of World Records* cited Marilyn as the smartest person alive from 1986 to 1989, then with so much controversy, future editions left out this category.

We used to believe IQ and intelligence were fixed, but in the last few decades we've realized this simply isn't true. Intelligence can increase or decrease at any age. In Dr. Norman Doidge's book, *The Brain That Changes Itself,* he cites examples of individuals believed to be hopeless cases, who increased their IQs through sheer tenacity. According to Doidge, the brain is no longer viewed as something which has "unalterable limits on memory, processing speed, and intelligence." Doidge refers to our brain's ability to increase at any age as plasticity, and like plasticine, our brain's learning capacity isn't fixed, it can stretch. We also believed if you were born with a set amount of intelligence it didn't change throughout life. Now we understand the brain as a dynamic organism, stretchable, renewable—a miracle of hope. Our brains are constantly adapting and "learning how to learn." According to Doidge, the brain is not "an inanimate vessel that we fill; rather it is more like a living creature with an appetite, one that can grow and change itself with proper nourishment and exercise."

We started viewing intelligence quite differently in the 1980s thanks to Howard Gardner, an American psychologist and Harvard professor, who wrote *Frames of Mind.* Gardner believes we've evolved to exhibit seven different types of intelligence; linguistic or language based intelligence, logical mathematical intelligence, musical intelligence, spatial intelligence, bodily-kinesthetic intelligence, and two forms of personal intelligence, one directed towards others, and one towards ourselves. He also believes that some form of "spiritual intelligence" may well exist.

This paved the way for Daniel Goleman who published *Emotional Intelligence* in 1995. Goleman also believed intelligence could encompass factors such as music, artistic ability, athletic ability, and social skills. Goleman found that teaching self-awareness, confidence, how to manage emotions and impulses, and increasing a sense of empathy and compassion, pays off in measurable academic achievement. He believes our traditional view of intelligence is limited, ignoring a critical range of emotional abilities that "matter immensely" as to how we do in life. These emotions, self-awareness, self-discipline and empathy, are perhaps a truer method of defining smart. They aren't fixed at birth, but can be nurtured and developed throughout life, with real benefits to our health, work, and relationships. And this isn't a radical new philosophy. A thousand years ago, Aristotle, in *The Nicomachean Ethics* was examining virtue, character, and what constituted the good life. Aristotle was concerned with getting emotions to a healthy, productive balance. He believed our real task was not simply to be smart, rather, to manage the intellect with emotions. When passions and emotions are in balance, they guide our thinking, values, and survival as a species. He wrote, "Anyone can become angry—that is easy. But, to be angry with the right person, to the right degree, at the right time, for the right purpose, and in the right way–that is not easy."

Artificial Genius

First and last what is demanded of genius is love of truth.
Goethe

How do we develop personal genius? We know you can't transform babies into little geniuses by sitting them in front of educational television. For over ten years, The Baby Einstein Company marketed DVDs as educational tools that would make babies smarter up to age two. This was challenged by The Campaign for a Commercial-Free Childhood, an advocacy group that complained to the U.S. Federal Trade Commission. They believed claims on Baby Einstein packaging and their website were not supported by scientific research. The American Academy of Pediatrics recommended that children under two years old watch no television. Instead, child development expert Melanie Gushnowski advised parents, "Play with them; experience their world with them. Use their senses and have an active learning component, not passive learning, which is something like baby television." In 2009, Baby Einstein removed any wording from its packages claiming their products could make babies smarter, testimonials claiming educational benefits from the DVDs, and offered cash refunds on any DVDs bought during a six year period.

To boost their brain power, students at college and university campuses have been taking the drugs Adderall and Ritalin, even though both drugs were originally developed to treat attention deficit disorders. Adderall, an amphetamine, came on the market in 1996, and Ritalin, which has an identical chemical compound as cocaine, has been around since the early 60s. In one study, Alan DeSantis, a communications professor at the University of Kentucky, found that up to 80 percent of students were using these drugs. Students feel it assists them in staying awake and being productive, makes boring work interesting, and helps them become more focused and detail oriented. But Ritalin has resulted in several deaths; it can cause heart and blood pressure problems, and long term effects on the developing brains of young people without an attention deficit disorder is still unknown. It's a highly addictive drug and psychosis is a known side effect. With some users, it actually hurts their performance, and others become so overly focused they have tunnel vision and lose creativity. Rather than taking drugs to stimulate brain power, students could obtain a mental edge naturally, by getting adequate sleep, journaling their dreams, meditating, balancing life and having fun!

Sleep expert, Dr. James B. Maas, explains in *Power Sleep* that dreaming or REM sleep is essential for peak mental performance. He says, "REM sleep plays a major role in facilitating memory storage and retention, organization, and reorganization, as well as new learning and performance. Without this power of REM sleep, we would literally be lost mentally." Without adequate sleep, information doesn't move from our short term memory to our long term memory. The edge that dreaming gives is still not understood, and definitely underutilized. When I was writing my doctoral thesis and was stumped on how to proceed, I would sleep and literally dream pages and pages verbatim of what I needed. It was all I could do to get it down on paper fast enough, but the ideas, concepts, and connections were definitely there. As we'll discover meditation actually does make chemical changes in the brain that make us smarter and more alert, and we don't need an expensive prescription to do this. Popping pills, the quick and easy, never leads to true and lasting genius.

We've also realized that intelligence can't be created in a test tube. In the next chapter we'll examine the genius of Alfred Nobel, the man who created the Nobel Prizes. In 1980, eccentric American millionaire, Robert Klark Graham came up with a scheme to breed a race of super humans, eugenics, a repeat of the concept Francis Galton devised back in 1883. Graham believed because the weak were not killed off before they reproduced, this was creating a "genetic catastrophe" in America. "Retrograde humans," those on lifelong social welfare, the incompetents and the imbeciles, were swamping the intelligent, and something needed to be done. He believed we could only be saved by "intelligent selection—our best specimens—our great white menmust have more children." To accomplish this, he set up The Repository for Germinal Choice, nicknamed the Nobel Prize sperm bank. Its sperm donors were an elite group of Nobel-laureate scientists, mathematicians, successful businessmen, and star athletes. For almost two decades women flocked to its doors believing they could spawn geniuses and child prodigies. But when Graham died in 1999, the bank quietly closed its doors, and no one knew if his genetic experiment had achieved its intended results. The bank had produced approximately 240 children, but records were sealed, and the identities of donors remained a secret. It took years of research, a lot of digging, many interviews with the children themselves and their parents, before writer David Plotz uncovered the facts in his book, *The Genius Factory.* Plotz discovered that trying to breed intelligence simply doesn't work. He writes, "To answer the obvious question: no, they are not all geniuses. Some are dazzling...But the kids are spread in a bell curve, slid a bit to the right of average. Some are brilliant. Most are very good students. And some are quite mediocre. Three of the 30 I know have severe health problems."

The most public story was Doron Blake, one of Graham's genetic experiments, whose mother put him in front of television cameras from the age of two weeks old, allowing the press to watch him grow up—always for money. Doron's life was a living Truman Show; by the time he was eighteen he'd done 100 media interviews including *Good Morning America* and *60 Minutes.* Doron has become increasingly disillusioned with the genius sperm bank theory. He says it's what in your heart, not your brain, that matters–a concept that would shock and outrage Graham.

"I was his ideal result," Doron says. "It was a screwed-up idea, making genius people. The fact that I have a huge IQ does not make me a person who is good or happy. People come expecting me to have all these achievements under my belt, and I don't. I have not done anything that special. I don't think being intelligent is what makes a person. What makes a person is being raised in a loving family with loving parents who don't pressure them. If I was born with an IQ of 100 and not 180, I could do just as much with my life. I don't think you can breed for good people."

The Repository for Germinal Choice was designed to prove the importance of nature over nurture—but Doron's life proves exactly the opposite—largely due to his adoring mother. She named him Doron, the Greek word for gift, and worshipped him like a demi-god. Doron was the center of her universe and the only person she wanted to spend time with. She indulged him, breastfeeding until he was six, and until he reached adolescence they were best friends. She encouraged all of his interests, and never judged or criticized. Her son ended up loving music and playing piano, guitar, and sitar. He majored in comparative religion—again something that would outrage Robert Graham. Doron was genetically programmed to be a math-science whiz, but he rejected those subjects, choosing what was closer to his heart—music and spirituality. With an IQ of 180, perhaps this is his true genius.

Creating True Genius

Do not go where the path may lead, Go instead where there is no path and leave a trail.
Ralph Waldo Emerson

One is not born a genius, one becomes a genius.
Simone de Beauvoir

American psychologist Dr. Thomas Armstrong advocates the theory of multiple intelligence, and believes every child is a genius. His books include *The Radiant Child, Awakening Your Child's Natural Genius, You're Smarter than You Think,* and *7 Kinds of Smart.* He says believing every child is a genius, doesn't mean they will all paint like Picasso, write music like Mozart, or score150 on an IQ test. The original meaning of genius was "to give birth," related to the word genesis, "to be zestful or joyous." The true meaning of genius is to "give birth to the joy" within each child, and all children have this innate capacity. When we examine the life of Albert Einstein we'll see, this *is* a major ingredient of genius, holding onto a childlike awe, fascination, curiosity and innocence. When we allow children to express this innate joy I believe they do amazing things. Armstrong says young children have "vivid imaginations, creative minds, and sensitive personalities" and it's important to encourage children to carry these traits into adulthood, a process called "neotony" or "holding youth." It's crucial to preserve this genius of childhood with its wonder, wisdom, playfulness and flexibility, but instead, our schools dampen natural genius with "testing and grading, tracking and labeling, talk and tedium." He reminds us that "Creativity can't thrive in an atmosphere of judgment." Armstrong hopes parents recognize each child's genius is unique, and can't be quantified with an IQ test. The media represses the natural genius of children "through its constant onslaught of violence, mediocrity, and repugnant role models." He tells parents and teachers there are three basic ways to preserve the genius of children. First, adults need to be adequate role models by reawakening their own natural genius, a source of creativity, vitality, playfulness, and wonder. Second, they need to provide simple activities to activate the imagination. Einstein's love of a compass awakened his love of learning as a young child. Third, create an atmosphere where children can learn free of criticism, comparison, and pressure to succeed. "Treat each child as a unique gift from God capable of doing wonderful things in the world." Armstrong explains as infants we have twice as many brain connections as adults, but if we don't stimulate or use these connections, we lose them. We're all born with the potential to be little geniuses, but a steady diet of television, violence, noise, constant activity, and pressure to succeed, dampens our spirits and innate intelligence.

Carol Dweck, psychology professor at Stanford University, has spent more than three decades researching the theory that intelligence is something we work towards. In her book *Mindset: The New Psychology of Success,* she tells parents and educators intelligence is not something children are handed on a silver platter, rather, it's a skill that can be developed. She's received letters from adults labeled "gifted" as children, but were never encouraged to work hard, or push past their natural abilities. Many never graduated from college or found meaningful careers, and as adults, they felt cheated, bitter, and disappointed. With intelligence, that old adage is true, "use it or lose it!" Dr. Dweck says, "More research is showing that it's really about dedicated effort and passion. That's what leads to success. Talent has to combine with passion and effort to flower...the brain isn't static, it's something that grows, neurons form new connections every time we work hard and learn something new."

In 2010, *Toronto Star* reporter Leslie Scrivener interviewed an elite group of geniuses dubbed the "100-percent-club," students who had obtained either 99 or 100 percent in their final year of secondary school. What she found wasn't surprising, unless one considers a teenager earning 100 percent a social misfit or recluse. She discovered these teens were "poised and sociable," and even though they tended to have a small group of friends, and usually weren't dating, they could put sentences together crisply and play Mozart sonatas. Their volunteer hours, like their marks, were outstanding; many had up to 600 hours. "They are fascinating students anyone would enjoy a real conversation with," said Don Klinger, an associate professor in education at Queen's University. They're also humble; Simon Babakhani who graduated with 100 percent, said, "I don't believe I'm an extremely intelligent person. Drive and motivation are more important than IQ. It's (high school curriculum), not complicated material." Bob Garton, a retiring principal of Turner Fenton Secondary School in Brampton, with the largest International Baccalaureate or IB program in the province of Ontario, knows many of these elite students. "I don't think their minds are any different," he says, "What is really different is they are highly organized." Even from childhood, Simon had the ability to focus intensely. He was curious and loved learning. In grade two it was cars; he wanted to know everything about them, and would methodically organize lists, grouping cars by horsepower, or if they were built in Europe or North America. In Grade 8, he decided to acquire every *National Geographic* ever published.

Unlike their peers, these teenagers were not slaves to cell phones, Facebook, social media, being popular, or late night gaming. They had good relationships with teachers, viewing them as allies in learning. One male student said, "I had a great relationship with most of my teachers. You have to invest the time. You have to get inside the teachers' minds. I had to adjust my writing and work skills, depending on how they marked." Another student said he was always willing to discipline himself because he didn't want to let his teachers down. "I never wanted to disappoint. I like it when people like me. I want to do well for them. It's the same with my friends." Because they're highly motivated, curious, and love learning, when these students reached grade 12, parents didn't need to supervise their studies at all.

Albert Einstein, the greatest genius humanity has known, wasn't created in a laboratory, didn't rely on DVDs as a baby, and didn't take neuroenhancing drugs, nor do any great genius's. As a young boy he was so brilliant he didn't rely on teachers—reading, reflecting, studying, and physics were his passion. Young Albert was the classic self-motivated scholar—learning was exciting and stimulating; it was his balm in troubled times, and it kept him grounded and intensely focused. But even Einstein worked like a Trojan horse to come up with his theories. In fact, he worked so hard, he often compromised his health. In his book, *Einstein,* Jürgen Neffe, explains that a super high IQ of over 150 can be more of a hindrance than a help, thwarting real creative genius because they're out of balance or left brain dominated. He says, "Creative people are propelled by a high-octane motor: the sheer force of will. They feel the overwhelming need to be creative, and are distinguished by their determination and boundless perseverance." Einstein fit this pattern perfectly, and freely admitted to having a "mulish stubbornness." He rarely backed down, but always had the inner fortitude to grit his teeth and push through. He once said, "God created the donkey and gave him a thick hide."

Neffe also explains that "Einstein's genius did not blossom overnight. As a rule, future geniuses go through a ten-year phase of ongoing practical and theoretical work—a kind of maturation process. Einstein required exactly one decade of mental toil, daily contemplation, and poring through books, often until the wee hours of the morning, to get from his high school diploma to his revolutionary discoveries in 1905, including the special theory of relativity. Mozart, Einstein's favorite composer, composed music for ten years before he was able to write the kind of music that made history." Creative geniuses need time to think, solitude, reflection, meditation, being alone in nature, and listening to the music of the cosmos. But this meditative time is always accompanied by hard work, hence we have Thomas Edison's famous phrase, "Genius is one percent inspiration and ninety-nine percent perspiration.

Dean Simonton, a professor in the department of psychology at the University of California, has also been studying the nature of genius for over 30 years. He agrees with this "10-year rule" needed for anything truly original to develop. "I call it the drudge theory of genius. Just keep sweating away and you, too, will have your eureka moment." He's discovered that discipline and work ethic are not enough; a genius needs creativity—the ability to make the type of connections that lead to breakthroughs. He reminds us that German physicist Max Planck said great scientists, "must have a vivid intuitive imagination, for new ideas are not generated by deduction, but by an artistically creative imagination." He also believes our notion of the lone genius is a myth, because they build on the theories of all the geniuses who have come before them. "Creative genius is almost always embedded in a rich network of distinguished predecessors and contemporaries...Newton famously said that he stood on the shoulders of giants. Even so, he still saw farther than all the rest."

New Understanding of Genius

We appeal as human beings to human beings; remember your humanity...If you can do so, the way lies open to a new Paradise; if you cannot, there lies before you the risk of universal death.
Appeal by Albert Einstein & Bertrand Russell

True genius is something we're just beginning to understand. The ancient Romans were astute in their belief that genius sprang from the soul, and that everyone had this potential. If we all cultivated personal genius, the world could be a different place. This is why we're all here in the first place—every one of us is meant to attain the genius that is part of the enlightened state. When we do, we will understand there is truth and beauty in all religions and there will be no religious wars or persecution. No religion will claim to solely represent God, because we will understand that God, truth, spirit, inner genius have always been inside us. We will not deplete our rainforests or exploit Mother Earth. We will not set off atomic bombs or stockpile them. We won't mistreat animals, cull them, or imprison them in zoos. We will eat healthier. Women will finally find their place in society as equals; they will be respected and honored, not raped, robbed, murdered and mutilated—and so will men. There will not be widespread poverty instead, the will would be balanced. More billionaires and millionaires will have a social conscience, not just a select few. Decisions in business and government will be based on a common good, rather than accumulating power or making profit. Businesses will co-operate rather than compete since they will realize there is enough work for everyone. Workplaces will exist without bullying and exploitation—everyone will be paid a fair wage well above the level of poverty. We will rely less on fossil fuels, and more on renewable resources—water, wind, and sun. Hospitals will be quiet healing places, with organic food, less noise, and more compassion. Schools will focus more on creativity, compassion, curiosity, and imagination, and become less mark and results oriented. Success in education will not only be equated with marks, grooming young people to understand that success in life is far more than a paycheck. Success will be seen as a balance of head and heart, the capacity to love, and to provide needed services to humanity. Greed and inequality will be eliminated. We will embrace all countries and ethnic groups as brothers and sisters—there will be no ego based illusions of superiority. We will spend more time understanding the messages in our dreams, meditating for insight, and being energized and revitalized by nature—this will be a vital part of every day. Although this may seem dreamlike or utopian, it is possible to take small steps towards this type of inner genius.

We've based genius on intelligence and logical, rational thinking, or the ability to acquire enormous sums of money. This is what we've always strived for, often leaving out the soul, intuition, or spirit. A true genius is always a visionary, which is why their work stands the test of time. True genius is learning to think with the heart and soul, not just linear, left brain logic. It's not always studied in school. It's working humbly but tirelessly to serve and support others. It's dissolving the ego or mind enough to operate with a heightened awareness. It's operating with the deepest respect, and regard for everyone and everything on this planet. It's elevated brain waves, connection to soul or spirit, the ability to transcend time and space and grasp infinite possibilities. It's what allows us to be extraordinary and stupendous rather than ordinary, mechanical, and egocentric. At its core, true spiritual genius is the ability to love deeply, without conditions, and to work at something you are passionate about. Passion and com-*passion* is genius.

A true genius is not concerned with making a fast buck, or making themselves famous, although this may certainly happen; geniuses are concerned with a future that is sustainable, where we don't destroy, where we work together for a common good. Individual genius doesn't necessarily mean we become rich, famous, or wealthy. No one has ever proved that millionaires have higher IQs. We all know that an enormous house, fame, or money in the bank, is not an automatic ticket to peace or happiness. What I'm writing about is the type of personal genius that fulfills us throughout life because it's exciting, rewarding, and sustains and gives back to the world. Riches or material gain are merely a fringe benefit.

Every true genius throughout history was connected to their soul or spirit. This doesn't mean they had to believe in God, or even be religious or spiritual. But they had a vision, and they knew how to isolate themselves sufficiently from the insanity of the world to bring their vision to light. Genius requires great inner resolve and courage, which always comes from spirit. Spiritual geniuses work tirelessly in isolation, with no praise, glory, or kudos. Michelangelo spent seven years on a scaffold, on his back, painting the Sistine Chapel. Leonardo da Vinci spent seven years perfecting *The Last Supper.* Geniuses have staying power. One discovery or success leads to another. They rarely rest on their laurels, because their work is just too darn exciting, challenging, and rewarding. True geniuses see through the illusions, seductions, and insanity of society, refusing to conform. Neffe says, "A desire to go it alone and great independence of thought distinguish people whose creative breakthroughs succeed." This was certainly the case with Einstein whose rebellious streak began as soon as he entered school. Albert wanted his mentors to stimulate a love of learning and free thinking. Instead he saw his instructors as drill sergeants and criticized the "mindless and mechanical teaching methods, which, because of my poor memory for words, caused me great difficulties...I would rather let all kinds of punishment descend upon me than learn to rattle something off by heart." Because of this, his defiance of authority was permanently etched in his character. "He rebelled against any kind of authoritarian structure; against rigid rules in school and at the university; against the dictates of bourgeois life; against conventions such as dress codes; against dogmatism in religion and physics; against militarism, nationalism, and government ideology; and against bosses and employers. His opposition to all forms of opportunism was one of the most remarkable of his personality traits."

Many geniuses are ignored or rejected, because their ideas are so outlandish. Our minds believe they're crazy, stupid, dunces, addled. It's their spirit, a well spring of energy, not their minds that keeps them going. Einstein was told his Ph.D. dissertation was fanciful and irrelevant. Walt Disney was advised to give up drawing and was fired by a newspaper editor for lack of ideas. Dr. Seuss' first children's book was rejected 23 times. Most geniuses never give up; since they're fueled by spirit, they're like a bionic Ever Ready Bunny. They just keep going because they don't need approval or praise from society telling them they're right or brilliant. Their motivation is internal, unwavering; they simply know they're on the right track despite the rumblings of society. One of my favorite geniuses is Dr. Seuss, or Theodor Geisel—magazine writer, cartoonist, film maker, and advertising agent. Despite being one of the most famous "Drs." in the world, Geisel never finished his graduate studies in literature at Oxford. Not wanting to disappoint his father, who had great hopes for his son, he put "Dr." before his pen name. He began his career as a writer and propagandist during the American war effort against Nazi Germany. His cartoons were social statements against racism, and leaders such as Hitler and Mussolini; he also made several films about peace. He wrote and illustrated 46 children's books, along with several humorous books for adults. With high ethical standards, Geisel wouldn't allow his characters to be marketed into products that would impact children negatively. He had a brilliant sense of humor, and was a true visionary. Each children's book packed powerful messages: *The Lorax* showed the effects of corporate greed while advocating environmentalism and anti-consumerism, *The Sneetches* is a satire on the injustice of racial discrimination, *Yertle the Turtle* profiled Hitler and anti-authoritarianism, *How The Grinch Stole Christmas* criticized the materialism and commercialism of Christmas, *Thidwich the Big-Hearted Moose* was an anti-hunting statement, and *Bartholomew and the Oobleck* heralds the wisdom and beauty of nature, along with the dangers of greed, ego, playing God and dabbling in magic. When he completed *"Horton Hears a Who"* in 1954, who knew 50 years later, his book would become a blockbuster movie. But his spirit must have known the ageless wisdom in his book's core message, that everyone is important no matter how small or seemingly insignificant. Horton protected the residents of Whoville, tiny creatures who couldn't be heard or seen by the rest of society–who were living in a parallel dimension. The book is actually a fictionalized account of string field theory, the "theory of everything" that states several unobservable dimensions in the universe must exist—however we can't see them. Geisel's spirit had the ability to peer into the future and understand how important this message would become. And, as we'll see, there were many similarities between Dr. Seuss and Einstein: both were German, advocated the American war effort against Germany and anti-Semitism saw the necessity for the Second World War, but were essentially pacifists. They were both married twice and had affairs, believed in Christianity, were prolific writers, wrote poetry, adored humor, bequeathed much of their fortunes to their favorite university, and became increasingly popular after their deaths. Both men were introverts at heart and were most productive when allowed solitude. In her book *Quiet: The Power of Introverts in a World That Can't Stop Talking*, Susan Cain explains that Geisel was "a more quiet man than most of his jocular rhymes suggest," who spent most of his days sketching and writing in his private studio a bell-tower-like room at his La Jolla, California home. "He rarely ventured out in public to meet his young readership, fretting that kids would expect a merry, outspoken, Cat in the Hat-like figure, and would be disappointed with his reserved personality. 'In mass, (children) terrify me,' he admitted." Ironically Geisel who delighted and inspired countless children, never had children of his own. When asked about this, he would say, "You have 'em, I'll entertain 'em."

Many geniuses don't grow up into hardened adults—they display a childlike innocence, a sense of awe and a delight in simple things. They don't need all the trappings of adulthood to make them content; they are rich in their inner worlds. Ghandi preferred a loincloth over his lawyer's business suit, and Einstein, who reluctantly donned a tux for state occasions, was happiest when he was sockless, in sloppy old clothes. As an adult Einstein laughed at corny jokes, played like a child, and delighted in practical jokes. Hardened or cynical adults usually judge this trait as stupidity or naivety. According to Howard Gardner, intellectual giants like Einstein, Mozart, Picasso, and Ghandi, each remained a "perpetual" or "victorious child."

If enough people understand this, one budding genius at a time, we can change the world. One determined genius can make a huge difference. Jesus was an enlightened genius whose philosophy can be summed up in a few words; love, respect, and have compassion for one another. We don't have a single book, letter, or discourse written by Jesus, still, more than two thousand years after his death, for two weeks every December the entire world shuts down to honor Him because His teachings contained simple yet powerful truths that apply to every religion, atheist, or agnostic. That is genius. We live in a highly technical age, a time when we've been socialized to believe that without a laptop, tablet, blackberry, smart phone, iPod or GPS, we're at a disadvantage.

But technology, as we'll discover, can do marvelous things or it can drastically depress and dumb us down. Historians speculate that Atlantis possessed a highly sophisticated technology, beyond anything we've achieved, but it was the misuse of this technology that led to its demise. Atlantis, despite its brilliant minds, imploded or self-destructed. Before we had speed dials, people memorized and knew telephone numbers. Before the mass media, people had the time and capacity to wait several minutes for something important. Before multitasking, everyone focused on one thing at a time. Before GPS, we read and studied maps and charted our own courses. After reading the next few chapters you'll learn that Alfred Nobel, who patented 355 inventions, traveled the world by boat. Einstein, whom we can thank for much of our technological breakthroughs, like laser, GPS, digital technology, and computer chips, never used anything remotely electronic, not even a telephone—he meditated with a pencil and paper. He tapped into secrets of the universe without the use of a sophisticated telescope. He came up with his theory of relativity before he was awarded his Ph.D. Canadian Craig Kielburger was traveling in India and holding press conferences to raise awareness when he was thirteen-years-old. His impetus for this trip didn't come from the Internet, or television. He read a newspaper article that changed his life. Jesus travelled mostly on foot, and never went to college or university. Mohammad was illiterate; he could neither read or write, which was why he instructed his followers to memorize his teachings. Buddha reached enlightenment by quietly sitting under a Bodhi tree. Perhaps if we all meditated as much as the Buddha, we'd all be peaceful, insightful and enlightened.

Meditation Makes Us Smarter

Activities involving meditation and intensive prayer permanently strengthen neural functioning in specific parts of the brain that are involved with lowering anxiety and depression, enhancing social awareness and empathy, and improving cognitive and intellectual functioning. The neural circuits activated by meditation buffer you from the deleterious effects of aging and stress and give you better control over your emotions. At the very least, such practices help you remain calm, serene, peaceful and alert...
Andrew Newberg and Mark Waldman in *How God Changes Your Brain*

Until recently, we believed when you reached a certain age, your brain was fully developed; in other words, by age five or six intelligence was fixed. We also believed the older we got the more brain cells we lost, gradually depleting our intelligence. Medicine hadn't discovered plasticity, or recognized the brain's remarkable ability to grow and develop neurons at any age. In the last few decades we've learned from magnetic resonance imaging, or (MRI) technology, which provides a picture of the brain, (fMRI) functional magnetic resonance imaging, showing areas of increased blood flow so that we know which part of the brain is active when we're thinking a particular thought or performing a specific task, positron emission tomography (PET), which gives us 3-dimensional color images of the body, and magnetoencephalography (MEG), which measures magnetic fields generated by neuronal activity in the brain. Researchers can now observe different areas of the brain lighting up, illuminating changes in neuronal growth. We've realized it's not carved in stone that getting older depletes brain cells, and these discoveries may significantly change the rate of people who succumb to diseases like Alzheimer's and dementia.

In the past, to sharpen the brain, experts would advise typical left brain activities such as taking courses, crossword puzzles, brain teasers, Sudoku, or learning a new language. But this is not enough. Now we understand the critical importance of sleeping and dreaming to accelerate and consolidate the learning process. The brain is a huge storage facility or library—it needs time to determine where to store, keep, organize, and reorganize new material. The more we sleep to allow this storage and assimilation to take place, the smarter we are, because we've given our brain the necessary time to save and organize files. If we don't get adequate sleep while we're learning something new, the previous day's files may be lost, or never stored properly, and we can't remember the information. Sleeping and dreaming are incredibly important to accelerate learning and retain information long term.

What we've never really understood in the Western world, is that we desperately need down time during the day in the form of some meditative activity—and there are literally hundreds of enjoyable ways we can do this like going for a walk, yoga, running, painting, drawing, watching a fireplace, cooking, sweeping, gardening, feeding a baby, or watching a sunset. Any task we do alone with a single pointed focus does two critical things. One, it relaxes the brain—allowing it to rest, recuperate, and be more efficient—the same way taking frequent rests allows us to go a greater distance when taking a long walk or hike. This is why in the workplace we have coffee breaks–but we've been socialized to have caffeine, cigarettes, and conversation to stimulate us—rather than truly resting and relaxing. Secondly, this quiet time allows the wisdom of your spirit, soul, God, the Universe, a higher power, the force, whatever you want to call it, to come in and guide, inspire, inform, give insights, ideas, and solutions to problems. Understanding this is critical, because true genius needs this meditative down time to achieve those flashes of insight that the left brain is not capable of giving us. The left brain only processes, reprocesses, and repackages what it already knows—anything new, innovative, creative, even joyful is a right brain/heart/soul/spirit/God function. If we want to be wise, we need to meditate.

It wasn't until the twenty-first century that we finally had the scientific proof that meditative practices could make us smarter. We lacked the hard core data and studies of the human brain to back this up. Recently, new fields have exploded into awareness, neurotheology and affective neuroscience, both blending neurology, brain scans, positive emotions such as compassion, meditation, spirituality, and religious experiences. Two leaders in this field are Dr. Andrew Newberg, director of the Center for the Spirituality and the Mind, at the University of Pennsylvania, and Mark Robert Waldman, therapist and author. They've been studying the brains of Franciscan nuns, Buddhists, Pentecostal practitioners, Sikhs, Sufis, yoga practitioners, and advanced and beginning meditators, to further understand the neurochemical changes resulting from prayer, meditation, spiritual, and religious practices. They started with the premise of Hebbian learning, also called Hebb's rule, or Hebb's postulate, developed in 1949 by Canadian neuropsychologist, Donald O. Hebb. His theory, explaining the neuronal changes that occur during learning, is often simplified by the statement, "cells that fire together wire together." If we repeat any new task enough times it creates new pathways, or neuronal connections that fire and wire together, until this new skill is hard wired in the brain. When we meditate, which quiets the mind and creates fertile ground for new growth, it changes the activity at the end of a neuron, eventually changing the structure of the cell. When the mind is overly stressed or busy, new connections don't form at the same rate. A busy, highly stressed mind is like a car stuck in gridlock; a relaxed mind is like a car quickly finding new roads and routes. It's the same with our brain; when we cultivate quietness, or meditation, new growth and connections take place. Under a microscope, a single neuron in your brain looks a bit like the intricate structure of a tree's branch system. Each neuron can have as many as 10,000 branches reaching out to other neurons. These are called dendrites, derived from the Greek word for the branches of a tree. While chronic stress impairs memory by stopping dendrite growth, meditative activity can reverse this by allowing new dendrites to form. Neurons are capable of changing all the time; in less than two weeks a neuron can grow new axons and dendrites, and these changes can occur suddenly, just as new shoots can emerge in a garden overnight. In their book, *How God Changes Your Brain,* Newberg and Waldman suggest eight proven strategies to exercise and improve the neural functioning of your brain; having faith, talking with others, aerobic exercise, meditation, yawning to stimulate alertness, relaxing every day, staying intellectually active, and smiling!

Newberg says, "Spiritual practices, even when stripped of religious beliefs, enhance the neural functioning of the brain in ways that improve physical and emotional health." He believes contemplative practices such as meditation or yoga, "strengthen a specific neurological circuit that generates peacefulness, social awareness, and compassion for others." They've discovered a particular area of our brains, the anterior cingulate that is stimulated by meditation and increases our ability to be compassionate and to show empathy. Several studies have also shown that a regular meditative practice can actually reduce the cognitive decline that may result from aging. With the use of brain scans, Newberg has shown that after only eight weeks of meditative practice, and just twelve minutes a day, we can actually slow down our aging process. He writes, "Our brain-scan study showed that meditation...strengthens a specific circuit—involving the prefontal and orbital-frontal lobe, the anterior cingulate, basal ganglia, and thalamus–that would otherwise deteriorate with age. This circuit governs a wide variety of activities involved with consciousness, clarity of mind, reality formation, error detection, empathy, compassion, emotional balance, and the suppression of anger and fear. When this particular circuit malfunctions or deteriorates, it contributes to the formation of depression, anxiety, obsessive-compulsive behavior, and schizophrenia." Newberg also found that movement based meditation like yoga, or even hand movement during meditation increases the activity in the basal ganglia, lying deep in the center of our brains. "The basal ganglia helps control voluntary movements, posture, and motor sequencing, but it also plays an important role in memory formation, behaviourial control, and cognitive flexibility. Abnormal functioning in this area is associated with movement disorders like Parkinson's, Alzheimer's, Tourette's and Huntington's disease." He believes movement based meditation, such as walking or yoga, more than passive sitting meditation, will strengthen those parts of the brain normally associated with aging. His research also suggests that academic performance could be improved if meditation was widely used in our school system.

Meditation although enjoyable *is* a discipline—and like all other disciplines from weight lifting to running, the more you do it, the better you become. After examining numerous studies, Newberg found the effects of meditation are cumulative. If you decide after reading this book that you're going to take ten or fifteen quiet minutes every morning to slowly sip your coffee, you'll probably feel better after the first week, calmer, more alert, and peaceful. After a month your clarity will increase even more, but, if you make meditation a daily practice for a year, the effects get even better. He says "the longer and more frequently you meditate, the more changes you'll notice in the brain...Those who practice daily for thirty minutes or longer, and for many years, show the greatest difference in neural activity, not only when they are meditating, but when they are at rest."

Several universities, including Harvard, Princeton, Berkeley, and Madison, Wisconsin, are carrying out meditation research, and these studies are showing that daily meditation does rewire the brain. Over time this produces a higher frequency brain wave, gamma, increasing our ability to focus, pay attention, learn, and remember. Studies with Buddhist monks who meditate daily have shown gamma brain waves stay ramped up permanently—particularly in the region where you experience pleasant thoughts. These findings were made public in 2004 by neuroscientist Richard J. Davidson, at the University of Wisconsin, working in partnership with the Dalai Lama and eight experienced monks from India. The Dalai Lama, the spiritual leader of Buddhism, has a keen interest in science, but he has a greater reason for teaming up with researchers from Western universities—to alleviate suffering. Buddhism is a centuries old system of practices used to reduce misery and perfect humanity through quieting the mind and cultivating compassion. The Dalai Lama hoped the world would understand these methods don't have to be associated with a religious practice. He's hoping they'll be more widely accepted, once their relationship with the science of the brain is established. This partnership began in 1992, when Davidson, a distinguished scientist and spiritual seeker with research interests in psychology, neuroscience, and meditation wrote the Dalai Lama. Davidson was invited to the Dalai Lama's home in Dharamsala, India, to interview monks and gain a better understanding of how a lifetime of meditative experience affected thoughts and emotions. A decade later in 2002, the Dalai Lama allowed eight of his most accomplished monks from Dharamsala to travel to Davidson's lab where they were hooked up to electroencephalograph (EEG) testing and brain scanning equipment. These monks had an estimated 10,000 to 50,000 hours of meditation accumulated over 15 to 40 years. When Richardson hooked up the first French-born monk, Matthieu Ricard, he immediately noticed higher than normal brain activity–brain waves around *40* cycles per second. We normally operate at four brain wave frequencies; delta or very deep sleep where our brain waves are between 0.5 and 4 cycles per second, theta or deep sleep between 4 and 8 cycles per second, alpha the realm of light sleep, daydreams, and meditation with brain waves between 8 and 12 cps., and beta, the awake state with brain frequencies between 14 and 20 cycles per second. So brain waves above 20 cycles a second were a complete anomaly. But, if we delve into Ricard's life, it becomes apparent his elevated brain waves are the stuff of genius, right and left brain in perfect balance. After earning a Ph.D in molecular genetics at the prestigious Pasteur Institute in France, he traveled to the Himalayas to become a Buddhist monk. He's an accomplished writer, photographer, and translator. Ten days of talks in Nepal with his philosopher father, Jean-Francois Revel, became a best seller, *The Monk and the Philosopher* which was translated into 21 languages. After his book *Happiness: A Guide to Developing Life's Most Important Skill*, co-authored with Daniel Goleman, also became a bestseller, he's referred to as "the happiest person in the world." His entire book royalties are used for 30 humanitarian projects, in Tibet, Nepal, India and Bhutan, which earned him the French National Order of Merit. He's now a subject, collaborator, and consultant on numerous scientific studies around the world examining the effects of meditation on the brain.

Little wonder that Dr. Ricard's brain waves were off the scale; since gamma waves are normally weak and difficult to distinguish, the researchers had never seen anything like this before, and were worried there may be something wrong with their equipment or methods. But when they brought in the other monks, along with a control group of 10 students who had never meditated, they realized the monks produced gamma waves 30 times stronger than the students! Larger areas of the monks' brains were active, especially the left prefrontal cortex, the area responsible for positive emotions. The researchers also found the movement of the monks' brain waves was synchronized, or more coordinated, compared to the students. Some of these monks produced gamma wave activity more powerful than anything previously reported in a healthy person, and the most experienced meditators had the highest levels of gamma waves. Mental activities such as focus, memory, learning, and higher consciousness are associated with the types of enhanced neural coordination found with these Buddhist monks, since gamma waves knit together or synchronize brain circuits, leading to greater mental acuity. Since these monks had gamma waves even when they weren't meditating, it's clear meditation enhances brain power short term, and produces permanent changes leading to higher levels of intelligence, focus, energy, better memory, and more consistently positive thoughts and moods.

Davidson's book, *The Emotional Life of the Brain,* chronicles his thirty years of research into affective neuroscience—studying the brain to determine ways to enhance wellbeing, peace, and positive qualities of mind such as compassion and empathy. He says these gamma waves firing in the brains of Buddhist monks are "like Rockettes kicking as one from one side of the vast Radio City Music Hall stage to the other." When gamma waves are present and neurons are firing in sync there is greater clarity as if a mental fog lifts. Regions in the brain associated with empathy, were higher with these Buddhist monks, particularly a brain circuit that switches on at the sight of suffering, along with regions associated with movement, as if their brains "were itching to go to the aid of those in distress." The 15 meditation studies taking place at Davidson's Wisconsin lab, attracted the attention of Danish filmmaker Phie Ambo, who treated her own panic attacks with meditation rather than medication. This led to her film *Free the Mind: Can You Rewire the Brain Just by Taking a Breath?* It shows how mindfulness meditation helped treat emotional trauma in Iraq war veterans suffering from Post Traumatic Stress Disorder, and children with Attention Deficit Disorder. Davidson believes meditation is "the brain changing the brain," intentionally helping the mind "to be happier and suffer less." And his research has shown we don't have to have 40, 000 hours of meditation under our belts like Buddhist monks to reap its benefits. Half an hour of mindfulness based meditation for three months, decreased anxiety and depression, boosted immune systems, and reduced cortisol levels which cause elevated levels of stress. If meditation is continued, depression may be reduced by about 30 percent which is significant.

A 2003 study at the University of Wisconsin, by Richard Davidson and Jon Kabat-Zinn, showed that meditation not only revs up the brain, it seems to increase our body's immune system. They found increased antibodies to influenza in a group who had meditated for only eight weeks. In 2005, researchers from the Psychiatric Neuroimaging Research Program at Massachusetts General Hospital, Harvard Medical School, Yale University, and Massachusetts Institute of Technology, published "Meditation experience is associated with increased cortical thickness." They used a group of experienced meditators, who incorporated meditation into a daily routine; participants were not monks, but had between seven to nine years of practice, and spent four to six hours a week meditating. Researchers discovered that long-term meditation leads to structural changes in the areas of the brain that are important for sensory, cognitive, and emotional processing. In meditators these brain regions were actually thicker. They also discovered that when we meditate, we grow older and smarter, since daily meditation helps produce more brain cells and slows down age-related thinning of your frontal cortex. The longer you meditate, the thicker this prefrontal cortex (an area just behind the left forehead) becomes, welcome news for anyone wanting to ward off dementia. It would appear with meditation, being "thick in the head" or a "fathead" is definitely a good thing!

Research at universities around the world is also showing another way to boost brain power is to exercise on a regular basis—regardless of age, it's not only good for our bodies but equally good for our brains. There are many movement-type meditations that we'll discuss in the final chapter like yoga, tai chi, qigong, walking, hiking, running, swimming, and biking—almost any sport we do alone can be meditative. And what better way to balance or counter a sitting meditation than to exercise afterwards. Unfortunately, most people's brains are as out of shape as their bodies. The latest Statistics Canada report found that only 15 percent of Canadians are active for the 150 minutes of activity recommended per week, despite consistent evidence that regular exercise with middle-aged and older adults is associated with better brain function. Since the late 1990s we've known that the human brain can grow new neurons, a process called neurogenesis. This takes place in the hippocampi, the tiny seahorse-shaped structure tucked into the base of each lobe of the brain. The hippocampus is an important area for memory and learning; although it is not where memories are stored, it helps to form memories after receiving input from other areas of the brain. Research on animals has shown that exercise produces more neurons in the hippocampus. We now understand that active children with higher fitness levels have larger hippocampi, a strong reason to advocate daily physical education in schools. But, rather than increasing the amount of movement children receive, especially with non-competitive types of movement like yoga, quigong, and tai chi, that further stimulate the right brain, many schools are slashing budgets for fitness, often considered a frill or non-essential subject. In older adults the hippocampus usually shrinks by one to two percent a year, but exercise can actually offset that loss. Art Kramer, a neuroscientist at the University of Illinois explained in *Macleans*, "The interesting thing about exercise is that it has effects all over the brain—various measures of cognition, short-term and long-term memory, decision making, attention, executive function. You see improvements across the board."

True Spiritual Genius—Balance of Head and Heart

People who learn on logic and philosophy and rational exposition end by starving the best part of the mind.

J.B. Yeats

Historically we've had many geniuses who were quirky, cruel, obsessed, isolated, mad-professor types, however I believe we're moving towards a time of more socially balanced genius. Perhaps one can see how far we've come by examining the genius presented in Clifford Pickover's book, *Strange Brains and Genius: The Secret Lives of Eccentric Scientists and Madmen.* Here nine men are examined who were brilliant but unbalanced. In fairness to these men, it's clear many suffered from a host of mental illnesses; obsessive-compulsive behavior, bipolar disorder, manic depression, and phobias which contributed to their antisocial behavior, so this is in no way a judgment. It is only in the last century that we've taken a more humane approach to mental health and its treatment, and we still have a long way to go. Examining their lives shows the fine line that often exists between genius and insanity. Perhaps we can look at their lives keeping in mind Carl G. Jung's theory that many forms of mental illness result from complete disconnection from spirit. In some cases connecting with spirit may prevent an individual from warding off their personal demons and tipping into insanity. None of these men married or even developed a lasting friendship. Although they contributed greatly to society, their isolation made them social misfits and they certainly didn't have the social support, admiration, or love from society like Einstein who followed them.

Our first example, Nikola Tesla, 1856 to 1943, was the inventor of the induction motor and alternating current or (AC) transmissions. Because of Tesla we have AC motors, generators, transmission lines and a high voltage generator known as the "Tesla coil." Tesla Motors, an American electric-car maker, based in Palo Alto, California, named its company after this illustrious inventor. He's also famous for his work in developing radio communication. When he demonstrated a radio-controlled boat during an exhibition at Madison Square Garden in 1898, this was so revolutionary, awed spectators believed it must be magic, telepathy, or even a trained monkey hidden inside piloting the boat!

But Tesla's personal life was tragic. As a young man studying at the Austrian Polytechnic, he became addicted to gambling, billiards, chess and card playing and like many brilliant individuals never graduated. To cover up that he had dropped out of school, he broke off contact with his family. Throughout his life he was stricken with many illnesses. However, it seems he was a true visionary—something still completely misunderstood and undervalued. Biographer Margaret Cheney describes him seeing blinding flashes of light often accompanied by a vision. As a child he frequently had flashback to events that had happened earlier. Tesla like Einstein worked intuitively often seeing visions or pictures of his inventions. These visions often provided the solution to a problem he was working on, or he might see an invention with exact precision, including all the necessary dimensions he needed before he began construction. Tesla possessed a photographic memory and was able to memorize complete books. He spoke eight languages; Czech, English, French, German, Hungarian, Italian, Latin, and Serbo-Croatian. It's believed he suffered from obsessive-compulsive disorder (OCD) because he had an intense fear of dirt, germs, jewelry and round objects. He couldn't bear to touch anyone's hair, and didn't like to shake hands. He preferred darkness to light and was obsessed with the number three. He felt compelled to walk around the block three times before entering a building, and would demand 18 napkins (6 x 3) to polish all his eating utensils until they were spotless. If he read one book by an author, he was compelled to read everything they had written. In his lab after observing unusual signals from his receiver, he believed he was receiving extraterrestrial messages from Mars. He loathed anyone overweight, was openly critical of people's clothing, and fired his secretary because he felt she was too fat. Tesla never married and believed that chastity boosted his scientific abilities. He lived most of his life in a series of New York hotels, and most days walked to the park to feed the pigeons, often bringing injured birds to his room to nurse back to health. He fell in love with one of these pigeons, explaining, "There was one, a beautiful bird, pure white with light grey tips on its wings; that one was different. It was a female. I had only to wish and call her and she would come flying to me. I loved that pigeon as a man loves a women, and she loved me. As long as I had her, there was a purpose to my life." In his final years it's rumored he lived solely on milk and Nabisco crackers which he stacked in numbered cookie canisters. Despite his left-brained brilliance and the fact that he sold many patents, he died alone, impoverished, and in debt. A maid found him in his hotel room two days after he has passed away, when she ignored the "do not disturb sign" he had placed on the doorway.

Another eccentric genius was mathematical physicist Oliver Heaviside, a contender for the 1912 Nobel Prize. It was Heaviside's research that gave us the ability to make long distance telephone calls. A solitary figure, he never married, and was at odds with the scientific community for most of his life. His eccentricities included a love of working in dark, small, swelteringly hot rooms. He painted his finger nails cherry pink, and replaced his comfortable furniture with large granite blocks. After writing his name he added the initials "W.O.R. M." He was antisocial and referred to his neighbors as "insolently rude imbeciles." He needed a female housemate to look after him, but kept her as a virtual prisoner or slave, forcing her to sign a contract agreeing never to marry, and demanded she not see friends, "You must write to your friends and tell them not to come to see you."

Henry Cavendish, a physicist and chemist who lived from 1731 to 1810, attended the University of Cambridge, but didn't finish his degree—he didn't need to. Despite his lack of formal education he has been lauded as the successor to Isaac Newton, who died four years before Cavendish was born. Pickover describes Cavendish as a "virtual Donald Trump." He was born into one of England's wealthiest families, and at age 40 inherited a huge sum of money from an aunt, making him one of the richest men alive. But this wealth had absolutely no bearing on his lifestyle. Rather than becoming a hedonist, he used every penny to buy books and laboratory equipment. Cavendish is described as a shabby, eccentric man, who rarely spoke, and when he did it was with the squeaky, hesitant voice of a cornered mouse. Tall, gaunt, Cavendish chose 50-year-old clothing, usually a faded crumpled violet suit with a high collar, frilled cuffs, and a three-cornered hat. But while he lacked right brained social graces, he excelled in left brained experimentation, including geology, magnetism, optics, pure mathematics, mechanics, and industrial science. His most celebrated work is perhaps his discovery of the chemical composition of water. He was the first to state that water consists of oxygen united with hydrogen. Cavendish gave us the chemical composition of air and water, the nature and properties of hydrogen, the specific heat of various substances, and numerous properties of electricity. He measured the density and mass of the Earth in an ingenious experiment now known as the Cavendish experiment. At age 70, Cavendish "weighed" the world using highly sensitive balances, determining that the earth was 5.45 times as dense as water. Today, using highly sophisticated techniques, we've found that the earth is precisely 5.5268 times denser than water. Other lesser known research included, work on the altitude of the aurora, a reconstruction of the Hindu civil year, a calculation of nautical astronomy, and a method of marking divisions on circular astronomical instruments. Cavendish also improved the accuracy of the mercury thermometers, discovered nitric acid, paving the way for Alfred Nobel's famous research with explosives, and designed ways to protect gunpowder from lightning.

Since he shunned the limelight and was mortified at the thought of public acclaim, his work spanning fifty years was mostly unpublished except for a few papers he wrote for the Royal Society of London. Because he didn't write any books or publish the bulk of his findings, his electrical experimentation was discovered in notebooks and manuscripts nearly a century later by mathematical physicist James Clerk Maxwell. Since the scientific community was not aware of his work, others had been given credit for Cavendish's discoveries.

Despite his scientific brilliance, he was bereft of social skills. He was celibate, never marrying because social interaction of any kind terrified him. Cavendish rarely appeared in public, and the only people he uttered a few squeaky words to were scientists. The rare times he ventured out, anyone he spoke to was instructed to look away while talking to him. If this rule wasn't followed, he would jump in a cab, and escape to the safety of his home. Cavendish was so shy around women he preferred writing notes rather than talking to his female housekeeper, and a second staircase was built in his house to avoid any interaction. He ordered housekeepers to keep out of sight, and if they had the audacity to violate this rule by exposing an arm, leg, or their face, they were immediately fired. Before his death, he ordered everyone out of the room; he wanted to die alone, the same way he had lived.

Although these men all possessed left brain brilliance, they were severely challenged when it came to personal relations and the ability to love. Their eccentric lopsided intelligence was only half of the equation needed to possess true genius. As we'll see, many of the geniuses of the last one hundred years have gone beyond being book smart. They are humanitarians with a social conscience, helping the world evolve to a place of greater balance. We'll examine perhaps the more enlightened genius of Alfred Nobel, Albert Einstein, Craig and Mark Keilburger, Roxanne Joyal, and Ricky Martin, individuals who possessed left brained brilliance, along with a right brain social and humanitarian approach to life. Hopefully these stories will enlighten and inspire, because every genius is a visionary; they stir up passions, promote a sense of awe, show us a better way, and give reason for hope.

CHAPTER THREE
Twentieth Century Genius

*The intuitive mind is a sacred gift and the rational mind is a faithful
servant. We have created a society that honors
the servant and has forgotten the gift.*

Albert Einstein

EVER WONDER WHY, IN THE last one hundred years, we've made more
progress in every conceivable area than the last thousand years? For a
thousand years, we were literally in the dark, no light bulbs, computers,
antibiotics, cars, telephones, indoor plumbing, or refrigerators. In 1900,
in North America, the average life expectancy was 48 for men and 51 for
women, only 14 percent of homes had a bathtub, and 8 percent of homes
had a telephone. Our ancestors traveled by horse and buggy, and the
speed limit for the few cars that existed was 10 miles per hour. Shampoo,
toothpaste, and deodorant hadn't been invented, and most people washed
their hair once a month with an egg and Borax mixture. Only 6 percent of
people graduated from high school. Marijuana, heroin, and morphine were
prescription drugs, with heroin prescribed to regulate stomach and bowels.

Historians tell us that in the last 100,000 years, the average life span
was around 30 years. Between 1850 and 1900, the Victorian area, it grew
to 40 years. But it has doubled in the last 100 years; instead of people
dying in their 40s, the average life expectancy is now the mid-80s, and
we have thousands of people living well into their 100s, a virtually
impossible feat a hundred years ago. World Future Society tells us in the
year 2000 there were 135,000 centenarians, and predict that number will
rise to 2.2 million by 2050. Perhaps we're preparing for the notion of
living for eternity, or at the very least extending our lives considerably.
This notion of living longer was prophesized before the time of Christ; in
Isaiah 65:17 we're told, "The Lord says, 'I am making a new earth and
new heavens. The events of the past will be completely forgotten. Be
glad and rejoice forever in what I create. The new Jerusalem I make will
be full of joy, and her people will be happy. I myself will be filled with
joy because of Jerusalem and her people. There will be no weeping there,

no calling for help. Babies will no longer die in infancy, and all people will live out their life span. Those who live to be one hundred will be considered young. To die before that would be a sign that I had punished them…Like trees my people will live long lives. They will fully enjoy the things that they have worked for. The work they do will be successful, and their children will not meet with disaster. I will bless them and their descendants for all time to come. Even before they finish praying to me, I will answer their prayers."

We now have teams of researchers around the world investigating longevity, trying to determine the secrets of people who are living happily into their hundreds just as the Bible predicted. This quest for the fountain of youth began with Lewis Terman, a Stanford University psychologist with a lifelong interest in genius and gifted children, who had teachers hand-pick their most gifted students from California classrooms in 1921. Terman was hoping to find the factors or traits that led to intellectual leadership, and collected a staggering amount of data over 35 years. However, he was working on volume five of *Genetic Studies of Genius* in 1956 when he passed away. Because IQ tests and the study of genius was relatively new, few researchers had accumulated so much information into the everyday lives of gifted students. His data was of great interest to a host of researchers, particularly those investigating longevity, since many of these students nicknamed "Termites," led productive lives into their eighties and nineties, while others died relatively young. Terman's gifted students were studied over 80 years, and the findings became the subject of the book *The Longevity Project* unlocking the secrets to living a long, healthy life. Co-authors Howard Friedman and Leslie Martin debunked many myths on longevity, finding with the 1,528 subjects they followed, it wasn't a carefree attitude or being popular and outgoing, taking life easy, playing it safe, or avoiding stress that added years to life. Instead it was those who had a lifelong pattern of persistence, prudence, conscientiousness, dependability, hard work, organization, and close involvement with friends and community. It seems this is that magical fountain of youth we've been searching for, combined with, "an active pursuit of goals, a deep satisfaction with life, and a strong sense of accomplishment…having a large social network, engaging in physical activities that naturally draw you in, giving back to your community, enjoying and thriving in your career, and nourishing a healthy marriage or close friendships." In Einstein's case, persistence certainly paid off, "It's not I that I'm so smart," he once said, "It's that I stay with problems longer. This type of genius adds not just years but often decades to lives. Longevity studies are taking place around the world in what are termed Blue Zones, most notably Sardinia off the coast if Italy, Okinawa in Japan, Nicoya in Costa Rica and Loma Linda in southern California in the United States. Many of these people lived simply and poorly; a 102-year-old Sardinian farmer interviewed for a CBC radio documentary, said the secret to his life happy life with his 100-year-old wife was that they were always laughing, "poor but happy." Many were farmers and shepherds leading lives of simplicity, hard work, and no doubt hours of meditation each day as they watched their sheep! Dan Buettner, a writer for *National Geographic,* is regarded as a longevity expert with his bestselling book *Blue Zones.* Not only did he interview centenarians, but younger men and women, to get a truer idea of the lifestyles that lead to longevity. One of these youngsters was 75-year-old Sardinian shepherd Tonino Tola, who had already been up since 4 a.m. the day Dan interviewed him. When Dan arrived at 9:45 a.m. he had "already pastured his sheep, cut wood, trimmed olive trees, fed his cows," and was butchering a cow! Every day for 70 years he had walked or ridden his donkey the incredibly steep five-mile trip to watch his sheep on his mountaintop pasture. Atop this mountain with its stunning vistas, Dan impulsively blurted out, "Do you ever get bored?" but realized he'd "uttered a heresy" before the words left his mouth. In our fast-paced westernized world we're not completely comfortable with such a meditative, simple lifestyle—this is probably akin to those Buddhists monks discussed earlier with gamma brain waves. When we're immersed in a world that's constantly doing, and never take time to rest, relax, meditate, contemplate, or enjoy nature, we get incredibly bored as soon as we stop doing things— tranquility and peace appears boring because it's never been part of our experience. Our jittery left brain gets nervous, and revolts at the thought of slowing down and allowing the right brain or spirit to take over, soothe, and inform it for thirty minutes. An over-stimulated left brain is much like a three-year-old rebelling against their much needed afternoon nap. "I've loved living here every day of my life," Tonino replied. "I love my animals and taking care of them." And how could he not? When we truly link into the genius of simplicity and the meditative state, our brain waves have essentially migrated into the higher realms of heaven on earth. Tonino explained that without this lifestyle, "I would be sitting in my house doing nothing. I would have little purpose in life."

The longest recorded life span belongs to a French woman, Jeanne Calment, who reached 122 years! She lived in the south of France, the same idyllic territory as Vincent Van Gogh whom she met in the 1880s. At 21, she married a wealthy businessman and never worked, but played the piano, went to operas, rode in hunting parties, played tennis, swam, and bicycled. Jeanne biked to her 100th birthday party! She took up fencing at 85, rode her bike until she was 100, and after her husband died of food poisoning when she was 67, she lived on her own. She had one daughter Yvonne, who died of pneumonia at 36, leaving her an eight-year-old grandson to raise. There is speculation her longevity had a lot to do with her healthy Mediterranean diet and the wine she enjoyed drinking. Calment believed it was because of the olive oil she liberally poured on her foods and rubbed on her skin. She joked, "I've never had but one wrinkle, and I'm sitting on it!"

All these advances are coupled with an exploding population; data from the UN tells us in 1800 there were one billion people living on earth, in 1900 this had only grown to 1.6 billion, by 2000 it jumped to 6 billion, and by 2011 we had over 7 billion people. Perhaps every soul that ever lived wants to return to earth for some important event! We are embarking on an unprecedented time in history—a time of tumultuous change, and many individuals have been preparing the way. We're moving into an era where many of the old rules will be eliminated; old systems of business and government based on corruption, greed, half-truths, and exclusion, are crumbling daily. Earthquakes, tsunamis, tornados, tropical storms, and hurricanes, are literally shaking up the earth, the same way a building shakes in its foundations when it is demolished, making way for something new. As painful as these events may be, many believe they're ushering in much needed change—perhaps a golden age, the new Jerusalem we're promised in the Bible—indeed a time when "those who live to be a hundred will be considered young."

Information travels from the heavens or spirit world when the earth is ready to receive it. Insight is released when there's a need for change, a shift in consciousness, or when we're capable of understanding new concepts. When we're ready for heightened awareness, it's downloaded from elevated dimensions while we sleep. But new information is usually met with considerable resistance, since our left brain desperately clings to the past, routine, and what it already knows. There's usually vehement opposition to spiritual genius, because it challenges the status quo. It's no easy task rewiring or building new neuronal circuitry in the brain, like going to the gym each day and lifting weights—it takes time, discipline, and vision. Einstein spoke from experience when he said, "Great spirits have always encountered violent opposition from mediocre minds."

There have been many times in history when the alignment of the stars and planets caused shifts in human outlook and perception. The fall of the Roman Empire marked the end of a military era characterized by left brain oppression, domination and desire for supremacy and control.

To balance this, during the Italian Renaissance there was a right brain revival of classical art, philosophy, science, architecture, literature, and learning, that lasted from the 14th to the 16th century. The age of Enlightenment followed, another right brained philosophical movement of the 18th century. The industrial revolution of the 19th century activated our left brains once again. In the early 20th century, when people were ready for cars, airplanes, abstract art, Eastern philosophy, and scientific breakthroughs, information was filtered through the dreams of scientists, inventors, artists and spiritual leaders—perhaps for the first time activating both right and left hemispheres. Two of these brightest stars, bursting into human consciousness were Alfred Nobel and Albert Einstein.

Alfred Nobel's Genius (1833-1896)

Justice is to be found only in imagination.

Alfred Nobel

Nobel is a classic example of an individual who balanced both head and heart. He was instrumental in producing dynamite and explosives, a mind-based task, but, also created the Nobel Prizes from his heart inspiring countless individuals to work towards a common good. Although labeled the "merchant of death" for inventing explosives, Nobel was a pacifist. Born in Stockholm, Sweden, in 1833, it was his destiny to choose a family who dabbled in explosives, since he would undoubtedly shake up the world. His father, Immanual Nobel, an engineer, inventor, and businessman, experimented with underwater mines and different methods of blasting rock which led to frequent explosions and fires in the Nobel family factories.

One of these early explosions destroyed Immanual's Swedish factory, leaving him bankrupt. He fled to Russia hoping to re-establish himself, leaving behind a wife and young family. During this time, young Alfred helped run a small milk and produce store, while his older brother, seven-year-old Ludvig, sold matchsticks. Back in St. Petersberg, Immanual was enormously successful, having convinced the Russian government to support his scheme to develop naval mines. When the family reunited in 1842, Immanual had accrued wealth and power, employing over one thousand workers in his factory—quite a feat since Russia was technically lagging behind the rest of Europe. During this era of the Crimean War and Florence Nightingale, his factory made iron components for steam engines and industrial machines, armaments, mines, cannonballs, and mortars.

As a boy, Alfred was shy and withdrawn, seldom playing with other children, but he was an excellent student. When eight-year-old Albert moved to Russia, he never formally attended college or university, instead, his father hired teachers to educate his four sons. Immanual wrote, "My good and industrious Alfred...is held in high esteem by his parents and brothers, both for his knowledge and his untiring capacity for work, which is excelled by no one." Alfred was taught literature and philosophy, and learned to speak six languages fluently: Russian, French, English, Italian, and German, besides his native Swedish. He received his natural science training from two professors, experts in chemistry, mathematics and physics. From an early age Alfred loved chemistry and physics, often carrying out his own experiments—all left brain functions. He was also an avid reader of fiction, philosophy, English Romantics, and enjoyed writing his own drama and poetry, which developed his right brain. Despite his early genius, young Alfred didn't excel in physical strength. He's described as being sickly, scrawny, weak, and prone to illness, a condition that would last his lifetime. After being bedridden for a prolonged time, he wrote this poem in English.

> *When fellow boys are playing*
> *He joins them not, a looker-on,*
> *And thus debarred the pleasures of his age*
> *His mind keeps brooding over those to come.*

His mother encouraged his interest in poetry, but his father believed this was flighty stuff and the boy was too introverted. Hoping to groom his son to join the family business as an engineer, his father sent Alfred to Germany, France, and the United States to study chemical engineering. But, this education continued to be informal and experimental; Nobel never attended college or university. While in France, he met an Italian chemist, Ascanio Sobrero, who had invented the explosive liquid nitroglycerine, by combining glycerine with sulphuric and nitric acid. Although nitroglycerine was more explosive than gun powder, it was still too dangerous to be widely used, since chemists hadn't found a way to keep it from exploding when subjected to heat and pressure. Given Alfred's family background in explosives, the possibilities of nitroglycerine intrigued him. When he returned to his father's business in Sweden, he continued experimenting using nitroglycerine.

But a year later, tragedy struck when an explosion in their factory killed his brother Emil and four workers. Immanual was so grief stricken he became temporarily paralyzed, and a month after his son's death, he suffered a stroke, and remained bedridden for eight years until his death. After the explosion, Alfred's older brother Robert advised him to "quit as soon as possible the damned career of an inventor, with merely brings disaster in its train." Alfred also had to contend with mobs of angry citizens who were chanting, brandishing pitchforks, and calling his factory a "deathship." Historians believe railway and mining interests, desperate for this explosive, prevented the police from charging the Nobel family with murder. A settlement was reached, fines were paid, and Alfred was prohibited from experimenting or manufacturing nitroglycerin within the Stockholm city limits.

Despite his father's collapse, his brother's warnings, and the wrath of the people of Stockholm, Alfred was driven to continue experimenting to make nitroglycerine safer. To escape the angry mobs, his factory became a covered barge, anchored in the middle of Lake Malaren outside the city limits, where Alfred worked alone, often bundled against the cold. He knew nitroglycerin was superior to gunpowder, so Nobel began peddling his product to mining districts throughout Europe, carrying padded suitcases containing his blasting oil. Eventually, it was used in the United States throughout the Sierra Nevada, for the Central Pacific Railway, saving millions of dollars and months of time that would have been spent shoveling out tunnels and in Australia for mining, England for slate quarries, and Norway and Sweden for mines and railways.

But the next few years were volatile, with several mining accidents and explosions, and millions of dollars of property damage as nitroglycerine exploded while being transported. Alfred built factories that were demolished by explosions, until the Nobel name became a nasty word, and many of his operations were shut down. The United States considered making any deaths linked to transporting nitroglycerine punishable by hanging, railroads refused to carry it, ships refused it as a cargo, and longshoremen wouldn't handle it. Undaunted, Nobel continued his research. It was tedious, lonely, and nerve-racking work, along with the knowledge that he could be blasted to bits any second! Often he was locked in his lab for weeks, breathing stale air and chemical fumes which gave him such excruciating headaches, he had to lie on the floor with a cold compress wrapped around his head. He deprived himself of a normal life, social contact, and adequate exercise, all in his quest to solve this dynamite dilemma.

Eventually, he discovered that mixing nitroglycerine with absorbent silica would turn it from a liquid into a paste, and this paste could then be inserted into long rods to create an explosive. After successfully devising a blasting cap for this invention, Alfred named his brainstorm dynamite, after the Greek *dynamos,* meaning "powerful." In 1867, at age thirty, Alfred obtained the patent for dynamite, unleashing powers that would explode worldwide. Since it was used in drilling tunnels and building canals, railways, ports, bridges, and roads, he never viewed his patent as destructive. Naively, he said, "My dynamite will sooner lead to peace than a thousand world conventions. As soon as men will find that in one instant, whole armies can be utterly destroyed, they surely will abide by golden peace."

As his dynamite ignited the world, so did his fortune. He was an inventive genius possessing a mind constantly erupting with new ideas. Work was his passion. Despite ill health, he never gave up his love of research, working nonstop in his 93 laboratories and factories in 20 countries around the world. Alfred said, "Home is where I work and I work everywhere." He was an experimenter and inventor, managing director, engineer, chemist, traveling salesman, public relations correspondent, treasurer, and advertising manager. He also invented synthetic leather and silk, tools for aerial photography, and blood transfusions, and improved explosives and firearms, racking up 355 patents and becoming one of the wealthiest men in the world. Alfred worked tirelessly to safeguard his patents, while continuing research, building new companies, and carrying out his business before telephone, fax, or airplanes were available. He led a hectic, stressful life, traveling the world by train or boat.

Despite his money, Alfred was never healthy; he suffered from epilepsy and experienced migraines, rheumatism, stomach problems, and bronchitis. When he developed angina pectoris, doctors prescribed nitroglycerin since highly diluted forms had been found to dilate blood vessels and increase oxygen supply to the heart. "It sounds like the irony of fate," he wrote, "that I should be ordered to take nitroglycerin internally. They call it trinktin so as not to scare pharmacist and public." He never married and viewed himself as a melancholic loner. "I am a misanthrope and yet utterly benevolent, have more than one screw loose yet am a super-idealist who digests philosophy more efficiently than food." At 43, hoping to find a wife, he placed this ad in a Paris newspaper, "Wealthy, highly-educated elderly gentleman seeks lady of mature age, versed in languages, as secretary and supervisor of household." The ad was answered by thirty-three-year-old Austrian Countess, Bertha Kinsky. Bertha had been employed as a governess, but answered the ad after her affair with the family's eldest son was discovered. She and Alfred developed an immediate rapport, but Bertha only stayed in his employment for one week. When Nobel was in Sweden, she eloped with her lover, Baron Arthur von Suttner, becoming

Bertha von Suttner. But this brief employment created the spark for a lifelong friendship, and historians believe Bertha's personal beliefs had a great effect on this "wealthy gentleman." Both shared an interest in pacifism. He once wrote her that the weapons he was creating would bring peace because, "On the day when two army corps will be able to annihilate each other in one second, all civilized nations will recoil from war in horror and disband their forces." But Nobel lived long enough to realize that the explosives he patented had the opposite effect; the power they unleashed created an insatiable demand.

By the time Nobel was in his fifties, his heavy work schedule had compromised his health, his heart was weakening, and doctors advised him to put his personal affairs in order. He wrote, "For the last nine days I have been ill and have had to stay indoors with no other company than a paid footman; no one inquires about me...My heart has become as heavy as lead." Another time he wrote, "I have no memories to cheer me, no pleasant illusions of the future to comfort me, or about myself to satisfy my vanity. I have no family to furnish the only kind of survival that concerns us, no friends for my affections or enemies for my malice." Perhaps it was during this lonely, melancholy period, that he began pondering the legacy he wanted to leave. Around this time, another event shook Nobel; his obituary appeared in a Paris newspaper. The reporter had confused the Nobel siblings, since it was his older brother Ludvig who had passed away. But even more shocking was his portrayal as a calculating monster. The obituary described how he had risen to great power and wealth after discovering dynamite, profiting from death, misery, human mutilation, lost eyes, arms and legs, all resulting from his explosives and weapons.

The Nobel Prizes

Contentment is the only real wealth.

Alfred Nobel

Historians believe this obituary and Nobel's ill health led to the creation of the Nobel Prizes. Although work had been his entire life, work alone was no longer sustaining him. A year before his death Alfred wrote, "I have great things to think about...at least one great thing—the passing from light to darkness, from life into the eternal unknown or, as Spencer calls it, the unknowable." Nobel was 63 when he died from a stroke. He was found early one morning slumped in his chair. Although he'd been advised by a heart specialist to stop working, Alfred continued experimenting with ballistics and guns in his Italian lab where the climate was warmer. When Nobel died, he owned over 93 factories, shares in factories and businesses in nine countries, six mansions in five European countries, real estate, numerous patents, intellectual property, and many other assets.

Historian Stephen Bown explains, "He was a man so driven to succeed that it damaged his health and ruined his chances for a family of his own, yet he took little pleasure in the trappings of wealth...In addition to being a persistent technical genius, Nobel was an introspective, poetic, and somewhat gentle soul. He did not want to believe that the source of all his wealth, success, prestige and honor was merely greater power for destruction and better methods for killing...he had a conscience, and as he aged and began thinking of his own death, he wanted more than to be known as an eccentric multimillionaire who made his fortune as a merchant of death...His last will and testament merely reflected the polarized inconsistencies that he wrestled with throughout his life, the irreconcilable contradictions between his head and his heart."

Alfred rewrote his will several times to ensure his wishes be carried out. Since he distrusted lawyers, he handwrote a four page document in Swedish, witnessed by four members of the Swedish Club, and deposited this will in a Stockholm vault where it quietly ticked away his explosive ideas. The administration of his estate was entrusted to two Swedish men he had known only briefly. He wanted Swedish executors because "it was in Sweden that he had met the greatest proportion of honest men." These two men had absolutely no legal experience, but Nobel believed in their integrity and honesty. Ragnar Sohlan, who Nobel described as "one of my few most favorite people," was twenty-six, and had worked for Nobel as a personal assistant in Italy and Sweden. His second executor, Rudolf Lilljequist, was forty, and had met Nobel twice.

There were undoubtedly times when Lilljequist wished he'd never met Nobel. Administering his will was a five-year saga, spanning the nine countries where he owned real estate and stocks. It involved struggles with Nobel's angry relatives, and with the institutions Nobel had selected to receive his prizes. All this was carried out before electronic money transfers, or reliable international agreements. Nobel's assets were sold, collected, and physically transported. His executors spent years traveling, negotiating, converting money, and hauling briefcases containing huge sums of money from country to country, before depositing them in Swiss banks. Both men knew that hold-ups and robberies were possible, so they developed a system of watching each other's backs, with the aid of loaded revolvers (possibly models improved by Nobel).

Although a small portion of Nobel's fortune went to relatives and friends, his will stated that $9 million be used as "prizes to those who, during the preceding year, shall have conferred the greatest benefit to mankind." Alfred's altruistic will attracted worldwide attention. In the 1890s, it was unprecedented to give away money for scientific or charitable purposes. He was criticized for the international aspect of his philanthropy; people believed the prizes should remain in Sweden.

But on December 10, 1901, the fifth anniversary of his death, the first Nobel Prizes were awarded in physics, chemistry, medicine, literature, and peace, the five areas closest to his heart. Alfred specified that the peace prize be awarded to the person who had done "the most or the best work for fraternity among nations, for the abolition or reduction of standing armies, and for the holding and promotion of peace congresses." A sixth award in economics was added in 1969, financed by the Swedish National Bank. Today, the Nobel Prizes are the most prestigious in the world. Originally denominated in Swedish kronor, they have multiplied 66 times since their inception. Each winner receives 10 million kronor ($1.5 million Canadian or $1.5 million US), a diploma, gold medal, and there is a lavish banquet, with Swedish royalty in attendance.

However, many still believe that Nobel's interests were more self-serving than altruistic. Bown reminds us that dynamite has caused terrible injuries, death, and irreparable environmental damage. Just before his death, Nobel bought a Swedish ironworks which he turned into the prominent ammunition manufacturer, Bofors. Bown says, "One of the greatest ironies of Nobel's endowment of the peace prize was that it represented a radical departure from the ideas he held throughout most of his life." His philosophies and work ethic seemed completely at odds. A few years before his death, Alfred said, "I wish all guns with their belongings and everything could be sent to hell." But he continued to experiment with more reliable fuses, silent firing arms, more stable and predictable projectiles, and better sealed firing chambers. His lifelong friend, Countess von Suttner, also didn't accept Nobel's theory that weapons would bring peace. She advocated an international tribunal to handle disputes between nations, eventually becoming President of the Permanent International Peace Bureau. In 1889, she published a bestselling anti-war novel *Die Waffen Nieder* (Lay Down Your Arms), which was translated into several languages, making her famous throughout Europe. Her book was a passionate plea for peace and disarmament, and Nobel, writing to congratulate her, said she was "an amazon who so valiantly wages war against war." Bertha became the first female to win his Peace Prize in 1905. Whether Nobel designed his prizes due to a guilty conscience, or the sincere desire to help humanity, or both, we'll never know for sure, but the Nobel Prizes have had a tremendous positive impact. In the last century the Nobel Peace Prize has been awarded to people like Martin Luther King, Bishop Desmond Tutu, the Dalai Lama, Mother Teresa, and international groups such as Doctors Without Borders, The Red Cross, The United Nations Peace Keeping Forces, and Amnesty International. Perhaps after a lifetime of working on explosives, his greatest act of genius was realizing he could inspire others. Whatever your opinion, this man with a left brain passion for chemistry, physics, science, and business, but with an equal right brain love of poetry, literature, drama, philosophy and peace, continues to inspire humanity more than a hundred years after his death. His prizes have become the most esteemed rewards internationally, not only for their monetary value, but for the honor and integrity they bring. When international philanthropy was unheard of, it was Nobel who gave birth to the concept of a more balanced genius.

Albert Einstein's Genius (1879-1955)

Nothing that I can do will change the structure of the universe. But maybe, by raising my voice I can help the greatest of all causes —
goodwill among men and peace on earth.

Albert Einstein

It was time for a new messiah to arise after the hardships and horrors of World War I. This messiah was a secular saint; a brilliant clown who could make the world laugh by sticking out his tongue at reporters, advance the world forever through his scientific theories, and foster compassion and respect for humanity. Max Born, one of Einstein's friends, explained, "People who had lost all faith in higher values during these years of misery, murderous warfare, lies and slander saw their hopes revived by the appearance of a simple, modest man who calmly contemplated the nature of space, time, and matter in the thick of all these hellish circumstances, and helped lift the veil of mystery surrounding creation." Perhaps the world had been waiting in silent desperation for this new messiah. Before Einstein, science had given us scant hope; instead, it issued a triple threat to our dignity. Copernicus discovered the sun, not the earth, was the center of the universe, Darwin believed we weren't created by God, but had evolved from apes, and Freud declared we were soulless creatures, controlled by a base animal instinct called the id, which was violent, self-serving, and brutal.

Then Einstein floated down, seemingly from another dimension, restoring our shattered dignity. Biographer Jürgen Neffe calls him "a breaker of taboos, part Galileo and part Gandhi, he succeeded in synthesizing artistic freedom with philosophical power." Einstein is a stellar example of combining right and left brain, head and heart, since he was both scientist and humanitarian. His life offers countless clues on how to cultivate genius, not a nerdy isolated type of intellect; he was definitely not a hermit, as you'll see, quite the opposite—a people's saint and a ladies' man. When Alfred Nobel passed away in 1896, Einstein was only seventeen—but tacitly the torch was passed. By 1921, when Einstein was in his early forties, he received the Nobel Prize in Physics. Einstein has been named *Time* magazine's "Person of the Century, and is often referred to as "the greatest physicist of all time," "the greatest scientist of the twentieth century," and "one of the supreme intellects of all time." His discoveries are so important, that the world of physics can be referred to as "pre-" and "post-Einstein." Neffe says, "Today, Einstein's popular image—a craggy face encircled by a white mane, with a bulbous nose and a look of wide-eyed innocence—is better known than that of any other human being...Even his name seemed tailored to work its way into people's memories and take root there. It is a strange, catchy German name pregnant with meaning (it translates as "one stone"), mighty as a monolith. The two syllables of 'Einstein' even rhyme."

Neuroscientist Sandra Witelson, from McMaster University, says, "Genius is not a sufficient word for this man. He had a rare combination of brilliance, confidence, gentleness and a piercing intellect. Even his name has extraordinary charisma." Einstein has shaped our understanding of everything from the smallest nuclear particles to the structure of the universe. He proposed new ways of understanding time, space, mass, and energy, light, motion, gravity, and electromagnetism. Astrophysicist Clifford Will credits Einstein's theory of relativity for changing modern physics. "Special relativity underlies everything we understand about light, atoms, nuclei and quarks, and is now part of the standard toolkit of every working physicist. General relativity has been part of a sea of change in astronomy. Whereas once the universe was seen as a quiet place of steady, fixed stars and wispy nebulae, it is now a jungle out there, with its exploding supernovae, colliding galaxies, mysterious black holes and, of course, the most violent of all events, the Big Bang." We owe much to Einstein. He laid the foundations for modern physics, modern chemistry, microelectronics, cellular phones, the "photoelectric effect" used for today's digital photography, computer chips, the Internet, superconductivity, and nanotechnology. He provided the theory needed to develop the laser (light amplification by the stimulated emission of radiation), gave us the formulas to develop GPS Global Positioning Systems, and laid the foundations for modern cosmology, the study of our universe as a whole. He even answered questions such as why rivers bend and why the sky is blue.

Science writer, Ed Regis, has called him "science's one and only saint: Saint Albert." His scientific biographer, Abraham Pais, a colleague of Einstein's and renowned physicist, speaks of his friend in a manner usually reserved for biblical prophets. "He carries the message of a new order in the universe. He is a new Moses come down from the mountain to bring the law and a new Joshua controlling the motion of heavenly bodies. He speaks in strange tongues but wise men aver that the stars testify to his veracity." Ed Regis says, "It's hard to avoid the holy connotations that hang over the man. Einstein's nimbus of silvery hair evokes a halo. His preserved eyes and brain are like saintly relics. And what did he do in his "miracle year" but perform scientific miracles? ...the Einstein museums, houses, and reconstructed offices may be regarded as shrines to his memory." Perhaps for Einstein science was not merely a job; it was his priestly calling.

Early Years

Imagination has always had powers of resurrection that
no science can match.

Ingrid Bengis

Einstein, a Pisces, was born March 14, 1879, in Ulm, Germany, where he lived for just over a year, but Ulm still carries the motto, *Ulmenses sunt mathematici,* proclaiming, "the people of Ulm are mathematicians." His parents wanted to name their son Abraham, after his paternal grandfather, but feeling this sounded too Jewish, they kept the initial A and called him Albert. There are accounts of his mother gazing at her firstborn son's "extremely large and angular head," and initially, they believed he was deformed. Also disturbing was his trouble with speech, similar to that of some autistic children. Little Albert would form complete sentences in his head, try them out in a low voice while moving his lips, and only after a practice run, would he voice his words out loud. "It is true," he wrote in 1954, "that my parents were worried because I began to speak relatively late, so much so that they consulted a doctor." I can't say how old I was then, certainly not less than three." The family maid called him "der Depperte," the dopy one.

His mother, Pauline, was an accomplished pianist who fostered his lifelong love of music. His father, Hermann, ran a thriving business selling featherbeds in Ulm, until his younger brother Jacob, an engineer, convinced him to move to Munich to become his partner in a high-tech electrical engineering company that provided generators and electrical lighting to municipalities in southern Germany. In the early 1900s technical innovations were rare; so this was a daring move. But in one decade, electrical lightening became ubiquitous—much like the Internet. Their company brought the first street lighting to Schwabing, Bavaria, and to Oktoberfest. Albert spent his early years in Munich, Germany, but also lived in Italy as a child where he attended a Catholic elementary school. Here he was required to take religion classes which he thoroughly enjoyed—he did so well that he helped classmates with their lessons. He was raised by secular Jewish parents in a non-religious household—his parents didn't keep kosher or attend a synagogue, and his father felt Jewish rituals were "ancient superstitions." But he was taught some Judaism from a distant relative. This early Catholic and Jewish instruction awakened "deep religious feelings" in young Albert, who would write and set to music songs in praise of God, which he sang at home and on the streets.

Since Albert was shy and slow in learning to talk, many of his teachers considered him a misfit. His classmates had two nicknames for him, "Big Bore" because he disliked competitive games and roughhousing, and "Straight Arrow" because he was devoted to fairness and compromise. One governess nicknamed him "Father Bore" because he was content playing alone, daydreaming, meditating, working on puzzles, playing with a steam engine, using his toy building set to erect complex structures, and building houses with cards—according to his sister he could build fourteen storey structures. In Munich, there was a strong military presence, and many children would run out into the streets when the Prussian soldiers marched by in lockstep—but Albert, watching this display, would burst into tears.

When he was five, his father showed him a pocket compass, beginning what would become a lifelong fascination for Albert, who realized something in space must be moving that needle. He said that experience made "a deep and lasting impression." It's a myth that Albert was a poor student. He finished his first year of school at the top of his class, and excelled throughout his academic career. He had a passion for learning and an insatiable appetite for books, never required any encouragement, and eventually surpassed his teachers. When he was 10, a medical student and family friend, Max Talmud, 21, recognized the boy's genius. Talmud began showing Alfred science, math, and philosophy books, including Kant's *Critique of Pure Reason* and Euclid's *Elements,* which Einstein called his "holy little geometry book." Initially, Talmud helped Albert, but after a few months, "the flight of his mathematical genius was so high that I could no longer follow." By the time he was twelve, Albert was pursuing independent studies in mathematics and science, teaching himself Euclidean geometry, and investigating calculus. He was brilliant in mathematics and physics, but unlike Nobel, had no gift for languages. By his sixteenth birthday he knew more about science than many experienced professors. And it was books that discouraged twelve-year-old Albert from organized religion. "Through the reading of popular scientific books I soon reached the conviction that much in the stories of the Bible could not be true."

His father Hermann, now a salesman and engineer, wanted Albert to pursue electrical engineering, so he enrolled his son in the Luitpold Gymnasium. But Albert didn't enjoy his studies there and clashed with authorities. He felt creative thought and the true spirit of learning had been replaced by dull regimentation and tedious rote learning. At the height of his fame he told a reporter, "The value of a college education is not the learning of many facts but the training of the mind to think." Near the end of his life, when asked what schools should emphasize, he said, "A society's competitive advantage will come not from how well its schools teach the multiplication and periodic tables, but from how well they stimulate imagination and creativity."

When Albert was fifteen, his father's business failed and the Einsteins moved to Italy, leaving Albert behind with relatives to complete his last three years of high school. He never finished high school in Munich; instead he ingeniously used a doctor's note (through Max Talmud's older brother) to convince school authorities he was suffering from nervous exhaustion, allowing him to join his parents in the Italian Alps. If he had remained one more year until he was 17, he would have been required to join the German army, which according to his sister, "he contemplated with dread." Soon, he would also ask for his father's help in renouncing his German citizenship. That summer at age 16, Einstein wrote his first scientific work, *"The Investigation of the State of Aether in Magnetic Fields."* When Albert was reunited with his parents, he wanted to apply directly to the ETH Zurich, the Swiss Federal Institute of Technology in Zurich, instead of finishing high school. But without a high school certificate,

Alfred was required to write an entrance exam, which he didn't pass. However, destiny intervened.

He ended up attending a high school in Aarau, Northern Switzerland, based on the philosophy of Swiss educational reformer Johann Heinrich Pestalozzi, who advocated the importance of visual imagery. "Visual understanding is the essential and only true means of teaching how to judge things correctly," Pestalozzi wrote, and "the learning of numbers and language must be definitely subordinated." Students were encouraged to reach their own conclusions; even math and physics were taught with hands-on observation, intuition, conceptual thinking, and visual imagery. Rote drills and memorizing facts were not considered useful. In Aarau, education was about nurturing the "inner dignity" and the individuality of each child. Here Einstein thrived, because it was the opposite of the left brain, structured German education he despised. Aarua stimulated his right-brain, possibly rounding out his genius. Einstein later said, "it made me clearly realize how much superior an education based on free action and personal responsibility is to one relying on outward authority." It may have been the influence of Pestalozzi, and Aarua, that led Albert to his teenage dream, where he saw himself traveling alongside a beam of light, a vision that later inspired his theory of relativity.

I was sledding with my friends at night. I started to slide down the hill, but my sled started going faster and faster. I was going so fast that I realized I was approaching the speed of light. I looked up at that point and saw the stars. They were being refracted into colours I had never seen before. I was filled with a sense of awe. I understood in some way I was looking at the most important meaning in my life.

When Albert graduated at age seventeen, he renounced his German citizenship to avoid military service, and enrolled in the mathematics program at ETH, The Zurich Polytechnic, a teachers' and technical college. Here he met Mileva Marić, the only woman studying math at the Institute. Young Albert was definitely a head turner—according to a female friend, he had "masculine good looks of the type that played havoc at the turn of the century...The lower half of his face might have belonged to a sensualist who found plenty of reasons to love life." Walter Isaacson, author of *"Einstein: His Life and Universe"* said, "He had wavy dark hair, expressive eyes, a high forehead, and jaunty demeanor." Albert fell madly in love with the dark, intense, intellectual Mileva. In 1900 he wrote to her, "How was I ever able to live alone, my little everything? Without you I have no self-confidence, no passion for work, and no enjoyment in life—in short, without you, my life is a void." She became pregnant with his daughter, prompting Albert to marry Mileva. Two sons followed Hans Albert, and Eduard.

Academics may have led Albert to Mileva, but after graduating in 1900 with a degree in physics, he couldn't find a job. Seventeen-year-old Einstein, realizing he was intellectually ahead of his instructors, was a sassy rebel. He constantly questioned authority, and called his teachers by their last names, considered quite impudent, since he was expected to address them as "Herr Professor." Since his professors didn't give him glowing recommendations, he spent *two* years working as a tutor and substitute teacher while trying to find a permanent position. He took up sailing in the Alpine Lakes around Zurich, a meditative pastime that, like music, became lifelong pursuits. He never gave up hope. While job hunting he wrote, "Strenuous intellectual work and looking at God's nature are the reconciling, fortifying yet relentlessly strict angels that shall lead me through all of life's troubles."

Finally, the father of a former classmate, Marcel Grossman, helped Albert find employment in Bern, at the Federal Office for Intellectual Property. Grossman's father knew the director of the Swiss Patent Office, and was willing to recommend his son's friend. Albert worked as an assistant examiner, evaluating patent applications for electromagnetic devices. Even here, Einstein wasn't accepted for a promotion, because he hadn't "fully mastered machine technology." But, his seven years at the patent office was perhaps the most creative and productive period of his life. He discovered that he could work on the patent applications so fast, it left time for his scientific inquiry. "I was able to do a full day's work in only two or three hours. The remaining part of the day I would work out my own ideas." This work often carried over to the wee hours of the morning, until, at the age of 26, Einstein published five ground-breaking scientific papers that are still sparking innovations more than 100 years later.

When Einstein published his papers, they were disregarded by most physicists, and the few scholars who did take notice, completely rejected his ideas. The first paper dealt with radiation and the energy properties of light, asserting that light was not just a wave as most scientists believed, but a stream of tiny particles of light or photons called "quanta" paving the way to quantum physics. He imagined each singular point of light surrounded by a field or force. This eventually earned him the Nobel Prize, for explaining the photoelectric effect—when light shines on a metal surface, the surface emits electrons—the principle used today in solar cells. The second paper was a determination of the true size of atoms. The third paper described the motion of microscopic particles, establishing that atoms and molecules exist. The fourth paper contained his theory of relativity $E=mc^2$ or energy equals mass times the velocity of light squared, explaining that everything from a feather to a rock contains matter, and even tiny amounts of mass can be converted into huge amounts of energy. When explaining his theory to an audience, he said, "It follows from the theory of relativity that mass and energy are both different manifestations of the same thing—a somewhat unfamiliar conception for the average man. Furthermore, $E=mc^2$, in which energy is put equal to mass multiplied with the square of the velocity of light, showed that a very small amount of mass may be converted into a very large amount of energy...the mass and energy in fact were equivalent." Einstein understood that since light is constant, two of our pillars in the natural world, space and time, are not. He helped the world understand that all energy reached a vibratory rate faster than even the speed of light $E=mc^2$, and that matter is energy and energy is matter—they just vibrate at different frequencies. A fifth paper clarified and added information to his Special Theory of Relativity. Because his theories were light years ahead of their time, 1905 has become known as Einstein's *annus mirabilis* "Wonderful Year" or "Miracle Year," or as Neffe says, "his canonization into the temple of science." Einstein continued studying and churning out papers, eventually receiving his Ph.D in Physics from the University of Zurich that same year. What is most astounding about Einstein's life is the difficulty he had getting jobs. He was the only graduate in his section of the Polytechnic who didn't receive a job offer. Eventually he landed a job as a junior professor, but it was nine long years after his graduation from the Polytechnic in 1900, and four years after his "Miracle Year" before his doctoral dissertation was finally accepted.

However by 1919 Einstein's life had moved forward at warp speed. He was internationally renowned, and visits to any part of the world became media events, drawing capacity crowds, with photographers and reporters in tow. This superstar status peaked in 1921, during his first two-month visit to the United States. Isaacson describes his fame as "the sort of mass frenzy and press adulation that would thrill a touring rock star. The world had never before seen, and perhaps never will again, such a scientific celebrity superstar..." When he attended the Metropolitan Opera in New York, the *New York Times* reported, "Every seat...from the pit to the last row under the roof, was filled and hundreds stood." When he visited Hartford, Connecticut, his procession included a band, more than a hundred cars, marching war veterans, standard-bearers carrying American and Zionist flags, and an estimated fifteen thousand cheering citizens lining the street. During his second visit to the United States in 1930, when his ship arrived in San Diego, dozens of press clamored to get on board, two of them falling off the ladder as they rushed on deck. Five hundred uniformed girls were waiting to serenade him, and the entire ceremony, including presentations and speeches lasted four hours. While Elsa (Einstein's second wife) and her husband were on tour, she charged $1 for her husband's autograph and $5 for his picture, and then donated the money to children's charities.

He once wrote to a friend, "...I've been so deluged with questions, invitations, and requests that I dream I'm burning in Hell and the postman is the Devil eternally roaring at me, hurling new bundles of letters at my head because I have not yet answered the old ones." In 1952, when Israel's President Chaim Weizman died, he was asked to become their second president, to which Einstein replied, "I am deeply moved by the offer from our State of Israel, and at once saddened and ashamed that I cannot accept it...All my life I have dealt with objective matters, hence I lack both the natural aptitude and the experience to deal properly with people and to exercise official function." At the height of his fame, he was also offered film roles which he graciously declined.

War versus Peace

I am not only a pacifist, I am a militant pacifist.

Einstein

As Einstein was born in Germany, he was acutely aware of the darkness Hitler was unleashing. When Hitler was appointed German Chancellor in 1933, one of his first actions was implementing the Law for the Restoration of the Professional Civil Service. This removed Jews and "suspicious" government employees including university professors from their jobs, unless they had demonstrated loyalty by serving in World War I. The Nazi's also demanded a boycott of all Jewish-owned businesses, stationing storm troopers outside their doors. Jewish teachers and students were banned from the university in Berlin, and their identification cards were confiscated.

Einstein had been a welcomed visitor to America on three occasions, so to escape oppression, at 54, he moved permanently to the United States. Before leaving Germany, he was one of the Nazis primary targets. Authorities raided his Berlin apartment several times, taking his valuables, carpets and paintings, and seizing all of his assets. They even took his beloved summer home in Calputh, raided on the pretense that it concealed communist weapons; his sailboat was confiscated on the pretense it might be used for smuggling. All this, despite Einstein traveling the world as a German scientist superstar, perhaps the best public relations figure the country had ever known. Instead, he was viewed as "an agitator in foreign countries." Before World War I, he was Einstein the scientist, who shunned public activism—a gentle man so adverse to conflict, he disliked playing chess. Now, with Hitler on the rise, he wrote a friend, "Europe in its madness had now embarked on something incredibly preposterous...At such times one sees to what deplorable breed of brutes we belong." In a 1935 unpublished manuscript he says, "In Hitler we have a man with limited intellectual abilities, unfit for any useful work, bursting with envy and bitterness against all of those whom circumstance and nature have favored over him...He picked up human flotsam on the street and in the taverns and organized them around himself. That's how he became a politician."

In 1939, Einstein signed his name to a letter written by renowned physicist Leo Szilard, and addressed to President Franklin Roosevelt. This became one of the most important letters in history. The letter warned that based on Szilard's research, Hitler might be developing nuclear weapons, and it urged Roosevelt to take action. "Recent work", he told the President "leads me to expect that the element uranium may be turned into a new and important source of energy in the immediate future....This new phenomenon would also lead to the construction of the bomb." He believed if the Nazis developed the bomb first, it would mean "inconceivable destruction and the enslavement of the rest of the world." But after the bombing of Hiroshima and Nagasaki, it became clear that Germany was not making bombs as America had feared. A few months before his death, Einstein told chemist Linus Pauling, "I think I have made one mistake in my life, to have signed that letter."

A popular misconception is that Einstein was responsible for developing the atomic bomb, when his only contribution was signing that letter. Einstein must have realized the bomb was being developed, because many of his fellow physicists had disappeared to obscure towns to work. Among those forced to flee Nazi Germany were fourteen Nobel laureates and twenty-six professors of theoretical physics. As refugees they were instrumental in assuring that the Allies developed the atom bomb before the Nazis. But Einstein was not a nuclear physicist, didn't have close ties with military or political leaders, and was considered a security risk, so was never asked to join the Manhattan Project which developed the bomb, nor was he officially told about it. Confusion resulted when a *Time* magazine cover, a few months after the bomb exploded, ran Einstein's picture, with an explosive cloud behind him, and his famous equation $E=mc^2$. *Newsweek* also ran a cover story entitled, "Einstein, The Man Who Started It All." These implications weighed heavily on Einstein's conscience. He told *Newsweek,* "Had I known that the Germans would not succeed in producing an atomic bomb, I never would have lifted a finger." In 1952, he explained to the editor of *Kaizo,* a Japanese newspaper, "My participation in the production of the atom bomb consisted of one single act: I signed a letter to President Roosevelt in which I emphasized the necessity of conducting large-scale experimentation with regard to the feasibility of producing an atom bomb...I felt impelled to take the step because it seemed probable that the Germans might be working on the same problem, with every prospect of success. I had no alternative to act as it did, although I have always been a convinced pacifist."

After the war, Einstein campaigned actively for peace, supporting Szilard, who vigorously opposed the bomb. In March 1945, he sent another letter to Roosevelt, this time urging him to heed Szilard's warning. When the war ended he said, "We delivered this weapon into the hands of the American and British people as trustees of the whole of mankind, as fighters for peace and liberty. But so far we fail to see any guarantee of peace...The war is won, but the peace is not." In another letter he said, "My pacifism is an instinctive feeling, a feeling that possesses me because the murder of people is disgusting. My attitude is not derived from any intellectual theory but is based on my deepest antipathy to every kind of cruelty and hatred." Einstein believed Gandhi's views of non-violence were the most enlightened of any political figure. He said, "We should strive to do things in his spirit...not to use violence in fighting for our cause, but by non-participation in what we believe is evil." He cautioned humanity with these famous words, "I do not know how the third world war will be fought, but I do know how the fourth will: with sticks and stones." He understood the need for consequences or karmic retribution when individuals or nations commit atrocities. In 1944 he wrote, "The Germans as an entire people are responsible for these mass murders and must be punished as a people...Behind the Nazi Party stand the German people who elected Hitler after he had, in his book and in his speeches, made his shameful intentions clear beyond the possibility of misunderstanding." Einstein was brutally honest in admitting that his efforts to prevent future wars were motivated by his deep pacifist instincts but also by guilt—knowing that the letter he signed had altered history. At a dinner given by the Nobel Prize committee in 1945, he reminded us that Alfred Nobel, the inventor of dynamite, had created his prizes "to atone for having invented the most powerful explosives ever known up to his time." Einstein saw the parallels. "Today, the physicists who participated in forging the most formidable and dangerous weapon of all times are harassed by an equal feeling of responsibility, not to say guilt," he said.

One week before his death, on April 11, 1955, he joined Bertrand Russell and nine other scientists in producing the Russell-Einstein Manifesto, denouncing every aspect of nuclear weapons and demanding their abolition. It warns, "A war with H-bombs might quite possibly put an end to the human race...Shall we put an end to the human race; or shall mankind renounce war?" But it was also written in the spirit of hope, "There lies before us, if we choose, continued progress in happiness, knowledge, and wisdom. Shall we, instead, choose death, because we cannot forget our quarrels? We appeal, as human beings, to human beings: Remember your humanity and forget the rest." The Russell-Einstein Manifesto laid the foundation for the Pugwash Movement, (named after the village where it was founded) considered the most important peace initiative in the past fifty years. From that document the Pugwash Conferences emerged, where scientists gather each year to discuss the control of nuclear weapons.

Scientist with a Heart

Use for yourself little, but give to others much.

Einstein

People around the world admired Einstein, the brilliant scientist, but a deeper respect emerged because of his humanitarian nature. The midpoint of his scientific career was in 1925, when at 46, he made his last great contribution to quantum mechanics. He spent 30 years revolutionizing science, then the remaining 30 years working for peace, freedom, and social justice. Isaacson explains "He was allergic to nationalism, militarism, and anything that smacked of a herd mentality...This led him to embrace a morality and politics based on respect for free minds, free spirits, and free individuals. Tyranny repulsed him, and he saw tolerance not simply as a sweet virtue but as a necessary condition for a creative society." Unlike Alfred Nobel, his social conscience was evident throughout his public life. The two social movements receiving his constant support were pacifism and Zionism, preserving the Jewish people and state. From childhood, he despised military regimes, but during the second half of his life, with his scientific discoveries behind him, he turned his attention to peace. After World War I, this became a passion. In New York, in 1930, he gave a famous speech outlining his radical pacifism platform, "If even two percent of those called up declare that they will not serve, and simultaneously demand that all international conflicts be settled in a peaceful manner, governments would be powerless." Although many labeled him naive, Einstein promoted this policy until the Nazi takeover of Germany. Then, like all true scientists, Einstein changed his mind. Isaacson explains, "The rise of anti-Semitism after World War I produced a counter reaction in Einstein: it made him identify more strongly with his Jewish heritage and community." As he was gaining superstar status, he returned to his roots becoming an advocate of the Zionist cause, even though neither he nor his family had ever belonged to a synagogue or carried out Jewish traditions. "I am really doing whatever I can for the brothers of my race who are treated so badly everywhere," he wrote a friend. Later, he said "My relationship to the Jewish people has become my strongest human tie." Einstein advocated a new Jewish university, a place where Hebrew scholars could work and study without the discrimination he experienced in Germany. "The prospect of establishing a Jewish university fills me with particular joy, having recently seen countless instances of perfidious and uncharitable treatment of splendid young Jews with attempts to deny their chances of education," he said. When Hebrew University in Jerusalem or HUJ was established in 1925, Einstein was one of the first governors, and when he died, most of his estate was left to the university. The university decides whether any Einstein product from posters to playing cards meets its approval. This has proved quite lucrative; by 2008 HUJ had earned $10 million.

Now all 80,000 items of Einstein's complete archives—everything from personal correspondence to his notebooks scribbled with his groundbreaking theories can be found online at websites the university has created.

Although Einstein maintained close ties with Zionism, his humanistic outlook excluded no one. He was deeply concerned for the Arabs being displaced by large number of Jewish residents pouring into what would become Israel. Speaking to a Jewish politician in 1955 he said, "The most important aspect of our (Israel's) policy must be our ever-present, manifest desire to institute complete equality for the Arab citizens living in our midst...The attitude we adopt toward the Arab minority will provide the real test of our moral standards as a people." He proposed that a council be set up consisting of four Jews and four Arabs to resolve any disputes, and warned Zionist friends if they didn't take measures to assure that both sides lived in harmony, the outcome would haunt them for decades. His views were considered naive. Believing strongly in freedom of speech, Einstein didn't hold back on issues he considered important. He spoke on any relative social topic. "Abortion up to a certain stage of the pregnancy should be allowed if the woman so desires. Homosexuality should not be subject to prosecution except where necessary to protect young people. And, in regard to sexual education: No secrecy!"

He believed in racial equality, and saw through the veneer of upscale Princeton University. Einstein worked at the Institute of Advanced Study in New Jersey, next to, but not formally affiliated with Princeton. Twenty percent of its residents were black African Americans who were segregated, lived in poor conditions, sent their children to separate elementary schools, and sat at the back of movie theaters. Princeton University didn't accept black students, and very few Jewish. During his first year living in New Jersey, he published an article lamenting, "Minorities, especially when their individuals are recognizable because of physical differences, are treated by the majorities among who they live as inferiors." He believed only by "closer union" and "educational enlightenment" would the "emancipation of the soul of the minority...be attained. The determined effort of the American Negroes in this direction deserves every recognition and assistance." In 1937, when African American opera star Marian Anderson came to perform, the Nassau Inn refused to rent her a room, so Einstein invited her to stay in his home. When he visited Ceylon in 1922, he was picked up by a customary rickshaw. In his travel diary he wrote, "We rode in small one-man carriages drawn at a trot by men of Herculean strength yet delicate build...I was bitterly ashamed to share responsibility for the abominable treatment accorded fellow human beings but was unable to do anything about it."

During the 1930s and 40s, with the assistance of his loyal secretary Helen Dukas, Einstein developed a second career, ensuring the safe passage of persecuted Jewish refugees to America. Together they saved hundreds of lives. "Miss Dukas and I run a kind of immigration office," he wrote his sister. Einstein wrote countless letters, testimonials, affidavits, and financial guarantees to help people relocate in the United States. He also paid a small fortune of his own money to help Jewish artists and scientists come to America. When people were accused of being Communist spies and sympathizers during the McCarthy era in the United States, Einstein again became a defender of civil liberties. If they were asked to give names and testify, implicating their neighbors and colleagues, Einstein urged them not to cooperate. When his friend Fritz Haber pioneered the use of chlorine gas as a weapon, Einstein said, "All of our exalted technological progress, civilization for that matter, is comparable to an ax in the hand of a pathological criminal." When both world wars were over he asked, "What good is a formula if it does not stop men from killing one another?"

In a famous speech to students at the California Institute of Technology in 1930, his approach was humanistic, stressing that science had not achieved its objective of doing more good for humanity than harm. During the war science gave people "the means to poison and mutilate one another" and during peacetime it "has made our lives hurried and uncertain." Rather than being a liberating force, "it has enslaved men to machines" making them work "long wearisome hours mostly without joy in their labor." "Concern for man himself must always constitute the chief objective of all technological effort…to assure that the results of our scientific thinking may be a blessing to mankind, and not a curse. Never forget this when you are pondering over your diagrams and equations!"

At sixty, Einstein wrote an essay for the first issue of *Monthly Review*, "Why Socialism?" He argued that capitalism led to great disparities of wealth, cycles of boom and depression, unemployment, and was a system based on selfishness and acquiring wealth, rather than cooperation and service. He objected to people simply being trained for careers; instead, he believed it was more important to love your work and be creative. He also felt political parties were being corrupted by huge contributions from wealthy individuals and companies. Americans had become complacent with a society where the rich just get richer, at the expense of the poor, unemployed and under-privileged. He said, "The conquering peoples establish themselves, legally and economically, as the privileged class of the conquered country. They seized for themselves a monopoly of the land ownership and appointed a priesthood from among their own ranks. The priests, in control of education, made the class division of society into a permanent institution and created a system of values by which the people were…unconsciously, guided in their social behaviour." He felt we live in a society where "egotisical drives" are constantly being accentuated, at the expense of our "social drives" which are weaker and are progressively deteriorating. "Unknowingly prisoners of their own egotism, they feel insecure, lonely, and deprived of the naïve, simple and unsophisticated enjoyment of life. Man can find meaning in life, short and perilous as it is, only through devoting himself to society. The economic anarchy of capitalist society as it exists today is, in my opinion, the real source of evil." His words written over half a century ago still reflect our present economy. He talks of an "oligarchy of private capital" with "enormous power of which cannot be effectively checked even by a democratically organized political society." This private capital he says is largely responsible for donations which support and influence our political parties, and these "private capitalists inevitably control, directly or indirectly, the main sources of information (press, radio, education). It is thus extremely difficult, and indeed in most cases quite impossible, for the individual citizen to come to objective conclusions and to make intelligent use of his political rights." He says that "technological progress frequently results in more unemployment rather than in an easing of the burden of work for all," there is always an "army of unemployed" and workers are constantly in fear of losing their jobs. "An exaggerated competitive attitude is inculcated into the student, who is trained to worship acquisitive success as a preparation for his future career." Rather than helping students enhance their innate abilities, or helping them "develop a sense of responsibility for his fellow man," or working out of joy or self-fulfillment, we have a society that encourages the "glorification of power."

Einstein's humanistic policies sought to unite; they were inclusive of everyone and everything, down to the tiniest subatomic particles in the universe. Neffe explained, "Einstein sought to unite not only mechanics and electrodynamics, mass and energy, space and time, gravitation and spacetime, and ultimately all theories in a world formula, but also to unite researchers in all countries, the Jews of the world, the nations and religions in a world government. He wanted to put an end to boundaries and barriers, especially between his own religious and scientific views." Although deeply committed to the Jewish people, in a 1938 speech before the National Labor Committee for Palestine, Einstein made it clear he did not advocate a Jewish state. "My awareness of the essential nature of Judaism resists the idea of a Jewish state with borders, an army, and a measure of temporal power...I am afraid of the inner damage Judaism will sustain—especially from the development of a narrow nationalism within our ranks, which we have already had to fright strongly even without a Jewish state...A return to a nation in the political sense of the word would be equivalent to turning away from the spiritualization of our community that we owe to the genius of the prophets." In the last decade of his life Einstein was a fierce supporter of one world government, which he felt was the best way to prevent future wars. This passion for creating a unified government was perhaps similar to his quest for finding a unified field theory, uniting all the forces of nature. Both had the potential for creating a universal order or oneness. He believed this world authority would work best if it had the military power to resolve disputes. Einstein suggested the three great powers of that time, the United States, Britain, and Russia, could establish this new world government and invite other nations to join. When the United Nations was formed in 1945, it didn't come close to the type of "supranational" military might Einstein has envisioned. He didn't want to impose a Western-style liberal democracy, instead he believed a world legislature could be created that would be elected directly by the people in each member country by secret ballot, rather than being appointed by existing rulers.

Einstein the Comedian

The only thing that interferes with my learning is my education.
Albert Einstein

People loved Einstein for his genius, humanity, and also for his sense of humor. Physicist Bernard Cohen said, "The contrast between his soft speech and ringing laughter was enormous...Every time he made a point he liked, or heard something that appealed to him, he would burst into a booming laughter that would echo from wall to wall..I had been prepared to know what he would look like...but I was totally unprepared for this roaring, booming friendly, all-enveloping laughter." Even on dreary occasions he told jokes, exploded with laughter when listening to silly stories, and one of his favorite books was *The Hundred Best Jewish Jokes.* Due to his voracious appetite for honey, "whole buckets" were purchased for his household, and he joked that he resembled a bear with a Buddha like belly. Under his picture, sketched by an artist, he wrote, "This big fat swine is Professor Einstein?" Once, when asked his profession, he replied, "fashion model." Whenever he saw photographers approaching, he mussed up his hair to perfect that famous fly-away demeanor. During his second trip to the United States he visited Riverside Baptist Church in New York, where a full size statue of Einstein had been carved, along with a dozen great thinkers. In the church bulletin he joked, "I might have imagined that they could make a Jewish saint of me, but I never thought I'd become a Protestant one!" When asked by a reporter if there was a conflict between science and religion, he answered, "Not really, though it depends, of course, on your religious views." While living in Princeton one of his pets, Chico, a white terrier, took a dislike to letter carriers. "The dog is very smart," Einstein said. "He feels sorry for me because I receive so much mail. That's why he tries to bite the mailman." One of his Princeton neighbors was an eight-year old girl, Adelaide, who, carrying a plate of homemade fudge as a bribe, would ring his doorbell and ask for help with math. Einstein graciously assisted, and gave her a cookie in return for the fudge. When her parents realized that Einstein was tutoring their daughter, they apologized profusely. "That's quite unnecessary," he said, "I'm learning as much from your child as she is learning from me." He loved to tell friends of her visit. "She was a very naughty girl, "he laughed, "Do you know she tried to bribe me with candy." While his sister Maja lived with him in Princeton, she was a vegetarian but loved hotdogs; Einstein decreed they were a vegetable, making everyone happy.

Einstein's Religious Feelings and the Perfect Universe

The situation may be expressed by an image: science without religion is lame, religion without science is blind.

Einstein

What humanity owes to personalities like Buddha, Moses, and Jesus ranks for me higher than all the achievements of the inquiring and constructive mind.

Einstein *The Human Side*

Einstein's theories on God, religion, and spirituality are widely misunderstood, because atheists, organized religions, and spiritual groups, *all* quote him to support their beliefs. However, Einstein flatly denied any illusions of being an atheist. Unlike his contemporaries Sigmund Freud, who believed religion was the opium of the masses, or Bertrand Russell and George Bernard Shaw who criticized people for believing in God, Einstein was never critical of anyone for expressing faith. He didn't have kind words for atheists. "There are people who say there is no God," he said to a friend. "But what makes me really angry is that they quote me for support of such views." Two years before his death he wrote, "What separates me from most so-called atheists is a feeling of utter humility toward the unattainable secrets of the harmony of the cosmos."

In 2008, a handwritten letter on Einstein's religious theories sold at Bloomsbury Auctions in London, England for $404,000. Einstein had written this letter to philosopher Eric Gutkind, a year before his death in 1954. In the letter, Einstein describes himself as an "agnostic," (someone who believes there is no proof God exists, but doesn't deny the possibility there may be a God), but "not an atheist" because he felt atheists were similar to religious fanatics. "The fanatical atheists are like slaves who are still feeling the weight of their chains which they have thrown off after hard struggle. They are creatures who–in their grudge against the traditional 'opium of the masses'–cannot hear the music of the spheres." The subject of God, he said, "is too vast for our limited minds." The Bible is "a collection of honorable but still primitive legends which are nevertheless pretty childish." Judaism, he said, like other religions, is "an incarnation of the most childish superstitions." He felt a deep affinity for the Jewish people, but explained, "As far as my experience goes they are also no better than other human groups, although they are protected from the worst cancers by a lack of power. Otherwise I cannot see anything 'chosen' about them."

Einstein was religious as a child, but at age 12, with science his new creed, he gave religion up, while still retaining a sense of awe for something larger than life. He held a profound respect for what he believed was an order, beauty, or unifying whole to the universe. For forty years he rarely discussed religion, but around the time he turned fifty, there was a resurgence of interviews, essays, and letters, expressing religious and spiritual views, although he admitted the subject of God was completely beyond comprehension. While living in Berlin, he said, "Try and penetrate with our limited means the secrets of nature and you will find that, behind all the discernible laws and connections, there remains something tangible and inexplicable. Veneration for this force beyond anything that we can comprehend is my religion. To that extent I am, in fact, religious."

Just after his fiftieth birthday Einstein granted an interview with German poet and propagandist, George Sylvester Viereck. When asked how he was influenced by Christianity, he answered, "As a child I received instruction both in the Bible and in the Talmud. I am a Jew, but I am enthralled by the luminous figure of the Nazarene." Viereck asked if he accepted Jesus, to which he replied, "Unquestionably! No one can read the Gospels without feeling the actual presence of Jesus, His personality pulsates in every word. No myth is filled with such life." Einstein's answer to "Do you believe in God?" was, "I'm not an atheist. The problem involved is too vast for our limited minds. We are in the position of a little child entering a huge library filled with books in many languages. The child knows someone must have written those books. It does not know how. It does not understand the languages in which they are written. The child dimly suspects a mysterious order in the arrangement of the books but doesn't know what it is. That, it seems to me, is the attitude of even the most intelligent human being toward God.

We see the universe marvelously arranged and obeying certain laws but only dimly understand these laws."

Einstein didn't believe in a personal God, but often used the word God as a reference, convenient metaphor, or easy to grasp shorthand "for the structure of the world so far as our science can reveal it." He didn't try to humanize God or blame God for the earth's calamities. Although he rejected organized religion, he perceived the universe as sacred. He rejected the idea of an Old Testament God, and could see no sense in trying to win favor with any deity through rituals or sacrifices. He believed any religious system where a priestly caste sets itself up as a mediator between a god and its people was "a religion of fear." He also didn't believe in what he called "the God of Providence, a moral conception of God" who "protects, disposes, rewards, and punishes..." Einstein said, "I cannot conceive of a personal God who would directly influence the actions of individuals or would sit in judgment on creatures of his own creation." He felt all religions were a blend of these two concepts of God either as provider or punisher. But he didn't reject God outright, which is probably why he saw himself as an agnostic. In his philosophy God was indeed a living presence, and he flatly rejected Nietzsche's famous philosophy that God was dead. He said, "If I am capable of hating anything, it is his writings."

In 1929, Rabbi Herbert Goldstein sent him a telegram, asking, "Do you believe in God?" Stop. Prepaid reply 50 words. His eloquent yet concise German reply did not require 50 words. "I believe in Spinoza's God, who reveals Himself in the lawful harmony of the world, not in a God who concerns Himself with the fate and the doings of mankind." Einstein's sincere response did not humor everyone, particularly those of orthodox, fundamental, or traditional religions; Spinoza like Einstein was a rebel who had been excommunicated from the Jewish community in Amsterdam for his beliefs, and had been condemned by the Catholic Church.

To many, Einstein was a paradox—his friend, writer Friedrich Durrenmatt, said, "Einstein was prone to talk about God so often, that I was led to suspect he was a closet theologian." He clarified this in a letter, "It was, of course, a lie what you read about my religious convictions, a lie which is being systematically repeated. I do not believe in a personal God and I have never denied this but have expressed it clearly. If something is in me which can be called religious then it is the unbounded admiration for the structures of the world so far as our science can reveal it."

Perhaps there is such a sea of contradictions because he was breaking new ground–until the beginning of the twentieth century, science, religion and spirituality had been mutually exclusive, all enshrined in their separate altars. Einstein was the first scientist in the 21st century to begin breaking down these barriers by merging God with science. He reshaped physics from a completely secular science, to one that both spiritual and religious believers could appreciate in a new way. "I am a deeply religious nonbeliever...this is a somewhat new kind of religion...I am of the opinion that all the finer speculations in the realm of science spring from a deep religious feeling." Einstein believed in "cosmic religious feeling." He said this is when, "The individual feels the futility of human desires and aims and the sublimity and marvelous order which reveal themselves both in nature and in the world of thought. Individual existence impresses him as a sort of prison and he wants to experience the universe as a single significant whole." Einstein wrote "The religious geniuses of all ages have been distinguished by this kind of religious feeling, which knows no dogma and no God conceived in man's image; so that there can be no church whose central teachings are based on it." He also said, "In my view, it is the most important function of art and science to awaken this feeling and keep it alive in those who are receptive to it." When a grade six girl from a New York Sunday school asked, "Do scientists pray?" Einstein replied, "Everyone who is seriously involved in the pursuit of science becomes convinced that a spirit is manifest in the laws of the Universe–a spirit vastly superior to that of man, and one in the face of which we with our modest powers must feel humble. In this way the pursuit of science leads to a religious feeling of a special sort, which is indeed quite different from the religiosity of someone more naïve."

Einstein may have revolutionized science because his deep faith both informed and inspired his work. "The cosmic religious feeling," he said, "is the strongest and noblest motive for scientific research." Einstein believed in "religious feeling," "mystery," and a "perfect" universe. He said, "While it is true that scientific results are entirely independent from religious or moral considerations, those individuals to whom we owe the great creative achievements of science were all of them imbued with the truly religious conviction that this universe of ours is something perfect and susceptible to the rational striving for knowledge." As a scientist, he found each discovery as "beautiful" as it was "correct." In the summer of 1930, while sailing in Calputh, he composed a personal credo entitled *"What I Believe."* "The most beautiful emotion we can experience is the mysterious. It is the fundamental emotion that stands at the cradle of all true art and science. He to whom this emotion is a stranger, who can no longer wonder and stand rapt in awe, is as good as dead, a snuffed-out candle. To sense that behind anything that can be experienced there is something that our minds cannot grasp, whose beauty and sublimity reaches us only indirectly: this is religiousness. In this sense, and in this sense only, I am a devoutly religious man." Four years later, at 55, in his book *Mein Weltbild* (My World View), he asked, "What is the meaning of human life, or for that matter, of the life of any creature? To know an answer to this question means to be religious. You ask: Does it make any sense, then, to pose this question? I answer: The man who regards his own life and that of his fellow creatures as meaningless is not merely unhappy but hardly fit of life."

He admitted to having "a rapturous amazement at the harmony of natural law." Einstein remained in awe of these mysteries science had not yet unraveled, telling friend and biographer Peter Bucky, "I sometimes face this mystery with great fear. I think there are many things in the universe that we cannot perceive or penetrate and that we experience some of the most beautiful things in life in only a very primitive form."

His Human Side

People are like the ocean, sometimes unruffled and friendly, sometimes stormy and treacherous–but essentially just water.
Einstein letter to son Eduard 1933

There is a myth that Einstein was detached, uncaring and aloof, but he was passionate about family, friends, humanity, and science. He was close to his one sibling, a younger sister, Maria, or Maja, who followed him to the United States and according to Isaacson was his "most intimate soul mate." When Maja died in 1951 Einstein was grief stricken. "I miss her more than can be imagined," he wrote a friend. Maja and his stepdaughter Margot preferred living with Einstein rather than their husbands when they got older. Margot worshiped her stepfather, and they grew increasingly close with age. The attraction was mutual, "When Margot speaks," Einstein said, "you see flowers growing."

Although there was a fractured relationship with his first wife Mileva, and his youngest son Eduard, he cared deeply. Eduard, nicknamed Tete, was schizophrenic, attempted suicide more than once, and spent most of his life institutionalized. The more troubled Eduard became, the more concern Einstein had for him. He once wrote his son, "People who live in a society, enjoy looking into each other's eyes, who share their troubles, who focus their efforts on what is important to them and find this joyful–these people lead a full life." Einstein was always deeply shaken and troubled by his son's illness, "This sorrow is eating up Albert," Elsa wrote, "he finds it difficult to cope with." When he and Mileva, his first wife, could not reconcile their marriage, she moved to Zurich with the boys. Albert "bawled like a little boy" all afternoon and evening.

His oldest son, Hans Albert, remembers him as an excellent father, "When my mother was busy around the house, father would put aside his work, and watch over us for hours, bouncing us on his knee...I remember he would tell us stories—and he often played the violin in an effort to keep us quiet." His second wife Elsa, his first cousin, was a lifelong friend and collaborator. When she died, he cried in front of one of his close friends, said he would miss her terribly, and returned to work "ashen with grief." He had deep lifelong relationships with many men and women. Einstein didn't simply like his friends, he adored them. One of his scientific heroes and friends was Hendrik Lorenz. He once wrote, "I admire this man like no other; I might say, I love him." Another of his scientific buddies was Niels Bohr; after their first meeting, he wrote, "Not often in life has a human being caused me such joy by his mere presence as you did," and he added that he took pleasure in seeing his "cheerful boyish face." Einstein once wrote his first wife, "I have to have someone to love, otherwise life is miserable." Isaacson explains, "There were times when he could be callous to those closest to him, which shows that, like the rest of us humans, he had flaws...He had deep friendships lasting for decades. He was unfailingly benevolent to his assistants. His warmth, sometimes missing at home, radiated on the rest of humanity. So as he grew old, he was not only respected and revered by his colleagues, he was loved."

Brain Drain—The Almost Perfect Ending

It is tasteless to prolong life artificially. I have done my share, it is time to go. I will do it elegantly.

Einstein

Einstein faced death the same way he lived life—humbly, gracefully, and with humor. Ironically, his stepdaughter Margot was a patient in the room next door when he was brought to Princeton Hospital. "I did not recognize him at first–he was so changed by the pain and blood deficiency," she said, "But his personality was the same as ever. He...joked with me and was completely in command of himself with regard to his condition; he spoke with profound serenity–even with a touch of humor—about the doctors, and awaited his end as an imminent natural phenomenon." As fearless as he had been all his life, so he faced death humbly and quietly. He said to her, "I have accomplished what I came here to do." Einstein's will stipulated that his body be cremated the day of his death, with his ashes be sprinkled at an undisclosed location. Einstein's funeral could have been a media event, with the same honor and dignity reserved for presidents, kings, popes, and bishops. Instead, he left without fanfare, being cremated the afternoon he died, with twelve people attending the ceremony. A few lines were recited from one of his favorite writers, Goethe, and his ashes were scattered in the nearby Delaware River. These wishes were carried out, but with glitches; two doctors were compelled to snatch their own holy relics. When lifelong "friend" and ophthalmologist Henry Adams learned Einstein's autopsy had been completed, he rushed to the morgue, plucked Einstein's eyes from their sockets, and preserved them in formaldehyde in a safety deposit box at a New Jersey bank, where they allegedly remain today. A second body snatcher was forty-two-year old Princeton pathologist, Thomas Harvey, who after determining Einstein had died of a burst abdominal aneurysm, decided he would use Einstein's brain to uncover the secrets to genius. Biographer Jürgen Neffe explains, "Removing and examining the brain of a dead person does not go beyond the purview of standard autopsy procedure. Harvey, however, has been neither asked nor authorized to do what he does next to Einstein's body, nor does the Hippocratic oath endorse his actions. He saws off the head of the dead man and scoops out its contents. He holds the brain in his hand the way hamlet held Yorick's skull. In these two and a half pounds of nerve tissue, he is certain, lies the key to understanding the greatest, intellectual creative power. If it were possible to elicit the trade secret from this organ, he, the pathologist, would gain fame and honor. He decides to walk off with it and never give it back."

Harvey was oblivious to the consequences of his actions. Rather than becoming an increasingly respected doctor or scientist, his life spiraled into that of a lonely man on the run. When it was discovered what he had stolen, he lost his job, but, insisted on keeping Einstein's brain preserved in jars for his own experimentation. Neff tells us, "how the jars, packed away in rags in the carton, accompanied him on his travels all over the country. How he had to keep hiding the brain in unlikely locations, underneath a beer cooler or in a closet of a student apartment, when his impoverishment after having lost his medical privileges drove him to seek employment in a factory in Kansas. And how, after more than forty years, he ruefully returned the infamous stolen goods to the safekeeping of his former workplace." Years after Harvey's brain theft, he still claimed to be doing research, but produced no conclusive results. He cut Einstein's brain into 240 pieces and began mailing samples of the brain around the world to scientists, neurologists, and pseudoscientists in alcohol-filled Ziploc bags, hoping they could collaborate and discover the secret to Einstein's genius. All this, despite Einstein's words, "We should take care not to make the intellect our god. It has, of course, powerful muscles, but no personality."

The most cited paper, and the only study that has drawn attention, was written in 1999, by Professor Sandra Witelson, and a research team at the Michael G. DeGroote School of Medicine, at McMaster University. When Harvey weighed Einstein's brain during the initial autopsy he discovered it tipped the scales at 2.7 pounds. Witelson found the average male brain weighed 3.1 pounds, suggesting that a large brain is not necessarily an indication of higher intellect. When she compared Einstein's brain to a group of men and women of "average" intelligence, she found Einstein's brain was the same, except for the area responsible for mathematical reasoning, and the ability to think in terms of space and movement. This part, in the left brain, was 15 percent wider than "average" brains, and contained more glial cells, believed to support and nourishes neurons. Einstein's brain also lacked the deep groove, a normal Sylvian fissure, which normally runs through this area. Researchers speculate this absence allowed his neurons to communicate more effectively. Another piece of Einstein's brain ended up in the hands of renowned neuroanatomist Marian Diamond at the University of California at Berkley. In 1985 after comparing it to samples of 11 other adult male brains, she announced that Einstein's brain had 73 percent more glial cells especially in the left parietal lobe, the area responsible for personal movement and mathematical reasoning. Although Einstein's brain has been poked, prodded, and examined for decades, there isn't one definitive theory as to why he was a genius. Neuroanatomists have discounted most of these studies, calling them shoddy, unconvincing, seriously flawed, or based on false assumptions. Neffe says, "they demonstrate a longing for simple formulas that encapsulate the life and work of a mental giant of Einstein's stature....Neither his brain tissue nor any other physical remains, such as his genes, reveal a thing about his extreme creative powers. The key to understanding Einstein lies not in biology, but in biography."

Despite our theories, scientific advances, and sophisticated scanning equipment, when it comes to understanding the brain, we are still fumbling in the dark—literally. It's fascinating that Einstein's brain had more glial cells, because those dark little cells remain a mystery. Glial cells, quite unlike neurons, were first discovered in the 1800s and called *glia*, the Greek word for glue. But it's just in the last few decades that we've realized the importance of these diminutive cells. Once regarded as mere insulators, waste removers, fillers, and bonders like glue, scientists now realize their function is more complex because our brains contain about a trillion glia; we have 10 times more glial cells than neurons! It's believed this may be the reason behind the now discredited theory that we only use 10 percent of our brains. Researches had underestimated glial cells, assuming they were deaf and dumb because they couldn't transmit electrical signals, but, they actually communicate through chemical signalling with neurons. Neuroscientist, Andrew Kobb, believes glia may be responsible for "our creative and imaginative existence as human beings." Science writer Carl Zimmer draws a connection between the dark matter in our brain and the dark matter of the universe. He writes, "There is something marvelous in the fact that we barely understand what most of the cells in our brains are doing. Beginning in the 1930s, astronomers realized that all the things they could see through their telescopes—the stars, the galaxies, the nebulas—make up just a small fraction of the total mass of the universe. The rest, known as dark matter, still defies their best attempts at explanation. Between our ears, it turns out, each of us carries a personal supply of dark matter as well." Neurologist Kevin Nelson tells us "less than 5 percent of the universe is detectable by our instruments," the remainder is this mysterious dark energy. He compares our huge untapped consciousness to this behemoth of dark matter—which I believe are the untapped worlds of meditation and dreams. We truly are a microcosm of the macrocosm.

Einstein's Genius–Simplicity, Silence, Solitude

*I have just three things to teach; simplicity, patience, compassion.
These are your greatest treasures.*

Lao-Tzu

Simplicity is the hallmark of truth.

Einstein

We've never understood Einstein's genius intellectually, because it's not something that can be observed and studied under glass–that was only the left-brained half of the equation. When Einstein was asked about his mental accomplishments his explanation was simple—insatiable curiosity. Near the end of his life he said, "I have no special talents, I am only passionately curious." Perhaps Einstein was quantum leaps ahead of other scientists because he followed his intuition, imagination, and spirit, where all true genius resides.

In fact, Einstein was misunderstood by his contemporaries because he trusted intuition, not logic, as his starting point. He never relied entirely on left-brain methodical, step-by-step, quantitative experiments. Instead, he made imaginative leaps and created new theories through visualization or thought experiments, in German, *Gedankenexperiment.* This became the hallmark of his career. Einstein must have dreamed a great deal because he slept a lot—rarely under 10 hours a night, usually strolling into his office between 10 or 11 a.m. Perhaps he activated his genius when his brain waves were in the alpha state—while he was daydreaming, meditating, musing, dreaming. After arriving in Princeton, and being shown his new office, he was asked what equipment he needed. "A desk or table, a chair, paper and pencils," he replied. "Oh yes, and a large wastebasket, so I can throw away all my mistakes." Paper and pencil were his sole scientific equipment. He would arrive at work, sit back in his chair, balance a large pad on his knee, clear his mind of all distractions, and write his equations in small neat script. When stumped by a problem, he calmly stayed with it. In other words, he meditated. He knew answers could be discovered because, "God is subtle, but never mischievous." He believed in the simplicity and logical order of nature. "It is a kind of faith that helped me through my whole life not to become hopeless in the great difficulties of investigation." He would ask, "Could this be the way God created the universe?" "I am not interested in this or that phenomena, in the spectrum of this or that element. I want to know God's thoughts," he said, "The rest are details." In a 1926 letter to physicist Max Born he wrote, "Quantum mechanics is very worthy of regard. But an inner voice tells me that this is not yet the right track. The theory yields much, but it hardly brings us closer to the Old One's secrets. I, in any case, am convinced that He does not throw dice."

Despite international fame, Einstein didn't let all this attention go to his head. From childhood until his death he followed the three S's; simplicity, silence, and solitude. Despite the complexity of his mathematical calculations and theories, he reveled in simplicity, believing that "nature is the realization of the simplest conceivable mathematical ideas." It was this mathematical simplicity, a unified whole or oneness that also guided his search for a Unified Field Theory, (which absorbed him for thirty years) and echoed Isaac Newton's declaration in *Principia* "Nature is pleased with simplicity." He believed that simplicity and unity were the trademarks of God's universe. "A theory is more impressive the greater the simplicity of its premises, the more different things it relates, and the more expanded its area of applicability," he wrote. When the German regime was burning books, and suppressing intellectual freedoms, he stressed the importance of solitude, "The monotony of a quiet life stimulates the creative mind." Similar to Buddhist monks, he also suggested that scientists seek work as housekeepers, so they might "devote themselves undisturbed" to thinking.

His ego never expanded like the universe he observed, and he never succumbed to depression or desires for wealth and fame. Neffe says, "He was utterly lacking in the three major forces he saw ruling the world: stupidity, fear, and greed—although he did confess...I am only getting more stupid with fame, which is quite a common phenomenon, you know." Einstein's ability to stay focused, never give up, revel in the mysteries of the universe, and never succumb to the doom and gloom around him, were a huge aspect of his genius. He once said, "One must divide one's time between politics and equations. But our equations are much more important to me, because politics is for the present, while our equations are for eternity." Despite his superstar status, his life was never easy—but he always laughed, loved, and found inspiration and solace in his work. He said, "To dwell on the things that depress or anger us does not help in overcoming them. One must knock them down alone." During the Nazi occupation in Germany he was asked how he could remain so cheerful. His reply, "We must remember that this is a very small star, and probably some of the larger and more important stars may be very virtuous and happy."

He was exceedingly humble, never comfortable with ceremony, pomp, or formality. Knowing he had to attend a formal event cast a dark cloud over his day. He hated collars and ties, preferring unbuttoned shirts, baggy trousers, and no socks. His trademark comfortable clothes, slightly disheveled appearance, and fly away hair, reflected this love of simplicity, utter lack of pretense, and a mild act of rebellion. "When I was young I found out that the big toe always ends up making a hole in a sock. So I stopped wearing socks," he confided to photographer Philippe Halsman, and to a neighbor he said, "I have reached an age when, if someone tells me to wear socks, I don't have to." Leopold Infeld, an associate at Princeton, explained, "One of my colleagues in Princeton asked me. 'If Einstein dislikes his fame and would like to increase his privacy, why does he...wear his hair long, a funny leather jacket, no socks, no suspenders, no ties?' The idea is to restrict his needs and, by this restriction, increase his freedom. We are slaves of millions of things...Einstein tried to reduce them to the absolute minimum. Long hair minimized the need for the barber. Socks can be done without. One leather jacket solves the coat problems for many years." He never learned to drive, or owned a car. When he didn't have a car available from a wealthy friend, he was content to walk, or take the subway or bus. "Possessions weigh you down," he said, "There is nothing I would have trouble giving up at any time."

"Humility is Einstein's religion," his son in law Rudolf Kayser said, "It consists of a childlike admiration of a superior mind." Once when he was taking a train from Prague to Vienna, three thousand people were waiting to hear him speak. His host was waiting where the first-class patrons were disembarking—assuming an esteemed scientist would travel that way. After much searching, he finally saw Einstein, strolling from third class at the far end of the platform. Carrying his violin case, and wearing his customary shabby clothes, he looked more like an itinerant musician. "You know, I like traveling first, but my face is becoming too well known," he explained to his host. "I am less bothered in third class." On his first trip to the United States in 1921, to keep things simple and inexpensive, Einstein said he was willing to travel steerage–instead he was given a stateroom. When his ship arrived in lower Manhattan, Einstein was standing on the deck wearing a faded gray wool coat, clutching a pipe in one hand, and his faded violin case in the other. The *New York Times* reported "He looked like an artist." In 1935, on a trip to Bermuda, he was greeted by the royal governor who suggested he stay in one of the island's best hotels. But Einstein, feeling they were too stuffy and pretentious, settled for a modest guest cottage he discovered while walking through town. He declined several invitations from Bermuda gentry, choosing to spend his time with a German cook he'd met at a restaurant.

Meditation in Motion

Neither a lofty degree of intelligence nor imagination nor both together go to the making of genius. Love, love, love, that is the soul of genius.
Wolfgang Amadeus Mozart

From childhood to death Einstein was a classic introvert, gravitating towards the solitary meditative activities he loved; reflecting with paper and pen, walking, music, poetry, and sailing. He loved to walk, and since he never owned or drove a car, he walked to and from work each day. Music soothed his soul. The violin was his real passion; he began taking lessons at age 6, a gift from his musical mother, and also played the piano. He played is violin daily until his 70s, when he switched to playing the piano daily. As a young man, he had frequent jam sessions with fellow students and colleagues, and while working in Berlin, he would sometimes go to three concerts a week. Wherever he traveled, his beloved violin, "Lina" accompanied him, a constant companion, along with his pipe. In a 1929 interview for *Saturday Evening Post*, he said, "If I were not a physicist, I would probably be a musician. I often think in music. I live my daydreams in music. I see my life in terms of music...I get most joy in life out of my violin." He felt music was "for the soul, not the intellect." At 13 he fell in love with Mozart who was his favorite composer; his sonatas evoked magic and emotion in Einstein. "Mozart's music is so pure and beautiful that I see it as a reflection of the inner beauty of the universe." He believed there wasn't a single superfluous note—with its perfect balance between harmony and melody—it came close to the purism of the formulas of physics. Neffe explains that music can be "mathematics poured into notes, and it may have afforded him insight into the harmony of the world... doesn't science discover the unknown in nature, just as music discovers the unknown in the human soul?" Einstein once said, "Music does not *influence* research work, but both are nourished by the same sort of longing." According to his son Hans Albert, playing music helped him think, "Whenever he felt that he had come to the end of the road, or faced a difficult challenge in his work he would take refuge in music and that would solve all his difficulties." A friend who knew Einstein in Berlin while he was working on his theory of relativity recalled, "He would often play his violin in his kitchen late at night, improvising melodies while he pondered complicated problems. Then suddenly, in the middle of the playing, he would announce excitedly, 'I've got it.' As if by inspiration, the answer to the problem would have come to him in the midst of music."

To express his deepest emotions, joy, triumph, sorrow, pain, and frustration he wrote poetry. Unfortunately, no one has compiled these philosophical musings into a book. Apity because they display his genius and his wit. While receiving copious amounts of mail each day he penned this;

A thousand letters in the mail
And every journal tells his tale
What's he to do when in this mood?
He sits and hopes for solitude.

In 1929 he wrote this poem summarizing his sentiments on turning forty;

Wherever I go and wherever I stay,
There's always a picture of me on display.
On top of the desk, or out in the hall,
Tied round a neck, or hung on the wall.
Women and men, they play a strange game,
Asking, beseeching: "Please sign your name."
From the erudite fellow they brook not a quibble
But firmly insist on a piece of his scribble.
Sometimes, surrounded by all this good cheer,
I'm puzzled by some of the things that I hear,
And wonder, my mind for a moment not hazy,
If I and not they could really be crazy.

His happiest times were in the solitude of the countryside at his summer house in Caputh, Germany, where he sailed his beloved sailboat the *Tümmler* or Dolphin. He loved this sailboat the way a young boy loves his favorite toy, and enjoyed going out on the water alone, spending hours letting the boat drift as he played with the rudder. Einstein's log cabin on Lake Timplin had a spacious terrace, shady porch, fruit trees, flowers and berries. "The sailboat, the expansive view, solitary autumn strolls, relative peace and quiet; it is a paradise...This paradise unfortunately lacks only one thing: There are no archangels to drive off curious gawkers and wearisome visitors with a fiery sword." Einstein would have been blissfully content growing old here, but this lasted just three summers before the Nazis drove him from his little paradise.

When he moved to Princeton, his cabin yacht *Tümmler* was replaced by *Tinnef*, a seventeen-foot dingy. *Tinnef* is Yiddish for piece of junk. A member of the local yacht club who went to retrieve Einstein on several occasions remembered, "Frequently he would go all day long, just drifting around...He apparently was just out there meditating." When the breeze stopped he would happily take out his notebook and scribble equations. Einstein described his own thought process as visual images, which were prolific. Neffe tells us, "He constructed his experiments inside his skull. He rode atop imaginary beams of light, traveled on superfast trains, whizzed in elevators through the cosmos, made blind beetles crawl, and established a new order with signs and numbers." He explained his theory of relativity to his nine-year-old son, Hans Albert by saying, "When a blind beetle crawls over the surface of a curved branch, it doesn't notice that the track it has covered is indeed curved. I was lucky enough to notice what the beetle didn't notice." In other words, spacetime is curved just like the branch to the beetle.

Perhaps Einstein's brain has eluded all the great scientists because he was simply too complex and multi-faceted. Only heart and spirit can infuse the brain with genius , eventually making it whole or holy, and this is something that can never be measured, dissected or quantified, just as we can't slice up a gust of wind, a surge of emotion, a creative insight, or a piece of a rainbow. The genius of spirit defies physical logic or precise measurement. Neffe writes "no other scientist has come close to his degree of fame and mythic transfiguration. His seemingly paradoxical nature–bourgeois and bohemian, superman and scalawag–lent him an air of mystery... he was a walking contradiction... He was a friend to some, an enemy to others, narcissistic and slovenly, easygoing and rebellious, philanthropic and autistic, citizen of the world and hermit, a pacifist whose research was used for military ends." The fact that his eyes and brain were illegally snatched, have only added to his priestly allure.

Evolving Genius

If you have not become more just, more peaceful, and generally more rational than we are (or were)–why then, the Devil take you.

Einstein

Einstein was just as human as the rest of us, and all earthly geniuses have their limitations. In his book, *Driving Mr. Albert*, Michael Paterniti says, "He laughed like a barking seal, snored like a foghorn, sunbathed in the nude. And then took tea with the queen." Einstein was a genius who never learned how to drive a car, had difficulty balancing his check book, used uncashed checks as bookmarks, and forgot his luggage on train platforms. He once showed up to work at the Patent Office in green slippers trimmed with flowers. He loved to sail, but never learned how to swim, and refused to wear a life jacket. On his second trip to the United States, he and Elsa were staying at the Waldorf Hotel, where they had two sprawling suites connected by a massive private dining room enabling him to greet a steady entourage of visitors. When a friend arrived and asked Elsa where Albert was, she replied with exasperation, "I don't know, he always gets lost somewhere in these rooms." When they discovered him, trying to find his wife, his friend suggested they lock the second suite off. This made Einstein much happier. He also didn't have an aptitude for languages. On his third visit to the United States, in his travel diary he wrote, "I am learning English, but it doesn't want to stay in my head."

Like Nobel, Einstein spent much of his time alone. Near the end of his life he said, "I am truly a lone traveler, and have never belonged to my country, my home, my friends, or even my immediate family with my whole heart...I have never lost a sense of distance and a need for solitude" He also said, "Everyone likes me, yet nobody understands me." But, in an amusing article entitled "Lady's Man", writer Kenneth Kidd presents him as "Einstein the rake, the blade, the swordsman who bedded many, only the tiniest fraction of whom happened to be his wife at the time." Einstein and Maric had two sons, and a mysterious daughter Lieserl, born before they were married. Some accounts say she was given up for adoption, while others suggest she died before her second birthday. Einstein was a magnet for women. They were attracted to his wisdom, wit, and unpretentious warm personality, and so he became entangled in many passionate relationships, despite wanting the freedom to work without commitments. Before Einstein's first marriage was over, he had embarked on a series of affairs. The results of this scientific experimentation led to his cousin, Elsa, whom he married in 1919. While married to Elsa, he developed a serious affair with the niece of a friend. This young women, Betty Neumann, was hired as his "secretary" and Elsa agreed to let Albert see this mistress twice a week, provided they were discreet. In his mid-fifties, he had a ten-year affair with Russian spy, Margarita Konenkova, whom he met when her husband, sculptor Sergei Konenkov, was making a bust of Einstein. Observing the insanity around him, he wrote to Margarita seven months after the war ended in 1945, "People are living now just as they were before ...and it is clear that they have learned nothing from the horrors they have had to deal with. The little intrigues with which they had complicated their lives before are again taking up most of their thoughts. What a strange species we are." In his sixties, he had a relationship with Johanna Fantova, who had immigrated to the United States from Prague. "Hanne" as he called her, was twenty-two years younger. Even the most esteemed geniuses and peacemakers still grapple with deeper issues of the heart. Einstein married twice, but didn't share a bedroom with his wife in both marriages. When one of his best friends, Michelle Besso died, Einstein said Besso's most admirable personal trait was his ability to live in harmony with his longtime wife Anna, "an undertaking in which I twice failed miserably."

Every genius is a work in process. Neffe says, "He had a blind spot when it came to the female half of humanity. He carried moral authority, but he was rumored to have illegitimate children and syphilis. With his marked sense of justice, he had as much in common with a queen as with a vagrant, but the equality of the sexes was of no concern to him. Quite the opposite: he valued and used women as lovers, but never really accepted them as companions on an equal level (except perhaps as musicians), and could not tolerate displays of femininity... Einstein loved the company of many women, but resisted a deeper emotional commitment."

When it came to relationships with women Einstein never really regarded women as equals. He grew up in an era when women were regarded as so intellectually inferior they weren't considered intelligent enough to vote. But we're evolving beyond a time where women are not respected equally as men. There is little genius or wisdom in misogyny or mistreatment of women since it ignores the heart, love, and compassion. In the more balanced definition of genius proposed in these pages both women and men would respect and honor each other as equals. This has always been a fundamental part of the equation for true genius. Any individual, society, or religious group that diminishes the gifts of women is deficient in their genius genes. Without feminine energies keeping balance, the world becomes harsh and chaotic; countries and religions are constantly at war, and large corporations rape and rob Mother Earth. The genius of both men and women has never been allowed to emerge, giving us that balance we desperately need. The geniuses profiled in the 21st century have achieved more balanced, respectful relationships—we are in fact getting smarter. For the first time since intelligence testing began more than a century ago, women have now surpassed men on IQ tests, and the average IQ scores for many populations have been rising. This was first reported in 2012 by James Flynn, emeritus professor of psychology and philosophy from New Zealand's Otago University, who based his results on IQ tests from western European countries: the United States, Canada, New Zealand, Argentina, Estonia and Israel. Flynn's observation that IQ rates have been rising consistently at an average rate of three points per decade has been dubbed the Flynn effect. He suspects that historically women have been disadvantaged and now with higher education we're reaching an equitable balance. Israel was the only country where women's IQ scores remained two points behind men. Flynn believes this is "entirely due to the Orthodox women who are cloistered from the world."

Einstein never balanced his health, and might have lived longer if he had looked after himself. Working long hours compromised his health and he began having problems in his late thirties. He boasted in a letter to Elsa, "I have firmly decided to bite the dust with a minimum of medical assistance when my time has come, and up to then to sin to my wicked heart's desire. Diet: smoke like a chimney, work like a horse, eat without thinking and choosing, go for a walk only in really pleasant company, and thus only rarely unfortunately, sleep irregularly..." Over the years he had gallstones, a severe stomach ulcer, jaundice, enlargement of the heart, and elevated blood pressure. At 39, he had lost 55 pounds and was so sick, he gave up his bachelor's apartment, and moved in with his cousin Elsa to be nursed back to health. He succumbed to his cousin's pressures to marry her, not out of romantic love, but because he realized he needed someone to look after him. By the time he was 49, he was in such bad shape he feared for his life, and wrote a friend he "came close to kicking the bucket."

Although most of what is written about Einstein, is a combination of awe and gratitude, there are exceptions. According to American science writer Tim Folger, "Albert Einstein–creator of relativity, godfather of quantum physics, bender of space and time—had a little problem that dogged him all his career: lack of vision." He contends many of the greatest ideas associated with the theory of relativity, weren't actually developed by Einstein, rather by scientists who came later and interpreted his work. Einstein rejected many of these theories because they seemed too outlandish. This may be why he's famous for saying, "If at first, the idea is not absurd, then there is no hope for it." One of Einstein's staunchest supporters, British physicist Arthur Eddington, said, "Not only is the universe stranger than we imagine, it is stranger than we can imagine." Einstein was convinced the universe was static. But after his version of general relativity was published in 1916, German physicist, Karl Schwarzschild, used Einstein's equations to determine if the mass of a star was compressed into a small enough volume, time froze and space became infinite, what physicists now call "singularity", where the laws of nature break down. Believing a star had to remain stable; Einstein tried to disprove this theory. Meanwhile, one of Einstein's students, J. Robert Oppenheimer, discovered that massive stars could implode under their own gravity, becoming denser, until their gravity trapped their light. Astronomers now believe this is how black holes form. A decade later, American astronomer Edwin Hubble discovered galaxies appeared to be hurtling away from each other at tremendous speeds. The universe was not static, and Einstein publicly admitted his error. By1998 astronomers discovered the universe was expanding at increasing rates, driven by an unknown force, which physicists refer to as that mysterious dark energy. French physicist Carlo

Rovelli says, "If you look at the history of physics, almost every epoch has the feeling that 'we know everything now.' I think what we don't know is probably huge. We are still far away from knowing all the ingredients." He believes a key element in Einstein's genius was his ability to completely change his mind so many times. "That's a sign of a great scientist. A great scientist is not somebody who believes his own ideas; it's somebody who does not believe his own ideas. He's ready to change his mind. What Einstein did was bring back science to its true soul, which is to change our view of the world, not just explain things. Einstein reminded us that what we don't know is much more than what we know."

We're all capable of realizing our individual genius if we understand the potential of heartfelt guidance. Einstein and Nobel were brilliant—but quite different. Nobel was a recluse who never married or even dated, while Einstein, an international celebrity, married twice and attracted women like a magnet. Nobel spoke seven languages fluently, while Einstein had no propensity for language. Nobel was self-taught never receiving any degree, while Einstein earned a PH.D. Clearly, there is no one magic formula for genius. Einstein read voraciously, but his spirit used that academic foundation to visualize, and leap to new frontiers. Meditation, dreamwork, music, long walks, living your passion, simplicity, dedication, hard work, solitude, and asking for heartfelt guidance are essential keys to genius. Now let's leap forward to examine genius in this century. We'll look at five individuals, who are humanitarians and social activists, more balanced in relationships and health, definitely movers and shakers, but in a different, perhaps more evolved fashion.

CHAPTER FOUR
Twenty-First Century Genius

The best way to find yourself is to lose yourself in the service of others.
Mother Teresa

Craig Kielburger One Kid Changing the World

The secret of genius is to carry the spirit of childhood into old age.
Bertrand Russell

MOST GENIUSES BEGIN DISPLAYING EXTRAORDINARY abilities in childhood. This was the case with Craig Kielburger, who at age twelve, rallied his friends and began Free The Children, now an international charity and educational partner. Destiny arrived one morning in 1995, as twelve-year-old Craig was sitting at the kitchen table, eating a bowl of cereal, and searching for his favorite newspaper cartoon. He was struck by a front page story, "Battled child labor, boy, 12, murdered." It told how four-year-old Iqbal Masih, from Islamabad, Pakistan, had been sold into slavery by his parents for less than $16. For six years Iqbal's life became one of forced enslavement, shackled to a carpet-weaving loom, tying thousands of tiny knots. Finally, freed at age ten, he began a personal crusade to let others know the atrocities suffered by child laborers. Angry members of the carpet industry threatened Iqbal, until one day, while riding his bike in his village, he was shot. Many believed his murderers were the people in the carpet trade who had been threatening him; true or not, Iqbal had been silenced.

This one paragraph story was the catalyst that changed Craig's life. After school he went to the public library to do research, reading about children like Iqbal sold into slavery in the carpet trade, children working in underground coal mines, and children killed or maimed by explosions in fireworks factories. Craig left the library bewildered and angry that the rest of the world was allowing this to happen. He was shocked that no one was trying to stop this injustice.

He kept that newspaper story. Riding the school bus, he would often uncrumple the article and study the picture of Iqbal in his bright red vest with his hand raised in the air. Finally, even though public speaking was not his forte, he mustered enough courage to ask his teacher if he could speak to his grade seven class. Like all of us, Craig had challenges. He was a shy and self-conscious kid who struggled with a speech impediment and had difficulty pronouncing many sounds, including R's, which made even saying his first and last name difficult since it contained three. He was teased mercilessly because he couldn't enunciate clearly and often spoke too quickly. (Interesting that Einstein also had speech problems as a child.) Sweating and nervous, he talked about Iqbal, passed out copies of the newspaper article, and shared all the alarming statistics he had learned. Craig ended his talk by asking for their help–probably without any expectations. To his surprise, eleven hands shot up, igniting what would become one of the most powerful social justice movements in the world.

Using Craig's Thornhill home as headquarters, these children began researching, giving speeches, writing petitions, and holding garage sales as fund raisers. Before long, Free The Children chapters were starting in other schools. They also started receiving mail from human rights organizations around the world with pictures of children who had been released from bonded slavery. One of their first success stories came after learning that Kailash Satyarthi had been imprisoned in India after fighting for children's rights. They collected 3,000 signatures on a petition, and wrote a letter to the prime minister in New Delhi demanding that Kailash be freed. All of this was inside a shoe box which the children had carefully wrapped and mailed. A year later, when a freed Kailash was speaking in North America, he said that little shoe box was, "one of the most powerful actions taken on my behalf." Remarkably, at age twelve, Craig discovered what would become a lifelong career and passion by following what tugged at his heart. In his book, *Me to We*, he says, "Working with a team toward a common goal, I felt a sense of accomplishment and joy. I was happier than I'd ever been in my life."

Despite these early successes, Craig felt he lacked the important experience of observing firsthand what was happening around the world. He shared these feelings with friend and mentor, Alam Rahman, a twenty-four-year old University of Toronto student and human rights activist. They often talked about whether Craig should make a trip to Asia himself, although Craig admits, since he was only twelve, he never thought it would actually happen. A short time later, Alam planned to visit relatives in South Asia, and asked Craig to join him. Craig's mom pointed out he'd never even taken public transit to venture downtown, and was thinking of traipsing around the world! His parents were incredulous, but Craig was determined. He began raising money for his trip and faxing organizations in Southern Asia. Intuition must have told the Kielburgers, two level-headed professionals, that their grade-seven-son would be fine on a seven week trip to some of the most impoverished places on the planet because they let him go. Little did they know, their son would make history.

His first stop was Dhaka, Bangladesh, a slum that was a sea of corrugated tin, woven reed, and cardboard huts. These people wore rags, owned next to nothing, had little food, and human and animal waste filled the gutters. When Craig saw this abject poverty he wanted to stay there the entire seven weeks to help out. He asked a human rights worker how he could help and was told, "Continue your journey. Learn as much as you can. And then go back home and tell others what you have seen and ask them if they think it is fair that places like this exist in the world. Because it's the lack of action, the refusal from people at home to help, that allows this to continue."

Craig met children working in metal factories, pouring metal without any protective clothing, five-year-olds slaving in brick kilns to pay off debts taken out by poor parents or grandparents, a ten-year-old boy covered with scars from an explosion that had killed fourteen other children in a fireworks factory, and an eight-year-old girl in a recycling factory forced to take apart used needles and syringes with her bare hands.

Before Craig's visit to Asia, Free The Children members had repeatedly written the prime minister's office, asking for a meeting to address child labor issues. They'd been told Mr. Chrétien was extremely busy, and a meeting would be impossible. Then destiny stepped in. While twelve-year-old Craig was in Asia, the Canadian Prime Minister, Jean Chrétien, was also there with eight provincial premiers and 250 business leaders, hoping to drum up trade. Craig couldn't believe the prime minister was signing billion dollar trade deals, without mentioning the abused and exploited children making these products. Child labor laws weren't even on their agenda. Craig was convinced if the prime minister saw just one of these horrendous stories first hand, he would help. His short time in Asia had showed there was a direct relationship between Asian children working in deplorable conditions, and our North American tendency to consume, throw away, and never question how or why products can be made so cheaply. Just after his thirteenth birthday, Craig called a press conference. Canada's major television stations and newspapers were there, covering the prime minister's visit when Craig, with scruffy hair and a dirty blue t-shirt spoke passionately about the deplorable lives of child laborers in Asia. Then he introduced Nagashir, who spoke through a translator, a friend he'd met at the Mukti Ashram, a rehabilitation center for former child slaves. The word *mukti* means release or liberation; every child from this ashram had been forced into labor and abused by their slave masters. Nagashir's parents had allowed their two sons to leave, believing a man who came to their poor village promising education and a good job for their children. Instead, Nagashir was chained to a weaving loom, working twelve-hour days. His good-paying salary was a small bowl of rice and watery lentils at the end of the day. If he fell behind in his work because of hunger or exhaustion, he was whipped and beaten. Nagashir showed the cameras the scars covering his body. His hands were a mangle of cuts from the carpet knife. His master, not wanting to lose time and money, filled these cuts with gunpowder paste, lit them to cauterize the wounds, then sent him back to work. But most shocking were the scars on his legs, arms, and against his throat, where he'd been branded with hot irons as punishment for helping his younger brother escape.

Thirteen-year-old Craig never imaged the impact this press conference would have—it was carried by networks around the world, including CNN. While in Islamabad, he discovered the prime minister's handlers were looking for him—Mr. Chrétien wanted a meeting. After their meeting, the prime minister agreed to address child labor with the heads of South Asian governments. Craig said, "It was exhilarating and strange. I was only a kid, but people were listening to me. I remember the feeling when I first realized I could actually make a change in the world. It floored me. I felt as if the laws of gravity had been broken. It left my skin tingling with excitement. It still does."

That excitement has propelled Craig into a dynamic and charismatic public speaker. In 2012 Free The Children released an annual report detailing the rapid growth of their organization. From a group of 12-year-olds sitting around the kitchen table, they grew into an international charity and educational partner who have built 650 schools in developing countries. In 2012 they had established more than 6,100 Free The Children groups across North America. They have provided $16 million worth of medical supplies, and helped more than 30,000 women become self-sufficient through loans, and provided one million people with improved access to clean water, health care, and sanitation. Free The Children works through its development model called Adopt a Village, which focuses on five pillars; education, clean water and sanitation, health, alternative income and livelihood, and agriculture and food security.

In 2007, Craig and his brother Marc organized the first ever We Day event for 8,000 Toronto area students in grades 7 to 12. By 2013, these events now held across Canada and the United States, were so popular that over 160,000 students earn their way to attend. These huge stadium events for empowerment, social awareness, and responsibility, are a combination of heart-wrenching stories, motivational speeches by social activists and celebrities, and musical performances. Young people earn their way to these events through service and volunteering. There are full-year programs running in many schools getting students fired up around service. Craig believes that learning social issues is just as important as reading, writing and arithmetic—and this is the true genius behind his organization. He's made being a humanitarian the coolest thing on earth. These are coveted events for teens since they have an opportunity to listen to humanitarian stars such as: the Dalai Lama, Al Gore, Desmond Tutu, Richard Branson, Justin Trudeau, Mia Farrow, Martin Sheen, Reverend Jesse Jackson, Dr. Jane Goodall, Chris Hatfield, Queen Noor of Jordon, and Magic Johnson. The event is also a rousing rock concert, largely by musical stars, so inspired by this movement that they have volunteered their time for We Day: Jennifer Hudson, One Republic, Hedley, Nelly Furtado, Joe Jonas, Demi Lovato, Avril Lavigne, Serena Ryder, Down with Webster and Imagine Dragon. Students hear speakers like Michel Chikwanine who was abducted in the Democratic Republic of Congo at age five while playing soccer with his friends. He was thrown in a truck and taken to their camp where his initiation began. Michel's wrists were cut, and while he was bleeding, the soldiers rubbed a mixture of cocaine and gunpowder into the wounds to make him literally go crazy. He was blindfolded, handed a gun, and they began screaming "SHOOT, SHOOT SHOOT." When the blindfold was removed, Michel realized he'd been forced to kill one of his best friends, Kevin. Later he was forced to watch the rape of his mother and two sisters.

By 2013, We Day events had spread to twelve cities across North America, with an additional We Day scheduled for the UK in 2014. In 2006, Craig was awarded the World's Children's Prize for the Rights of the Child. Free The Children has also been awarded: The Human Rights Award in 2006 from the United Nations/World Association of Non-Governmental Organizations, The Skoll Award for Social Entrepreneurship in 2007, the World Economic Forum Medal, and the Roosevelt Freedom Medal. In 2008, at age 25, Craig became one of the youngest Canadians in history to be honored as a member of the Order of Canada. That's pretty impressive for a shy twelve-year-old, who once struggled with a speech impediment.

Marc Kielburger & Roxanne Joyal: One Couple Changing the World

The one thing we haven't globalized is compassion.
                                             Craig Kielburger

When you see an injustice, you have the responsibility to act.
                                             June Callwood

Marc Kielburger, Craig's older brother, began shaking up the world at age thirteen when he turned his passion for environmental issues into a grade-eight science project. Marc researched and tested the harmful effects of popular cleaning products on our water system, then proposed natural alternatives that cleaned as effectively—environmentally friendly products like lemons, vinegar, and baking soda. He founded an environmental club, began giving speeches, created petitions, and collected thousands of signatures, becoming the youngest person in the province to receive the Ontario Citizenship Award.

Before his last year of high school Marc wanted to be student council president, so he came up with catchy campaign slogans like, "It's not a burger, it's a Kielburger." However, he lost by a handful of votes—perhaps because he had a different destiny. When Marc was eighteen, he began working as a page in the Canadian House of Commons, and like brother Craig, one small event changed his life. While delivering a note to a man he describes as a "formidable and balding gentlemen," he was asked, "What kind of legacy do you want to leave son?" When Marc didn't have a clear answer the "gentleman" started describing a charity that he volunteered for in the slums of Thailand, and asked if Marc was interested. Marc politely said, "No thank you." But this man was so persistent and "persuasive" that when the school year ended, Marc was on a plane to Bangkok, Thailand. He had put his scholarship on hold, and used all of his savings to buy the ticket.

Marc was taken to Klong Toey, on the edge of wealthy Bangkok, where tens of thousands of people live on less than a dollar a day—worse than anything he had imagined. He described it as a "sprawling sea of corrugated tin, mud and cement bricks, zinc roofing, open sewers, and garbage heaps." His volunteer position was in the AIDS ward of a hospice. Two Thai nurses greeted him, hoping he was a doctor or medical student because they hadn't had a day off in three weeks. Marc confessed his only medical experience was watching the television show

E.R. every Thursday. Desperate for help, they began giving him a four-hour crash course in medical procedures. Marc said, "I learned how to clean wounds, administer IVs, treat bedsores, and dispense medicine. The work was punishing, made worse by stifling heat, frequent blackouts, and an incredible stench in the air. I tried desperately to hide my weak nerves and queasy stomach, and more than once dashed for the bathroom to throw up." Before the end of the first day those overworked Thai nurses left Marc in charge.

After they left, a patient with fluid in his lungs began having difficulty breathing. When he started choking, Marc ran frantically to the street, yelling and pleading for anyone passing by to help. No one responded. The only thing he could do was return to the ward, sit by the man's side and hold his hand as he looked into his eyes, and watched his life slip away. He was still crying when the nurses returned, but was told, "Marc, people die all the time. That's why we're here." That evening, emotionally exhausted, he called his parents and arranged a flight back home. But that same night, a group of street children knocked on his door and invited him to a birthday party in a few days. These street kids didn't know their parents, ages, or birth dates, so every year they pooled their money, mostly from shining shoes, and held a huge birthday celebration. Not wanting to disappoint them, Marc agreed to stay until the celebration was over. At the party, he feasted on peanuts and watermelon and was overwhelmed by their laughter, warmth, singing, dancing, storytelling, and generosity. These boys were too poor to buy shoes, but willing to share everything they had. Marc ended up living in Klong Toey for almost a year, teaching English, and working in that AIDS ward.

When Marc returned to Canada, he put his professional life back in motion, moving to the United States, where he was accepted on a full scholarship to study international relations at Harvard. After graduating, he moved to England, earning a Rhodes scholarship, and a law degree at Oxford University. This story would usually end with Marc being courted by several large companies, and accepting a job with a starting salary close to $200,000 plus fringe benefits. His lifestyle would include lavish parties, a fancy sports car, lots of golf, and sitting on the board of governors for large corporations. However, Marc walked away from this, since most geniuses never trod a conventional path. When Marc explained he was returning to Canada to run a children's charity, his classmates thought he was crazy. Back in Canada he co-founded Leaders Today, which would eventually become Me to We, with his younger brother. Me to We is a social enterprise that works co-operatively with Free The Children. Me to We offers socially conscious and environmentally friendly products and life-changing experiences. It reached more than 520,300 people in 2012, providing opportunities to travel and learn through international volunteer trips, those same experiences that changed Marc and Craig indelibly. However, these trips are for shorter periods of time and with experienced support!

Marc may not be driving a Mercedes like his classmates, but he says, "I'm humbled to be able to do this work on a daily basis. Unlike my friends on Wall Street, I don't have a $5,000 watch. My $100 model works great. I don't dine in five-star restaurants every night. And I still do make spaghetti using canned spaghetti sauce. But I can look in the mirror at the end of the day and see myself smiling back. I am simply happier helping people...I still feel that I learned more about compassion, caring, and leadership from my street kid friends than I have from any of my tweed-clad professors with endless letters after their names."

Free The Children has been successful because of the commitment of its founding members. One of these remarkable people, is Roxanne Joyal, now married to Marc Kielburger. They met as teenagers while working as parliamentary pages in Ottawa, and started dating when Marc was 18, and Roxanne was 17. Perhaps Marc was able to get through his year working with AIDS patients in the slums of Klong Toey, because Roxanne had agreed to join him. She spent six months in Bangkok, Thailand, caring for mothers and children afflicted with AIDS, then went on to earn a degree in international relations at Stanford, a Rhodes scholarship, and a law degree from Oxford where she specialized in labor and family law. After competing her legal training in Canada, like Marc, Roxanne turned all her talents and attention to Free The Children. Her initiatives in a few short years, are more than most people accomplish in several lifetimes. She has worked with the World Bank on poverty-alleviation projects in Zimbabwe. With Free the Children she has worked on social and economic empowerment initiatives in Kenya, Ghana, and Sierra Leone. Roxanne divides her time between Toronto, Canada, and Nairobi, Kenya. She spearheads a micro-lending program in Kenya, helping women start their own small businesses, and Me to We Artisans, beadwork, jewelry and original accessories handcrafted by artisans around the world. This started in the sprawling Massai Mara region with the women of Kenya, who begin beading beading circles beneath acacia trees as young girls. Roxanne explained, "Inside their small huts, the mamas showed me their intricate beaded handiwork. They did not think of it as art, but necessity. These objects played a major role in rituals surrounding birth, circumcision, marriage, warriorhood and death. These very practical women could not believe I wanted to sell their work and return the profits to them and their families." She added, "In helping empower these women, I found my calling." The program has been enormously successful. Free The Children staff member Katie Hewitt found after just a year in the program, one women, Narripol Pariken, referred to it as her "savior from poverty." She was able to buy two goats that provided milk and cheese for her husband and seven children, along with clothes and utensils. That extra income also meant her children could stay in school and plan for their futures instead of going to work. Before the Artisan program her children rarely attended school, and when there was little rain, her husband, a farmer, could not provide enough food for the family. Roxanne also created the Bogani Cottages and Tented Camp, a first of its kind facility where youth, families, or corporate groups can stay while volunteering in Kenya. This was so successful, she established a similar facility in Rajasthan, India. In 2011 Marc and Roxanne had their first child, a daughter, Lily-Rose, who made her inaugural trip to Kenya when she was just four months old. Roxanne has accomplished much of this by the age of thirty—that's genius.

Ricky Martin—One Celebrity Rocking the World

Setting an example is not the main means of influencing others;
it is the only means.

Albert Einstein

Barbara Walters once interviewed singer Ricky Martin at the pinnacle of his fame and asked if he was really happy. With his handsome demeanor, talent, adoring fans, and money, it seemed inevitable he would laugh and say, "Yes Barbara, I've been incredibly fortunate, I couldn't be happier." But Ricky stopped smiling, became deadpan serious, and said something profound; no one could possibly say they were happy all the time, unless they were being dishonest, or using drugs. Ricky was in his late twenties during this interview, and this is the wisdom we usually attribute to holy men, sages, or budding geniuses.

Ricky's genius is that he is absolutely right. It doesn't matter how gorgeous or wealthy we are, everyone experiences emotional and physical pain: the death of loved ones, accidents, illness, and the insanity around us. What gives us a greater degree of peace is becoming aware of why we're really here, cleaning up our karma, and following a more dharmic path where we give back or serve humanity. Living any other way is putting in unnecessary time, and contributing to the chaos of our soul, as we'll see in the next chapter. How would he know this? Many go through lifetimes never grasping this essential truth.

Ricky, born Enrique Martin Morales, is a musician, singer, composer, actor and philanthropist. Instinctively, he always knew he was born to be a singer; at six he would grab a wooden kitchen spoon using it as a microphone. He's sold more than 65 million albums, won two Grammys, American Music Awards and Billboard Awards, and is a Goodwill Ambassador for UNICEF. And like all geniuses he has worked incredibly hard. He says, "…there is no doubt that I have come to where I am, and accomplished what I have, because I worked hard to get it. If anything is true in this world it is that destiny is something you have to help." Ricky began working nonstop hours at the age of twelve. After auditioning three times for the first Latin American boy band Menuda, he became the youngest member of the group to sing around the world. They performed concerts to screaming fans in the United States, Japan, the Philippines, Europe, and South America, and during these trips Ricky began what would become a lifelong career as a goodwill ambassador. His band managers wanting to make the most of these travels, enlisted the boys as UNICEF ambassadors. They began visiting orphans and homeless children who lived on the streets and invited them to their shows. At 17, when Ricky left Menuda after five years with the group, what he wanted most was simplicity—freedom from the private jets, entire hotels to himself, private chefs, personal bodyguards, tutors and assistants. In his autobiography *Me* he writes, "My happiest memories in life are from my childhood. The time I spent with my father. Going for coffee with my grandparents in the afternoons. Being with my grandmother in the living room as she worked on one of her projects. Listening to music with my mother."

There are many sides to Ricky Martin. In 1994, he played the part of singer Miguel Morez in General Hospital, and in 1996 he played Marius Pontmercy on stage in "Les Miserables." Because of his interest in eastern culture he spent his 28th birthday on a spiritual quest in the Himalayas. He refers to this time in India learning meditation and yoga as "an awakening." In *Me,* he explains, "In India I found what I consider to be the three keys of life; serenity, simplicity, and spirituality. I was able to comprehend the enormous blessing that is my life, and I discovered that true wealth does not exist outside, but instead lives inside of me."

Ricky speaks Spanish, English, Portuguese, and some Italian and French. He's come close to death on at least four occasions. The first time, while making a video, his motorcycle smashed into a barrier and caught on fire. He suffered only a bruised leg. In the second incident, he had just left a plane, which crashed after takeoff, killing the pilot. His third escape from death occurred in Buenos Aires when his car was rammed by a truck and sent hurtling off the road. Another time in the mountains of Italy, racing at 120 miles per hour to attend the music festival of San Remo, his car turned upside down. He survived with minor injuries; obviously he still had important work to do.

In his late twenties, after returning from India, Ricky began reading and researching, and discovered his destiny involved more than music. He life took a far different path after learning that each year more than one million children become victims of trafficking. Every day 3,000 children are kidnapped, sold and abused—mostly innocent young girls because men are willing to pay $15,000 for the virginity of an eight-year-old child. While traveling in Cambodia he met a beautiful fourteen-year-old girl. Her abductors had told her, "If you come with us, we'll make you a model and the money you earn will be sent to your grandmother so that she will be able to get the medicine and therapies to treat her condition." Instead, she was kidnapped, put in a brothel, raped, became pregnant, and given HIV.

This was why at the height of his career, Ricky walked out of the spotlight and focused on issues closer to his heart. He established the Ricky Martin Foundation in his home country Puerto Rico, with a mission to promote education, health, and social justice for children. His organization is active in battling every aspect of human trafficking; factories that exploit workers, prostitution, pornography, forced labor, sexual exploitation of children, servitude, even organ trafficking. In Puerto Rico, his Foundation provides scholarships for low income students. One of its first tasks was partnering with Yamaha and FedEx to raise enough money to purchase one million dollars worth of musical instruments for public schools. Partnering with Easter Seals, it funds programs to educate and rehabilitate disabled children and adults. Another project in Puerto Rico is a holistic youth center in Loiza, a town on the north coast with gang-related problems. This center offers classrooms where youth can learn meditation, yoga, arts, and activities to keep them off the streets. It has built a rehabilitation Center in Aibonito, a small town in the center of the island, to provide early stimulation and therapy for children with physical and intellectual disabilities. For the children of San José (with one of the highest criminal rates in Puerto Rico) it provides tutoring, theater, dance, drawing, and sports lessons, and purchases medical equipment for children in need. His foundation has launched a project called *Llama y Vive* (Call and Live), a toll-free hotline where victims of trafficking can call for help.

Globally, his foundation also makes a difference. He explains, "Traffickers often take advantage of extreme situations, such as earthquakes, floods, or wars, to abduct the children who are most vulnerable...When they come upon a child who is crying for his mother, they know that this child will believe anyone who says, 'I know where your parents are. Come with me.'" When the tsunami hit Thailand in 2004, Ricky was there determining how he could help. In partnership with Habitat for Humanity, his foundation built 224 homes for victims in Phang Nga province in Thailand. That same year he addressed the United Nations as part of an international panel of philanthropists dedicated to the education and prevention of child trafficking. And when Haiti was ravaged by earthquakes in 2010 Ricky's foundation came to the rescue.

In 2008, he became the father of twin boys Matteo and Valentino with the help of a surrogate mother. There had always been speculation around Ricky's sexual preferences, but for the longest time he remained silent, meditating on what to do. It was the subject of his 2003 album, "*Almos del Silencio*" or Souls of Silence. "I really needed to go back to focus, to my center, to the beginning. I had the need to search within, and really dig deep, and find these emotions that, because of the adrenaline and the euphoria that I lived for a couple of years, were probably sabotaged." At age 38, Ricky went public about his personal life. He needed "many years of silence and reflection to understand" what he carried in his heart. On his website he posted this message, "I am proud to say that I am a fortunate homosexual man. I am very blessed to be who I am... These years of silence and reflection made me stronger and reminded me that acceptance has to come from within and that this kind of truth gives me the power to conquer emotions I didn't even know existed." He also posted a quote by Martin Luther King. "Our lives begin to end the day we become silent about things that matter." It was writing his memoirs and thinking about his twin sons that led him to go public. It certainly has not affected his popularity and influence.

Ricky has learned to blend what he was always passionate about, singing and performing, with his humanitarian efforts. His time away from concerts and recording only added to his popularity. One concert reviewer applauded his "capable voice," "tremendous physicality" and called him a "former teen heartthrob" who was still "an energetic, entertaining force." He also commended his humanitarian efforts, describing how "he delivered a sombre five minute spiel on gratitude, faith and the pursuit of simplicity as an introduction to Somos La Semilla (We Are the Seed), which he sang before a scrolling photo montage depicting poor, ill and war-torn people."

Ricky was raised a devout Catholic, but studied Buddhism, and practices kriya yoga which focuses on spiritual action. When asked why, he replied, "When you're surrounded by noise all the time how can you hear God? It helps to bring the silence that is needed to hear God." He writes, "Life's most valuable lessons are learned in absolute silence. It is when we are deep in that silence that we have the ability to think about and connect with our most intimate nature, our spiritual being." A life of simplicity, silence, and finally peace, three often misunderstood traits needed for wisdom, insight or genius. He says, "The only thing I desire in my life, and in the lives of all other human beings, is to find inner peace. It doesn't matter what path you choose to reach it. Be it Catholicism, Islam, Buddhism, Hinduism, Christianity, Judaism, quantum physics, Taoism, atheism—what matters is to find what works for each of us...no one religion is more effective or more valid than another...If I limited myself to being only a Buddhist or a Catholic or a Hindu, to a certain degree I would be closing myself off from receiving other lessons from other beliefs and philosophies." Ricky has found his destiny or dharma, purpose and peace through his music and foundation. He says that giving back feels wonderful, better than anything else he's done before. "If we, who are all here together on this earth, don't take care of one another, then who else will? It is our duty. All of us have some responsibility on the spiritual path. It could be fighting against human trafficking; helping the elderly; assisting the helpless; fighting for the rights of the LGBT community (Lesbian, Gay, Bisexual, Transgender); or feeding the hungry—but we all have the obligation to stand up for what we believe in and help the less fortunate and take care of the neediest." Ricky Martin is not merely singing his way through a superficial or self-indulgent life. His head and heart are connected, working in harmony to end that "la vida loca" he sings about, the crazy life or chaos of the soul—musical genius at work.

PART TWO
ACTIVATING THE WISDOM OF SPIRIT

Earth's crammed with heaven,
And every common bush afire with God.
Elizabeth Barrett Browning

CHAPTER FIVE
The Soul in Chaos

No one goes his way alone; all that we send into the lives
of others comes back into our own.

Edwin Markham

Karma or Hell on Earth

WHILE I WAS TRYING TO be rich, smart, and successful, I believed I had little control over my life. My mind wanted me to believe I was a victim, so I could stay in the little prison it had created for me. To ensure its place of control, my mind convinced me of many things; life wasn't fair, I was a victim of circumstances I couldn't control, and bad things happened to everyone, but mostly to me, and no one really suffered or had as much pain and bad luck as I did. If your mind has told you any of these things, you've been seduced, deluded, tricked, or trapped, just as I was. There's a term for this type of thinking in Twelve-Step circles. It's called "terminal uniqueness."

Terminal uniqueness is that "woe is me" mindset that no one in the universe has it quite so bad. Unique in our pain and suffering, we become the center of our self-absorbed mini-universe, and everything revolves around our emotional or physical pain. Terminal uniqueness bolsters the ego or mind. We may take great pride in our pain, and ability to endure it; we may even become attached to this pain, so that it defines who and what we are, completely pushing aside our spirit. The mind desperately wants to become its own isolating universe, but in this state we only become more desperate, depressed, lonely, and isolated from others who may provide guidance and support. But spirit sees the world as a place of infinite possibilities and connects us to others, providing shared wisdom, love that energizes, and renewed hope. If the mind is like a prison, spirit provides the keys or way out. Terminal uniqueness is well-named. The mind with its dark, deluded thinking can overshadow our core or spirit. Without being aware of what's happening, this can compromise our soul's very reason for being here.

But in truth, we're more in control than we think. God or spirit is not controlling our life. The desire to control is a human, mind-based quality. Each of us writes our own blueprint or life script; it's not something imposed on us. It's not God's will; it's our spirit's will. Life is not a cruel game we're thrown into to see whether we'll sink or swim. It's not survival of the fittest. It's an incredible opportunity to return to our original state of balance and grace, a time when our body did not break down and experience physical death. God has no direct plan for any one person. Each person has their own plan. Everyone has a personal plan based on the needs of their soul. Their soul knows. Prior to entering life the soul sits down with God and says okay, this is the level to where my soul's grown to, perhaps this soul is at level five, and I need to accomplish these ten things in this next life in order for my soul to grow to the next level. God looks at their ideas and basically they write it out as a book. The soul might say for items one to thirteen, I'll grow up in New York, go to college, meet my future wife there, get married, have three children, work as a teacher, and really tackle my ego issues, fears around money and failure, will try to respect my wife, will spend more time with my children, and work on greater faith and humility, and not judging and criticizing others. I'll get this illness, maybe item fourteen is their death. The soul shows God their book of life, their novel. And God says, okay, I agree with you, maybe I'm going to change item, five, because it would serve you better to work through karma with only two children, but finally they reach an agreement. The soul tucks that information into their DNA and goes into a body, is born, and the conscious mind goes about meeting the needs of that physical body, and is fuelled unknowingly by the subconscious, because only the soul knows exactly what the purpose of the life is. It's as if a veil is drawn between the spirit worlds and the physical worlds and our minds have absolutely no idea why we're really here and what our book of life is all about. This is sometimes referred to as spiritual amnesia. In many ways it is a form of grace or a blessing. If we were consciously aware of all of our karma and what we needed to face, we might be consumed with so much fear, guilt and self-loathing, that we wouldn't be able to get out of bed in the morning! It's like being in a witness protection program, where we're given a whole new identity, and a different place to relocate so we can start anew. Meanwhile God has the plan up in heaven, or another dimension, and watches down on every soul as they move along. He's aided by the archangels, and there's a guiding angel for each soul.

This guiding angel makes sure each step is followed as closely as possible and will check into the subconscious and say,

"Do you still want to do this?"

And the subconscious might say, "You know what, I'm not sure, I had plan A for a career, I think it would be better if I worked in another school in the same city."

And God says, "Okay, fine, we'll make sure plan B works for you then. In plan B you were going to meet these five people rather than these five people."

In a nutshell that's how it works. In Hinduism this Book of Life is referred to as the *akasha*, Sanskrit for sky or space. It's also referred to as our akashic records—the book for each soul kept in a library on the akashic dimension or astral plane—a dimension we may frequently travel to while dreaming. There is even reference to this Book of Life in the Bible. In Psalms 139:15:17, it says, "When my bones were being formed, carefully put together in my mother's womb, when I was growing there in secret, you knew that I was there—you saw me before I was born. The days allotted to me have all been recorded in your book, before any of them ever began." So, it's not that God plans it entirely—we co-create this sacred book under God's guidance. God has a master plan for the universe. He gives us free will which actuality comes into play prior to birth. The soul takes its own responsibility for knowing what it needs to accomplish in a life. God is certainly not a puppet master, and so we are given the greatest autonomy, trust, and respect. Meanwhile the conscious mind hasn't a clue about the needs of the soul. Left to its own devices it would completely screw up!

Within this blueprint or book of life our soul is attempting to work through or clear away all its unresolved karma or unresolved debts. The Law of Karma is one of the tenets of both Buddhist and Hindu philosophies, but is not completely understood in the Western world. The word karma is believed to have first appeared in the Rigveda or Rig Veda the oldest religious text on the planet, and one of four sacred Hindu texts. Depending on the source, its origins vary considerably; it may have been first recited between 4,000 and 12,000 BC. The word Rigveda is a combination of the two Sanskrit words, praise and *vedu* or knowledge. Karma is a universal spiritual law that governs everyone—there's no escaping it! The law of karma follows us like a shadow. We take it with us from lifetime to lifetime, all of our previous thoughts, words, and deeds. This is what Buddhists refer to as the law of cause and effect. At death we leave our physical body beyond, but not our karma and our spirit. The good news is we also take our dharma, spiritual merit, or virtuous deeds with us. The Buddha said, "If a king or householder shall die, His wealth, family, friends, and retinue cannot follow him, Wherever we go, wherever we remain, The results of our actions follow us."

It's exceedingly important to understand that karma is not divine retribution or punishment from God. Instead God gives each soul the free will to self-educate, and experience what it needs to experience in order to reach enlightenment. Depending on the alignment of the planets, we decided when we would arrive on earth, who our parents, siblings and friends would be, whether we would marry, have children, what types of work would best help us and others, and how and when we would die. The purpose of this script is to cleanse away all of our karma, fears, illusions, chaos, and emotional and physical pain, and arrive at a place of clarity, understanding, and peace. Understanding the laws of karma and dharma can be our ticket out of much of the pain, suffering, and craziness we experience.

Let's imagine Henry was a 15th century feudal landlord in France, living a life of luxury, while peasants work his land and live in abject poverty. He might be reincarnated into the 21st century and inherit a huge high rise apartment building from his father. Between incarnations his soul decided this may be the best way to reverse his karma. The people who were his peasants are now tenants in that high rise apartment. He's really here to learn how to honor and respect these individuals. Instead, he charges unreasonably high rents to make a fast buck, and fails to maintain the building, causing them to live in shoddy bed bug infested units. Henry dies suddenly at 43 in a car accident. His spirit determined that he needed a quick exit plan because his mind had absolutely no awareness of how amoral his actions were, and he showed no desire to change his ways. He was repeating the same karma and making absolutely no spiritual progress. It would serve him better to exit from earth, review his life, and start anew.

Another hypothetical example might be Ralph who lived in the 18th century as a wealthy English baron or lord. He owned a large estate, divided into farms, inherited from his family, and charged his tenants exorbitant taxes to maintain his wealthy self-indulgent life style. His henchmen would beat or set fire to the homes of these peasants if they couldn't pay his taxes. Ralph is also a womanizer; he marries in this early twenties and has four children, while continually having affairs. In his forties he casts out this wife, for a naïve beautiful, younger, women, and abandons his children leaving them impoverished. Ralph never changes his ways and dies ten years later of syphilis and gout. He reincarnates in the United States in the 21st century, into another wealthy family, eventually becoming the CEO of a large prosperous fast food chain. His soul's plan was to turn things around and run the company ethically allowing employees to purchase shares in the company that would be a model for other businesses. Instead, disconnected entirely from his heart and spirit, his greed resurfaces. He comes up with what he believes is an ingenious plan to continually reap billions, and never invests any of this money in philanthropy. All of his employees work part time at minimum wage with no real job security, benefits, sick pay, or holidays. He gets away with this because unemployment is high, so people are desperate for jobs. He marries in this lifetime and again has four children, (the same children he abandoned in his past life) but this time, his wife deserts him for another man, leaving him a bitter, lonely billionaire. He fails to do any soul searching. A few years later, he dies of a sudden heart attack at work, because his soul had determined he has made absolutely no progress in his book of life, or spiritual blueprint. Ralph had become hopelessly caught in a web of endless incarnations. Eastern religions refer to this as the wheel of karma—becoming caught in a revolving wheel of suffering. Without the wisdom and awareness that comes from prayer, meditation, and dreams, your mind convinces you this is simply life. Except there's no genius in living the same cruel pattern repeatedly. Ralph's paltry pleasures of earth, are nothing compared to the joy and fulfillment he could be experiencing on more elevated dimensions and places of greater harmony and beauty.

In simple terms, karma is disconnection from the wisdom of spirit. It's like being a majestic horse that gets so accustomed to the comforts of that corral it forgets it was once a free spirit. The word karma in Sanskrit means something that we do, a deed, or action that is not in alignment with our core nature or spirit. In the Western world the closest equivalent to karma is sin, spiritual consequences, or unmoral or unethical behavior. Karma is usually self-serving behavior that helps no one. The more karma we have, the more our soul paces in frustration like that wild stallion trapped in a corral. On earth, karma is a universal spiritual law that *no one* escapes. And this is a huge part of the problem; our mind has tricked us into thinking we can get away with murder! In the Western world, we understand karma through the phrases, "whatever you sow you reap," or "what comes around, goes around." This is a spiritual law we *all* abide by, whether we're consciously aware of it or not. Spiritual records are kept and they're very real, even though we can't physically see them. No one can pull a fast one, deceive, or trick God. Every single karmic deed needs to be repaid sooner or later. It's like needing to repay all your debts on earth to have a good credit rating. Since earth is largely karmic, many people commit karmic acts, and temporarily get away with it. No one figured out they were running an illegal business; no one saw them abusing family members—except God. No one makes a fool of God. In the realms of spirit—our karmic debts follow us when we die, and we keep coming back over and over until they're all repaid—and it is our soul or spirit, *not God,* that determines how and when we will do this. God does not control our destiny; control in any fashion is a human ego based quality. Our spirit writes our life script; and only when it is viable, and not impossible or too difficult for a soul to complete, is it sanctioned or agreed to by God. This also means that life is not unfair as many believe; it's just that our mind, ego, or limited left brain has no idea what transpired before we were born.

To understand how karma works, it's helpful to understand the law of cause and effect, one of the most ancient teachings on the planet. The law of cause and effect came to us several thousand years ago from ancient Egypt and the Hermetic philosophies. The Basic Hermetic Doctrines, passed on from teacher to student, were also known as the Seven Hermetic Principals. Principal six states, "Every Cause has its Effect; every Effect has its Cause; everything happens according to Law; Chance is but a name for Law not recognized; there are many planes of causation, but nothing escapes the Law." Simply put, every one of our actions has an equal or opposite reaction, effect, or consequence. If we kick our dog he may bite our ankle, distrust us, or become aggressive. If we're late every time we meet our best friend, we may find we've lost a friend. If we consistently drive over the speed limit, putting our life and others in jeopardy, the effect may be a speeding ticket or car accident. We usually keep repeating the same karmic deeds, until our mind finally realizes these actions don't serve us, and we change. But this knowing or understanding must be deep enough, intense enough, that our mind can't trick us into repeating the same self-serving actions. It is extremely difficult work cleaning up karma. For example, it's karmic to judge others, but we all do it. We judge people if our mind tells us they're another nationality, too fat, skinny, religious, not religious enough, conceited, stingy, poor, egocentric, slovenly, gossipy, or lazy. Imagine you change so much that you live with absolutely no judgment of another human being. You accept everyone conditionally with honor and respect–difficult, but not impossible. This is changing or releasing your karma.

The more we are connected to our spirit, the more aware we become of everything—what we're doing, why we're doing it, and the effects it may have on others. We achieve this heightened awareness through prayer, meditation, and journaling dreams, so that we're not an automaton controlled and led solely by the mind. The mind can go on autopilot, so that we do really stupid things repeatedly and mindlessly without awareness. Old habits die hard, as the saying goes. But when we're led by spirit, instead, we are guided, awake, and aware. The mind really needs spirit to wake it up, and only spirit has the capacity to inform the mind wisely. This is what "awakening" truly is. The more we meditate, reflect, or contemplate the more awake we become, because we're shutting down our mind, and allowing the genius of spirit to come through.

When we live karmically, we're ego or mind-based, and our mind convinces us we're the center of our little universe. We live in a "me mentality," without the inherent awareness that we're all connected and dependent on each other. So it's important to understand the ramifications or ripple effect of each karmic action, because we're also responsible for these ripples. To understand this better, I've changed the details slightly of an actual event that took place while I was a teacher. Imagine that during lunch, a teenager, Jane, beats up her rival, Sarah, because they're both dating the same guy Jason, and Jason has declared that Sarah is "hotter." Jane takes scissors, viciously stabbing Sarah and cutting her hair. Sarah is rushed to the hospital with critical stab wounds, while a crowd helplessly watches. This act of aggression affects all twenty people who witness the fight and they all have difficulty concentrating for the rest of the day. A few students, close friends of Sarah, fail a test in the afternoon because they're so distraught. The two teachers on cafeteria supervision, who witnessed this, are completely unhinged, and during their remaining afternoon classes lose patience with many students. The parents of the victim fly into a rage. Several social workers and the police become involved. The victim's siblings and friends are afraid to attend school the next day. Jane's parents, who are both store managers, are angry and humiliated, and for several weeks take it out on their employees. The principal cancels a musical concert celebrating their best talent, and begins planning an assembly helping students deal with bullies and assault. Every teacher at the school becomes involved in the assembly, and every student is expected to attend. Every friend of every student and teacher attending this school hears this story and becomes fearful and upset. When the story hits the local paper many parents reading it are shocked and afraid to send their children to that school. Thousands of people are negatively affected–all the result of one karmic act that took a few seconds.

It's also important to understand every physical action or karmic deed usually begins with a decision carried out *in the mind*. We may drive dangerously over the speed limit because our mind tells us it's okay, everyone else does it, or if we don't, we'll be late, or it's okay because we won't get caught. The minds of most bank robbers convinced them they deserved the money, or they could get away with it. If they were jailed their minds may have convinced them they'd been treated unfairly, they didn't deserve this because of a tough childhood, or they could pull their next robbery without getting caught. If our lifestyle is largely karmic, we're connected to our minds rather than our spirit, decisions come solely from the mind, without the wisdom or ethics of spirit, and our lives usually revolve around mere survival, holding onto money, power, or self-indulgent activities.

Karma is like suffering from a serious infection, without knowing you even have it; and if you do, you have no idea how to get rid of it. This isn't such a longshot, if we think of the many infections that plague earth; colds, flus, viruses, meningitis, AIDS, cancer, sexually transmitted diseases, even pimples and cold sores are a type of infection. Each of us comes to earth with several different types of infection or karma. For some of us the infection is fear, or low self-esteem. Fred may not be able to get through a day without lying. Your next door neighbor's infection may be gossiping, or cynicism. We're here to clean up our individual infections until we reach a place of physical and emotional balance. It's tough because we were born with these karmic diseases, so we think it's normal, and everyone else on earth has some form of the same disease or infection. Being on earth is like living in a hospital where everyone has some form of illness. But these karmic infections do not exist in more elevated dimensions, where beings are clean of infection or enlightened. Karmic infections include: fear, worry, addiction, ego centricity, anger or rage, inability to forgive, arrogance, jealousy, denial, depression, greed, control or manipulation, intolerance, contempt and judgment, to name a few. None of these attitudes, emotions, or karmic infections were our natural, original, or pure state.

In any of these karmic states we go through life virtually asleep, or unaware, like walking zombies repeatedly going through the same motions. Live becomes robotic; we get up, go to work or school, put in long hours, come home, go to bed, never reflect, meditate, journal or remember our dreams, and the whole cycle continues. Karma is smoking two packages of cigarettes a day to relieve stress, then getting infected with lung cancer. Karma is trying to get revenge over and over. Karma is staying in a toxic relationship with anyone who abuses or disrespects us, because we've never learned to experience true love—often our ticket to higher states of awareness. When our life is karmic we may be immersed in pain, fear, denial, lies, illusion, low self-esteem, addictions, or abuse. The list of karmic activities humans engage in is almost endless: abusing ourselves or others, anger, cheating, controlling, deceiving, disrespecting, dishonoring, envy, gluttony, gossiping, greed, hating, infidelity, inability to forgive, laziness, lying, lust, killing, judging, manipulating, polluting, pride, raping, stealing, swearing, tricking, wasting. Unfortunately, we're all familiar with karma. And we're familiar with the emotions that accompany a karmic lifestyle: fear, low self-esteem, self-centeredness, anger, bitterness, disillusionment, disappointment, betrayal, doubt, envy, jealousy, greed, depression, stress, restlessness, boredom, anxiety, and despair.

Karma can be active or passive. Active karma are the obvious things like cheating on a test, lying to your teacher or boss, getting drunk and smashing into a telephone pole, hitting a child, openly criticizing an ethnic group, or robbing a bank. But, karma may be passive, or not as obvious. For example, karma can be the mind believing we're right, someone else is wrong, and trying to force our beliefs on another person. It's karmic if we disrespect, dishonor, have silent contempt, or judge anyone, even if it's not openly expressed. It's karmic if we haven't learned to honor and respect ourselves, because we haven't recognized or become aware of the part of us that is of God or spirit. It's karmic to live immersed in fear or worry, rather than faith. It can also become karmic if we fail to achieve our individual destiny, that place of personal greatness where we give back to the world in some way, big or small. If it was our destiny or blueprint to be a great politician, but we idled away our life, then this inaction becomes our karma, because we had a responsibility and the skills to help others. It would be karmic if someone stands by and failed to take action as they watched a sleeping man being robbed.

Fundamental Christians believe we come to earth as sinners, Catholics believe we arrive with this black spot or original sin on our souls, and Eastern philosophies believe our karma follows us like a shadow. Regardless of what philosophy we subscribe to, we come with the enormous task of wiping the slate clean, cleansing ourselves of spiritual infection, or correcting our karma. Our spirit knows it must wake up this incredibly dense mind that wants to repeat the same stupid karma over and over, because it's easy and familiar. When soul sees us immersed in fear, self-doubt, or depression it wants to shout, "Stop this insanity! If you leave that job, partner, neighborhood, fear, guilt, pattern of low self-esteem, you'll stop being miserable. You're here to see and break this pattern. You've been a victim for countless lifetimes. You've suffered for an eternity. I want to guide you. Listen to your heart and emotions. Trust your gut feelings and intuition. It's so hard when you try to control with your mind. You're so afraid that if you take that leap of faith you'll lose everything. But what you lose is pain, suffering, disease, and depression. I want to show you joy and peace. Why can't you write down your dreams? Why do you never meditate, pray, or just go for a long walk to clear your mind? Why can't you relax and have fun? When was the last time you prayed for clarity or guidance?"

Many souls come here in utter despair knowing they must somehow reach a mind that is dense and highly repetitive. Our souls are often in constant chaos because of the stupidity of our minds. But soul can't tell our mind what to do because of free will. Our souls must follow spiritual laws which means respecting free will, regardless of how crazy or self-destructive the mind may be. However, there is always hope and a way out—dharma.

Dharma—The Path to Heaven on Earth

I slept and dreamt that life was joy. I awoke and saw that life was duty.
I acted, and behold, duty was joy.

Rabindranath Tagore

Dharma, the opposite of karma, is connection to our core or spirit. This connection is vital, because it's our spirit, not our mind that knows and understands how to go through life in an ethical, honest, compassionate, peaceful, and loving manner. The mind, without the guidance of spirit, is like a barbarian, a bohemian, a mere seeker of pleasure or stimulation; it will constantly lead us away from our true path or purpose for being here, while spirit always brings us back on course. Dharma is sometimes referred to as our ultimate path or the way—it is the path or way out of insanity to a place of greater purpose and peace. There are numerous definitions for dharma; righteous living, sustaining society, lawfulness, right action, truth in action, good works, correct course of conduct, morality, virtue, and conformity to one's duty and nature. If karma is disconnection from our spirits, then dharma is being awake, aware, and connected to our core truths. The word dharma comes from the Sanskrit root word *"dhri"* meaning to support, hold or bear. Dharma is support from *within*—from spirit or heart rather than the physical mind or external forces. If our focus is external our behavior is guided by what our mind believes is fate, good or bad luck, or external circumstances beyond our control. It lacks the awareness, wisdom and faith of knowing that we are constantly receiving assistance and guidance. We may do things blindly, without questioning our motives. Someone may stay in an unhealthy relationship or job for years believing there are no alternatives, they're a 'victim" or not "good enough" to move on.

When our spirit, rather than the mind, begins guiding us, we begin to be "awake" or aware and experience clarity rather than confusion.

When our orientation is internal, we're heart focused and our behavior is guided by our gut feelings, intuitions, and internal longings. We act with greater faith and conviction, and this conviction comes from spirit. We're the masters and guides of our destiny, rather than being bounced around by the mind and external forces. But operating from the heart or internally often means we choose to defy the status quo or "acceptable" route in life, like those geniuses we just read about. Many of the greatest politicians, scientists, inventors, teachers, painters, sculptors, artists, musicians, poets, philosophers, dancers, and writers, have stood apart from society, followed their hearts, but never quite fit in. Their spirit knew, there was no great merit in being swallowed up by a cruel or chaotic world.

There have been many times in history when people blindly followed external laws that were far from compassionate, wise, or just. These laws were always made with the mind, and were based on power and control rather than co-operation and compassion. Slavery which existed for thousands of years is perhaps the best example. After slavery was abolished there was still widespread segregation and discrimination, all products of karmic minds rather than compassionate spirits; all motivated by power, control, and greed rather than internal wisdom or justice. Our greatest advances in society have often come when people were brave enough to stand up for what they believed was just, right, compassionate and fair, rather than following external laws or belief systems. If this shift had not occurred we would still be experiencing human and animal sacrifice, gladiators fighting to the death, crucifixion of thieves, political executions, torture, stoning people to death, public hangings, honorable duels, disemboweling, whipping, and placing people in stocks as objects of public humiliation. There would still be feudalism, the caste system, and women would not be allowed to own property, vote, or attend school. We'd still be going to slave auctions on Saturday afternoon because we were following the crowd and status quo. We'd pay money to attend circuses to stare at fat women, Siamese twins, bearded ladies, and anything deemed "freaks of nature" because circus owners intent on making money, told us it was "the greatest show on earth." Sadly, some of these practices still exist—but are slowly being eradicated as the global consciousness is waking up.

One of the best examples of operating from our hearts, or in a dharmic fashion, is the 1955 story of Rosa Parks, a black seamstress from Montgomery, Alabama, who defied the law by refusing to give up her seat on a bus for a white man. The bus driver had demanded that four black people relinquish their seats in the middle of the bus, so that one white man could sit down. Three of them complied; Rosa, who wasn't a sheep, refused. She said, "When he saw me sitting, he asked if I was going to stand up and I said, 'No I'm not.' And he said, 'Well if you don't stand up, I'm going to have to call the police and have you arrested.' I said, 'You may do that.' Rosa's act of civil disobedience was dangerous in the 1950s; she was risking legal sanction and possibly physical harm. She was arrested, convicted of violating the segregation laws, and fined. Rosa was simply tired of being humiliated, of having to follow archaic rules that reinforced the position of blacks as inferior. E.R. Shipp has written, "Parks refusal to move back was her intrepid affirmation that she had had enough. It was an individual expression of a tireless longing for human dignity and freedom. She was not 'planted' there by...any other organization; she was planted there by her personal sense of dignity and self-respect."

This single courageous act from her heart catapulted the nation, and caused a major ripple effect. The buses in Montgomery were boycotted for nearly 13 months, and twenty-six-year-old preacher Martin Luther King, was transformed into a major civil rights leader. A year later in 1956, the U.S. Supreme Court outlawed segregation of the city's buses. When Rosa Parks died at the age of 92, thousands attended her funeral. She became the first women to lie in honor in the Capital Rotunda in Washington, and was bestowed the same honor as Abraham Lincoln and John F. Kennedy. Fifty five years later, the United States elected its first black president, all mysteriously interconnected to this one dharmic act of courage.

Rosa Parks story demonstrates how the ripple effect applies not only to karma, but to dharma. A single act of bravery, justice, kindness, love, compassion, or good will, goes a long way. At 6:30 a.m. if you smile or give your seat to one stranger on a bus, it could have a ripple effect of 100 people receiving unexpected smiles or good deeds that day, all generated from the energy of one sincere action. Looking at the big picture, *dharma* can be understood as the essential order of things, an integrity and harmony in the universe. It's really all those noble things we strive for, right action, honesty, ethics, compassion, justice, and heartfelt purpose. As we move into dharma there is a greater understanding that all things are interconnected—we all come from the same Creator, energy, or higher power. Hence John Donne's words, "No man is an island, entire of itself, every man is a piece of the continent, a part of the main;...any man's death diminishes me, because I am involved in mankind; and therefore never send to know for whom the bell tolls, it tolls for thee." While karmic thoughts are selfish and self-centered, dharmic insights always work toward a common good.

Living dharmically also means we recognize that we each have special abilities, talents, or assets which are meant to contribute to this common good. Einstein said, "Man can find meaning in life, short and perilous as it is, only through devoting himself to society." A dharmic life is one where we share these gifts for the betterment of society. We understand that the purpose of our work is not solely to make money, achieve the greatest sales in our department, outdo the competition, build the biggest company, or become famous. Each of these outcomes is a product of the mind or ego. When we're connected to our heart, we understand the intrinsic benefits of our job, how it helps or assists others, or enables the world to run smoothly without friction or chaos. Because of this, dharmic work is usually so rewarding and fulfilling we do it gladly. Our paychecks become an added bonus. From this perspective it doesn't matter what we do, it doesn't matter how great or humble our job appears to be, because there are so many needed services in the world. There is a saying, "Don't worry if your job is small, and your rewards are few, remember that the mighty oak, was once a nut like you." Ideally, as our lives become more dharmic, we end up doing something we love and enjoy. When we're connected to our core, often our "work" is who or what we are, the gifts, loves, or innate passions inside us needing to be expressed. Artists, dancers, singers, nurses, chefs, writers, teachers, healers, and politicians, who work from their hearts, all have the ability to inspire and uplift others.

Former Beatle, Paul McCartney, obviously doesn't still sing and perform to make money, or become famous–music is deeply embedded in his DNA. While writing this section I was listening to a radio interview with singer Cyndi Lauper who became popular in 1983 when her first album sold millions of copies and produced five hit singles. Twenty years later she still enjoyed enormous success and was launching another CD. During the interview, Cyndi was asked why she didn't just retire and enjoy her money. She said the reason she became a singer, wasn't to make millions, in fact, she never expected this to happen. She sang because she loved it, and that's why she was continuing her career. Interesting, one of her hits was, "Money Changes Everything", and "Girls Just Want to Have Fun."

Living dharmically means we're living and working responsibly, but also having fun and enjoying life. The emotions accompanying a dharmic lifestyle are: self-esteem, self-worth, vision, faith, fulfillment, purpose, satisfaction, unconditional love, compassion, tolerance, patience, understanding, clarity, insight, flow, focus, balance, wisdom, peace, serenity, tranquility, connection, contentment, creativity, energy, joy, passion. Our goal in life is to find these emotions from within, then to sustain them for longer periods of time, until they become more of who we are. When we achieve this state, we've returned to our essence, who we originally were before the infections set in. Sometimes we believe these higher emotions are reserved only for people on acid trips, drugs, alcohol, or yogis, mystics, or saints. But dharma is the birthright of everyone created by God. No matter how disconnected, dark, or karmic we've become, it's always possible to turn karma into dharma. There's always hope. That teenager Jane, who terrorized her rival, could grow into a responsible adult who teaches anger management. The rock bottom alcoholic, who loses his wife and job, may find AA, eventually stop drinking, and become a mentor and inspiration to other alcoholics. From the depths of our darkness it's possible to draw our greatest wisdom, compassion, and strength. Who understands anger better than someone who has flown into many rages? Who understands the tricks and denial of the mind better than a former alcoholic, workaholic, or drug addict? Regardless of our karmic patterns, there are endless opportunities and there is always hope.

Walking the Steps

We make a living by what we get, but we make a life by what we give.
Sir Winston Churchill

Reaching peace, enlightenment or heaven on earth is a lengthy process. We return to earth countless times until we completely rid ourselves of the infections of a karmic mind. Like graduating from high school, we work through twelve levels of correcting karma, releasing more illusion, pain, and suffering with each step. Once we've completed these twelve levels of karma, we begin working through seven stages of awareness or dharma until we're fully enlightened. Achieving this state of freedom from the endless cycle of karma is referred to as *moksha*, or liberation in Sanskrit. One might compare this to twelve years of high school, then spending seven more years to complete a Ph.D. Those initial twelve steps are similar to the Twelve-Step program that Alcoholics Anonymous and other groups have been so successful with. Working through their twelve steps is incredibly similar to working through karma and dharma. In the first three steps of Alcoholics Anonymous or AA, individuals become aware of their issues or karma, see a glimmer of hope towards a solution, and are willing to work toward change. Steps four through eight are the "action steps," but rather than action being the old karmic patterns, they try to make amends to anyone they have hurt, harmed, or offended. After making a list of anyone they have hurt, they're encouraged to write a letter, apologize, correct their behavior, or if the person they've hurt has passed away, they work at acknowledging their wrongdoing, feeling remorse, and moving on. When they reach step nine, they've taken the necessary action to make amends; turning karma into dharma. Steps ten through twelve, known as the maintenance steps, are like walking into dharma or grace. Step eleven says, "Sought through prayer and meditation to improve our conscious contact with God as we understood Him, praying only for knowledge... and the power to carry that out." And it's not necessary to believe in the God of organized religion for this to be effective. In AA the word God can be understood as: good, orderly direction, ethical principles, the courage of fellow AA members, or the harmony and intelligence of nature. Step twelve talks of having a "spiritual awakening as a result of these steps," and of carrying these practices and principles in all affairs. Perhaps AA has been so successful because the focus is not on an outside expert fixing anyone. Instead, each member takes responsibility for their own actions. It's important to understand that dharma is cumulative, the more dharmic your life becomes the more brownie points with God you have. This is like accumulating a huge spiritual bank account, grace, or what the mind believes is "good luck." Dharmic reserves give us a more peaceful, meaningful, and balanced life. We have more frequent "highs" in life, or episodes of walking in heaven on earth, and it's done naturally.

Many of our classic books and movies where the hero is pitted against the villain are really studies in the laws of karma and dharma. True heroes and heroines are seldom swayed by the crowd or popular opinion, always following their heart or inner convictions. They don't let fear overtake them, and because of their faith, they miraculously prevail. They know with God or spirit, anything is possible. In the original *Star Wars* movies it was Hans Solo, Princess Leia, and Luke Skywalker using *the force* within to wage against that lord of darkness, Darth Vader. In *The Wizard of Oz*, Dorothy, a young girl, destroys the Wicked Witch of the East, and the Wicked Witch of the West. A small unassuming hobbit, Frodo, in the *Lord of the Rings*, outwits the evil lord Saruman. In the *Harry Potter* series, Harry, a teenager, manages to outsmart the dark Lord Voltemort through the strength of his convictions. In fiction, and in life, good always prevails. Light is always stronger than darkness. Universal spiritual laws tell us that karmic individuals never "get away with it." Does our mind really know what happens after death? The truth is that darkness has this nasty habit of self-destructing or being destroyed by another dark character, just like in the movies. Karmic actions may continue for years, decades, even centuries, but like the Roman Empire, they eventually fall.

When I taught English there were a few novels that every student loved; *To Kill A Mockingbird,* by Harper Lee, was always high on the list. Maybe this was because Atticus Finch, the main character, a 50-year-old single father, was simply the most dharmic being imaginable. It was impossible not to draw inspiration from him, which is probably why The American Film Institute rates him the "No. 1 film hero of all time." In creating Atticus, Harper Lee wove elements of her own father, Amasa Coleman Lee, into the novel. Her father, a newspaper editor, lawyer, and representative in the Alabama State Legislature, was a man of keen sensibilities and principles. Amasa Lee defended two black men, accused of murder in 1919, who were found guilty. After they were hanged and their bodies were mutilated, he never tried another case.

In the novel, Atticus Finch is a lawyer in Maycomb, Alabama, during the 1930s, a time when prejudice against blacks was rampant. Atticus doesn't follow the crowd. He agrees to defend a black man, Tom Robinson, accused of raping a white woman, Mayella Ewell. Atticus knows there is absolutely no way he can win the case; prejudice against blacks was ingrained in the minds of this community—a deep karmic infection. He's compelled to take the case, not for fame or money, because he wasn't really paid; he defends Tom because like Rosa Parks, he knows in his heart it's the right thing to do. He explains to his daughter Scout, "Simply because we were licked a hundred years before we started is no reason for us not to try to win...This case, Tom Robinson's case, is something that goes to the essence of a man's conscience—Scout I couldn't go to church and worship God if I didn't try to help that man...before I can live with other folks I've got to live with myself. The one thing that doesn't abide by majority rule is a person's conscience."

One of the best lines from the novel is when Atticus tells Scout "You never really understand a person until you consider things from his point of view–until you climb into his skin and walk around in it." This may be the key to truly leading a dharmic life always putting yourself in someone else's shoes—leading your life with a deep respect for others and with compassion. Atticus frequently seems superhuman, simply because he doesn't act like most karmic people. In his youth, Atticus was "the deadest shot in Maycomb county," and his nickname was Ol One-Shot, but he refused to use a gun, believing it gave him an unfair advantage. After the trial, Mayella's father, Bob, wants revenge, a common karmic trait. He waits until Atticus leaves the post office, then curses, spits on him, and threatens to kill him. However, "Atticus didn't bat an eye, just took out his handkerchief and wiped his face and stood there and let Mr. Ewell call him names wild horses couldn't bring most people to repeat." Jem, Atticus's son, doesn't understand his father's behavior, because the normal or karmic behavior is to strike back or seek revenge. But Atticus explains, "See if you can stand in Bob Ewell's shoes a minute. I destroyed his last shred of credibility at that trial, if he had any to begin with."

At the end of the novel, Atticus doesn't win the case. Tom Robinson is sent to prison and dies a short time later. Scout and Jem are attacked in a further act of revenge, and Jem's arm is broken. Life seems cruel and unfair to the children, however, the karmic characters wrap themselves into deeper webs of lies, deceit, anger, and despair. Their lives became a cruel, dark place of their own making. There is absolutely no genius or wisdom in repeating the same karma over and over. In contrast, dharmic individuals always survive because they're able to look in the mirror each morning knowing in their hearts they've done the right thing, and they receive support, energy, and solace from spirit. Atticus may have lost the court case, but he won great respect, admiration, and love, which no amount of money can buy. At the end of our lives, it's not human judges, relatives, neighbors, or friends we must face with a clear conscience; it is an all knowing God. With this simple yet profound knowledge in our hearts, when we lead a dharmic life, death is nothing to fear. Working through karma is our destiny. It's why we came to earth in the first place. Earth is like one huge hospital or opportunity to heal, and do community service. When we connect to our spirits, we understand that healing is possible, no matter how great the karmic infection and that is reason for optimism and hope.

Typical Contract of a Soul

What you know in your head will not sustain you in moments of crisis...confidence comes from body awareness, knowing what you feel in the moment.

Marion Woodman

Imagine Mark Freeman has scripted a life of approximately ninety years, growing up in a wealthy home where he has everything material, but his parents are egocentric and emotionally distant. With their high powered jobs as a priority, the Freemans spend little time with their son. Mark's father works long hours, and his mother leaves Mark in private boarding schools or with nannies. Growing up, he's rarely hugged, kissed, or played with. He has everything material a child could desire, but money doesn't replace the warmth, nurturing, and companionship he desperately needs. The Freemans worship success, money and status, and Mark is raised to revere these false gods. To fill his emotional void, at twenty-three he marries Jessica, a woman his parents adore. Her family are business associates, and Jessica will inherit a lucrative family empire. Although Jessica is physically attractive, she's also condescending, flirtatious, and doesn't respect her husband. They have two children, a boy and a girl. After the children are born, Mark suspects his wife is having affairs, but says nothing because Jessica has a violent temper, and he wants the marriage to work to keep appearances up. To escape and deny how much he despises his life, he buries himself in his job as a lawyer at a major legal firm, working 50 to 60-hour weeks. Mark attempts to get all the kudos and attention at work he's never gotten from his parents and wife. By working long hours, he repeats his parent's karmic pattern, emotionally neglecting his two children.

When Mark is in his late forties, his first wakeup call occurs. He develops a heart condition, a blocked artery, possibly because of the blocked emotions, bitterness, and resentment he carries inside towards his wife and parents. He's literally worked his heart out. He also hasn't learned to love himself or others, or to act from his heart, so this illness infects or affects the heart, that part of the body associated with nurture and love. Mark has carried this neglect of his heart from several previous lifetimes. He has surgery to repair the artery, believing this is entirely a physical problem, and it seems life will be fine. A few years later, he's in a car accident where he injures his knees because he's inflexible and literally afraid to move forward. He also fractures his shoulder because he feels he must shoulder all family responsibilities alone. Rather than giving himself time to rest, recuperate, journal his dreams, meditate, and reflect and make changes, Mark buries his anguish in work, and becomes increasingly driven.

In his late forties, Mark loses his high profile legal position to downsizing during a major recession. His soul wrote this into his life script, giving him valuable time to reflect, recharge, and seek balance. But his mind believes it's the worst thing that could happen. He has enough money to take a few years off, live comfortably, and spend more time with his teenage children, but joins another prestigious company right away. He's worried what people will think if he doesn't work, and the money in this new company is even better than his last job. Just when it seems he has his life back on track, Mark's son announces he's homosexual and pleads for support. In anger, Mark distances himself further from his son. His daughter decides to elope with a man Mark believes amounts to nothing because he's a musician. He's devastated and feels this can't be happening to his wealthy, high profile family. But Mark's soul planned all this in his spiritual contract to help him develop humility and respect. Shortly after, he discovers an Internet correspondence confirming his wife is having an affair with his best friend, Charlie, a salesman. A few months after this discovery, he develops sciatica, inflamed nerve endings in his back and legs, resulting from anger and frustration over a life he literally can't stand; he feels afraid and powerless to change anything. Deep inside Mark wants to leave his wife, knowing their marriage was built on illusion and is completely loveless. Its foundation of money, ego, and appearances is collapsing, shaking Mark's psyche. He craves a companion who genuinely loves and respects him. He also needs to see that Charlie only desired the money, status, and affluent lifestyle connected with their family; he was never a sincere friend.

We could say that in earthly terms Mark has a normal life—nothing out of the ordinary—the same brutal life of many earthlings. He even has lots of perks: two parents, wealth, beautiful house, world travel, dinner parties, glamorous job, and a million dollar family, two children, a boy and girl, and an attractive, sexy, wife. If Mark has scripted a life of approximately ninety years this gives him another forty-five years to see through the seductions and illusions, to correct his karma, and reconnect with his spirit. Ninety years seems like a long time, except Mark's karmic infections go deep because like many people, he's repeating similar scenarios from many previous lives. What he may need to do in this lifetime to clean up his karmic infection is: understand that money is an illusion or trap if it has never brought him happiness or peace. Understand that money can bring great satisfaction and pleasure if we use it dharmically to help others. Realize that if he's leading a dharmic life he will always have enough money when it's needed. Give from his heart with compassion without expecting anything in return. Eliminate layers of ego he's held regarding money and wealth. Understand that marriage is another illusion if there is no honor, love or respect. Understand that by staying in a loveless marriage, he's adding more karma to an already karmic life. Honor himself and learn to empower himself by leaving the marriage. Trust that he can move on to find a more dharmic partner who respects him, once he begins to respect himself. Understand that although he was never nurtured by his parents, he has both the ability and responsibility to nurture his children. Realize his musician son-in-law may not have financial wealth, but this is not the ultimate measure of a human being. Forgive both parents, his wife, and friend Charlie, understanding they're actors in the play of life, and have incurred huge karmic debts they will have to repay. Recognize that holding on to hatred, anger, or a need for revenge, just keeps him trapped in their karmic spider webs. They may have played out a similar drama over and over in previous lifetimes, and the only way to break free is to release these people from his life without bitterness. Realize that by breaking free he may find true love and peace with another partner. Rise above his cold emotional distance, especially with his homosexual son, and learn compassion, empathy, and love. Integrate humility. Communicate honestly, openly and without ego. Let go of his notions that he is superior to others because of his money, education and family. Express his emotions rather than bottling them up. Integrate tolerance and understanding regarding his son; understand he has agreed to play the difficult role of being gay possibly to open up Mark's heart. Recognize the importance of living a balanced life and taking time to journal dreams and meditate. Learn to enjoy simple pleasures and nature. Learn to have fun, and relax, rather than working all the time. Understand that bitterness, resentment, and anger were the causes of his heart problems, car accidents, and sciatica, and that he can speed up self-healing by releasing these emotions. Understand that he came to rise above and transcend everything that has happened, not to be swallowed up by it. Rather than feeling frustrated, unfulfilled, and depressed every day, it's his destiny to feel self-esteem, self-honor, and satisfaction with his work. Once this happens, he'll find fulfillment in giving back to humanity, wherever he sees the greatest need—it could even be in his chosen profession, law. Understand his greatest need is not money but love.

Facing these challenges would be a tremendous learning curve. It would require rewiring Mark's left brain and thinking in a different way—difficult, but not impossible. None of us were meant to suffer for an eternity, or live devoid of any real love or joy. We suffer when our lives are largely karmic, and *all* of this suffering is mind-imposed. Our souls are frantic because this is a seemingly impossible task and if we don't "get it" our souls must come back over and over again and watch us wallowing in misery. We come to earth with the best intentions, like that kindergarten student eager to learn and experience, but often get trapped or seduced by the desire for money and power. Earth can be a terrible prison for the soul if we're living karmically, chained to routine, suffering, and pain. Since our mind believes the only way to be happy is to buy external things, we go on vacations, buy the new car, camera, laptop computer, or clothes, knowing these things are short lived diversions, preventing us from taking the time to meditate long enough to figure out why painful things keep happening.

There may be times when our soul is so frantic to help us achieve something dharmic that it doesn't seem to use logic or common sense. Our soul may want us to leave someone who has never loved or respected us, when we have no logical idea of how we could possibly afford it. Spirit doesn't concern itself with physical details. That's the job of the left brain. Our soul sees the big picture, our potential and possibilities. It's often not the job of spirit to follow earthly logic. It knows our blueprint; perhaps we scripted in a way to receive the money, but first we need to have faith and just leave. We don't do crazy, hurtful, or irresponsible things when we follow our spirit, but we do often step out of our comfort level and beyond the limited horizons of the mind. This is why it's so important to allow our mind and spirit to work together in harmony, and when we achieve this, we end those meaningless cycles of painful incarnations.

It's also important to realize this is a fictitious example—I don't really know Mark. It's a story to illustrate the way life may work when viewed with spiritual awareness and not just our minds. This insight or understanding can drastically turn around our lives from a living hell, to a virtual heaven. *However, sometimes it's absolutely impossible to understand, comprehend, or rid ourselves of illnesses, no matter what we do.* There is a new-age belief that if you understand the root causes of every illness, you should be able to cure them yourself, and if you can't, you really haven't done the right inner work. This I believe is a cruel twist of the truth. There may be cases where you can—but certainly not in every case. I really wish I had the answers to why I've had debilitating migraines my entire life, and a host of other ailments. Sometimes, someone we love dearly dies of cancer at a young age. Sometimes that was scripted into their spiritual blueprint—they only needed 32 years to accomplish what they came to do. This is what makes life so mysterious. Why does one person's cancer heal miraculously, while another suffers and dies? It is absolutely impossible to understand the reasons for everything—nor should we even try. This only occurs when we've reached the upper levels of enlightenment—all the more reason to strive for the genius of this state. In the meantime, it helps enormously to stay connected to spirit, because this is where we get the strength, faith and perseverance to shield us through the toughest of times.

Peace, Heaven on Earth, or Enlightenment

It is not wisdom to be only wise,
And on the inward vision close the eyes...
But it is wisdom to believe the heart.

George Santayana

No pessimist ever discovered the secrets of the stars, or sailed to an
uncharted land, or opened a new heaven to the human spirit.

Helen Keller

Like Ricky Martin we're all here to end "la vida loca" the crazy life or chaos of our soul. Achieving peace, and more glimpses of heaven on earth, is possible, yet few beings reach this state. But we are entering an unprecedented time of hope. As we transition into the Age of Aquarius, the planets are aligning in ways that make waking up a greater possibility than ever before. These galactic alignments have not occurred for over 2000 years, since the birth of Christ. The 60s and 70s the era of hippies, flower power, peace, expanded consciousness, and love, perhaps was a precursor to this golden era. It seems we're trying to relive this consciousness again. Rather than feeling we need to spend enormous amounts of money on designer jeans, it was incredibly cool in the 60s to wear faded and ripped jeans. We've tried to recapture this golden essence, but haven't quite gotten it right–now we have costly designer jeans that are faded and ripped, rather than the authentic thing.

This Age of Aquarius has been prophesied as a time of greater equality, brother-and-sisterhood, love for all, truth-seeking, independence, freedom, non-judgment, experimentation and discovery. People will no longer conform to the same norms, and we'll respect and appreciate life as sacred. We may not all completely clean up our karma this time around, but we may make enormous progress, throwing away karmic crutches that have crippled us for centuries. Perhaps, we'll be inspired by a handful of people, showing us the potential, and encouraging us to move forward in ways we never imagined.

We've explored how balanced genius is a synthesis of both left and right brain functions or head and heart. It's hard work, but its benefits are tremendous, even if not fully reached in this lifetime. If we read the stories of many saints, sages, prophets, and enlightened beings, they developed these abilities or became enlightened while still living on earth—it's not just science fiction or fantasy. If you've been raised as a Taoist, Buddhist, or Hindu, the concept of enlightenment is often embedded into the culture, but in the western world it's largely misunderstood. This is why we often read about people reaching retirement with feelings of great emptiness who ask, "Is this all there is to life?" The answer is an emphatic NO. In the west we're not aware that the entire purpose or goal of life is to eventually become enlightened and live permanently in dimensions like heaven—and this was never intended to be the destiny of just a chosen few—we all have the potential to reach the spiritual genius of enlightenment–it's embedded in our DNA. Derek Lin explains that *Fo Shing* in Chinese, meaning *Buddha Nature,* refers to the potential within everyone to awaken into enlightenment and become a living Buddha. He says, "It is not a question of *if* you will ever attain Buddhahood; it is a question of *when*...It lives in your heart regardless of your education, intelligence, compassion or any other attributes, and one day it will manifest its full expression as you awaken to a greater reality."

Understanding this is critical to our well-being, sanity, even our pocket book. We spend enormous sums of money on makeup and cosmetic surgery to look younger, because few people realize that as you work towards enlightenment, you don't age as quickly. Enlightenment is a lofty goal; it means we're not subject to the rules of earth. We have transcended physicality and all its limitations—we have what appears to be super powers! Our body no longer grows old, gets sick, and dies. When we reach enlightenment, our body isn't heavy and dense, so we're not trapped by physical boundaries; like Neo in the movie *The Matrix* we can fly. Our bodies are between 70 to 98 percent water, depending on how evolved we are. As we move towards enlightenment, we lose our heavy physical mass, like a butterfly shedding its cocoon. We literally become less dense and lighter; our body chemistry changes and we take on the fluidity of water allowing us to merge, flow and slip into other dimensions. We've mastered crossing dimensions and can travel at will. We don't need planes, buses, or cars, because, just as in dreams, we can transport ourselves to wherever we need to be. We can walk through walls, or walk on water, or dematerialize. We can bilocate or split our energy, and be in two places at once. We don't need money because we can materialize or create what we need. In the higher dimensions there is no need for money—we have whatever we need to live and carry out our work. We're not dependent on phones since we can communicate telepathically. Because our thoughts are elevated, without judgment, we know what people are thinking. Our hearing is more acute. We can talk with and understand animals, understand and speak multiple languages, and take in vast amounts of information. We have the knowledge and understanding from all of our previous lives. We don't really need to sleep, although we have periods of rest and rejuvenation. We no longer need food to sustain a physical body, but we may choose to eat for enjoyment. We don't work just for money, status, power, or to pay the bills, but we do necessary work in other dimensions, often similar to the highest work we did on earth, that is rewarding, energizing, and an expression of our core talents. We don't work insane hours, damaging our health, just to build up a large pension plan, because we live forever. Hard to imagine how freeing and exciting this would be. Yes, this sounds like science fiction, except for the fact that in our dreams we're already doing many of these things! As we dream, we're already trying to understand, work through, and clean up karmic infections and enact our dharma. Sleeping and dreaming is our present state of genius.

In the movie *K-Pax*, based on a novel of the same name, Prot, an enlightened alien appeared to be trapped in a psychiatric hospital. Except he wasn't trapped at all. Prot would announce to his doctors he'd be leaving on a trip to Africa or Greenland, then disappear for a few days. Doctors thought he was a crazy patient on a psychiatric ward, but on these trips, Prot was researching and learning about earth, gathering information, having fun, helping people, aiding humanity. Prot was an evolved being from another dimension trying to teach any doctor who would listen.

Our goal is to evolve so that we're *not* trapped on earth. When we're fully enlightened we have a body just like Prot did in *K-Pax,* or as Jesus did when he came to earth, but it's a light body composed of energy. Because it's pure energy, rather than heavy, dense physical matter, it's impossible to shoot, kill, or destroy. This state is true freedom, because in our light body we're no longer subject to physical laws or restraints. If someone on earth tried to harm us we could simply disappear. Once we reach full enlightenment, we may visit earth temporarily the way we might visit our old high school. Some enlightened beings choose to stay on earth because they have an important service to provide. Others have a job, destiny, service; they carry out in other dimensions, just as a sales representative living on earth travels to many countries. Full enlightenment is challenging, exciting, ever-changing, and without physical pain. However, getting there is a process; it takes lifetime after lifetime. Our goal is not endless incarnations, rather ending these endless incarnations!

If we don't believe that reaching heaven on earth is possible, we close many doors of adventure and opportunity. If Michelangelo never believed he had artistic ability he would never have painted. If J.K. Rowling didn't believe she could write, *Harry Potter* would never have inspired millions of children and adults. If Christopher Columbus hadn't believed in a new world, we wouldn't be living in it, and if Edison hadn't believed in his inventions, there wouldn't be light bulbs and we'd still be floundering in darkness. The first critical step is understanding this is our destiny; it's why we come to earth. To achieve this we need to have faith in what we can't always see, touch or understand. The most sacred, precious things in life can't be measured or quantified—love, respect, compassion, joy, vision, endurance, persistence, awareness, the wisdom of eternity. What we believe becomes encoded in our DNA; it becomes part of who we are. We are the sum total of all the emotions, experiences, thoughts, and beliefs we've carried from lifetime to lifetime. If we go into the next life knowing enlightenment is our destiny, our choices may be quite different. Like Edison we need to believe in the power of light to illuminate and bring clarity, and like Columbus to hold on to a vision of a new, exciting world.

Waking Up—Getting Rid of Infection or Getting Enlightened

"It is with the heart that one sees rightly; what is essential is invisible to the eye."
Antoine De Saint-Exupéry, *The Little Prince*

I once read an honest but wise account by Andrea Ferretti, editor for the magazine, *Yoga Journal*. During her yoga teacher training Andrea had learned about enlightenment. She listened as her teacher talked about "the great seers, sages and mystics who had come before us. They could stop their heartbeat and control their brain activity; they could even transcend time and space and transport themselves anywhere they wished." She left class that day feeling dizzy, discouraged and worried, wondering, "If enlightenment is the goal...how would I ever attain it? And, perhaps more important, did I really want to?" As the years went by, Andrea put aside her fear of what she called "the big E," and learned instead to value the small things in life. "One of the first changes I noticed was simple–that creaky twinge I felt in my upper back disappeared....A few years into my practice, the panic attacks that tormented me in my early 20s had all but faded." Andrea doubts she'll ever experience the type of enlightenment that allows her to bilocate or appear in two places at once. She says, "For now, I'll focus on becoming aware of the small transformations–truly listening when a friend is in need, being more compassionate with my family, breathing calmly in the face of panic. All of those smaller actions add up to more ease, comfort, and joy than I could ever have imagined." Wise counsel for everyone.

The concept of living forever, flying through galaxies, and disappearing, may sound daunting, scary, and farfetched. We fear what we haven't experienced or don't understand. Many are afraid of leaving home for the first time, getting married, attending college or university, or starting their first job, but these weren't necessarily scary experiences, or detrimental to their well-being. If you're ten years old, the thoughts of getting married might appear impossible, but twenty years later, it may not. We grow into these roles, step by step, day by day, until they become part of who we are. Marrying someone who loves and respects us can be the most dharmic experience possible. But feelings of deep love and mutual respect don't happen overnight. Similarly with enlightenment, it doesn't happen in just a few years—or a few lifetimes. We grow into it like our favorite jeans, until it becomes a comfortable fit. Enlightenment isn't like a shot gun marriage; we don't go into it kicking and screaming. It's what naturally happens if we stay true to ourselves and our deepest longings and loves; it's what we earn, it's grace, a final state of balance. Because we can't imagine what it feels like to be fully enlightened, perhaps we can start with whatever small step brings us peace, hope, or joy. Would you like to never have a really bad cold or the flu again? Wouldn't it be nice never to worry about passing an exam, but instead, having faith in yourself? Imagine the peace of never worrying about having enough money—instead trusting you'll always have enough to live on. Wouldn't it be amazing to understand exactly what your cat or dog is trying to tell you? Imagine the bliss of never feeling afraid, insecure, or insignificant again. If the word enlightenment seems unattainable, try substituting it with any word that does. Perhaps you'd like greater peace, love, awareness, understanding, clarity, purpose, or joy. It's possible you want to just stop having pimples or bad hair days, getting sick every winter, or always getting parking tickets. Perhaps you want to feel loved and respected, or feel that your ideas are valuable and worthwhile. If you've become a workaholic, maybe you want to start by having more fun, or doing something you enjoy for an hour every day.

Rather than focusing on any outcome, it's more important to lead our lives honorably, ethically, and with love and respect. This allows everything to happen naturally. One day, you'll realize that karmic things just aren't happening as often, and when difficult times happen, you handle them with greater ease. When fully awake, we experience greater moments of heaven—states of peace, heightened awareness, greater balance, and beauty. We've no longer stuck in the chaos of soul, the dark, disjointed, jarring, ugliness of karma. We're drawn to the symmetry and harmony in all things beautiful; there is more movement, rhythm and flow. Beauty awakens, inspires and literally moves us. As we awaken or move towards enlightenment, we notice, appreciate, and fill our world with more of the finer things in life—be it art, music, nature, or people. We're also moved and inspired by the little things as if tiny unobservable dimensions suddenly open up. The world becomes a place of awe and beauty as we observe, as if for the first time, the warmth of a friend's laugh lines, the light or aura reflecting off the moon, the deep blue within a candle's flame, the intricate design on the wings of a dragonfly, the iridescence of a pigeon's wings, fascinating patterns in clouds, or the symmetrical pattern of a sea shell or leaf. True beauty is always synonymous with purity of spirit. Have you ever seen an ugly angel? Einstein said, "Know what is impenetrable to us really exists, manifesting itself as the highest wisdom and the most radiant beauty. Dante believed that "beauty awakens the soul to act." English poet, John Keats wrote, "Beauty is truth, truth beauty—that is all ye know on earth, and all ye need to know." There is a famous Navajo prayer that describes walking and being in this state of awareness—part of the process of enlightenment—reaching, then walking in places of greater beauty—heaven on earth.

AS I WALK IN BEAUTY

In beauty may I walk.
All day long, may I walk.
Through the returning seasons, may I walk.
Beauty will I possess again.
Beautiful birds...
Beautiful joyful birds...
On the trail marked with pollen, may I walk.
With grasshoppers about my feet, may I walk,
With dew about my feet, may I walk.
With beauty may I walk.
With beauty before me, may I walk.
With beauty behind me, may I walk.
With beauty above me, may I walk.
With beauty all around me may I walk.
In old age, wandering on a trail of beauty,
lively, may I walk.
In old age, wandering on a trail of beauty,
living again, may I walk.
If it is finished in beauty,
In beauty it is finished.
In beauty it is finished.

Navajo Prayer

CHAPTER SIX
Illusions of the Mind and Ego Dreams

Those who live as their human nature tells them to, have their minds controlled by what human nature wants. Those who live as the Spirit tells them to, have their minds controlled by what the Spirit wants. To be controlled by human nature results in death; to be controlled by the Spirit results in life and peace.

Romans 8:5–7

ONE OF THE GREATEST BLOCKS to peace, insight, genius, and enlightenment is the mind. When the mind works in co-operation with spirit it's brilliant, but left to its own devices the mind can be like a dull or flickering light bulb. Like a sophisticated computer it's great in retrieving facts or data, but many computers break down, malfunction, and develop nasty viruses rendering them useless. Even geniuses may develop Alzheimer's, essentially losing everything stored in their brains. Compared to spirit, the mind is fleeting, short lived, and sadly, downright stupid in many areas. Our minds can become forgetful, fuzzy, muddied, overcrowded, facts can become distorted, and we can become so bombarded with fears, anxieties, and hallucinations, that we literally lose our sanity. The mind also sets up its own belief systems that can be faulty and fraught with illusions. Neuroscientist, Dr. Andrew Newberg, tells us "The human brain seems to have difficulty separating fantasies from facts. It sees things that are not there, and it sometimes doesn't see things that are there. In fact, the brain doesn't even try to create a fully detailed map of the external world. Instead, it selects a handful of cues, then fills in the rest with conjecture, fantasy, and belief." Jungian analyst John Sanford contends, "For all of our highly sophisticated consciousness, the human mind is sick. We need a healing, a balance, and a revelation for our minds that our rational consciousness cannot provide us."

In 2005, Malcolm Gladwell wrote an entire bestselling book about this, *Blink: The Power of Thinking Without Thinking.* Through countless examples, he explains how the greatest minds can spend weeks, months, years, even decades, gathering realms of data, yet often be duped; while our spirit or intuition can arrive at genuine truth in a flash, second, or the blink of the eye. Spirit just knows without having to do all the mental gymnastics. Gladwell begins with the story of an art dealer, Gianfranco Becchina, who approached the J. Paul Getty Museum in California in 1983, trying to sell a nearly seven foot tall marble statue. It was known as a kouros, a nude male youth, dating back to the sixth century BC. Since this was a rare find with about 200 kouros in existence, the asking price was just under $10 million, and The Getty Museum spent fourteen months investigating the authenticity of this statue. They brought in a geologist from the University of California, who used a high-resolution stereomicroscope, electron microscope, electron microprobe, mass spectrometry, X-ray diffraction, and X-ray fluorescence. Their conclusion was that the dolomite marble used to craft this statue was indeed ancient; it couldn't be a sophisticated fake. The statue was purchased, becoming part of their 1986 fall collection, and the Getty's curator of antiquities, Marion True, was enamored with this rare find. "God or man, he embodies all the radiant energy of the adolescence of western art," she gushed.

However, other scholars and historians smelled a rat. Rather than seeing "radiant energy," they knew something wasn't right, and they didn't need an electron microscope to prove it. To resolve the issue, the statue was shipped to Athens, Greece, where one senior sculpture expert felt an "intuitive repulsion" on seeing the kouros. They determined the statue was a fake, fashioned in a Roman forger's workshop in the early 1980s. One geologist said it might have been "aged" in a matter of months using potato mold.

Just like those scholars who sensed something was wrong, we all have this ability to rely on our intuition, sixth sense, gut, or emotions. However, we live in an age of needing facts, data, reports, quantitative results, before we will believe anything. The mantra of the masses is "seeing is believing," and most people need solid, physical proof. But relying on the mind, rather than spirit, is contrary to our true nature. Our minds have befuddled us and turned things upside down. We go through life trying to rely on our minds, which is often a long, arduous, and disappointing journey; many of us have forgotten that in a blink, we can access what is authentic via spirit, and this wisdom never lets us down.

As children, we wanted to believe our parents were perfect. It's often a painful and humbling experience first realizing our parents are only human, and so we search for things to invest our faith or allegiance: government, religion, science, institutions, movie stars, singers, sports stars, even fabricated heroes like Batman, Superman, or Spiderman. But, the truth is, *there is no ultimate authority on earth*; religions, institutions, science, governments, and celebrities all made mistakes and major blunders—they've all committed acts which are unethical and amoral—anything created by karmic individuals in a karmic world will at some time disappoint or let us down. Instead, we need to rely on a combination of evidence, facts, gut feelings, God, and intuition or spirit. We're all familiar with gut feelings—simply *knowing* something is right for us. Intuition is having a deeper understanding that goes beyond the limited awareness of our minds. To achieve balance, harmony and genius, we need to cultivate spirit through intuition, because it is the only authority on earth that doesn't let us down.

Muddle of the Mind

Imagination is more important than knowledge.

Einstein

The mind has no social conscience, ethics, warmth, compassion, or sense of humor, and it's not capable of anything exciting or creative. The mind could eat spaghetti every night for supper for twenty years, or never venture past the same cartoon collection its entire life. It wouldn't experiment with nutritious foods or wines, get the urge to travel, try a new hairstyle, or spontaneously dance, sing, paint, draw, or play music, because true inspiration comes via the soul or spirit. Einstein couldn't have discovered his theory of relativity if he relied only on logical equations and his mind. His hunches, theories, visions, pictures, thought experiments, dreams, always came first. He was light years ahead of other scientists because he theorized intuitively, then took those images and proved them using math and logic—using right, then left brain genius.

Dream psychologist Sigmund Freud called the ego or mind "the executive of the personality." The ego is really our conscious mind, but it's completely *unconscious* or unaware of the genius, insights, and guidance of spirit, and it's a bully, always wanting complete control. Like an impetuous two-year-old, the ego doesn't want to share its power or self-serving interests with spirit. It has tunnel vision; it's stubborn, obstinate, and short sighted, like a small child who won't share toys. Our spirits have the memories of hundreds of incarnations, everything we've ever done, and been. And our spirit knows why we're here, what karma we need to work through, and what our dharma or destiny is. The ego has mental amnesia, but still insists on being the boss. As executive director of our personality the ego or mind has **three** chief functions:

1. It protects the body and keeps it safe.
2. It carries out routine day to day tasks.
3. It makes ALL of our decisions.

Since the ego or mind is responsible for protecting the physical body, our mind tells us to wait until that truck has passed before we cross the street. The mind tells us to wear a coat when it's cold outside, or it could tell us not to wear that coat, even when it's freezing, so we'll look cool and trendy. The mind also carries the memories and information to help us carry out day to day tasks like eating, working, or driving. It's a computer bank filled with needed information to navigate through life; get up at 6:30 a.m., take a shower, take highway 410 to work, pick up groceries on the way home, cook chicken for supper, drive to your night class at 7:30 p.m. If we're driving to work, we rely on all the data or information in the computer bank of our mind to get us there, like street names, and when to turn left and right.

It's important to understand that our ego or mind makes ALL of our decisions, regardless of how negative, self-defeating, faulty, self-destructive, or illusionary they may be. Maybe Jane isn't a great singer, but she auditions for *American Idol* anyway, because her mind and the collective beliefs of society have convinced her she should. If you decide you're too ugly, short, fat, skinny, unpopular, poor, or stupid, your ego made these decisions based on external data or someone else's opinions. It was dream psychiatrist Carl G. Jung who helped us understand the concept of the collective consciousness—all the belief systems, ideas, values, or traditions held by parents, teachers, institutions, and society. Collective thinking includes society's views towards almost anything: technology, religion, politics, education, war, sexuality, fashion, ethnic groups and media. Although collective thinking can be positive, such as trends to help those needy or sick, recycle, conserve the environment, or save animals, this is not always the case. Collective thinking isn't always based on truth, because it doesn't come from our heart, spirit, or emotional body; it's usually imposed on us by external forces and faulty karmic thinking. It's dangerous when minds get together with warped, misinformed or faulty belief systems–ideas that contain no love, compassion or social justice. This is exactly what the initial decision to start segregation and slavery was—the decision by calculating minds to take control without the guiding wisdom of spirit. It was the cruelty of collective thinking that enabled Hitler to carry out white supremacist policies and persecute 6 million Jewish people. Sadly he didn't do this alone. Hitler and all his henchmen believed they were doing the right thing in preserving the purity of society. The mind will always attempt to exclude in its quest for domination and power, while the spirit tempers this with justice, mercy, and compassion.

In decision making the ego might work two ways. Like a dictator, the mind or ego can assume sole responsibility for every decision. Or the ego can allow soul or spirit to work as an advisor, providing insights to inform its decisions. If this is the case, both ego and spirit work together as partners. Ego could allow spirit to use information from dreams, meditative experiences, insights, imagination, or gut feelings, to make the decision to start a relationship, get married, change jobs, start a new activity or hobby, take a new course, or travel.

When we dream, spirit may present us with several possible choices, but it is the ego that decides which choices to act upon, or whether to act at all. Spirit, like God, never tells us what to do; we always have free will. Inspiration and ethical guidance comes from the spirit, while decision making and action come from the mind or ego. After the ego or mind makes fun of that new person at work, a dream could help the ego understand these words were cruel or judgmental. If ego is open to accepting new information, other dreams might help it understand that making fun of others stems from deep feelings of insecurity. If it continues listening to spirit, through dreams it would rehearse and try out scenarios, where it apologizes, or sees that person in a truer fashion.

As young children we didn't have enormous egos because we were more connected to our core or spirit. Our thoughts were our own, because we hadn't yet been influenced and socialized by the collective consciousness. Young children don't criticize, judge, condemn, ridicule, or assume a superior or arrogant stance as much as adults. This is mostly learned behavior or socialization, something the mind observes, then imitates like a parrot. I'll never forget teaching grade one and talking about the prejudice that existed toward American Indians, assuming these six-year-olds understood what I was talking about. A classroom of puzzled faces stared back at me—they didn't understand the word prejudice, and when I tried to explain it to them, I was met with blank expressions, because it hadn't yet been programmed into their little left brains. These children lived in a close knit Italian country setting where family and friends were known, loved and accepted—that's all they knew.

Without our conscious mind, or ego, we would be pure spirit without the structure or grounding function of the mind and physical world. It's a blessing the mind has absolutely no idea just how tough it's going to be to work through lifetimes of karma, because if it did, it would revolt and check out! Spirit would be floating off to other dimensions, instead of partnering with the mind to clear away karma. But despite the limitations of the mind, it *is* important to develop a strong identity or ego. When we're babies our minds are like blank slates, or empty hard drives, so it's important to fill them with truthful and ethical information. One acronym for ego is *"Energy Grounding Organizer."* If the ego or mind has limited or faulty programming, such as, "You can never do anything right," or "You'll never amount to anything," it can be overwhelmed or bullied. Young people who allow themselves to be abused, ridiculed, manipulated, dishonored, disrespected, harmed, or taken for granted, may not have developed a healthy ego with sufficient convictions to support them. They too are running on faulty, illusion-based programming because we all have tremendous potential. If it was a girl's destiny to become a great scientist, but she allowed her parents and siblings to constantly batter and berate her, she may grow up believing she had no gifts or purpose. If we don't develop a sound ego in childhood, we struggle as adults to find the programs or belief systems to sustain us. And if this is coupled with total disconnection from spirit which will sustain, nurture and protect, that faulty mind will drive a teenager to drinking, drugs, self-mutilation, depression, withdrawal, or even suicide.

Our task as children, teenagers, and adults, is to develop an ego, mind, or database of information that will keep us grounded in physical reality. This is difficult for young children at first, because the ego or mind is *not* who we really are. Ego is what we develop to enable our brains to survive on earth. It's much like the programs or software that allows a computer to run efficiently. *The ego actually stops us from remembering who we really are at our core, and why we're here.* Even though we begin with no real ego identity, over time, the scales tip in the opposite direction, and most of us end up identifying ourselves completely as ego, believing our true personality is *only* the mind. One of our greatest tasks is to create that wise balance, where ego and spirit are balanced partners.

In *The Tibetan Book of Living and Dying,* Buddhist monk Sogyal Rinpoche asks us to imagine suddenly waking up in the hospital after a car accident to discover we're suffering from total amnesia. Our body is intact, our face looks the same, our senses and mind seem to be functioning, but we have no idea who we are, or where we came from. This is exactly what happens when we're born. We have spiritual amnesia, no memories of our true or original home, family and identity in other dimensions, or previous lifetimes. Ego compensates by developing personalities or masks, along with money and physical trappings keeping us earthbound. Our mind convinces us only physical things are real, and we need a lot of them to be secure and successful. This becomes our biggest trap. Rinpoche says the ego is, "The absence of true knowledge of who we really are, together with its result: a doomed clutching on, at all costs, to a cobbled together and makeshift image of ourselves, an inevitably chameleon charlatan self that keeps changing and has to, to keep alive the fiction of its existence." To activate real genius, peace, or heaven on earth, we need to slowly become aware of this, just as a patient with amnesia slowly pieces together their former life. Rinpoche says, "So long as we haven't unmasked the ego, it continues to hoodwink us, like a sleazy politician endlessly parading bogus promises, or a lawyer constantly inventing ingenious lies and defenses, or a talk show host going on and on talking, keeping up a stream of suave and emptily convincing chatter, which actually says nothing at all."

Who Are You?

Trippers and askers surround me,
People I meet, the effect upon me of my early life or the ward and city I
live in, or the nation,
The latest dates, discoveries, inventions, societies, authors old and new...
These come to me days and nights and go from me again,
But they are not the Me myself.
Walt Witman from "Song of Myself"

The body and mind are constantly changing, morphing from one identity into another; we begin as babies, become toddlers, adolescents, teenagers, young adults, middle-aged, then senior citizens. If you're a teen reading this, you probably feel your real identity is a teenager. But ten years from now you may take on the identity of a working adult. If you're thirty-five years old, you define yourself as someone in their thirties, or perhaps a mother or father. You may also define yourself as the sum total of everything you've done and accomplished; perhaps you're a computer animator, but ten years ago you were a college student. But, which you, is the real you, the baby, toddler, adolescent, teenager, twenty-year-old, or thirty-year-old, mother, father, or computer animator? At what age do you achieve your true identity? Are you less real at ten than you are at twenty? Does our nationality define us? Are we truly Danish, Dutch, Spanish, Russian, Canadian or American? What if you're born in Holland, then move to Canada as a teenager, you have Dutch and Canadian citizenship. Are you really Dutch or really Canadian? Does our job define us or having children? If you lose your children are you still a parent? What if you have several careers—which of these jobs defines you? Our name doesn't even define us, because we can change our name and be exactly the same person. Or, is there a being that is ageless, timeless, and inherently wiser, waiting to be discovered inside you? The real you, the true you, is not something physical we can see with our eyes, because it is your spirit, and this part of you is also constantly changing. Consider that the real you *is not* this person who inhabits your physical body, but the spiritual body that dreams and travels every night. This can be scary, because it means giving up everything we've believed, everything our mind has spent our entire lives trying to piece together, everything that seems to ground us, and give us security. Like the Mafia, we've all developed a complex, sophisticated "cover" that defines us and gives us purpose. Tapping into spirit begins to blow open this cover, revealing an extraordinary being of energy and light.

Looking at who we are from a physical perspective can be quite revealing, since our body is rapidly discarding old cells and recreating new physical versions of who we were. The human body consists of approximately 1,000,000 billion cells; of this cell population 600 billion are dying and regenerating every day—over 10 million cells per second! The only parts of our body that remain permanent are special cells in our brain and eyes. Nothing in the body is constant, although heart and brain cells endure longer than most. The chief chemical components of our muscles are proteins—these are broken down and built up again every 12 days. At this rate every 15 years we have an entirely new set of muscles. Each red blood cell in our body has a life of about 128 days. Bone cells are renewed every three months. Our bones, comprised mainly of calcium salts, are completely replaced every nine years. If we live to be 80, we've gone through 14 complete skeletons. So, we do have skeletons in our closet! In *Ageless Body, Timeless Mind*, Deepak Chopra tells us, "In order to stay alive, your body must live on the wings of change. At this moment you are exhaling atoms of hydrogen, oxygen, carbon, and nitrogen that just an instant before were locked up in solid matter; your stomach, liver, heart, lungs, and brain are vanishing into thin air, being replaced as quickly and endlessly as they are being broken down. The skin replaces itself once a month, the stomach lining every five days, the liver every six weeks. To the naked eye, these organs look the same from moment to moment, but they are always in flux. By the end of this year, 98 percent of the atoms in your body will have been exchanged for new ones...Einstein taught us that the physical body, like all material objects, is an illusion, and trying to manipulate it can be like grasping the shadow and missing the substance. The unseen world is the real world, and when we are ready to explore the unseen levels of our bodies, we can tap in to the immense creative power that lies at our source."

Ego Traps

Reason alone does not suffice.
C.G. Jung *The Undiscovered Self*

Intellectuals solve problems; geniuses prevent them.
Albert Einstein

We've all heard the terms, ego-maniac, ego-driven, ego-centric, driven, workaholic. One of the biggest human traps is when individuals develop such a huge ego they're out of balance, and out of control. Ego-centric is an apt description, since the ego becomes the center of the personality dominating everything at the expense of the spirit. Since the ego doesn't have truth, compassion, or the ability to express love, insight, or creativity, we think of egocentric people as selfish, self-absorbed, driven, and cold. But this can happen to anyone. Many people develop enormous egos because they're insecure, fearful, or feel powerless. Without conscious awareness, we can develop huge egos as a defense mechanism because we feel inadequate. The cycle works like this:

As a child or adult we may be *judged*, bullied, ridiculed or put down
↕
We begin to *feel sorry* for ourselves
↕
We feel like a *victim*
↕
We become *vulnerable*
↕
We feel *powerless* so we need a way to gain power again
↕
We attempt to gain power through *ego*

We've all heard stories of people who came from difficult, troubled childhoods, who overcompensated, becoming successful, rich, yet dysfunctional ego-driven adults. Celebrities often fall into this trap. Many superstars with great talent, and business people who accrue enormous wealth, incarnate over and over into privileged positions. Each time their task is to remain balanced, not to be overtaken or swallowed up by ego, perhaps to realize their talents were God-given rather than ego-driven. Their purpose in coming to earth was to connect with their spirits, rather than losing their core or spirit to an inflated ego. The stories we hear of celebrities committing suicide, or overdosing on drugs and alcohol, are often the result of out of control egos searching desperately for some form of true "spirit" or bliss, heaven on earth in that fame, drug, ecstasy, or bottle of alcohol or spirits.

Before this happens many out of control egos get wake up calls. They may experience physical problems resulting from unbalanced energies in the body. Things happen to slow them down, so they can reflect and connect with their spirit again. But when this happens, rather than seeing this time as necessary before they self-destruct or die, many ego-driven individuals complain bitterly about how they're losing valuable time from work and earning less money. It may be a serious car accident, or broken leg, literally giving them a "break" to focus on heart rather than head, a heart attack because they've literally worked their hearts out, a brain tumor because their belief systems were faulty, migraines, or nervous exhaustion or burnout because they're running to satisfy ego needs rather than spiritual needs. The way to wholeness and health lies in balancing our ego, but emotionally this is tremendously difficult. For many, it becomes our life's work.

Inflated Ego is the Enemy of Humanity

Because my mind thinks something–doesn't necessarily make it so.
Anonymous

We are all here because we aren't all there.
Anonymous

A man is what he thinks about all day long.
Ralph Waldo Emerson

Dreams and meditative experiences are always trying to help us break through the illusions of the mind so that we can reconnect with truth. They're like computer anti-virus programs, cleaning up infections that prevent it from running properly. This enables the mind to download new programs, replacing fear with faith, and dark sectors with light. If we never seek awareness, the mind shrugs its shoulders, tells us life is a bitch, the world is unfair, we're victims, and we must die of a heart attack because our father and grandfather did. We succumb to this faulty programming, and the insane dramas continue, until all these infected karmic programs are rewritten or corrected.

C.G. Jung believed that isolation from the unconscious was isolation from our souls. He felt that modern neurosis was the result of this ego/spirit split. As a psychiatrist he observed that our essential psychological problem was *disconnection from spirit*. This is why a second acronym for ego is *Edging God Out*. If we become ego-dominated, we don't allow the wisdom of spirit to filter through. This is life's continual challenge, finding that middle ground, balance, the melding or partnership of mind and spirit.

Another road block with ego is that it will convince us we're right, when we may not be acting in our best interests—it tells us we're not qualified for that job, and so we don't apply, when that very job might have been destiny. Ego is a sea of swirling contradictions; sometimes it has absolutely no confidence, and other times it doggedly refuses to admit it was wrong. Writer Karen Casey explains, "The unchecked ego is humankind's only natural enemy, and the only one we need worry about. It is a great hindrance to spiritual progress. Our ego is the accumulation of all our beliefs, beginning with those we formed in childhood, and it gives off confusing signals. It makes us afraid of failure, but it can also make us afraid of success. It makes us feel all-knowing at times, and then utterly stupid." She says even though ego tosses us around in a turbulent sea of conflicting notions, God's laws and spiritual truths are constant and based on mutual respect and love for one another. Wisdom and humility walk together; we absolutely can't know everything. When I was a high school teacher, I would experience the most extreme guilt, self-loathing, and sense of inadequacy when I didn't know an answer. My ego told me I was a failure, because I should know everything about English. But the mind can't always be right. In truth, until we're fully enlightened we're only human.

Ego lacks the wisdom, compassion, or creativity of the soul. It's the ego that ridicules someone at a gym deciding they're fat, ugly, clumsy, uncoordinated, or hopelessly out of shape. The ego could survey the entire gym and decide it already has a great body, so doesn't need to exercise. Or the ego could decide that exercising is too much work, and it would rather sit at home and watch television. The ego has no conscience, morality, ethics, or compassion because it's largely a data bank of facts and information. Any decision to gossip, ridicule, judge, shun, rape, kill, or rob a bank, came solely from the mind or ego. But since the ego can draw from vast amounts of information, data, and knowledge, it can appear brilliant. The reign of Saddam Hussein with pictures and statues of himself everywhere, was a perfect example of an out of control ego. Humanitarian Samantha Nutt, who often visited Iraq, describes portraits of "Saddam firing a Kalashnikov, Saddam saluting the masses, Saddam posing as a fighter pilot, Saddam carrying children on his shoulders." After his death, reporter Neil Macfarquhar, wrote, "While Saddam was in power, his statue guarded the entrance to every village, his portrait watched over each government office and he peered down from at least one wall in every home. His picture was so widespread that one joke quietly circulating among detractors in 1988 put the country's population at 34 million—17 million people and 17 million portraits of Saddam." For decades he escaped any type of law or justice because he was not a stupid man. Many criminals like Jack the Ripper who never get caught are intelligent with well-developed egos. There's a theory he was a surgeon, because he removed the internal organs from at least three of his victims. Perhaps this is the reason for poet Elizabeth Barrett Browning's famous quote, "Since when was genius found respectable?" This is why it's so important to allow spirit to balance and inform the decisions of the ego or mind. Without the guiding wisdom of spirit, ego causes death, destruction, and incredible pain.

All the dysfunction in our world actually stems from a split of ego and spirit. *Inflated ego is actually the enemy of humanity because it has caused all of our destruction and distress.* If we look at why most leaders go to war, it's often because they want power, control, wealth, natural resources, or they believe their way is the only way. Ego is a lone wolf. It doesn't want to feel connection to other human beings, because if it did, it would lose control. It's the ego or mind of men who rape or abuse women or children. It's the mind of suicide bombers igniting those bombs, believing their god approves, and they'll be rewarded in heaven. It's the ego or mind of men who kill their ex-wives, not wanting anyone else to have them. It's the mind that decides to buy that fifth house or car, while millions are homeless and starving.

If there is no wisdom or balance provided by spirit, two deadly things may happen to the mind—brainwashing or mind control. The mind may be brainwashed, or manipulated into believing something good, even noble, when it could prove fatal. This is like loading a computer program with faulty information. Let's use the example of smoking cigarettes, which millions of people do, even though there is a direct relationship between smoking cigarettes and cancer, emphysema, and chronic obstructive pulmonary disease—all fatal. It's been estimated that a single cigarette shortens one's lifetime by eleven seconds, and that for the average smoker this translates into eleven lost years. There are always the exceptions, the miracles, the people who defy all odds, but cigarette smoking is probably one of the best examples of an activity where our mind convinces us it's okay. Cigarette ads in the thirties and forties claimed their products were "fresh" and "pure." One ad for Camels pictured a distinguished doctor in a white coat, with a cigarette in his hand. The headline read, "More doctors smoke Camels than any other cigarette." In the movies of the sixties and seventies all the important people smoked. Smoking was especially cool if you were an artist or writer, as if each smoke ring ascended from the depths of your being, lassoing all this wisdom. Decades later most of these smokers had died. Dreams always show us when things are false or misleading. Dreams could have saved thousands of lives, because spirit is never duped by even the most sophisticated ad campaign.

Dr. William Dement is considered the world's leading authority on sleep and dreaming. As a young medical student back in the early 1950s, along with Eugene Aserinsky and William Kleitman, he was one of the first people to discover REM or Rapid Eye Movement sleep, the realm of dreams. In a Discovery Channel television series, *The Power of Dreams*, Dr. Dement describes a vivid dream he had as a young man when he was a heavy smoker. In the dream, he begins coughing up blood into a handkerchief, and decides to have chest x-rays taken. When his friend, a radiologist, shows him the x-rays on a viewing screen, he realizes he has lung cancer. Dement said, "In that moment I knew my life would soon end. It was just overwhelming. I wouldn't see my children grow up, wouldn't see green grass. It was just tremendously powerful. And then I woke up, and oh man, I can still remember, the *relief*, was so *real*. Ah. A second chance to be reborn. But the main thing was I had experienced cancer of the lung and I knew that was a totally unacceptable alternative. I never smoked another cigarette. That dream saved my life."

The secondly deadly thing, mind control, always takes place when we're in a vulnerable state. If we're stressed, depressed, sleep deprived, or feeling lonely, unloved, or insignificant, our mind can be skillfully manipulated by other powerful minds, or external forces, then completely taken over, pushing out the soul or spirit completely. These decisions completely lack common sense, compassion, or wisdom. Mind control is nasty business. It's what enabled Jim Jones, the self-proscribed leader of the Peoples Temple Church to move his congregation from San Francisco to the jungles of Guyana. He set up a community of nearly 1,000 followers which his ego named Jonestown. On November 18,

1978, he convinced 914 followers including 276 children, to commit mass suicide by drinking cyanide-laced Flavor Aid. This was also carried out by cyanide injection, or shooting. In his lengthy speech before this mass suicide, Jones convinced his followers they were doing something noble. He used a borrowed term, "revolutionary suicide," telling his followers this honorable deed was performed in ancient Greece, and was necessary to escape the violence and evil in the world. Most followed his instructions like programmed zombies—he had skillfully taken over their minds and excommunicated their spirits.

Each night we are flooded with several dream experiences, and it's the ego that decides which dreams to let into conscious awareness. Freud believed the ego or mind acted as a gatekeeper or censor, and that we might be completely overwhelmed if the ego allowed everything through. Most of us have at least five dreams each night, and often more, if we're working through complex issues. Another way of looking at the ego is to think of it as an overprotective parent. As children, we all need parents, but eventually we need to break away from the ego's total control, the same way teenagers need to break from parents to form their own identity. If we don't make this transition, the ego becomes that overprotective parent. It looks after physical and safety needs, but completely neglects emotional or spiritual needs. An overly controlling ego is like the seventy-year-old mother who still cooks, cleans and does laundry for her forty-year-old son, who has never married, or left home. The ego will never help us find our destiny or dharma, true love, or meaningful employment, all the things that fuel our spirit.

An example of this type of parent/child relationship is seen in the movie *Billy Elliot*. Billy is the eleven-year-old spirit striving to break free, and his father is the stubborn, ego driven, over protective parent. Billy's destiny is to become a dancer, but his father insists that Billy take boxing lessons and become a coal miner, just as Billy's brother, father, and grandfather did, because the ego is not creative and loves the security of what is known and familiar. The life of a coal miner would have literally suffocated Billy's spirit. The mind or ego of Billy's father doesn't understand his son's destiny or dharma. Since his father believed it was stupid, impractical, and embarrassing for a man to dance, he tries to dissuade his son, but Billy's is relentless and never stops dancing. Finally, his father's ego concedes, submitting to the longings and strength of Billy's heart. He takes his son to a prestigious ballet school for an audition, and Billy is accepted. The final scene is years later and Billy is now a young man. His spirit helped him to find a way out of the poverty and despair he was born into. We see his father entering an elegant theater to watch his son dance. The performance begins with

Billy leaping across the stage. His father gasps; the beauty and power of his son's movement literally takes his breath away. Like Billy, we all have the ability to leap and soar in life, if only we listen to our spirits.

Balancing Ego with Intuition

Conversion for me was not a Damascus Road experience. I slowly moved into an intellectual acceptance of what my intuition had always known.
Madeline L'Engle

People who lean on logic and philosophy and rational exposition end by starving the best part of the mind.
J.B Yeats

The mind doesn't really care that you need fun, rest, peace or solace, because it's incredibly self-centered. It's not concerned that you need a vacation, haven't seen your best friend in weeks, or that you're exhausted or depressed. If you ask the mind, it will convince you to keep on working to get the bonus, or to make the money to buy more stuff, because it operates like a child. It will tell you to get another degree, title or promotion, so you can look smarter and better. Ironically, the only guaranteed time our mind stops blaring, shuts up, or goes off line is when we meditate, or while we sleep and dream. During this time our spirit directs, guides, and helps us experiment and work through issues, in five or six dream scenarios a night. But when we wake up, our mind kicks in again, and tells us dreams are just nonsense, and we only have twenty minutes to get to school or work.

We're all naturally good at acting on feelings and hunches. It's what allows painters to create masterpieces, people to fall in love against all odds, song writers to compose music, stockbrokers to invest money wisely, friends to phone when you need support, and parents to know when something is wrong with their children. But many don't trust dreams or intuitive hunches because they're not logical or grounded in physical reality, and you can't prove them. Since it's natural for us to act on hunches, feelings, our gut, emotions, intuition—usually when we do the outcome is positive. How does Tom walk into a bar, see Sally across the room for the first time, and know instantly he wants to marry her? It's not logical because his mind doesn't know Sally—they've never even had a conversation. His deep "feeling" is a heartfelt memory of love for Sally from other lifetimes. This memory may be part of his spirit's contract with Sally. Our Book of Life, karma and dharma is deeply encoded into the body's tissues, cells, and organs, especially the heart—often referred to as "body memory." If Tom acts on his gut feelings and body memories, Sally may be completely dharmic, bringing him incredible comfort and happiness. But if his mind tells him it's crazy to talk to strangers, she won't like him, and no one respectable meets someone in a bar, he may remain lonely, miserable or unfulfilled.

Our egos are like radios, blaring all the time, loud and clear, so it's easier to follow the mind because it's right in your face. And like radios, our minds are usually hopping from station to station, commercial to commercial, talk show to talk show. It becomes difficult to shut our minds off, slow them down, and relax. We're so bombarded by constant chatter, noise and music, that silence feels strangely awkward. We're uncomfortable turning off our cell phones, not wearing our iPods, turning off the radio or television, having silence, and allowing those wisps of wisdom to filter through. While the mind is like a radio, repeating the same commercials, spirit or intuition whispers like a gentle wind and you need to be quiet before hearing it. These whispers don't tell us mundane things like where to find a parking spot, or which store has your favorite jeans on sale; ego can do that from experience. Instead, it gives you insights and ideas that genuinely help you to become more aware and insightful. Sometimes we need faith to carry this out, because it won't always make rational sense. And like everything else, developing or honing our intuition takes practice. There may be times when we're absolutely certain we're gotten an intuitive nudge, and other times when we really don't know if the message is from our mind or spirit. The only way to find out is to experiment, act on it, as long as it will not harm you or others. When something turns out in your best interests, and harms no one, it is *always* the gentle guidance of spirit or intuition. Over time you will get better at discernment, recognizing the guidance, and disregarding the rumblings of your mind. Over time you might develop the awareness that the mind and intuition have distinctly different qualities or feelings. Intuition is soft, indirect, gently leading you towards a hunch or feeling. In contrast the mind can be sharper, more direct, judgmental and uncertain. If it doesn't feel good, it's always the mind! In her book *Bird by Bird* Anne Lamott says, "You get your intuition back when you make space for it, when you stop the chattering of the rational mind. The rational mind doesn't nourish you. You assume that it gives you the truth, because the rational mind is the golden calf that this culture worships, but this is not true. Rationality squeezes out much that is rich and juicy and fascinating."

She tells us to "calm down, get quiet, breathe, and listen." It's spirit, not the mind that helps us make physical and emotional connections. Lamott says, "The conscious mind seems to block that feeling of oneness so we can function efficiently, maneuver in the world a little bit better, get our taxes done on time. But it's even possible to have this feeling when you see—really see—a police officer, when you look right at him and you see that he's a living breathing person who like everyone else is suffering like a son of a bitch, and you don't see him with a transparency over him of all the images of violence and chaos and danger that cops represent. You accept him as an equal." That's the beauty of spirit, it excludes no one, and has the wisdom to always act in your best interests, opening up a challenging, yet exciting world of possibilities.

Ego Dreams

Dreams do not deceive, they do not lie, they do not distort or disguise...
They are invariably seeking to express something
that the ego does not know and does not understand.

C.G. Jung

If I hadn't listened to my dreams during my early forties I'm sure I would have died from fatigue, exhaustion, high blood pressure, or self-destructed somehow. My ego wanted me to be the same as all the other teachers who were going to work each day. At its worst, my ego wanted me to be super teacher with a Ph.D. My ego didn't want to admit I had serious health problems, was exhausted, sleep deprived, and had been in chronic pain every day for years—it wanted to keep up appearances. Admitting I had serious ego issues was one of the most painful things I needed to face when I stopped teaching. Suddenly I wasn't super teacher or Mother Teresa any more. I probably had many of these dreams while I was working, but my ego pushed them aside. My ego certainly didn't want me to uncover that I could be a control freak. It wanted me to believe I was humble, hardworking, and unassuming. But anyone going to great lengths to appear humble is unconsciously trying to draw attention to their "virtues," usually because they're terribly insecure. This becomes a clever ego trap. For most of my life I've had a passive, but out of control ego. Like many people, I fantasized about doing great things to help humanity, probably to compensate for my inability to even get out of bed in the morning. Here are two of my ego unmasking dreams during this emotionally painful, yet illuminating time.

Asked to Speak
I'm somewhere with a group of people. There are a lot of high-powered business men here. One of the men asks me if I'll do a reading. It's from a small, dark, leather book that looks like a Bible. I immediately accept thinking this is a great honor. I think to myself, he's probably found out I'm a great reader or public speaker. Maybe someone has told him about me. Then I open the book and realize it's in a foreign language I don't understand. I start to read, believing I can just figure out the words and still appear impressive. This shouldn't be too difficult.

Before I can rehearse the paragraph I'm told it's time to go up to the podium to read. This is quite a formal, important affair. Everyone is well dressed. I stumble over the first few words. I'm really faking it. Then I realize I need help with pronunciation, so I have to stop and ask a man who is sitting to my right beside the podium. He tells me the word and I go back to speak. Then I realize I'm in way over my head. The words get progressively harder, and more foreign as the paragraph progresses. I realize now there is absolutely no way I can even fake it. The dream ends and I'm embarrassed and humiliated because I've had to admit publicly that I can't continue to read.

Waking up I realized I'd only agreed to do this dream reading because my ego felt I was a superior reader and I wanted the attention and recognition. I was also aware I was set up, because this man obviously knew my ego issues. He knew I wouldn't say no because I believed I was a great public speaker and could read well. He knew even asking me to do this would pump up my ego. I realized I'd fallen into a trap. He gave me a book with a familiar looking cover almost like a Bible. My mind thought this might be some sort of spiritual book and I could appear like a great teacher. If I wasn't under the illusion that no one could do the job as well as me, I probably would have declined and saved myself the embarrassment. In dreams there is usually one sentence that crystalizes or sums up its entire meaning—in this dream it was the phrase "I now realize there is absolutely no way I can fake it." Faking it was exactly what I'd been doing for several years—trying to appear like the "I've got my act together teacher," when I was a blubbering mess. Writing this I also became aware of what a vicious cycle this whole ego thing is. If this happened in real life, I probably would have wanted to read somewhere publicly again to restore my shattered ego and self-esteem. After I did my ego would be pumped again and the whole insidious cycle would start again.

Rebecca Does Yoga

I'm watching Rebecca teach yoga from behind a fence. I've taught her before. She begins to show a move more advanced than Downward Dog. She mentions other teachers names at her elementary school who have taught her. I'm momentarily thinking, "I'm the only one who can teach her, my way is the right way." I realize even in the dream this is my ego. Then I watch her and realize what I was teaching her was way too basic and easy. She does downward dog in an advanced one leg move that I've never seen or done before. Then she progresses into all kinds of advanced moves that are amazing. I'm in awe of her skill.

This dream occurred in my life when I was feeling incredibly insecure, fearful, and stuck. My spirit was trying to help me understand that I would remain stuck in life, unless I recognized ego issues that had become like a ball and chain around my neck. Rebecca is the daughter of a dear friend Shelley, and when I had this dream Rebecca was seven-years-old. A few months before the dream I learned that Rebecca had started gymnastics and she was doing well. I had listened to stories of her mother's amazement as she described advanced moves Rebecca could do with little formal training. Before this dream I had been taking yoga classes at a YMCA with a teacher for two years and wanted to believe I was good, really to cover up my own low self-esteem. There were a few yoga moves I could do well, but I was really just a beginner. After about a year and a half, I actually started investigating teacher training, way before I was proficient enough. Since I couldn't be super high school teacher, my ego was trying to be super yoga teacher. When I started going to actual yoga studios, a brand new experience, I could hardly keep up. I felt like a beginner and realized I'd only believed I was good enough to teach because my experience had been limited. It also made me aware of an ego trap I had fallen into my entire life as a teacher, wanting to believe I was superior or the best to cover up for the really deep sense of inadequacy I'd always felt. I'd carried this feeling of worthlessness from my childhood. When I found something I could do reasonably well, my ego tried to convince me I was great.

Something else I believe triggered this dream. A few days earlier I was at a spinning class at a gym. The fitness instructor was talking about her serious wrist and arm injury from the repeated stress of teaching this class. She was on pain killers, muscle relaxants, and needed to wear a tensor bandage. When I asked, "Are you going to stop teaching this class?" she looked at me as if I was crazy and replied, "I can't. There's nobody else who can do it." She was an excellent teacher, but there were at least six or seven other instructors at this gym qualified to teach her class. Her ego had convinced her she was indispensable. In a flash of realization, I saw myself in her. Not only do dreams provide mirrors, people in our lives can be our mirrors, revealing our deepest issues. In our spiritual contracts we've agreed to teach each other, through our mutual dysfunctions, although our minds are never aware of this. When my doctor ordered me to stop working a few years earlier, I believed I couldn't. I wanted to believe there was no one else who could teach my courses or mark my student's exams, so I actually finished off the semester against doctor's orders, and then literally collapsed. Ego is usually (but not always) that voice inside us saying, "If I want it done right, I have to do it myself," because it's not a team player, it may be a martyr, sometimes it has an exaggerated sense of responsibility, possibly wanting all the glory, it won't accept different points of view or innovative ways of doing things. This was a huge wake up call, because this fitness instructor's reply was almost laughable, yet she was convinced no one else could possibly teach her class. Her mind had convinced her she was indispensable, just as my mind had. Ironically a few years later, she was let go from this position—we both had our wake-up calls, but in a different fashion.

The Ego and Dreams

The ego wants to pin down a meaning for the dream so that it can hold a prize in its hands, but that is not always essential or even necessary for the evolution of the psyche.
Robert A. Johnson in *Balancing Heaven and Earth*

It doesn't take long for us to become quite adept at understanding our dreams. It's a normal, healthy, balancing function, just like eating, or drinking, or exercising, so with absolutely no knowledge of dream theory and little practice, we can all become little geniuses in unmasking these nightly dramas. I've constantly been amazed and humbled, when I've been teaching a class, or with a group of people, and someone relates a dream. After a lifetime of keeping a dream journal, I have absolutely no idea what it means, yet someone from the group, often a complete novice in dream work, comes up with this brilliant synthesis that gets to the heart of the matter. So, a word of caution. Your ego or mind will try to take all the credit for what your spirit has done in a fraction of a second. Your mind will attempt to convince you that you're brilliant, clever, a notch above the rest of humanity, because you have this amazing ability to penetrate deep beneath the layers of the unconscious and understand dreams. The mind will try to convince you that it's doing all the work, and because of this you must be exceedingly clever. It's easy to fall into yet another ego trap, as I did.

Once I had digested every book I could get my hands on concerning dreams, and completed a doctoral thesis on dreamwork, my mind wanted to believe it was an expert, and that I could somehow illuminate the lives of others with this brilliant insight. And so for years I actually wanted people to tell me their dreams, so that I would appear clever. This was a great boost for my insecure ego, but over time, it backfired. After a while I was inundated with people phoning—a friend, of a friend, of a friend, people I had never met, or would never meet, who wanted free dream therapy. I actually wished that I had never volunteered to listen to anyone's dream—and all because my over-inflated ego had wanted more pumping up. It was a hard lesson. It took a long time to realize ego can feel a real power trip when you tell someone the meaning of their dream, but this doesn't last very long, so the next day your mind just wants more of the same experience to keep it pumped. But when you teach someone how to understand their dreams and how to be constantly self-empowered, it's enormously satisfying, and feels a hundred times better than those puny ego pumps.

Understanding dreams was meant to be something we all do, never something reserved for a few experts. Our ancestors were well-versed in dreams, and this only changed about four hundred years ago, when our world became more external and everything became more scientific and technical. Most people can do basic things like operate a computer, drive a car, and program their phones, but we're illiterate when it comes to dreams. When this changes, be wary of ego insisting you have acquired some superior function. We all dream and dreams are meant to be understood, and treasured, not held up as trophies of the ego.

I've come to regard all the dreams I've journaled over the years, as something precious I've collected, just like people who collect jewelry, music, or art. It is sacred wisdom, and because dreams come from other dimensions, our egos will also try to conquer or understand every single dream, mastery of the mind over the spirit. In his book, *Balancing Heaven and Earth*, Robert A. Johnson says, "The key is not so much to interpret a dream as to appreciate it and befriend it." In *Care of the Soul* Thomas Moore says with dreams there is never a single definitive meaning. "I like to treat dreams as if they were paintings and paintings as if they were dreams…Over many years, a good painting will retain its power to mesmerize, satisfy, and evoke new reverie and wonder…The point in working with a dream is never to translate it into a final meaning, but always to give it honor and respect, drawing from it as much meaningfulness and imaginative meditation as possible. Entering a dream should revitalize the imagination, not keep it in fixed and tired habits…Dreams are watery: they resist all efforts to make them fixed and solid."

Every dream is like a gem you bring back from other dimensions. Many precious stones and gems do contain energetic and healing properties. We don't know how this works, but we still like to have them around—it's the same with dreams. We don't have to analyze every single dream, but we can appreciate them as sacred experiences, and record them, in the same way we keep a diary, or journal, when we travel. Consider how we collect music. Most of us can't play instruments, sing like Pavarotti, or understand the dynamic process that went into making that song we love so much, but it's still exciting to have it in our collection. Knowing this, we can begin collecting dreams the same way we may collect sea shells, art from other countries, jewelry, gems, music, or joke books—sometimes dreams are hilarious. Rather than pumping up your ego, try being grateful for each insight, and rather than feeling you must master every dream, instead treasure and appreciate their uniqueness. It's like going to several free movies every night that you've directed, produced, and starred in. Over time, more of those dreams you've collected will make sense—and when they don't, it keeps you humble and gives you another challenge to work towards, helping you walk the path of a more balanced genius.

THE MIND

We believe the mind is clever, with thoughts that make us smart,
But what if the mind has problems, like a hard drive that's falling apart?
We believe the mind is a genius; that thinking is where it's at,
But what if the mind is selfish, like a spoiled two-year-old brat?
The mind only wants to please itself, and get the best of you,
It doesn't care if you're stressed, depressed, or if you're feeling blue,
The mind is not creative, it can't compose a song or dance,
The mind is not adventurous, it's afraid to take a new chance,
It always wants to run the show, it may even drive you insane,
It can tell you lies about yourself, that cause you endless pain,
The mind will say you're ugly, that you're never good enough,
That life has never been that fair; and things are always rough,
The mind has no real wisdom, it's like a fancy fool,
And despite these limitations, it always wants to rule,
If we want wisdom or compassion, genius or real smarts,
Then connecting to your spirit is the only way to start,
Genius always comes from spirit, and all things that are wise,
But the mind will masquerade as smart, and wear a clever disguise,
Beethoven wrote his symphonies when he had gone quite blind,
When he composed this music; it wasn't from his mind,
We live in a time of madness, with wars, guns and knives,
When minds make decisions, to snuff out helpless lives,
Any decision to kill or hurt, or act in ways unkind,
Didn't come from spirit—it came from someone's mind,
Spirit needs to inform the mind, or violence will increase,
We need to listen to our hearts, or wars will never cease,
The way out of this insanity, the way to wisdom and peace,
Is giving our tired minds a break; this is a true release,
If everyone could meditate and give their minds a rest,
Then every human being would truly do their best,
If everyone could understand their truth from dreams each night,
These dreams would guide humanity, and help us set things right.

Marina 2006

CHAPTER SEVEN
Working Through Fear in Dreams

Fear imprisons, faith liberates; fear paralyzes, faith empowers; fear disheartens, faith encourages; fear sickens, faith heals; fear makes useless, faith makes serviceable.

Harry Emerson Fosdick

Be not afeard. The isle is full of noises,
Sounds and sweet airs that give delight and hurt not.
Sometimes a thousand twanging instruments
Will hum about mine ears, and sometimes voices
That, if I then had waked after long sleep,
Will make me sleep again; and then, in dreaming,
The clouds me thought would open, and show riches
Ready to drop upon me, that when I waked,
I cried to dream again.

Shakespeare, *The Tempest* 3.2 148-156

FEAR IS A DIMINISHING DISEASE, a horrible virus, a cancer that sucks the joy, vitality and spontaneity right out of us. We are never really free when we live in fear, because we're controlled, crippled, imprisoned by everything we're afraid of. In essence we're imprisoned by our minds since spirit is fearless. There is little wisdom or genius in fear, yet humanity has lived in fear for eons. In 1580, French writer Michel Eyquem De Montaigne said, "The thing I fear most is fear." In 1623, painter Frances Bacon said, "Nothing is terrible except fear itself." The Duke of Wellington, sometimes nicknamed "The Iron Duke", confessed in 1831, "The only thing I am afraid of is fear." And in 1841, poet and philosopher, Henry David Thoreau, said "Nothing is so much to be feared as fear." American president, Franklin D. Roosevelt, paraphrased this in 1933, when he said, "The only thing we have to fear is fear itself."

Close your eyes for a few seconds and try to imagine how your life would feel if you were fearless—you have complete faith and nothing to fear. Imagine absolutely no fears about walking alone at night, getting into college or university, finding a job you enjoy, having enough money, never getting sick or old, never experiencing physical pain, and having people in your life who love and respect you. These feelings are close to the authentic you or enlightened state. We might have felt this way when we were two or three-years-old, except we don't remember, we were literally another person then, sleeping and dreaming a whole lot, no sweaty palms, stress, insomnia, sleepless nights, panic attacks, hypertension, or high blood pressure. Every day was a new adventure and we had faith that we would be taken care of. When our minds began running the show, we caught the fear virus which had seeped deeply into every cell. However, this virus can be eradicated without making expensive trips to a doctor; in fact we're all working hard to diminish our fears every night as we dream. Unfortunately, we live in a world where great minds have built sophisticated and rational defenses to keep dreams and spirit at bay. Often we're afraid to acknowledge the very thing that will lessen our fears, allow us to laugh at their absurdity, and give us new perspectives. Awareness, our greatest ally, has become the enemy; we're often terribly afraid to bring our deepest fears, secrets, or insecurities to light. Dreamwork is tough. It's not for the faint of heart because it exposes our dark side, our deepest fears, insecurities, issues, and challenges. Dreams help us work through our karma, and this can be emotionally painful. To compensate, we build armor and fortresses around ourselves keeping out the very truth which may forever set us free.

In the most guarded fortresses is the belief that we don't dream, a clever trick by the mind preventing us from accessing nightly guidance. Ego will say, "You don't dream every night, or else you'd remember them, but there are foolish people who actually try to understand their dreams. These are merely fantasies and you don't want to associate with these feather brains who sway your rational judgment." The ego of a less guarded fortress might say, "Maybe other people dream, but I don't. Dreams really don't mean anything anyway. And even if they did, who has the time to write them down!" Another popular defense is, "Yes, we all dream. I've remembered many dreams, but when I try to decipher them, it's apparent they're all nonsense." We've got to give the mind credit, it's been exceedingly clever in convincing humanity we spend one third of our lives engaged in an absolutely useless activity!

But the truth is, every dream makes absolute sense over time, and although our mind may not be clever enough to figure this out right away, with a little knowledge, and faith we all have the innate ability to understand even the most cryptic dreams, as long as we're able to suspend our minds long enough to allow intuition or spirit to peek through with insights. It's far easier to say we don't dream, or that dreams are nonsense; this way we never have to face our shadow, issues, or fears. But when we're afraid of anything, it depletes us of much needed energy. We give away our power, without realizing this can be changed. When we're afraid we miss out on joys, awareness, and new experiences, and we can be controlled by people who are manipulative, uncaring, or ego-driven. Or we may compensate by developing a huge ego, appearing tough and cool, which is just another trap. Being trapped by fears is like being stuck in mud. When we're immersed in fear it's almost impossible to be aware or insightful; it's like going through life wearing fogged up glasses. Fear is absolutely disempowering.

Have you ever seen a picture of an angel, saint, prophet, or mystic who looked afraid? That's because as we get closer to enlightenment, or even wiser, we begin releasing our unfounded fears. It's like throwing out unneeded garbage. Most fears are illusions, which is why a popular acronym for fear is; False Evidence Appearing Real. I discovered these acronyms posted at a Toronto swimming pool; Failure Expected And Returned, and Finding Excuses And Reasons. Underneath was typed, "Each time we face our fear we gain strength, courage, and confidence in the doing," and "Courage is not the absence of fear but the mastery of it." Although this was on a message board for elite swimmers and divers, it's great wisdom for everyone. Think back to your childhood fears. Although some may have been real, you probably realized over time most fears were completely unfounded. When we live in fear we never discover our essence or spirit and never achieve our destiny or dharma. Imagine how different the world would be if Edison was afraid to test his invention the light bulb, if Einstein was afraid to write about his theory of relativity, if Michelangelo never painted, fearing he had no talent, if the Beatles never recorded a song fearing their music wouldn't sell, or if Martin Luther King never spoke in public fearing no one would listen. If we're immersed in fear we shortchange ourselves and the rest of the world. We all have an important destiny to contribute.

If we want to move forward, to reach what Jung called individuation, Buddha called enlightenment, Maslow called self-actualization, self-realization, or simply a life without constant stress, we absolutely need to work through fears. We need to face our fears and recognize that most are clever illusions just like those monsters we thought lived under our beds. Dreams are one of the most effective ways of doing this. Whether we're aware or not, our dreams are constantly helping us eradicate fears. Working through fears may be difficult, but it's also incredibly empowering.

In the workplace, the most dangerous disability is not something we can easily diagnose like dyslexia or Attention Deficit Disorder—it's fear. Dr. Edward Hallowell, a specialist in learning disabilities, explains that fear of our boss, co-workers, poor performance, or not being able to meet a deadline, puts us into survival mode, which is okay if a tiger is about to attack you, but in the workplace it prevents "fluid learning" and "nuanced understanding." Rather than being able to utilize your entire brain for answers, the lower centers of the brain recruit the higher centers to make sure you'll survive. Your body compensates by producing more adrenaline and cortisol, and we go into black-and-white thinking. It's yes or no, on or off, up or down. We lose those cutting edge functions, like flexibility, reading between the lines, dealing with uncertainty, being creative, coming up with innovative solutions, having a sense of humor, and entertaining new ideas. We quickly deal with things, in the easiest way possible, before the tigers devour us. If we're wanting to work intelligently, survival or fear mode is the last place we want to be.

Fear also prevents us from being compassionate, caring, and giving. In their book, *Me to We,* Craig and Marc Kielburger explain that millions are existing on just a few dollars a day, because people in wealthier countries are afraid to donate to reputable charities. We're afraid our money is not going directly to help the problem, which does happen, but mostly we're afraid if we give away even a fraction of our money, we won't have enough to live on. Fear is often (not always) one of the major reasons why people become seriously ill. The mind is a powerful manipulator, and if we tell ourselves enough times we're going to die of a heart attack, cancer, or AIDS we probably will. If we think positive or peaceful thoughts, we lower our brain waves to the alpha state, or the place of genius (8 to 12 cycles per second) where we operate like a boat on a steady, flowing river, and if we meditate on a regular basis, returning to that alpha state, all of these things boost our immune system. If our mind is focused only on doom and gloom, our brain waves increase to the beta state (12 to 20 cycles per second) where we're functioning more like a speed boat out of control. If we're constantly rushing and stressed, a complex chemical reaction takes place in our body, producing stress hormones such as cortisol, norepinephrine (noradrenalin), and epinephrine (adrenalin), weakening our immune system, and eventually leading to disease. In her book *Dying to Be Me,* Anita Moorjani, who developed a case of terminal cancer or lymphoma, believes pervasive fears created her illness. She had watched a close friend, Soni, and a brother-in-law die of cancer and was terrified this would happen to her too, but her fears had infiltrated every aspect of her life. She believes we're taught from an early age to be afraid, although we're not born this way, and these subtle fears creep up gradually until they can totally control us. She admits she was afraid of, "Just about everything, including falling, being disliked, letting people down, and not being good enough. I also feared illness, cancer in particular, as well as the treatments for cancer. I was afraid of living, and I was terrified of dying." Her fears increased until she felt completely caged and controlled by them. "My experience of life was getting smaller and smaller, because to me, the world was a menacing place. And then I was diagnosed with cancer."

Think back to September 11, 2001, when those planes hit the World Trade Center in New York City. Many were gripped with the fear that the world was an unsafe place, and there would be repeated terrorist attacks. This was quickly followed by anthrax scares—deadly white powders turning up in the mail. Many believe these events were planned, cleverly carried out by businessmen who wanted to profit by creating fear in the American people, justifying a reason for war, and war is big business—there's lots of money to be gained from selling jeeps, tanks, planes, helicopters, jets, stealth bombers, missiles, bombs, guns, rifles, ammunition, and army boots. Billions could be made by businessmen if we feared war was necessary. War did follow, but we didn't respond in complete panic and fear. Instead there were peace rallies, candle light vigils, and a great outpouring of compassion, support, and concern for the victims and their families. It would have been easy to push a button in fear and declare nuclear war. We could have reacted with hatred, vengeance, and despair, but instead we sought peace, and this energy or vibration had a global impact. Through this experience the people of the United States learned a valuable lesson—that they had been controlled and manipulated by their own fears. In time they elected a president, Barak Obama, who seemed to be confident and fearless, advocating the motto 'Yes we can." Yes, we can turn this around. Yes, we can have hope again. Yes, we can put these irrational fears to rest.

When the 18-day revolution took place in Egypt, in 2011, this fearless uprising was significant because Egypt is often compared to the United States of the Eastern world—when it does something major, many countries are affected and follow its example. Its leader was 30-year-old Google executive, Wael Ghonim, who orchestrated this uprising not with fear, terrorism, hatred, or tanks, but with Twitter, texts, Facebook, and satellite TV broadcasts. Three days after the protest began in Tahrir Square, Wael disappeared, and his family and friends feared he had been killed or kidnapped. Wael had been arrested by Egyptian authorities, and during that time he was blindfolded, handcuffed, and constantly interrogated. He was released after 12 days, in time to enjoy the celebrations throughout Egypt, and President Hosni Mubarek fled the country after 30 years of brutal dictatorship. After his release, Wael was interviewed in Cairo, by CBS News correspondent Harry Smith. In the interview, Wael said after being released from jail, he wrote a status message declaring they were going to win the revolution because they weren't playing nasty political games, their tears came from their hearts, and they had a dream; and if anyone stood in front of their dream, they were ready to die defending it. He was confident this would happen, because his followers were fearless. He said it was going to happen, "Because the only barrier to people uprising and revolution is the psychological barrier of fear. All these regimes rely on fear. They want everyone to be scared. If you manage to break the psychological barrier, you're gonna definitely be able to do the revolution." That wall of fear definitely fell, as Egyptians, mostly young men 30 years and under, fearlessly defied their government and demanded change. Wael was asked, if he was hit or beaten while jailed, "Yeah, but it was not systematic...It was individual based, and it was not from the officers. It was actually from the soldiers. And I forgive them, I have to say. I forgive them, because...they were convinced that I was harming the country. These are simple people, not educated...So, you know I'm sort of like a traitor. I'm de-stabilizing the country. So when he hits me, he doesn't hit me because... he's a bad guy. He's hitting me because he thinks he's a good guy...At the end of the last day, you know, I removed my...blindfold. And I said, 'Hi,' and kissed every one of them. All of the soldiers. And, you know, it was good. I was sending them a message."

Peace, love, faith, and compassion are always the high road. Fear, war, and knee jerk reactions just lead to greater fears, death, and destruction. Fear has always been the most powerful weapon of the dark side—because they know as long as we're afraid we become powerless, and in this state, we essentially turn our back on God and the light. Succumbing to fear is like saying, "I don't believe that light is stronger than darkness, I don't have any faith in goodness, peace, or guidance from God, I prefer the dark side, doom and gloom, and so I will remain afraid and powerless." Of course this is all unconscious, but fear lowers our vibration so much, that we spiral deeper and deeper into an abyss of faulty mental programs and illusions of the mind. Fear feels terrible, and it takes a lot of energy and mental power to keep fears alive. It requires far less energy to have faith and trust, but once in the abyss, it's tremendously difficult to crawl out. It's hard to choose new ways of thinking and responding and to stop listening to those fear tapes repeating in our minds.

Eradicating fears is tremendously difficult because we've been conditioned, brain washed, and socialized to be afraid. The natural state of the soul is peace, not fear. Fear is a learned behavior, a product of our minds; we're out of balance when are lives are dominated by fears. As babies or toddlers often we're taught to be afraid of strangers, kidnappers, robbers, monsters, witches, gremlins, bullies, the bogey man, and the list increases as we grow older. I'd love to tell you I'm a fearless individual. I know about fear intellectually, in my mind, but integrating this deeply and emotionally so that we banish all irrational fears is something I'm always working on.

For example, when first writing this chapter, I was planning a weekend away, driving my thirteen-year-old car, to celebrate my father's 95th birthday party. I was driving an old car because I was afraid I couldn't afford the car payments if I purchased a new one—another irrational fear which proved totally unfounded. I had put a lot of money into repairs, had the car tuned, the oil changed, but my incessant mind kept telling me over and over I was going to break down on the highway. It brought up visions of being stranded miles from nowhere, with no cell phone, and my cat's high-pitched howling. I had myself so riddled with fears, that for over a week I couldn't sleep. My mind was relentless replaying the same message, which is why I did have the courage to make the trip. A few days before, I'd reread what I'd written about the differences between the mind and spirit, how the mind is like a broken record which will drive us to the brink of insanity playing the same messages over and over, while messages from the spirit, which are always the truth, just wisp up briefly, respecting our privacy and free will, then leaving us in peace. This helped me understand those fears were all in my mind. I made the trip and my thirteen-year-old car ran just fine.

Since I have been a fearaholic for much of my life, it wasn't hard to come up with a list of things people are afraid of. I was so afraid I'd never get this book published I didn't even tell most people I was writing it. This is also where ego comes in—if no one knew I'd be spared the shame and humiliation of having to admit it was rejected by 40 publishers. This list is by no means complete, but I'm sure we can all identify with many of these fears. As children we're afraid of our parents going out and leaving us alone. Afraid of going to school. Afraid we won't have friends at school. Afraid we won't be popular. Afraid the teacher won't like us. Afraid of not doing well in school. Afraid of failing exams. Afraid of getting our report card. As teenagers we're afraid we won't be popular, have friends, or dates. Afraid we won't make the team. If we make the team, we're afraid we'll screw up somehow and disappoint everyone. Afraid we won't be accepted in college or university. Afraid we won't get a job. Afraid our lover will find someone else. Afraid we won't get married. Afraid we'll never afford a home. Afraid we won't make the mortgage payments. When we get married we're afraid our husband or wife won't love us or may leave us. We're afraid for our children's safety. Afraid our children won't do well in school. Afraid they'll be bullied at school and picked on. Afraid our children won't get into college, university, or land a good job. Afraid they'll announce they're a lesbian or homosexual. Afraid we might be a lesbian or homosexual. Afraid our children won't get married. Afraid we've been inadequate parents or our children don't like us. Afraid of dentist or doctor's appointments. Afraid of not having enough money. Afraid our homes will be broken into. Afraid our security system will malfunction. Afraid of walking alone or at night. Afraid we'll be attacked or robbed. Afraid we won't have enough money to buy a car or make the payments. Afraid our car will be stolen. Afraid of maxing out on our credit cards. Afraid we can't afford that holiday we want. Afraid of the dark; of being alone. Afraid of being late for that important meeting. Afraid no one will show up to our party. Afraid of not having enough money to retire. Afraid of losing our home. Afraid we might lose our jobs. We hate our job, but we're afraid to quit. Afraid to start a new profession because we might fail. Afraid of success. Afraid of making mistakes and looking stupid. Afraid we're too fat or skinny, too tall, or thin. Afraid our clothes or hair are not in style. Afraid of not being popular—of people laughing or making fun of us. Afraid of nature; rain, bugs, spiders and bees. Afraid of growing old. Afraid of looking old, getting grey hair, and wrinkles. Afraid of going bald. Afraid we've missed the meaning of life. Afraid of where we'll go when we die! Afraid of the devil, dark beings, witches, warlocks, monsters, and zombies. Afraid we'll go to hell. Afraid of living and having fun. Afraid of dying!

The majority of our fears are unfounded—elaborate constructions of the mind, media, or movies. Many fears are generated by the collective consciousness. Fear is the product of a mind operating without the guiding wisdom of spirit. Our soul sees the illusions. It knows our potential and understands our life script or soul contract. Our soul operates through faith, as well as determination, vision, and insight, rather than the illusion of fear. Many of us fear we'll never be successful at something—and so we never try. But with faith, the outcome isn't even important, as long as the soul is engaged in something it's passionate about. Every genius possesses a clear focused mind—linked directly to the guidance of their soul or spirit. Spirit doesn't follow the crowd; it follows its own instincts and longings. It may know we're destined to act in films and we've scripted in many acting jobs to help us evolve. Our ego or mind doesn't have this awareness. It tries to convince us that we'll never make it in acting because ego isn't creative or flexible and it doesn't like to take risks. It may trap us in fear by saying we'll be poor and penniless if we pursue acting. It will fill us with self-doubt and convince us we don't have any talent. We have tunnel vision if we're not guided by our spirits. To the extent that we're controlled by our mind or ego we will endlessly be afraid, and these fears will endlessly overpower us.

So why do we have fear in the first place if it's so spiritually crippling? Fear in small doses is a *safety mechanism*. If we're standing in the middle of an intersection and a huge truck races around the corner, a small burst of fear motivates us to run to safely. Fear can protect us. Some dreams will alert us to unsafe situations so we won't be harmed. Fears will always arise; it's part of living. Dreams and meditation prevent us from becoming overwhelmed or controlled by these fears. They *reward us with courage and faith*, and help put things back into perspective. There is a middle road where fear does not overwhelm or control our lives. The natural state of the soul is peace, connection, and freedom—not mind-based fears that cripple and victimize. Connecting to dreams enables us to work through these fears with clarity, insight and sometimes humor.

Meditating and Dreaming to Release Fears

One has really nothing in the world to fear.
One becomes fearless when one understands the power of the soul.
Gandhi

Buddhist monks, Zen masters, sages, and saints have been showing us for thousands of years that meditation reduces fear, stress and anxiety, but it wasn't until recently that we had the scientific proof to back this up and understand how it happens. Thanks to MRI's or magnetic resonance imaging, we know the tiny area of our brain, the amygdala, (pronounced a-mig-da-la) is like fear central, firing out signals that make us freeze in our tracks when confronted with our most powerful triggers: snakes, spiders, flying, or heights. Like a tiny webcam, the amygdala is constantly scanning our environment for potential threats to our safety. The amygdala is located deep in the limbic system of the brain, an ancient brain network even found in animals. It's an almond-shaped mass within the temporal lobe of the brain, originating from the Greek word for almond *amydale*. Small but mighty, the amygdala is sometimes referred to as the "emotional brain" since it processes emotions such as fear, anger, and pleasure, along with basic instincts like appetite and sex drive. It receives information from our five senses, then like an emotional switchboard, signals the rest of the brain and the nervous system on how to respond. It also determines what memories are stored in our brains, and usually the stronger the emotional response the more likely that memory will be held. Its partner in crime is the stress hormone noradrenaline, which works on the amygdala as a long-term-memory enhancer, locking in all those frightening details. But fear, fortunately is a learned behavior, and the more we meditate the more we eliminate those fearful memories. Scientists now understand that another part of the brain, the ventromedial prefrontal cortex, or vmPFC, actually overrides or modulates the amygdala's fear responses. When we meditate, there is more activity in the ventromedial prefrontal cortex which over time may reduce our fears considerably, making this area of the brain larger and more robust. When it comes to fears, meditation is mental weight lifting—helping us replace those fears which weaken us, with feelings of greater confidence.

And if we combine meditation to alleviate our fears with dreamwork, we become spiritual heavy weights. Not to mention that working through fears in dreams can be entertaining and hilarious. Dreams help us understand that spirit has a brilliant sense of humor. When we're trying to face our fears in dreams often the situations are *exaggerated* to extremes, simply to get the point across. That boss we're afraid of at work might become a three headed monster, a fire breathing dragon, Shrek, or King Kong. A dream might show you Shrek, wearing your boss's clothes, a huge, seemingly fearful ogre who may destroy you. This same dream might also show your Shrek-like boss cuddling his babies, being pushed around by ogre buddies, or being terrified by a little garter snake, so that in the dream you become aware your boss is not as fearsome as you thought.

If we're starting something new, dreams may provide all the worst case scenarios imaginable so we can work through every fear. Perhaps you're making a major sales pitch to a group of executives, or doing an important presentation at school. You may dream that everyone in the room falls asleep, confirming your worst fears—you're terribly boring. Or they start throwing food at you, then all get up and leave in the middle of your talk, and you're left standing there feeling stupid and inadequate. Or they start laughing at you, and you realize in horror that you're still wearing your pajamas and slippers. Perhaps you've dreamed of opening a French bakery and you've put your life's savings into this endeavor. Just before it opens you have a dream that a rival bakery opens across the street. People are lined up to get into this new bakery and your shop is empty. The next night you dream that everyone who bought your pastries has thrown them in the garbage and you overhear a customer complaining they taste like cardboard. These dreams are *not* predicting the future. They're dream therapy. In dreams, we work through every imaginable fear, anything that could possibly go wrong, so that when the time comes to face whatever we fear, we're emotionally prepared. To understand how this works let's examine some actual dreams.

Bitter Regrets *dream of a 17-year-old female student.*
I was in a <u>small room </u>that reminded me of a big box, or the solitary confinement room that you see in jailhouse movies. The walls were all colored <u>dull yellow.</u> The door, which was one of the walls, was being closed by a <u>person wrapped in bandages;</u> white bandages. I could see that person's face and one hand that was closing the door. Behind that person was just darkness. I felt scared, like I didn't want to be there. I felt like crying because I was so afraid of being locked in that room alone, forever. At the end of the dream I woke all sweaty and scared. The dream only lasted for five minutes or so until I awoke suddenly.

When I woke up after this dream I felt scared and a bit confused about the contents of it. After discussing it, I realized that there was nothing really to be scared of, that this dream might have been a positive one. I am in a small room confined there for life probably because the room symbolizes my father, who is terminally ill with a malignant tumor that affects his mobility skills and perception of his left side, and the effects it has on my life (this happened a year ago). Since this happened I have had to stay home more and definitely cut my social calendar. This room is the responsibilities that hold me down and keep my priorities straight towards my dad.

The color of the room is yellow to symbolize how I felt before, when my dad was first diagnosed, considering the fact that yellow can mean faithlessness and betrayal. I didn't really know what was going on, my mom was going to the hospital every day with friends of the family and my dad was staying there for about a week or so. I never knew his problems were so serious but I should have had some idea because of the length of his stay at the hospital. Instead I put it at the back of my mind so it wouldn't bother me while I took advantage of the situation of no parents. Considering it was summer, I was sixteen and there was no school, I didn't want anything to ruin it. I realized when the end of summer drew near how selfish and stupid that was. I have cried many a time over those decisions and hate myself for putting my father on the back-burner.

The color yellow on the walls may also be foreshadowing good times to come. My dad is a very optimistic guy when it comes to his sickness, he can laugh and talk about it, and he tells us that he is going to beat this thing no matter what. So maybe the yellow walls are his courage and hopefulness; but then shouldn't they have comforted me in the dream? I don't know! Last is the bandaged person who was closing the door. At first I believed this was my father but the more I thought about it I realized it wasn't at all, it was the tumor itself. When my dad came home after surgery, the top of his head was bandaged but nothing else, but the tumor attached to his brain was totally bandaged. That's how I came to the conclusion that it was the tumor. It is closing the door because it is the one that made this difficult situation and confined me to my house more often, and made me realize like a kick in the ass, to get my priorities straight. It is also the one who confined my dad to constant frustration and medical pills. But you know what? He always finds a bright side. I love my dad.

My Son The Amazing Swimmer
by Sabrina, a workshop participant in her thirties:

I was with my husband, my daughter and my son. We went swimming at my brother-in-law's house. In this dream his pool was very large, something like an Olympic size pool. Everyone was swimming, playing and having lots of fun. I could see my daughter swimming and laughing. I was helping my son swim. Suddenly, the sky became very dark and I could feel myself begin to panic.

We looked up and saw a small airplane fly right over our heads and crash into the tree by the pool. I looked around and could not find my son. I was frantic. Everyone was jumping out of the pool and running. I jumped out and searched the area. That's when I saw him ... my son, he was swimming! And it wasn't the doggy paddle, he was swimming this amazing back stroke and he was wearing a flowered swimmer's cap. He swam so fast, made it to the end of the pool, hopped out and gave me this great big smile (he was so proud). I was so relieved and happy to see him. I brought both my kids in the house, got them dressed and then woke up!

My feelings: Ever since the birth of my son, I have had a phobia of something terrible happening to him. I have had several dreams where he has gone missing, has been hurt or someone has taken him from me. When my son is not with me, I must stop myself from imagining the worst. I believe that this dream was showing me that my son can take care of himself. I just need to let go and have faith. The best part was waking up with a sense of relief and happiness.

UNFOUNDED FEARS

I've lived my life with so many fears,
With so much stress and too many tears.
I've been so afraid of everything,
That my soul could never sing.

I've been afraid of not being cool,
And breaking someone else's rules.
I've been so afraid I would fail,
That I've kept my spirit in a jail.

I've been afraid of being fat,
And not understanding where it's at.
I feared I'd be penniless and on the street,
Because my rent I couldn't meet.

I feared there was something wrong with my brain,
That caused my life to be so insane.
I feared there was nothing lovable in me,
If someone had the chance to see.

I feared I would die in pain and alone,
Too weak or confused to pick up the phone.
I feared my whole life had been for naught,
That I'd never learned what needed to be taught.

I feared I'd led a wasted life,
So full of tears and so much strife.
But the wasted time has been these fears
That eroded my spirit every year.

All these fears have come from my mind,
These programs that do trap and blind.
They sucked the goodness out of me,
Creating fears till I just couldn't see.

They're just illusions from a faulty left brain,
That doesn't care if I go quite insane.
I've got to focus on what is true,

Or I'll be in fear and forever blue.
I've got to remember I can turn this around,
In heartfelt wisdom, peace can be found.
So every time my brain puts on a tape,
I'll switch it off and find my escape.

I'll close my eyes and clear my mind,
And think new thoughts that will be kind.
I'll throw away those crazy fears,
That haven't served me all these years.

I'll turn to God and ask to be guided,
Instead of my mind where I'm always chided.
I'll repeat simple prayers that give me hope,
Or go for a walk, when I just want to mope.
I can release all these crazy fears,
Although it may take me many years.
In the meantime I'd pray for nurture and care,
As I banish my fears, till they're no longer there.

Marina 2008

CHAPTER EIGHT
The Shadow Side of Dreams
Working Through Karma

*A whole person is one who has both walked with God and
wrestled with the devil.*

C.G Jung

Turn your face to the sun and the shadows fall behind you.

Maori Proverb

Exercise: Take a moment and reflect on the things that drive you crazy about other people. What behavior or actions really get under your skin?

RECOGNIZING OUR SHADOW OR DARK side is one of the most difficult tasks facing humanity. We're all a bit like an alcoholic who won't admit there is a problem—it's easier and less painful to believe we're nearly perfect. Rather than acknowledging our dark side, the ego or mind convinces us we don't have issues. It's constantly trying to rationalize, defend, or explain away every karmic thought, word or action. Slave owners believed they were helping people who didn't have the intelligence to support themselves. Suicide bombers believe they're holy martyrs. Soldiers in religious wars believe their actions are in the name of God. Robbers believe they're entitled to this money because they grew up in poverty. Parents who hit their children claim the Bible gives them permission. Husbands who beat their wives believe it's their right, their wife deserved it, and women must be put in line. People judge others constantly believing they're better, more qualified, or it's part of life. Celebrities have become public property, and some make a living by judging the actions of every movie star, politician, singer, model, and athlete. The mind convinces gossipers this is mere conversation. Most of the world is infected with a belief that we have this right, making gossip and judgment part of our collective shadow. We're all a mixture of karma and dharma, darkness and light, but our inability to face this darkness causes much of the world's suffering and pain. This is why one of the most powerful dream characters is the shadow.

227

If we think about our shadow outdoors in sunlight, there are several similarities to our inner shadows. Everybody has one; we all see our shadow when we're exposed to the sun or light. Although it looks like us, and has the same form, it isn't an actual representation of who we really are—only a dark semblance. It's a distortion, not an actual reflection of what we look like—we're so much more than that dark specter following us around. As a child growing up in the Catholic school system, I was taught we come to earth with a black spot or original sin on our soul, making us all sinners. This never sat right with me, because like everyone else I wanted to believe it wasn't true. But there was more truth to this theory than I've wanted to admit, because we all carry our shadow, dark spots, karma, or sins with us from lifetime to lifetime. If you were an alcoholic in your last ten lifetimes, and never worked through this shadow side of your personality, it follows you into this life and you will have a propensity to drink. Karma, patterns, habits, addictions, issues, problems, follow us like a shadow from lifetime to lifetime.

It was Swiss psychologist C.G. Jung who first coined the term shadow, that part of our personality the ego or mind tries to reject or ignore. If we're an alcoholic our ego convinces us we're merely a social drinker. If we have issues with anger and rage, ego tells us the people we verbally attacked deserved it. If we're chronically late, ego will tell us it's because we're busy and important, and we have less time than other people. If we're prone to gossip, ego tells us other people have serious character defects, but we don't. If we lie all the time to our mother, our mind tells us we need to do this to protect her. If we're always getting speeding tickets, our mind will tell us the speeding limit is way too slow. Sometimes these rationalizations are quite humorous. Jung believed the shadow can also be our *unlived life,* or the aspects of our personality we're afraid to face and explore. If we've never learned to drive, our minds might convince us the roads are too dangerous, we'd be in an accident, or friends really don't mind driving us everywhere. If we've never married and the real issue is workaholism, our mind will tell us we prefer being on our own, we don't want to lose our independence, everyone we've dated is a loser, or that a husband or wife would just take all our money. If we've never had sex, then sexuality becomes our shadow. If we've never enjoyed a glass of wine, alcohol becomes our unresolved issue or shadow. If we've worked ten years without taking a vacation, ego has convinced us we're indispensable. If we're forty and have never left our parent's home, ego convinces us our mother needs us, or we're just staying there until we save for a down payment on a home. The dreams of these people would be exploring and trying to help them work through their issues, while their mind convinces them life is great, and there's no need for change.

One of the best examples of the shadow is Robert Lewis Stevenson's *Dr. Jekyll and Mr. Hyde*. Not surprising, the plot came to the author in a dream, after he'd been racking his brains for an original idea. In the story, Dr. Jekyll, a physician, drinks a potion transforming him into a classic shadow figure, the murderer, Mr. Hyde. During the day he's a kindly, respected physician, while at night he becomes a cold-blooded killer. In the *Star Wars* series, Luke Skywalker must crawl into a cave as part of his training to become a Jedi Master. In the cave he's instructed to confront whatever he discovers. He begins fighting with another warrior, Darth Vader, who represents total evil or darkness. When Luke lifts the helmet from Darth Vader's head, he sees his own face. Before Luke can realize the full power of the force or positive energy inside him, he must accept his dark side that exists simultaneously. This is a tough lesson for Luke who realizes that Darth Vader, the prince of darkness, is his own father. We're really no different from Luke Skywalker training to become a Jedi Master; we're training to become masters of our own destiny. Just like Luke, we become empowered only when we let go of fears and face our darkness. We all must walk through the darkness of our shadows before we reach the light.In her book *A Return to Love*, Marianne Williamson tells the story of how Leonardo da Vinci found a beautiful young man to model for a portrait of Jesus Christ. Several years later he was painting another religious picture, and needed a model to represent Judas Iscariot, the disciple who betrayed Jesus. He walked through the streets of Florence until he finally found the perfect dark, seedy looking character. When Leonardo asked this man to pose for him he replied, "You don't remember me, but I know you. Years ago, I was the model for your picture of Jesus."

Many actors and actresses are gifted in personifying both light and darkness. Actor Ben Kingsley played the role of Mohandas K. Gandhi, a lawyer from India, who fought to free his country. Through peaceful or passive resistance he ended years of British oppression. Gandhi was instrumental in proving that violence begets more violence, and there are more effective ways to achieve peace. In the movie Kingsley wears only a loincloth, true to the gentle, humble character of Gandhi. Kinglsey so convincingly transformed himself into this saintly man, that you almost believed this was Gandhi, acting in a movie about himself. Several years later, Kingsley played the role of sociopathic gangster Don Logan, in the movie *Sexy Beast*. However, in this role, Kingsley was described as "the anti-Gandhi" because he was so convincing as the darkest being imaginable. Kingsley swears, yells, bullies, manipulates, robs, kills with absolutely no remorse or conscience. If you saw him in *Gandhi*, it seemed impossible this could be the same man.

Since we all possess a shadow, it's one of our most defining features as human beings. But there was a time when we didn't possess a shadow, just as there was a time when we didn't have ego issues and fears—it's all part of being human. I've never bought into Darwin's theory of evolution that we all evolved from apes, because this gives us the perfect excuse to never totally address our shadows. However, I also believe there were ape like creatures roaming the earth closely resembling humans, but for the majority of us, our ancestors came from more evolved dimensions. I believe the story of Adam and Eve is a metaphor describing a time in our existence when we were without karma or shadow. The Garden of Eden, which many consider to be heaven, was an elevated dimension, where immortals or enlightened beings resided in harmony. The snake, darkness, or serpentine energy, were the clever, chameleon-like forces that tempted us with their greed and desire for power. The birth of shadow and ego, with all its infections, was one of the major factors contributing to our fall from grace. For eons we have been struggling to find our true nature again, and to connect with the purity and balance of our original state.

We all have a shadow; it's part of the human existence. Only when we've had the courage to face our shadow and release our karma, do we rid ourselves of all our inner viruses and infections. *Our shadow is basically our karma or disconnection from spirit.* We wouldn't be here in a human body if we didn't have karma to pay back. Freedom from fear, darkness, and death, begins when we become aware of this. Freedom from our shadow is only possible when we humbly and honestly admit we have a dark side. When we reach this level of awareness our next challenge is not to beat up on ourselves. We can clean up our karma without becoming stuck or immobilized by guilt or feelings of inadequacy. Shadow work can be emotionally painful, but our goal is to move beyond this pain, fear, guilt, remorse and negativity. It's far easier facing our shadow and moving into dharma or grace.

Freud, a pessimist, saw absolutely no hope for the human race. He believed our core, which he called the *id,* was dark, impulsive and incorrigible, the part of us that was violent and selfish. He also believed there was no way we could change or rid ourselves of this darkness, although we could become slightly more civilized. He believed the fundamental task of psychoanalysis was to "struggle with the demon," but there was no getting rid of it. Freud failed to realize it is our destiny to face and release this dark side. He didn't believe in a soul, spirit, or the part of us that was essentially dharmic or good. But Jung, his contemporary, had a different and more optimistic perspective. Jung believed that *individuation* or reaching our greatest potential in life begins with confronting our dark side. He understood the root of all human evil was our "refusal to meet the shadow." Jung believed an evolved person is someone who has both walked with God and wrestled with the devil. He said, "One does not become enlightened by imagining figures of light, but by making the darkness conscious."

In his book, *Be Careful What You Pray For,* Dr. Larry Dossey explains that if we ignore the "genetic roots" of our shadow we "underestimate its power." This may be why historically humans have always harmed others, or why we simply don't understand evil in the world. Dossey says we get ourselves off this "genetic hook" by projecting our dark ways onto something external. Hence the phrase, "the devil made me do it?" In *The Road Less Traveled and Beyond,* Scott Peck explains that karmic or dark individuals are often highly intelligent. Their worst crime is blatant refusal to face their shadow because it takes great courage and fortitude to experience the emotional pain that accompanies this. He says, "Those who are evil refuse to bear the pain of guilt or to allow the shadow into consciousness and 'meet' it. Instead, they will set about—often at great effort—militantly trying to destroy the evidence of their sin or anyone who speaks of it or represents it. And in this act of destruction, their evil is committed." The atrocities in Rwanda, Congo, Iraq, Afghanistan, and Nazi Germany are poignant reminders the human shadow exists.

Projecting Our Shadow Onto Others

If we were to make a list of the people we don't like...we would find out a lot about those aspects of ourselves we can't face.
Pema Chödrön

Our shadow can often be the characteristics we loathe or judge in others. If we're unaware of our dark side, we will invariably project it onto other people, and this is usually done unconsciously. We're completely unaware of the whole insidious process. It was actually Freud who first introduced projection to our vocabulary, one of many *defense mechanisms* he believed the ego uses to deflect anxiety and falsify or distort reality. Freud believed since it would create anxiety to admit we had issues, instead we unconsciously project our thoughts, feelings and impulses onto someone else. When we attack someone, we're unconsciously attacking ourselves; when we lash out at another, it's our mirror image we're assaulting. We don't like what we see, so we pick a scapegoat, and project our karmic qualities onto them. Phrases describing this propensity to project are, "you spot it, you got it," and "everyone is a mirror of yourself." But each time we project our shadow onto someone else, we reject, deny, or fail to take responsibility for our issues. We also inflate our ego and slip deeper into illusions of the mind. So if we find ourselves constantly criticizing our neighbor for being a meddling gossip, possibly we gossip. If we secretly love watching porno movies, we'll criticize them for being crude and distasteful. If we judge our friend for eating too much junk food and putting on weight, then this may be our biggest weakness and fear. If Ethel drives us crazy because she's afraid of traveling, taking risks, enjoying life, chances are there's a major life experience we're afraid of facing. If we think most people are liars and can't be trusted, we may be prone to telling little white lies to cover ourselves. If we detest a movie star or singer because we feel they have an enormous ego, it's usually because we have ego issues ourselves. If we despise our boss at work because we believe they're a control freak, chances are we control our friends, children or family. Students who don't do their homework blame teachers rather than taking responsibility for their learning. Teachers blame students rather than admitting they may be part of the problem. Children blame parents, parents blame children. Bosses blame their employees and employees blame their bosses. Life can become a vicious, unconscious cycle of denial and pain. Lack of respect or any form of dishonoring others is one of the most universal forms of shadow and ego working together. We will respect others, only when we totally respect ourselves. When we're aware of these shadow qualities, we start listening to gossip with greater awareness. As human beings we're really hilarious. Those who judge, blame, criticize, belittle, or dishonor, are experiencing the greatest self-denial. It's easy to blame others because when we're throwing stones we don't have to face our own shadows. That's why taking responsibility for our shadow is the hardest work we'll ever do. It's important to become aware that when we judge, blame, or criticize others, often these are the shadow aspects of our personality we hate to face. When we're in denial, it's easier to project it onto the closest victim. The alternative would be to consciously listen and reflect on everything we say, also to daily meditate, pray for guidance, and journal our thoughts and dreams. Often, the more highly evolved someone is, the more acutely aware they are of their shadow. Ignoring one's shadow breeds arrogance; having the courage to face one's shadow brings heightened awareness and humility. Ignoring one's shadows breeds isolation, a one-upmanship attitude, while examining one's shadow links us with the pain, suffering, and vulnerability of others. We don't lash out at someone for being late, recognizing we've been late too. We don't gossip about stupid Jane because we realize we all do silly things. We don't judge someone for becoming overweight, because we realize we all battle different weight problems. We don't criticize Ethel for being afraid of life, because we recognize we all have fears.

If we become overly defensive or have a strong emotional reaction to something, chances are this is part of our shadow. We're usually in denial of the things that are most painful for us to admit. Consider this when you reflect on your list of things that drove you crazy about other people. Let's say you wrote, "Mary next door is a complete slut who will sleep with any man who wears pants." Perhaps Mary is sexually promiscuous and this is part of the karma she needs to work through. Possibly she needs to work on self-honor in this lifetime or creating boundaries. If we were more enlightened, we'd understand this, and Mary's sexual encounters wouldn't get under our skin. We'd also be aware that Mary's sexual escapades might bring her great pain, she may be incredibly lonely or emotionally needy, so we'd have compassion for her rather than resentment. But let's say we had two or three sexual flings we were deeply ashamed of, and this was our deep, dark, secret. Her sexuality only bothers us if there's something we wish to cover up. So rather than doing our painful homework, we project; we judge, blame, ridicule Mary, elevating our ego, and making us seem almost perfect.

Reflect on what you wrote concerning the things that drive you crazy about others. Some may hit a nerve, others may not. If we write that our teacher or boss is insensitive and a tyrant, we may not be a full blown tyrant, but this may be an aspect of our shadow to a lesser degree. We may feel Uncle Jack is cheap, a Scrooge with his money, a cold hearted miserly type of person. But this will only hit a nerve if we're cheap too at times. Maybe we're cheap when it comes to spending money on ourselves, but generous when we buy for others. If it drives us insane when people are late at work, perhaps we're always on time when it's something professional, but when it comes to family and friends we're often late, a more subtle form of disrespect. We're really saying my time is more important than yours. And in matters of spirit it's never black and white, so there will be times people do things that justifiably drive us insane and *it's not part of our shadow* at all—if we're honest with ourselves we always know.

The shadow is clever, and hides under many disguises. One of my most humbling lessons was realizing I was teaching about the shadow, but still judging people in workshops who talked sincerely about their dark sides. If someone said, "You know I really judge people at work if they don't agree with my ideas," my shadow would rear its ugly head without my conscious awareness. My ego would say, "I would *never* do that, or I would *never* think that way." Maybe not, but we all have different sides to our shadows. My ego had done a brilliant job in convincing me I must be a great teacher. The truth is we often teach, study, paint, or write about what we need to understand about ourselves. As children we were in constant denial when we did something wrong and knew this inside. We lied, had temper tantrums, or ran away. As adults we still may experience the same pain in facing our demons, we just develop slicker, more sophisticated methods of covering them up.

Facing our shadows is the most painful, yet the most liberating work we do. Our shadow traps us like frightened children in the dark. It takes courage, time, humility, and great honesty to stand up to our demons and vanish them forever. We're all like children battling our monsters, demons, fears, and insecurities—until we're fully enlightened. Feeling guilty doesn't help. Sometimes the best anecdotes we can use are humor, compassion and love. Self-love rather than self-loathing can smooth out our dark corners. Compassion feels a whole lot better than guilt, anger, bitterness or resentment. When compassion for ourselves and others overtakes the shadow, we begin crawling out of that costume of darkness, and exposing our true self to the light.

Shadow Dreams

It is a common experience that a problem difficult at night is resolved in the morning after the committee of sleep has worked on it.

John Steinbeck

Let's turn to actual dreams to understand how spirit works in exposing the shadow. In dreams if we're working through karma or shadow issues, we may encounter shadowy figures with dark, hazy, or indistinct features. Often it's hard to make out their faces for a whole variety of reasons; they may be standing in shadows, mist or darkness, their head may be down, or they may be wearing a hood or veil. But if we've done the hard work of facing our dark side and making positive changes, those shadowy figures can actually transform into more positive dream characters, and when this happens we've literally turned shadow or darkness into light. Instead of the witch, hag, demon, warlock, murderer, shadowy figure, or horrible face in the mirror, we begin interacting with positive dream figures who guide and inspire us.

Sometimes this dream figure can be our alter ego, or alternate ego or self, which can take many forms. Our alter ego can be someone you'd like to be, and it can often be the *opposite* of who we are. If we lack confidence our alter ego might be a successful rock star, politician, or activist. The alter ego can also be a trusted friend, who seems part of you. For years after I stopped teaching and felt terribly depressed and stuck, I started to dream about a high school friend, Dianne whom I respected. I felt she was the most beautiful, intelligent, kindest person I knew. In reality she was happily married to a dentist, with two children, lived in huge home, had a Master's degree, and worked as a nurse and university teacher, helping and healing people. For me, she was the epitome of someone who was successful in all ways that were important. I felt she was as beautiful inside and out, and believed she had love and success in her life, because there wasn't an unkind, judgmental, or egocentric bone in her body. I admired her tremendously and she was everything I aspired to be. But for years my dreams contained a very different friend, my shadow, or mirror, the metaphor of all the things in my life that had gone wrong, or that I hadn't achieved. In my dreams this childhood friend had moved back to a small town, that I perceived as a horrible dead end place, she had left her husband and kids, and stopped working. She had completely isolated herself, never dated, didn't work, never had fun. I watched her in these dreams, amazed at how she had chosen to just stay in bed, when she had so much going for her. In every dream I was thinking, "Why is she doing this to herself, why is she limiting herself to such a dark, awful, dead end place? What a waste of potential." This was actually the message for me, only I couldn't see it. It took about eight or nine years for my dense brain to understand she represented me—my unlived life, all the things I might be capable of. A few years later, I started dreaming about another childhood friend, also a doctor and on disability for chronic pain like me. In these dreams my friend was always in great pain and distress, mirrors to my own emotions, and I wanted to call her, believing something was terribly wrong. I think because I didn't get it for the longest time, my spirit introduced this second friend, to reinforce the meaning. The whole time, there was something terribly wrong with me—these dreams were mirroring my own frustration, pain, hopelessness, and inability to help or serve anyone. Dreams are always about *us*, attempting to give *us* guidance, insight, perspective, and balance. These dreams changed around the time I started to get much needed emotional support from weekly visits to a pain clinic. They referred me to a compassionate doctor, Brian Kirsh, who convinced me to socialize more, despite the pain. He felt isolation just made the pain worse, and if I pushed myself to get out, I'd feel better with more social support. Desperate for relief I followed his advice. For ten years I dreamt about Dianne selling herself short—in the last dream she was working as a salesperson in a tacky shop, and I couldn't understand why she would "choose such a stupid job!" In year eleven, the turnaround took place—I'm not observing Dianne, we're friends and I'm thrilled because I "admire and idolize her." Days later, in another dream, "Dianne is waiting for me—smiling—she wants to be my friend—she wants to go to Ottawa with me for the day to go shopping." Eight months later, in a dream I called "Following Dianne," she shows up at a party with a friend, and I'm trying to spend time with her. My final words are, "I feel like a groupie idolizing Dianne instead of being myself...I should have done my own thing." In a dream a year later, I'm in a mall when I bump into Dianne and "she looks even more beautiful, her hair is the same style as mine now, and she tells me she's been trying to phone me and I realize I've had the ringer off, so she couldn't get through. She also tells me she's moving." This marked a time when emotionally things were "moving" in a more positive direction for me. After 15 years, in a humorous dream Dianne's life is definitely back on track, she's with her husband again, they're living in a mansion on the ocean, and are having a party with 3,700 guests! I guess my attempt to socialize more worked. As I was putting this manuscript to bed, I was still having Dianne dreams. I think my spirit has decided Dianne is the perfect mirror for my emotional state—if she's ever back in bed feeling sorry for herself—I'll know I'm in trouble!

One of my first dream therapy clients had just gone through a nasty divorce. Her husband, a wealthy man, wanted her back, but she was much happier on her own. She began the session by explaining she'd had a series of dreams where a monster was pursuing her. When I asked her to describe this monster, or to tell me anything unique about it, she said it had this unmistakable heavy breathing, *exactly* the way her ex-husband used to breathe! This monster represented her husband; it was part of her shadow, the unresolved emotional issues around this man she needed to face. Once we understand the concept of the shadow, many dreams that have puzzled us begin to make sense. However, it's always easier to spot the shadow in someone else's dream, and more difficult to face our own dark side! Let's look at some courageous dreamers who began confronting their shadows. Most are dreams that my former high school students generously and humbly agreed to share.

Everlasting Stairs

Everlasting Stairs was written by a grade twelve student who was repeating an English course for the second time. Her dream occurred near the end of the semester, when it seemed she would again lose her credit due to several absences. She realized she was overextending herself, trying to juggle a full time job, often working until 2 a.m., while attending school full time. In the dream, she confronts a female figure who says if she doesn't slow down "she is going to die a horrible death." The words, "I needed to hug her because the woman looked exactly like me," were such an important insight for her. Near the end she admits, "Something was wrong with my life." As is often the case, she brilliantly summed up the dream's meaning while retelling it:

I was sleeping in my bed hugging my pillow tight, sweating, tossing and turning and almost crying. . It all started when I watched a scary movie. I was walking down the stairs in my house and the stairs wouldn't stop going. They were continuous. Then I started running and still I couldn't get to the end. I was screaming and screaming and no sound came out. I could see someone behind me and they were calling my name telling me "It's my turn." I stopped and asked, "What do you want from me? I don't have what you want, please leave me alone." But still no sound. I was crying nonstop, asking for help. Then I felt someone touching my shoulders. I got so scared I was petrified. I slowly turned my face and it was a young woman that slowly turned into me!

She was telling me to slow down, realize that you're trying too hard. She was talking to me about my life. Then she said if you're not going to change you're going to die a horrible death. It was like a damn horror movie. But I needed to hug her because the woman looked exactly like me and I knew that something was wrong with my life. Then she slowly faded away and the stairs stopped moving and I walked back up them. I woke up feeling dazed and confused.

"Right now I'm going through a lot with my family and money. I have been working ever since I was twelve years old. I feel like I'm being pressured a lot, not too much by other people but more by myself. I'm trying my best. I never ask my parents for money. I want them to see that I'm responsible. I think that the voices that I heard in my dream were representing myself because of all the pressure that I'm putting on myself. I'm going through a lot of stress right now. I feel like if I quit working I still couldn't ask my parents for much. Walking downstairs at the beginning of the dream is symbolic of my frustration and setbacks. Walking upstairs at the end may signify solid achievement and progress."

The Monster (dream of a grade eleven female student)

I am in a small washroom at home. The lights are on. I can't really see what I'm wearing, but it looks white. I am looking into the mirror in front of me. I see my eyes. I feel something tugging at my hair. I raise my eyes to look at my hair. I see horns sticking out of my head. But they are alive. They're grasshoppers! Large grasshoppers! They're pulling my hair. Then a flash comes before my eyes. After the flash, I notice my hair turning grey from the roots of my hair and growing until it reaches my waist. My red hair was gone, replaced by the grey. I wake up feeling confused and a bit scared.

A washroom in a dream can mean a place of cleansing, or a place of isolation. The light enables me to see myself. When looking in a mirror, I see a different side of myself. I'm wearing white clothes which represents my virginity. I can see my eyes which represent the windows to my soul. In the mirror, I see grasshopper-like horns. My different side is a monster. The flash represents a change. My hair turns grey and grows longer. My red hair represents energetic youth. When my hair turns grey, it means that my monster personality could age me and also might kill me. When waking up from my dream, I felt scared. I knew what my dream was telling me. I have a truly horrible side to my personality, which I don't want anyone to see. My monster can eventually kill me.

CHAPTER NINE
Working Through the Shadow
And Karmic Loops

In this world everything changes except good deeds and bad deeds;
these follow you as the shadows follow the body.

Ruth Benedict

Pinocchio—Changing Karmic Loops to Dharma

THAT POPULAR PHRASE "WHAT GOES AROUND COMES AROUND" helps us understand that karma doesn't just happen, it often happens in loops, and only when we grasp this essential awareness can we begin breaking through these loops that bind us like handcuffs. Ancient Taoists believed everything in existence moved in a circular fashion; going out, coming around, and returning to its starting point. Even planets, stars, galaxies, satellites move in these circular orbits. No matter where we go each day, we always come around to the same point, completing the cycle. We see this too when people retire and often move back to the place where they grew up. Taoist Derek Lin, writes, ..."The circular principals of karma come into play so that whatever energies you give to others will eventually make their way back to you. This is why it makes sense to give everyone the best and most positive in you. It is the most natural thing to do when you can see the great circle everywhere."

The classic tale of *Pinocchio* has endured because it holds these deep internal truths. Most of us can relate to this naive little puppet struggling to overcome temptations in life, because in many ways we're like Pinocchio, still in a karmic, raw, or unfinished state, until we've gone through numerous karmic loops and life experiences that provide wisdom. We become finished, no longer shadow puppets to ego and darkness, when we learn to love unselfishly as Pinocchio did. When we achieve this, like Pinocchio, we become enlightened or real. Before he could be a boy, Pinocchio needed to explore the shadow side of life. Since he is naive, without a well-developed ego or mind, he becomes victim to all sorts of illusions, trickery, and seductions only after making a conscious decision to care for his father and change his ways, that he finally becomes real.

When the story begins, Geppetto knows he's in trouble well before the puppet is finished. As soon as he carves the nose, it begins growing, and before he completes the mouth, the puppet begins laughing and mocking him. Pinocchio is so anxious to see the world, he runs to the street the second he's finished. A police officer arrests him for running around naked and causing a disturbance, and when the officer discovers that Geppetto is responsible for this naked puppet, he throws Pinocchio's father into jail.

Pinocchio returns to Geppetto's home, tired and hungry, and meets a Talking Cricket, who becomes his conscience. When the Cricket tells Pinocchio he has lived there for over a hundred years, Pinocchio insists the room is now his, and yells at him to get out. This leads to the Cricket's first piece of advice; children, who disobey their parents and leave home, won't come to any good, and they'll be sorry for it. When he asks why he doesn't learn a trade so that he can earn an honest living, Pinocchio replies the only trades he likes are eating, drinking, sleeping, and having fun.

When the Cricket informs him that he's likely to end up in the poorhouse or in prison, Pinocchio picks up a wooden mallet and hurls it at the cricket, leaving him dead against the wall. That night Pinocchio falls asleep with his feet hanging over burning embers, and wakes up to discover his feet have been burned off. Geppeto returns from prison, makes new feet for Pinocchio, and even sells his jacket to buy the puppet a spelling book so he can go to school. Pinocchio promptly sells his speller for four pennies so that he'll have the money to attend a puppet show. At the puppet show he meets the puppeteer, Fire-Eater, who wants to use Pinocchio as firewood to roast his lamb dinner. But, in a turn of fate, he takes pity on the puppet, giving him five gold coins for his poor father.

When Pinocchio meets a lame grey fox and blind alley cat, he's introduced to the karmic side of money. They tell him there's a place nearby called the Field of Miracles, where you can dig a hole, bury your gold coins, water them, sprinkle a pinch a salt, and in the morning those coins will grow into a tree that is worth five hundred times the amount you buried! The fox and cat know Pinocchio has money, so at his expense they order a huge meal that night at the inn. They escape while the puppet is sleeping, telling the innkeeper they'll meet Pinocchio in the Field of Miracles at dawn. When Pinocchio leaves the inn, he meets a tiny transparent creature, the ghost of the Talking Cricket, who warns him to go back and take the four gold pieces to his poor father,. But

Pinocchio still believes his four coins will become two thousand. The Cricket warns him not to trust people who promise to make you rich overnight. When Pinocchio leaves, he's pursued by two masked assassins (the fox and cat) who demand he hand over the money hidden in his mouth. After trying unsuccessfully to pry open his mouth, they bind his hands, slip a noose around his neck, and hang him from the branch of an oak tree, telling him they'll come back for him tomorrow. He'll be dead with his mouth open and they'll take the gold coins hidden under his tongue.

In this helpless state, Pinocchio is spotted by a beautiful girl with blue hair, who is really the good Fairy. Pinocchio is taken down from the tree, and she nurses him back to health. When Pinocchio confesses his story, she asks him where he put his gold coins. Pinocchio begins a series of lies–the coins are really in his pocket, but he says he's lost them in the forest. With each lie, his nose grows bigger, until he can't even pass through the door—instant karma. Taking pity on the crying puppet, the good fairy claps her hands and a thousand woodpeckers work on his nose, in minutes bringing it back to its original size. When Pinocchio asks about his father, he's told Geppetto will be there by nightfall. Overjoyed, Pinocchio asks if he can meet his father. The Fairy agrees and Pinocchio sets off, but on the way, he meets the fox and cat again, who convince the gullible puppet to bury his coins in the Field of Miracles. They walk for half a day before coming to a town called Catchafool, then stop in an isolated field. Here Pinocchio buries his coins, then goes back to Catchafool where he's arrested and thrown in prison. After four months the puppet is let out of prison, only to be captured again by a peasant who owns a poultry yard. This peasant has just lost his watchdog, so decides to use the puppet in the dog's place. The man slips a collar covered with brass spikes around his neck, and attaches a long chain to the collar. Cold, hungry, and afraid, Pinocchio wails that it served him right. But when Pinocchio tells his owner about four thieves who are stealing eggs, the man is so grateful, he sets the boy free. Pinocchio immediately runs to the house of the beautiful little girl, only to find the home is no longer there; instead he finds a small marble slab with the words, *"here lies the little girl with the blue hair dead from grief for having been abandoned by her little brother Pinocchio."* Overcome with emotion he cries out, little Fairy, why didn't I die instead of you? While he's crying, a pigeon flies down and informs Pinocchio that he left Geppetto on the seashore three days ago. Geppetto had spent four months looking for his son, and fearing he'd gone to the New World, he built a boat to cross the ocean. The pigeon takes Pinocchio on his back and they journey to the place where Geppetto was last seen.

242 | *The Genius of Spirit*

Pinocchio jumps into the sea and swims frantically to find his father, ending up at the island of Busy Bees. Here he's reunited with the little girl who has now magically become a woman, old enough to be his mother. Pinocchio blurts out his overwhelming grief. The good fairy assures him she knows, and that's why he's been forgiven. The sincerity of his sorrow helped her realize he had a good heart and she has decided to be his mother. Pinocchio promises he'll go back to school. For the first time the puppet becomes a model student. He keeps his promise, and at final exams earns the honor of being the best student in the school. As a reward, the good Fairy announces that the next day he will no longer be a wooden puppet; he will receive his wish and become a real boy.

Pinocchio's only problem is that he still has schoolmates who are troublemakers. That night he meets one of his favorite schoolmates, Romeo, nicknamed Candlewick, one of the most roguish boys in the school. Candlewick says he's going to live in a beautiful, enchanted place, Funland, with no school, teachers, books, or studying. He tells Pinocchio there is no school on Thursday, and every week is made up of six Thursdays and a Sunday. This is just too irresistible for the puppet. He follows Candlewick to a place where a strange wagon is picking up boys destined for Funland. His first clue should have been that the wagon is pulled by donkeys wearing white leather boots. Funland is the home of boys aged eight to fourteen, and just as Romeo promised, there is laughter, games, and fun. He spends five carefree months here, until one morning he wakes up with donkey ears. Pinocchio has jackass fever, and in a few hours will become a donkey. He finds out it is written in the "Decrees of Wisdom" that lazy boys who hate books, schools, and teachers, and who spend their days selfishly having fun, end up turning into little jackasses.

Now Pinocchio is bought by a circus manager who tries to teach him how to dance and jump through hoops. But his circus career is short lived because during one show his hind legs are caught in a hoop and he falls. When the veterinarian determines that he'll be lame for life, the circus manager has him taken to the market to be sold. Pinocchio is bought by a man who notices he has a tough hide–he plans to use his hide to make a drum. He puts a stone around the donkey's neck, ties his legs to a rope, and throws him into the sea. Fifty minutes later, he's sure the donkey is drowned, but instead pulls up a wriggling puppet. The man wants to take Pinocchio back to the market to sell him as kindling wood, but the puppet escapes and swims out to sea.

At sea, he's swallowed by a sea monster. At first, he's in shock because all around him it's, total darkness, This whale, nicknamed "the Attila of Fish and Fishermen" is so enormous; his body is over a mile long. Far away is a light–a small table laid for a meal, a burning candle stuck in a green glass bottle, and an old white haired man chewing on some fish—Gepetto.

Pinocchio is delirious with joy at finding his father. He throws his arms around Gepetto's neck and cries, telling his father that he will never, ever leave him again! Realizing this whale is old, suffers from asthma, heart palpitations, and sleeps with his mouth open, Pinocchio devises a clever escape plan. While the fish is asleep, he leads Gepetto to its mouth, and they jump into the ocean. Pinocchio swims with his father on his back, until a large tuna takes Pinocchio and his father safely to shore. Back on land, the first creatures they meet are the same cat and fox who had tricked Pinocchio out of his gold coins. However, they look quite different—the effects of karma. The cat is blind, and the fox is old, mangy, completely paralyzed on one side, and missing his tail. When they ask Pinocchio for money, he repeats the proverb; "He who steals his neighbor's cloak is bound to die without a shirt." They walk until they come to a straw hut and meet the Talking Cricket who reminds Pinocchio he threw a mallet at him. But the cricket, ready to forgive, says he'll have pity. He wanted to remind him of his nasty actions to teach him that we must be kind to everybody, if we want to be repaid with equal kindness.

This hut was given to the Talking Cricket yesterday as a gift by a blue-haired Goat. When Pinocchio asks for a glass of milk, the Cricket explains he must earn his keep by turning a windlass to draw water for watering vegetables. Until now, a donkey has been doing the job, but the poor thing was near death. Pinocchio goes out to inspect this donkey and discovers his old buddy, Candlewick. In horror, he watches as Candlewick utters his last breath. This is the turning point, where Pinocchio's life goes from karmic to dharmic. He begins getting up before dawn to turn the windlass and earn the glass of milk his father needs to restore his health. In his spare time he weaves baskets and sells them. He builds a cart, and uses it to take his father outside for fresh air. During the evening he practices reading and writing. Pinocchio is so diligent he manages to save forty pennies to buy new clothes. But on the way to market he learns from a Snail that the Blue Fairy is in hospital, and she is so poor, she can't afford a loaf of bread. Pinocchio gives the Snail all of his money and asks him to give it to the Blue Fairy. That night, instead of working until ten o'clock making baskets, Pinocchio stays up until midnight. When he goes to sleep he dreams of the Fairy who kisses him and says, you did well Pinocchio! Because you had a kind heart, you are forgiven for all your mischief. Any boy who takes care of his parents when they are sick and in need deserves praise and love. In the future, you will be happy.

In the morning Pinocchio is transformed into a real boy. Putting his hands in his pockets, he finds an ivory money-case which tells him that the Fairy has returned the forty pennies . Instead there are forty gold pieces. Pinocchio, ecstatic , exclaims how foolish he was when he was a puppet, and how glad he is to finally be a real boy.

Transforming from Puppets to Being Real

The way to Heaven is fraught with demons on the side of the road, just as the fairy tale castle is surrounded by dragons.

Marianne Williamson

The story of Pinocchio helps us see the importance of experiencing life. At first Pinocchio is self-absorbed, naive, and easily manipulated. He hasn't developed the capacity to love in an unselfish way. It never occurs to him to think of his father, or to act with consideration or kindness. Even when he's taken in by the good Fairy and given a second chance at school, he chooses Funland or the Island of Illusi on. In contrast, Gepetto never traps, exploits, or punishes his boy. His love for Pinocchio is unselfish and unwavering—a parallel to our Creator or God. The little girl with the blue hair, the good Fairy who becomes his mother, is symbolic of our true Mother, Gaia, or Mother Earth, a constant, nurturing force. During most of the story, Pinocchio is intent on exploring the world and is easily seduced, literally becoming a puppet to darkness. His transformation into a donkey or jackass is a reflection of the asinine things we do, often spending our days in the pursuit of pleasure rather than giving back to humanity or living dharmically. When he's bought by the circus manager and expected to jump through hoops to entertain the audience, this is much the same as the hoops we jump through in life to please employers, relatives, and friends. These hoops or karmic cycles will just keep repeating until we wake up. Recurring loops are his encounters with the cat and fox who keep reappearing until he has the sense to understand their trickery. When Pinocchio, as a donkey, is thrown into the sea, and emerges as a puppet, he's once again transformed or trapped in an endless loop of karma. Being devoured by the whale, symbolizes being completely swallowed or trapped by darkness. Inside the whale, he sees a faraway light, Gepetto—this spark of light has the power to transform everything. Seeing the light doesn't always mean an angel sweeps into our homes, transforming us—often it's the little things, that proverbial last straw, flicking a switch in our brains and enabling us to follow a wiser course.

Pinocchio's salvation was found through meeting and accepting his father or creator.

Like Pinocchio, we come to earth to understand how to navigate through darkness without becoming its victim. Only when we've gained enough awareness to see through the illusions, seductions, and traps, do we earn the spiritual merit to return home. Geppetto could have kept his puppet locked in the house. But Geppetto loved his creation so much he allowed the boy to run free. Our Creator respects humanity so much we're given free will. We're not puppets and God is not a puppet master. Like Gepetto, God never wishes to control us. He knows we will explore and have many experiences before we choose the light. It is God's wish that we choose him freely of our own accord, just as Pinocchio did. We are never forced, coerced, or manipulated to choose God; that is how darkness works, not light. On earth, the only way we can become real or self-realized is to experience life so that we recognize characters like the Cat, Fox, and Candlewick, as opportunists rather than true friends. If we weren't allowed to experience the seedy side of life, we'd always wonder what it was like, if it was better, and why our father wouldn't let us go there. Like Pinocchio we may experiment with insincere friends, selfishness, gambling, power, greed, and money, until we understand these things lock us in an endless web of illusion, suffering, and despair. Until we consciously choose the light, we will be tricked, manipulated, and seduced just like Pinocchio was. Every time Pinocchio told a lie his nose would grow. Every time we choose darkness, our karma grows. Awareness turns everything around. When Pinocchio realizes his father had given up his life, and ended up in the belly of a whale—service and love transform him into a real boy. We're all puppets to darkness, until we say yes to our spiritual Father and leave the seductions and trickery behind.

Groundhog Day Endless Loops of Karma

When action grows unprofitable, gather information; when information grows unprofitable, sleep

Ursula K. LeGuin

The movie *Groundhog Day* is a hilarious yet brilliant example of how we repeat the same patterns or karmic loops until we finally wake up or get it. In the movie, Bill Murray plays TV weatherman Phil Connors, whose ego is so enormous, it can barely be contained in

Punxsutawney, Pennsylvania, where he's sent to cover famed groundhog, Punxsutawney Phil, and the annual Groundhog Day festivities. Believing he is superior, Phil calls the people of Punxsutawney "hicks." Ironically he has the same name as that famous rodent, which he refers to as the forecasting "rat."

After filming the Groundhog Day celebrations, a winter storm makes it impossible to return to the television station. Phil is forced to stay another evening in Punxsutawney with those small town "hicks" he despises. He wakes up the next morning at the same time, 6 a.m., to *I've Got You Babe* by Sonny and Cher, the same song as yesterday, with the exact same banter from the radio announcers. It's Groundhog Day all over again, and Phil is caught in an endless time loop—his worst nightmare.

When Phil realizes it's impossible to escape a perpetual Groundhog Day, he could have dissolved his ego immediately, and become completely dharmic, but this rarely happens—it's virtually impossible for any human being. We usually walk painfully through every element of our shadow before we wake up, so Phil lives out every aspect of his dark side. The second day he goes to a bar, steals a car, careens recklessly around town, and is chased by a police car. He drives on the railway tracks and narrowly misses being hit by a train. Phil is arrested, put in jail, but wakes up the next morning to *I've Got You Babe.* Believing he can literally get away with murder, Phil's shadow grows even darker. Over the next three days he assaults people, eats copious amounts of pastries, smokes, drinks, seduces every woman in town, and robs a security truck. He tries to seduce his producer, Rita, played by Andie McDowell, but is never successful, because Rita can't tolerate his enormous ego. Phil is desperate to leave this dismal loop of groundhog madness. He tries everything to commit suicide; electrocuting himself in the bathtub, jumping in front of a truck, and leaping from a building. Each morning he wakes up at precisely 6 a.m to *I've Got You Babe.* When Phil realizes this could be a nightmarish eternity something clicks in his brain.

He's ready for something different, so makes a conscious decision to change—he begins cleaning up his karma and enacting dharma. Phil gives money to the man he sees each day begging on the street corner. He begins reading and studying poetry, takes piano lessons, makes ice sculptures of angels, tried repeatedly to save a dying man, saves a young boy falling from a tree, changes a flat tire for three elderly women, saves a choking man in a restaurant, and entertains the townsfolk every night by playing the piano. Eventually he gains Rita's admiration, and she agrees to spend the night with him. This act of love transforms everything. When he wakes up the next morning *I've Got You Babe* isn't playing; it's a new day. Phil is freed from the endless karmic loop of Groundhog madness and his nightmare ends. Phil's dharmic ways and love for Rita makes the transformation possible

In dream workshops I often use the movie *Groundhog Day* as a humorous example. Thankfully Mimi, an insightful participant in one of my first workshops, agreed to share her story of a groundhog that mysteriously appeared at the daycare center where she worked.

Groundhog Story

I am open to the guidance of synchronicity, and do not
let expectations hinder my path.

Dalai Lama

"One morning I went to work very early, 7:15 a.m., and was a bit depressed. A friend I had worked with for a couple of years had left, and my spirits were down. I wondered why she was able to leave, and why I was still in the same location. I had worked with children for twenty-five years, and loved working with kids, and know they have been the source of much growth for me. My spiritual learning has truly been working with children. But at times you get low and wonder why you're in the same place, when someone else has moved on.

Once she said, "Thank you. I came here broken, and to meet you, and be healed."

We knew we were together for a reason, and I knew her time with me would be short. She just needed to be healed, and had to move on.

That morning my co-worker Karen was there and said, "Oh my it's Friday—yea!"

I responded, "It's Friday. So what it's Friday, another Friday, another weekend, week, month, year, season, it just keeps repeating itself all over again and we're still here."

She looked at me as if to say, "Oh my goodness, this is too heavy for first thing in the morning."

I looked at her and said, "Have you ever seen the groundhog movie with Bill Murray?"

She said no, and within a two minute span I capsulized the whole story. I knew it was spirit talking through me because it couldn't have been me so early in the morning!

I explained, "You know it's about this man who gets stuck in a twenty-four-hour period. He realizes that his day keeps repeating and repeating. He also realizes there is a great deal of freedom within that repetition, because there's no consequences. So he experiences the dark side of himself. He goes through the things he would normally not do because of consequences in life. However, when he realizes there are no consequences he laughs at it. Eventually this became very boring. He was the only one who could really change. He understands for the first time he can be of service to these people because he knew what was going to happen. Ultimately, he realizes his true joy is in loving and being of service to the people around him. When he understands this, his day changes, and he was able to go on to the next day.'

When I told her this story, she just looked at me and probably thought, "Okay Mimi."

I suggested, "Well you really should rent the video you know."

She said okay in a tone of voice that made me realize I had been too heavy for her. We talk about our faith all the time because we both have great faith, but I tend to go a little further, and unintentionally make her uncomfortable.

I said, "Don't you realize this is God's plan? We just keep on repeating the same things over and over again in our lives until we finally get it, until we finally get it right."

She looked at me as if to say, "Oh God!"

We left it, and I realized I was too heavy *again*. We went to our playrooms with the kids. She went on a break about 9:30 and came running back screaming, "Mimi, Mimi, you've got to come out here you won't believe it!"

Literally panicked she said, "There's a groundhog at our front door!"

I went and sure enough, there's this *huge* groundhog, and I'd never seen a groundhog in my life. When I got there he was in the driveway, and that's the first and last time I've ever seen a groundhog. I had been working at that daycare for twelve years, and it was the only time a groundhog appeared. She was shaking and couldn't talk about it. I just looked up and said, "Thank you God, you were listening to me and I guess I'm on the right track."

After this experience I thought, "Whatever you want God. Whatever you want, if I can be of service that's fine. I'll be here."

My Groundhog Loops

I asked for power that I might have the praise of men,
I was given weakness, that I might feel the need of God.
Prayer of an Unknown Solider

Groundhog Day has always been one of my favorite movies, because of its humor and deep insights. The years 2003 to 2006 were particularly difficult for me. Since childhood I'd experienced migraines, but they always went away—eventually. Sometimes they lasted weeks or months, but I could always count on that blessed relief from pain. But during these three years the pain was relentless, every single day, something even the strongest drugs couldn't remedy. I felt so incredibly stuck in a continuous loop of pain, just like Bill Murray in *Groundhog Day*. At that time I wasn't living in the best environment for a migraine sufferer: the top floor of the house I was renting was noisy, haunted, over a hundred years old, and I suspected there may be problems with mold or the insulation. I had lived in this same house for 22 years, and was really stuck in a loop of no change. But I was too sick, tired, and depleted to look for a new place. I survived day by day—until groundhogs started appearing in a two-week span—four of these little critters. The first groundhog appeared one June morning as I opened the door to go outside which was surprising since I'd never see a groundhog before in the backyard. There he was, calming sitting in the middle of the driveway, as if this was perfectly normal. And he didn't move when he saw me—just stood there staring me down.

A few days later, I visited a garden center, a place where I'd been many times before. This particular garden center was at a temporary summer site in front of a grocery store, on a major street with heavy traffic, just off an eight lane highway in Toronto, and miles away from any park, ravine, or forest. As I was looking at the plants, a groundhog meandered across the parking lot, and came directly up to me. It felt like he wanted to talk. The next week at the same garden center, the same thing happened. This time he came so close it really spooked me. I'd been there at least 10 times before because I love looking at plants, and there was never a groundhog.

That same week I was riding my bike on a path that started in downtown Brampton and made its way north into the Caledon Hills. This was a scenic path winding along a creek that I'd cycled hundreds of times. Not far from home, a huge groundhog ran right in front of me. It seemed to come from nowhere and there was absolutely no way I could swerve to avoid it. Then something truly bizarre happened. I actually ran right over the top of this groundhog's back as it crossed the path, and I don't know how, but I didn't fall off my bike. I screamed this guttural sound I'd never made before, like, "Urrrgggghhh" because I was so freaked out from running over a groundhog. I've fallen off my bike many, many times before, when I've seen snakes and dogs, or hit gravel I couldn't navigate. This wasn't a mountain bike I was riding, and I'm not exactly the most balanced cyclist. Miraculously, I didn't fall, but realized this poor groundhog was probably injured or in shock. I stopped, and turned around to see if it was okay, but my furry friend had vanished! After this fourth groundhog encounter, or "coincidence," I realized I really must be in an incredible loop of karma. The next summer I did muster up the courage to move, and it did break that three year cycle of endless migraines. I'll always be grateful to my furry friends, and to the humorous hand of spirit.

Thomas Harvey's Karmic Loop

If God is at the front door, the Devil will be at the back door.
                                                                    C.G. Jung

Let's go back to Thomas Harvey, that infamous doctor who snatched Einstein's brain, believing he'd find the true equation for genius. It would be easy to mercilessly judge Harvey—to call him a crook, thief, or immoral opportunist. But we're all in karmic loops and it's counterproductive to judge. However, we can understand a great deal from objectively examining someone's karmic patterns. The book, *Driving Mr. Albert*, by Michael Paterniti, is a humorous account of Harvey's trip across the United States, a quest to return the brain he had stolen to Einstein's granddaughter, Evelyn Einstein. Paterniti says, "Harvey seems to travel through life with far fewer regrets. If he's a sinner, he doesn't seem to know it yet. If he's a car, then he's the one doing fifty-five in the right-hand lane of the highway, forgetfully, unapologetically, flashing a blinker he long ago acted on—and he's been on this highway for over forty years..." Regardless of how much we're in denial, karma follows us like a ball and chain around our necks. Life breaks down, shatters, disintegrates—we become karmic fugitives on the run. No legal action was ever brought against Harvey; there simply wasn't a protocol in the courts for stolen brains. Still, there is a higher court no one escapes, the spiritual court of justice or karma. It follows us for eternity, and if we get away with murder in this lifetime, we're brought to spiritual court in the next—or the next. Justice and fairness always prevails.

The opportunity for international fame must have totally seduced Harvey—his ego or left brain won out over his heart, because his heart surely would have told him that stealing a dead man's brain was a violation of human dignity. But the ego is terribly persuasive, and a master at justifying its own rules. He was not a morally reprehensible man, just the opposite. Harvey's former partner in general practice, Patrick McAlinney, described him as "a cautious, conservative physician who was nothing but a gentleman." Fellow Princeton doctor, Lewis Fisherman, said, "He is a scholarly man, the cream of physicians, honest and sincere." When he performed the autopsy on Einstein, Harvey was a Yale-educated scholar, committed Quaker, a pacifist, chief pathologist at prestigious Princeton Hospital in New Jersey, a handsome forty-two-year-old man with a beautiful wife and two boys.

Harvey was eventually fired from his job for not handing the brain over to hospital authorities; he had been keeping this prized possession, his holy grail of brains, at home. He did give the occasional interview from 1956 to 1988, always reporting the same thing—he was about "a year from finishing study on the specimen." He believed his personal mission was to determine if this brain contained physical evidence of Einstein's genius. He sent more than a thousand slides or pieces of the brain to experts around the world, believing if he wasn't able to find something conclusive, someone else might—justifying his theft in the name of science. This quest continued into his eighties when he drove to Canada, and gave Professor Sandra Witelson about one-fifth of Einstein's brain. Although her study carries the greatest credibility, most have been mere speculations yielding no definitive results, perhaps confirming his worst suspicions, that Einstein's brain was simply a physical specimen. Without the spirit of a living, breathing man to animate it, and give it life, personality, humor and intelligence, it was no different from any other brain.

Harvey's first marriage collapsed shortly after Einstein's death, culminating in an affair with a pretty, blond nurse. He married and divorced three times, first to Ellouise, who gave him three sons, then Alison, from Australia, and finally Raye, who walked out on him in 1982, leaving Harvey a lonely old man. On the career front, there were many changes. After being dismissed from Princeton Hospital, Harvey held jobs in mental institutions and research facilities. He tried to start a nursing home, moved west setting up a family practice, provided medical services at Leavenworth Prison, then in his seventies, he failed the Kansas State medical exam, ending his career as a doctor. When his medical license was revoked, he found employment with E & E Display Group, a plastics factory in Lawrence, Kansas, where he worked his way up from assembler, to extruder's apprentice, then to extruder operator, manning the machine that produced angled plastic shelving used to display Hallmark greeting cards. He made $8.00 an hour, and no one at the factory knew of his illustrious past.

In his eighties, he came full circle, moving back to Princeton, New Jersey, where he lived in the basement of his girlfriend's house. When writer Michael Paterniti found Harvey living in Princeton, he offered to drive him across the United States to Berkley, California. Harvey had expressed a desire to meet Einstein's granddaughter, Evelyn, and Paterniti assumed that after forty years, he wanted to do the decent thing—return the brain to one of Einstein's few living relatives. *Driving Mr. Albert*, recounts this hilarious road trip in a Buick Skylark with Einstein's brain floating in a Tupperware container in the trunk. Eventually, they met Evelyn Einstein, who wasn't at all interested in acquiring her famous grandfather's brain. In fact, she considered Harvey's possession of the brain downright creepy. Her only interest was to answer one burning question. Evelyn was the adopted daughter of Einstein's oldest son, Hans Albert. She was born after Einstein's second wife had died, at a time when he had several intimate relationships with women. Rumors had circulated that Evelyn was the result of one of Einstein's many romances. She hoped the DNA from Einstein's brain, would give her answers, but the way Harvey had embalmed the brain made it impossible to extract DNA samples.

In 1998, Harvey completed his karmic loop—at eighty-six, he delivered what remained of Einstein's brain to Dr. Elliot Krauss, the pathologist at Princeton University who had taken his old job. On the 50th anniversary of Einstein's death, 93-year-old Harvey gave interviews on the amazing history and travels of the brain. He lived to be 95—dying at the University Medical Center in Princeton in 2007, the same city where 52 years earlier he'd performed the autopsy on Einstein. Perhaps this gave him time to reflect, understand how his life was karmically altered by that one fateful day, and finally released that karmic loop, earning dharmic redemption and peace of mind.

We're All in Karmic Loops

*It's not true that life is one damm thing after another—
it's one damm thing over and over.*
Edna St. Vincent Millay

Most of us are trapped in our own karmic loops just like Pinocchio, Phil Connors, and Thomas Harvey. Being caught in these loops is frustrating and painful, and the problem is compounded because we're often not aware we're even in them. When something karmic happens we might believe we're a victim, life isn't fair, we've had bad luck, we blame somebody or something, or we fail to realize we're stuck in the same cycle. We also have multiple loops happening at the same time. We may get another speeding ticket, receive another notification our rent check has bounced, and have a major fight with a parent, all in the same day. Until we gain awareness, realizing we're not a victim, instead, we're actually making all this happen, the karmic cycle just keeps repeating.

If I'm really honest about my life, sadly, I could show you how it's been a series of one karmic loop after another. I start one horrible cycle, become aware, attempt to work through the issues, then start a whole new loop, or go back to a previous loop, because I've fallen into that same all too familiar pattern again. The number eight, like all numbers, represents many things, but one of its symbolic meanings is the loop of karma. If you trace your finger around the number eight, it's an endless loop that repeats, with no beginning or ending. Eight can symbolize karma, and it can be quite an unlucky number, but it can also be fortuitous, symbolizing dharma—the state where you've worked through all of your karma, and are in a harmonious and smooth flow. With karma you're riding the loop in an old sputtering car that starts and stops, sputters, quits, then starts again. When our lives are dharmic you're riding in a new efficient car, no snags or speed bumps, just one flowing rhythm, like a piece of harmonious music.

If we examine local and world news, karmic loops abound. One example close to where I live was a February 18, 2008, train derailment near Burlington, Ontario, where a freight train skidded off the tracks derailing 19 cars. Four years later, almost to the day, on February 26, 2012, in the exact same block of tracks in Burlington, a train derailed killing three and injuring 46. Looking at global patterns, over-consumption, and pollution which has directly led to global warming, are the most obvious loops. The increasing trend of the rich getting richer while the poor get poorer is a catastrophic karmic loop, because it is those disadvantaged teenagers and young men, uneducated, unemployed, and angry who are willing to resort to war. And the senseless pursuit of war becomes a larger karmic loop. Each time a war occurs, it's not just a loop for the countries involved, it's a loop for humanity. We all know that violence begets violence. We cannot force anyone to be peaceful; it has to come from inside. There has to be an internal desire to end war. Physical wars will only stop when globally we reduce greed and poverty, stop the wars within, and become peaceful. If we blame, point our fingers, and accuse world leaders of being evil or wrong, we perpetuate the cycle. Instead, we need to look inside and examine the ways we are not at peace ourselves. Do we harbor jealousies or rivalry? Are we prone to anger? Do we battle and fight with family members, friends, or coworkers? Only when everyone individually addresses and corrects their own greed, anger, aggression, and hostility, will we begin to end karmic problems, fighting and wars on earth. If we were all peaceful beings without egos and judgment, who respected and had compassion for everyone, wars would not exist. When we become aware of these loops and how we can unravel them, we have the potential to create a different world.

Living Frees Us From the Loops

> *There are times when even to live is an act of bravery.*
> Seneca (4BCE–65CE) Rome

> *God does not ask you to be a Trappist monk or a hermit.*
> *He wills that you sanctify the world and your everyday life.*
> St. Vincent Pallotti

It takes incredible courage and perseverance to work through karmic loops. I once had the romantic notion that if I'd been a priest, monk, or nun, I would be free of karma, until a wise teacher explained the best way to unravel these loops is simply to live each day ethically and honorably. He said it's possible to do this without ever setting foot in a church or religious institution. We release these loops by praying or speaking daily to God, meditating daily, always being true to ourselves, honoring ourselves, honoring God, letting nothing sway us, and eventually, we reach dharma. Some people spend inordinate amounts of money, doing trendy things to find God: journeys to sacred countries or sites, sweat lodges, vision quests, or costly workshops with famous speakers. There is nothing inherently wrong with any of this, but for some, the impressive, glamorous stuff is done for the wrong reasons—to make them feel good, spiritual, or religious. All these spiritual and religious activities can become very self-absorbing. It can prevent people from facing their core issues and doing the difficult day to day work of cleaning up their karma, and having compassion for family, friends and community. Someone may spend their life going to work every day to support their children, or taking care of a sick, aging mother, or looking after a disabled child, while still honoring themselves, and maintaining a daily connection to spirit. These humble people just may self-realize in this lifetime. It's not about glamour. Often the biggest breakthroughs, those moments of clarity, ecstasy, and peace come amidst the seeming drudgery of life. When we're living entangled in karmic loops, life is frustrating, depressing, and painful. But if we connect to God each day through dreams, prayer, or meditation, we begin to get insights on how to unravel those loops. Slowly, as each loop is released, we feel lighter, until one day we wake up and realize those loops of karma just aren't happening any more.

The 2001 movie *Samsara* shows that living in a simple, honorable fashion, can help us work through karma even faster than becoming a priest or monk. *Samsara* is Sankrit for wheel of life, that endless repetitive cycle of birth and death before we reach liberation, enlightenment or *moksha*. The movie begins with a group of Buddhist monks trekking up a mountain to a distant hermitage to retrieve a young monk, Tashi, who has been in a deep meditative state for three years, three months, three weeks, and three days. After Tashi comes out of his trance, it takes weeks before he can walk, feed himself, eat, or even talk. When he has recovered, Tashi is honored in a special ceremony, and one would think this man was almost enlightened, a god with superhuman abilities, able to sustain himself for three years without talking or eating. Tashi has been a monk since he was five years old.

A short time later, he's sent to a neighboring village to take part in a harvest blessing ceremony. Tashi who has had limited exposure to the world, is completely captivated by a farmer's beautiful daughter, Pema, who shares this attraction. He returns to the monastery, and discovers his thoughts are no longer spiritual in nature—they have become sexual. Rationalizing that even Buddha was married, had a child, and lived in the secular world for the first 29 years of his life, Tashi leaves the monastery in the middle of the night without saying good-bye. When he arrives in Pema's village without his monk's attire, her father believes he's a transient worker and employs the young monk as a laborer.

When Pema sees Tashi again, her recognition is instantaneous, and they spent a passionate evening together. Her parents discover this, a great disgrace to their family, since Pema's marriage has been arranged to another villager, Jamayang. Unable to make a choice, Pema suggests that a traveling astrologer should decide on her true husband. Luckily for Tashi, the astrologer feels they have already consummated their love, and should marry immediately. Tashi and Pema are married, and have a son they call Karma–aptly named! But the life of a husband, worker, and father, proves overwhelming for Tashi, who has lived a sheltered monastic life, where decisions were made for him, and the necessities of life were provided. A short time later, someone sets fire to their fields, and when half of their crops are destroyed Tashi is outraged. Believing this is the work of Dawa, a powerful businessman, he storms into his warehouse, starts breaking everything in the office, gets in a fight, and only survives because Pema and her father intervene. Another karmic loop begins to unfold, as Tashi is attracted to Sejata, a beautiful migrant worker who helps with the grain harvest each year. When Pema has gone to town, and Sejata knocks at the door to collect her salary, Tashi can't contain his lust any longer. Their acrobatic sex, using a sari as a trapeze, is interrupted with Pema's unexpected return.

A short time later, one of Tashi's monastery friends delivers the dying words from Apo, who was Tashi's mentor. Apo asks what is more important, satisfying one thousand desires, or conquering just one. Consumed by guilt Tashi, repeats the same karmic act, leaving in the middle of the night without saying good-bye. Before returning to the monastery he spends time by the river shaving his long hair, and changing back into his monk's robes. But when he arrives at the monastery gates, his wife Pema is waiting for him.

She talks of Yashodhara, who was married to Siddhartha before he became the Buddha. In tears, Pema explains that Yashodhara loved him dearly, but he left his wife and son without saying good-bye. Yashodhara had shown compassion for the sick and dying long before Siddhartha was aware of the suffering outside his palace gates. Pema suggests that might have owed his enlightenment to her. She tells him that if his thoughts regarding enlightenment were of the same intensity, love, and passion he had shown towards her, he might become a Buddha in this lifetime. Despite Tashi's years in the monastery, it's obvious his wife possesses greater wisdom. She lives humbly and honestly, isn't prone to bursts of anger, is faithful to her husband, can honestly express her emotions, and her love for Tashi is pure and unconditional.

Love is often that invisible key towards enlightenment. We free ourselves from endless karmic loops through love and service to others, by experiencing life, not running from it. We don't need to join a monastery, become a nun, priest, rabbi, or guru, give away all our money, or meditate in a cave for years to understand and banish those karmic loops. Experiencing life, loving sincerely, and respecting one another, are powerful forces that set us free.

Old High School

It's possible to leave the karmic loops behind—in fact the whole point of life is to evolve beyond karmic loops into dharmic ones. We've all had our own versions of dharmic loops; a teacher who encouraged and inspired us that we bump into later in life, an old high school flame we meet years later and begin a meaningful relationship with, a childhood friend we truly loved who resurfaces years later when we need support after losing a parent, a former neighbor who offers you a job, or perhaps returning to a city or country where you've lived before and realizing it was the best place for you. Life is a complex, many faceted web of karmic and dharmic loops, running simultaneously, just like multiple roads and highways. As I was writing this book, and working to undo my own karmic patterns, I had this dream, teaching me that life can turn around. There was no hidden or cryptic meaning; it was simply giving me information, validating, perhaps helping me finish this chapter. Since I was a former teacher my spirit used the backdrop of a new secondary school.

I'm in a brand new high school that's just been built. It's beautiful, modern and I'm walking the halls with some young people. While I'm there, I meet Rita and Vern Adams, my former elementary school principal and her husband, and we embrace. Rita was an extremely positive role model for me, definitely a dharmic figure in my life. This was the site of their first high school and Vern is there again taking out an old history book. We talk for a long time and try to catch up.

While I'm there I bump into every group of people I've ever known. Among them are Sheri Bothwell and friends from my childhood, Joanne Crate and Smiths Falls friends from high school, and Laurie Personnet, a long-time friend from my first year at Ryerson University who now lives in France.

The dream ends with me being told that everything in life goes full circle again. You meet the same people again and again, from lifetime to lifetime. Sometimes they stay and you relish the experience and travel with them, sometimes you leave them and move on—but the loop always is there—part of your personal history.

CHAPTER TEN
Miracles and Visions Experiencing Other Dimensions

We live in a world of theophanies. Holiness comes wrapped in the ordinary. There are burning bushes all around you. Every tree is full of angels. Hidden beauty is waiting in every crumb. Life wants to lead you from crumbs to angels, but this can happen only if you are willing to unwrap the ordinary long enough by staying with it long enough to harvest its treasure.
Sister Marcrina Wiederkehr

It is not necessary to have a bolt of fire from the sky or the sound of a heavenly voice.
Miracles are happening all the time, at all hours of the day and night; and they come about quietly, just like this, with two men talking together, perhaps in a darkened room and the world asleep outside.
Thomas B. Costain *The Silver Chalice*

AMIDST THE DOOM AND GLOOM in the daily news, miracles abound—reminding us that with God or spirit anything is possible. One of these miracles was the story of Dutch athlete Monique van der Vorst, who was confined to a wheelchair with muscular dystrophy at age 13, and told she would never walk again. But Monique's spirit pushed forward, and she went on to compete in hand cycling at the Paralympics in Beijing, where she won two silver medals. Just when she seemed on top of the game, the worst tragedy imaginable happened—she was struck by a car while training. The doctor who arrived at the scene of the accident said she wasn't going to make it. Monique was in a coma with a spinal cord injury, further complicating her crippling muscular dystrophy. She did come out of that coma, but in the beginning was able to move only one hand. One day while exercising she balled that hand into a fist, and suddenly felt a strange sensation in her legs. A year later, at 25, she was walking like never before, had signed a pro contract with an able-bodied cycling team, and was training for the next Olympics. Monique says she can hardly believe this miracle herself.

Anita Moorjani, who wrote, *Dying to Be Me,* had suffered four anguished years with cancer, and weighed less than 90 pounds. Her breathing was so labored an oxygen tank was a constant companion, and she couldn't lie down, needing to be propped up all the time because of the suffocating fluid in her lungs. There was such an army of toxins invading her body that she was covered with lesions and her skin was forced to open everywhere to release these poisons. When her husband, Danny, could no longer care for her, he rushed Anita to the hospital, only to be told she wouldn't make it through the night. Her organs had already shut down. She had tumors from her skull to her abdomen as big as lemons. Her brain and lungs were drowning in fluid, and her entire body was weeping toxins. In what appeared to be the end, Anita's spirit slipped away, aware completely of everything happening around her while her body remained in a coma. While out of her body, she traveled to other rooms in the hospital, where she heard doctors, nurses, and her family discussing her imminent death. Her spirit drifted into other dimensions—in her words Heaven—where she met with her deceased father, and learned she would be returning to earth. Anita came out of her coma, more awake and aware than ever before. She recovered fully, a miraculous feat that baffled her doctors. Now Anita believes "that Heaven is a state and not a place, and...that our 'true home' is also only a way of being and not a location."

When a devastating earthquake hit Haiti in 2010, amid the anguish, pain, and horror, there were daily miracles—people pulled from the ruins, after authorities had given up all hope. Most human beings can live four to six weeks without food, but drinking water is critical since the body loses five or six cups of water each day. Without life-sustaining water, one rarely lives for more than three or four days. Six days after the earthquake struck, a two-year-old girl was pulled from the rubble physically unharmed. The newspaper story said, "Six days of no water, no food, no one to sing comforting songs to her. And she was not only alive, but apart from the long-term malnutrition, she was physically unharmed. Now it will take a miracle to find her family—if they survived." Three million Haitians were displaced in the earthquake, but weeks later another story reported her name was Lovely Avelus, and her family had survived and found her. The next miracle headline was Rico Dibrivell, 35, pulled from the rubble, 14 days after the earthquake hit, covered in dust and wearing only his underpants. Even more astounding, 15 days after the quake, a seventeen-year-old girl, Darlene Etienne, was rescued—dehydrated with a broken leg, but alive. She had been taking a shower when the earthquake struck, and was trapped in a space barely bigger than her body. Since she had access to small amounts of water, that shower may have saved her.

There are numerous airplane crashes where passengers survive against all odds. In 1972, flight attendant Vesna Vulovic fell from a disintegrating Yugoslav airliner, landing on a wooded hill, and survived with only broken legs. In 1995, a Columbian plane exploded in midair. The lone survivor was a nine-year-old girl found unconscious amidst lily pads. In 2010, a nine-year-old Dutch boy, Rubin van Assouw, was the lone survivor of a jetliner crash in Libya, when he was found still breathing and strapped to his seat. The same year a Columbian Boeing 737, believed to have been hit by lightning, crashed in a thunderstorm, exploding into several pieces as it careened onto a San Andres Island runway. The plane slid forward on its belly as the fuselage fractured and bits of landing gear and an engine were ripped off. The plane lay in crumpled pieces at the end of the runway with parts scattered everywhere. Miraculously, only one of the 131 people aboard died; authorities believed he may have had a heart attack. "When we fell, we wound up on the pavement still in the seats," said passenger Ricardo Ramiriz. "We tried to get out of the plane because the plane was starting to shoot flames." He described the crash as a "miracle of God," adding, "Thanks to God we are alive."

I witnessed a plane crash in August 2005, described in the media as the "Toronto Miracle," "Miracle Escape," and "Miracle on Runway 24L." I was driving across Highway 401 by Pearson Airport in Toronto to teach a yoga class half an hour away, when traffic became gridlocked. A stone's throw away Air France flight 358 had skidded to a halt, 200 meters past the end of the runway. It lay in three pieces, with its nose down a ravine, and the tail visible from the highway. Flames and black smoke were pouring off the tail. What I didn't know as I sat waiting, was that flight attendants had evacuated all 297 passengers through the emergency exits in just two minutes and there were no fatalities. Seconds after the evacuation the plane exploded into black toxic flames.

Most people believe that visions and miracles took place in the Bible. Christians accept that Jesus healed the sick, walked on water, turned water into wine, changed five loaves and two fish into enough to feed five thousand, and commanded the dead Lazarus to rise up and walk. We believe the angel Gabriel appeared to Mary, Moses parted the Red Sea, and Christ appeared to the disciples after he was crucified. We believe in modern day saints like Padre Pio, who could bilocate and be in two places at once. There's a famous account of how he appeared in the sky larger than life to ward off World War II German fighter planes, while simultaneously still back in his monastery. We believe that Joan of

Arc, an 18-year old uneducated peasant girl, with no military training, won back land for France that the English had captured and held for centuries. She said it was the voices of St. Michael and St. Catherine that guided her. These are mostly Christian accounts, but whether you are Jewish, Muslim, Hindu, Buddhist, or any other faith, miracles abound. The sacred texts of every major religion are filled with events that defy the rational mind: miracles, visions, and visitations by angels, sages, and enlightened beings.

Canadian physician Dr. Jacalyn Duffin, a hematologist, who teaches the History of Medicine at Queen's University, was by her own admission a skeptic and confirmed atheist before writing *"Medical Miracles: Doctors, Saints and Healing in the Modern World."* Her book describes 1400 cases of miraculous healing that took place from 1588 to 1999. She cites cases where a dead baby comes back to life, a crippled girl begins to walk, and a woman's painful breast tumor vanishes overnight. Her interest in miracles was sparked when she was asked to review a set of slides she thought were being used for a malpractice suit. Her conclusion was that the young woman had suffered from acute myeloblastic leukemia, the most aggressive form of this disease. Since the slides were ten years old, she assumed the woman had died, because that type of leukemia kills within two years. But the patient was alive and well. Later she found out that her testimony was being used by the Vatican to determine whether, Marie-Marguerite d'Youville, who became the first Canadian born saint, was worthy of canonization. That young women with leukemia had prayed to d'Youville and her cancer had gone into remission. The process of canonization, which began in the 1500s, requires medical doctors and other experts to agree there was no possible scientific explanation. Before any healing is considered a miracle, it must be "complete, durable and instantaneous." If the healing occurred naturally or through human intervention it does not qualify as a miracle. Duffin, completely intrigued, and realizing there was no scientific explanation as to why this woman was still alive after ten years, began doing some serious medical research which led to her book.

Michael Talbot in *The Holographic Universe,* devotes an entire chapter to past and modern day miracles. He talks of Sathya Sai Baba, who lived in Southern India until his death in 2011. At fourteen, Sai Baba began materializing objects out of thin air. He conjured up jewels, lockets, rings, and gold jewelry, giving them away as gifts to throngs of daily visitors. His miracles have been filmed and witnessed by millions, including scientists and magicians who couldn't come up with a rational explanation of how he does this. Talbot explains, "He also materializes vast quantities of food, and when the various delicacies he produces fall from his hands they are sizzling hot, so hot that people sometimes cannot even hold them. He can make sweet syrups and fragrant oils pour from his hands (and even his feet) and when he is finished there is no trace of the sticky substance on his skin..."

"Equally astonishing are his productions of sacred ash. Every time he walks among the crowds that visit him, prodigious amounts of it pour from his hands. He scatters it everywhere, into offered containers and outstretched hands, over heads, and in long serpentine trails on the ground. In a single transit of the grounds around his ashram he can produce enough of it to fill several drums." His followers applied this sacred ash, known as *vibhuti*, to their foreheads.

When Paramahansa Yogananda, a renowned yogi from India, passed away in 1952, his body lay in Los Angeles for twenty days, from March 7 to 27, before the bronze cover of his casket was put in place. In a notarized letter, Harry Rowe, the mortuary director, said during those twenty days there was no odor or decay from the body. "The absence of any visual signs of decay in the dead body of Paramahansa Yogananda offers the most extraordinary case in our experience...No physical disintegration was visible in the body even twenty days after death...No indication of mold was visible on his skin, and no visible desiccation (drying up) took place in the bodily tissues. This state of perfect preservation of a body is, so far as we know from mortuary annals, an unparalleled one."

Eleven years later a similar miracle took place with a Catholic pope. Although Pope John XXIII died in 1963, his body still hasn't decomposed. He can be seen by visitors to the Vatican where he is preserved in an air tight glass coffin. Masses are televised from the Vatican with the casket clearly in view—he appears to be sleeping peacefully. I was suspicious reading about this, until a good friend, Maria Watts, returned from a trip to the Vatican, and confirmed she'd been to one of these masses, and had seen his casket. I began relating this story to a very rational-minded relative, brought up as a Catholic, but he simply wouldn't believe me. The further I got into the story, the more skeptical he became. He argued the Vatican must be using a special air tight procedure so the body wouldn't decompose. But, the truth is, even in an air tight coffin, a body will eventually break down. And how does one explain that the bodies of other popes have decomposed, but his hasn't? We often have difficulty accepting the unexplained; we need physical or logical proof for everything. The ego or rational mind is often not willing to accept miracles because it challenges that logical, left brained, physical part of us. But to never hope for or believe in miracles is to be trapped in the prison of a logical left brain that declares,

"I'll believe it when I see it." The mind will cling desperately to what is known, routine, harmful, and sometimes illusionary or untrue. If we all accepted miracles as everyday occurrences, we'd have to admit that spirit really has more power. It can do virtually anything—extraordinary things our minds will never comprehend.

Vision, Miracle or Insanity?

None of you will ever believe unless you see miracles and wonders.
John 4:48

It is impossible on reasonable grounds to disbelieve miracles.
Blaise Pascal

As to me, I know of nothing else but miracles.
Walt Whitman

Miracles and visions don't happen *only* to saints, mystics, holy men, or Biblical characters. As we become aware of miracles we begin breaking through the illusions of the mind that trap and bind us, and realize miraculous events can happen to *everyone*. We discover more elevated dimensions do exist and rise from the mundane to the miraculous. The spiritual dimension is always interacting with us. *Visions and miracles are simply the presence of the spirit world coming through and giving us physical proof they are there.* There are angels, spirit guides, and enlightened beings interacting with us seven days a week, twenty-four hours a day. It's similar to a child at school who may be helped by their teacher, a music teacher, French teacher, guidance counselor, soccer coach, parent volunteer, secretary, social worker and principal. These people come and go when they need to play a role in the child's life. Similarly we have angels, archangels, and guides continually visiting when we need them; just because we can't see them doesn't diminish their presence, and doesn't mean they don't exist.

Many people believe in angels, but if someone tells us they speak to angels we question their sanity. We believe that to be sane, we must be rooted *only* in the physical dimension. If people have the ability to see into other dimensions, many believe they're crazy. But we certainly aren't crazy when we dream. It appears we're doing crazy things, like flying or talking to a horse, because we're subject to spiritual rather than physical laws. If we witness a miracle we aren't crazy; it's grace or a gift helping increase our awareness and propelling us forward. If we have a vision, for a short time we've been granted the privilege of seeing into the spirit world. A door to other dimensions has opened, enabling us to truly see.

In *The Emerald Tablet,* Dennis Hauck says there are no real miracles, rather miracles are "manifestations of the universe's hidden laws that we do not understand." He says "what we call the spiritual world is actually *more* real than physical reality." It's a question of faith—the spiritual dimensions are always there. If you believe, if you ask, subtle doors of grace and opportunity may open. We can rely on physical laws to try to explain everything, or we can have the faith to believe in spiritual laws which defy and challenge ego or mind-based logic. Spirit has its own set of laws allowing the miraculous to occur, and when it does, this is a tremendous spiritual gift. Faith seems to propel and encourage miracles, and this is not a left brain function. Faith is the spiritual muscle that develops from connection to spirit—the inner strength that enables us to weather all life's storms.

But how do we know the difference between a miracle and a sophisticated illusion? Psychiatrist Dennis Gersten explains this in his book, *Are You Getting Enlightened or Losing Your Mind?* He says there is something that allows us to know if we've witnessed a genuine vision or miracle or if we are certifiably crazy—*the emotions associated with the experience.* If we've had a true vision or miracle the emotions are *never* upsetting or disconcerting; they're spiritual: awe, awareness, clarity, comfort, joy, peace, and reassurance. True spiritual experiences are never accompanied by feelings of fear, despair, doubt, anxiety, or confusion, because these emotions usually come from the ego or mind. The mind wants to appear "superior" to spirit, so for many it completely disregards miracles and sadly misses out on the emotional benefits. Dreams, visions, and miracles always take place to help us heal, evolve, and carry out our dharma. They never harm us. We would never be instructed in a dream or vision to hurt or harm anyone. This is not how God or spirit works. Beings in the spirit world guide, reassure, comfort, and propel us forward. If we experience a true vision or miracle there's never any doubt, although we can't explain logically what just happened. Often there is a feeling of great reverence. Many are so sure of its authenticity; they don't need to discuss it with anyone for verification. They realize it doesn't serve them to talk about it right away, because others might diminish its sacredness. With visions there is rarely fear, although there can be exceptions. When the angel Gabriel appeared to Joseph in a dream, he was told, "Do not be afraid to take Mary to be your wife," and when Mary, did not understand the role she was to play, she was advised, "Fear not." Although there may be initial surprise or shock, by the end of the visitation or experience fear dissipates. There is clarity often accompanied by even greater faith. Suddenly, we understand things we couldn't before, and there is a knowingness that this was unexplainable, but real.

This doesn't dismiss the fact that there are unbalanced or "crazy" individuals. There are people who believe they are Jesus reincarnated. Some men claim their ministry involves having sex and impregnating women. There are stories of people who have brutally murdered a relative or loved one, claiming they were instructed by the devil or some supernatural being to do so. But killing and violence have nothing to do with God or spirit. C.G. Jung believed the true reason for mental disorders was disconnection from our spirit or core. Many people believed to be certifiably crazy have actually seen other dimensions and don't know how to deal with it, especially if they've disconnected from spirit—we're rarely given training or information on how to navigate or understand both worlds. So when they talk about interactions with other beings, most believe they are delusional or crazy. Sometimes they're having hallucinations because they haven't worked through their layers of ego and karma and are more connected to their minds. If someone hasn't done any inner work or dissolved their ego, it can become over inflated and out of balance, and their minds believe their illusions that they're the Messiah, Elvis Presley, or Marilyn Monroe. If they become terribly unbalanced and spiral into the lower vibrations of the mind and negativity, they may begin seeing negative entities or demons from darker dimensions. These beings taunt and haunt their victims because they vibrate at the lower vibrations of the mind, not the higher comforting vibrations of spirit.

The movie, *A Beautiful Mind,* based on the life of Nobel Laureate John Forbes Nash, a brilliant mathematician, who was believed to be a genius, illustrates this well. In the movie, Nash is working at prestigious Princeton University, but is handicapped by an enormous ego; he believes he's superior to everyone. He has no sincere desire to help or teach his students and is pompous and condescending. Eventually he's so inundated by demons, delusions, and hallucinations that he's hospitalized and diagnosed as a paranoid schizophrenic. If we rely only on the intellect, we're in danger of being led like a puppet by an unbalanced mind. If the mind is not tempered by the wisdom of spirit, like Nash in the movie, we can become so unbalanced it leads to insanity. And the feelings that accompany insanity are mind-based emotions; fear, paranoia, disorientation, distrust, depression, agitation. Disorientation and fragmentation occur because people have literally lost elements of their soul or spirit—that energy or information that holds everything together and provides guidance. This happens if someone tries to control their life with *only* the mind. There can be a fine line between mind genius and insanity. But insanity is highly preventable. Einstein was a genius with tremendous faith and a sense of awe. He wasn't ruled solely by his mind or ego; instead he was inspired and led by spirit which provided clarity and creativity.

Visions

There are only two ways to live your life. One is as though nothing is a miracle. The other is as if everything is.

Albert Einstein

Visions like miracles exclude no one. It's possible to experience a vision if you've led a completely secular life, and never set foot in any church, synagogue, mosque, temple, or religious institution. Such was the case with Bill Wilson, cofounder of Alcoholics Anonymous, who valued his rational, logical, scientific mind. Bill was at the end of his rope, a hopeless drunk repeatedly in and out of hospital, until, in 1934, while a patient in Towns Hospital, everything changed. In *Alcoholics Anonymous Comes of Age* he explains, "My depression deepened unbearably and finally it seemed to me as though I were at the bottom of the pit...All at once I found myself crying out, 'If there be a God, let Him show Himself now! I am ready to do anything, anything!' Suddenly the room lit up with a great white light. I was caught up into an ecstasy which there are no words to describe. It seemed to me, in the mind's eye, that I was on a mountain and that a wind not of air but of spirit was blowing. And then it burst upon me that I was a free man. Slowly the ecstasy subsided. I lay on the bed, but now for a time I was in another world, a new world of consciousness. All about me and through me there was a wonderful feeling of Presence, and I thought to myself, 'So this is the God the of the preachers!' A great peace stole over me and I thought, 'No matter how wrong things seem to be, they are still all right. Things are all right with God and His world." When Bill had this experience he had just turned 39, and for the rest of his life never took another drink. He had absolutely no desire to—instead he poured all his energy into what would become Alcohol Anonymous or AA. After what he called his "hot flash," Bill described his experience to the man caring for him, Dr. William Silkworth. His doctor knew something miraculous had happened because Bill seemed years younger, and was happy, relaxed, and energized. Fortunately, Silkworth didn't think Bill was crazy, and although they couldn't explain what had transpired, he suggested rather than trying to understand it, he focus on what the experience had given him.

Visions and miracles often appear to be one and the same thing. Such was the case with Edgar Cayce, often referred to as the sleeping prophet, father of holistic medicine, and the most gifted psychic of the 20th century. Cayce born in 1877, grew up on a Kentucky farm, and only attended school until the ninth grade, perhaps because his extraordinary talents emerged much earlier. By age five he was telling his parents about his visions and talks with deceased relatives, particularly his grandfather, who had died after being thrown by a horse. Edgar told his parents that his grandfather was still on the farm, working in the fields, and helping the farmhands by reminding them of important chores. He also recounted the history of the Cayce family's early years in Virginia, which he said his grandfather was telling him—accurate stories a five-year-old could never have known. Young Edgar was deeply religious, dreamed of becoming a preacher or missionary, and as a boy began reading the Bible from cover to cover, a practice he continued every year of his life. When he was thirteen, while reading his Bible in the woods, a beautiful women bathed in light appeared. She told him his prayers had been answered, and asked what he wanted most of all. Cayce replied his greatest dream was to help others, especially sick children. The women advised Cayce to sleep with his head on his books, and if he did, he would remember everything. Young Cayce had been having trouble in school, was frequently criticized for being a daydreamer. The day before his teacher, his uncle Lucian, made him stay after school to write the word "cabin" five hundred times because he misspelled it. He'd received several beatings that night from his dad because he couldn't remember his spelling, until he heard the voice of the lady from his vision urging him to sleep a little so that he could be helped. After Edgar slept with his head on his books, he had a photographic memory of everything he slept on from that day forward! As a young man this photographic memory enabled him to get jobs clerking in stores during tough times, since he could easily memorize entire store catalogues! Cayce visions continued throughout life and he went on to become the most prolific psychic in history. His wish of helping the sick was realized, first when he went into a trance and cured his own serious condition of laryngitis, then through thousands of readings containing medical cures and information that assisted the doctors he eventually worked with. In total Cayce gave over 14,000 readings, all archived and catalogued by the Association for Research and Enlightenment in

Virginia Beach, Virginia. He was exceedingly humble, never taking part in any public demonstration of his abilities or seeking publicity. He used his abilities only to prescribe cures for the sick, or to give spiritual advice. He worked as a photographer and Sunday school teacher for most of his life, and never charged for his readings, only asked for donations. Cayce never sought wealth despite having illustrious clients such as Thomas Edison, Nikola Tesla, Nelson Rockefeller, George Gershwin, Irving Berlin, and Gloria Swanson. He was committed to a life of compassion and service. Possibly his most miraculous vision took place when he was going through a rough time financially and decided to take a road trip to New Mexico with a friend. Here his deceased mother appeared to him, encouraged him not to worry about finances, or doubt the power and truth of his readings. Before the vision faded she handed him a silver dollar. Restored by his mother's words, Cayce returned to Virginia Beach where he lived with his wife and sons, determined "to be of greater service to his fellow man." But Cayce's son Hugh Lynn, was curious about this mysterious silver dollar. When he sent the coin to the Federal Treasury for investigation, he was informed it didn't have a mint mark, and only narrowly escaped prosecution for counterfeiting by pointing out that no counterfeiter would turn their own work in for examination!

As children, like Cayce, we were all visionaries. We knew where we came from, and hadn't yet lost our ability to see into other dimensions. Children talk and play with imaginary characters or friends all the time. They often tell us they've had a conversation with animals, angels, elves, fairies or a grandparent who has passed away. Children have just come from the more elevated dimensions of spirit which vibrate faster than the dense vibrations of earth. As children are exposed to the lower vibrations of this physical dimension they begin to take on that vibration. They're socialized to believe in only the physical, and told that these imaginary friends aren't real. They're exposed to the pain, fear, and illusions of the world. They begin accumulating karma and vibrating at lower levels. Finally, they stop seeing their real friends in the spirit world, and these guides are replaced by physical illusions created largely for profit; Santa Claus, The Great Pumpkin, The Tooth Fairy, The Easter Bunny. Their real friends provided conversation, companionship, advice, protection, information, and support. There was no ulterior motive. Gradually children are inundated with so many material things and illusions that the spirit world retreats until they're ready to believe in truth again. The spirit world can only wait and watch. They can't intervene without our permission; they must follow spiritual laws and respect our free will, hoping as adults we develop the insight to shed the illusions enabling us to truly see again. Have you ever sat down with a group of people and asked, "Have you ever had a vision or mystical experience?" Chances are almost everyone has, although they're usually not comfortable talking about it. We're reluctant to share these experiences because we fear people will doubt us. Since we can't prove it, they'll be skeptical and think we're crazy. But this reluctance is changing. We're entering a time in history when visions will become an acceptable part of life. Portals or spiritual highways are opening allowing the spirit world to break through like never before. Spiritually we're ready for this, the same way we were ready for air travel, telephones, televisions, and computers in the 20th century. Visions are just a higher form of information filtering through from spiritual dimensions. It's like opening windows where for the first time we can see dimensions that vibrate at higher frequencies. If we are approaching a time when we can actually step into and cross dimensions, then having glimpses or visions of these dimensions may be the first step. More people are dreaming of departed loved ones, angels, guides, and having visions. The time has come to understand we're not crazy or insane. This is a form of grace. For those few seconds the veils or walls between the physical and spiritual worlds are drawn open. Visions are doors or windows of sacred opportunities. With dreams or visions we embrace guidance and truth, and see without the shadows of ego or illusion. We're not crazy if we experience a vision—we're incredibly blessed.

A Vision of a Divided Self

Walls crumble, and we get to the essence of who we are.
Christine Northrup, M.D.

A vision of a divided self was related by Carole, a former teacher and school administrator, who had started teaching elementary school when she was nineteen, and was eligible for retirement in her early fifties. After over thirty years as a dedicated teacher, consultant, and administrator, she was experiencing severe guilt at the thought of leaving education. She had just become a vice-principal, and was respected and relied upon by colleagues, so this made it even more difficult to leave. But her soul longed to break free and move in a new direction. She had always wanted to paint and pursue art full time, but had never had the opportunity to do this, since teaching had been all consuming.

"I had decided to take early retirement from teaching but I was facing difficulty with my decision. Wasn't I too young to be retired? Shouldn't I continue in my career and achieve all the goals I had set for myself? Wasn't it self-indulgent to think that I could retire from a busy, responsible career and focus on my own interests? Although I had handed in my resignation and even had my retirement celebration, I increasingly felt that I had made the wrong decision.

"On a particularly beautiful May day I found myself very distressed. Convinced that I had made a mistake, and believing that it was too late, I felt a mounting dread and left work early to go home. I decided to go for a walk to help relieve my incredible stress. My emotions were in turmoil. I walked my usual route, but could feel the tears rushing to the surface. It was so ironic that I was crying in the middle of a beautiful, sunny, late afternoon walk. Many people were out walking, but they seemed oblivious to me. I walked to the bottom of the hill and with tears streaming down my face. I turned and walked back up.

Part way up the hill I suddenly saw, directly in front of my eyes, a transparent blue vision of two identical women. I could clearly see the women and through them I could see the street, the houses, the people walking. The woman on the right was reaching out and down to the other woman who was turned away. She was trying to comfort the woman on the left who appeared very sad. My creative side had been repressed so long by the demands of a very responsible career in education. Each year that I continued in administration drained me of creative energy. The latter part of my career in administration was all left brain dominated and I was working all the time. I was so consumed by my job I had no time to do the creative right brained things. I didn't even have time to draw a picture. I think that was why I was so unhappy because I was all left brain. I was two separate people, right and left brain. The right brain part was stifled by my career. In an instant, I knew that these two women represented the split in myself and that I needed to retire to be whole.

Lasting only seconds, the vision had a profound effect on me. I felt the stress immediately dissipate. I knew instantly that I must retire from teaching and move on with my creative life. I was also beginning to realize that my creative and spiritual paths are one. The vision is as clear today as it was on that sunny afternoon four years ago. It reassures me whenever I find that the 'shoulds' start to take over, and make me question my decision to focus my energy on my creative and spiritual journey. I never had a vision before that day and have not had one since. I believe it was a gift from the spirit world to help me in a time of great distress. Throughout my life I have had other pushes that have moved me along on my spiritual, creative path. This was the most dramatic and profound."

When Carole gave me permission to use this vision, she was enjoying a second career as a successful artist. She had taken part in many art shows, sold several paintings, and had just received honorable mention in a juried art show. Painting had become a means of self-expression reflecting her personal explorations and spiritual journey. She began painting realistic type canvasses, then realized her real passion and strength was in abstract work which focused on visions, light, dreams, intuition, sacred sites around the world, and sacred geometry. Her traveling, research, retreats, courses, and experimentation into other art media went far beyond the parameters of anything she had done before. Thankfully, she followed the guidance of her spirit.

"Everything is Going to Be All Right"

Miracles are unexpected joys, surprising coincidences, unexplainable experiences, astonishing beauties...absolutely everything that happens in the course of my day, except that at this moment I'm able to recognize its special value.

Judith M. Knowlton

Before my mother died of cancer in 1981, I had spent four months with her while I was between jobs. My Italian mother was the furthest thing from a calm, tranquil person you could imagine. She worried constantly, always expecting the worst to happen, and was definitely not an optimist. Before she passed away, my mother had suffered from cancer of the bowel for four painful years, and had undergone several surgeries. One afternoon while we were together, I'm sure she realized the end was near, and was able to let down her defenses. It was a few weeks before she died, and we were sitting together in the veranda of our cottage. It was a windy day and one of those rare times when neither of us were talking. My mother was lying down watching the wind drift through the trees. She became serene, and told me she was seeing the face of a man with a dark beard, who was up in the trees speaking to her. She said, "Look he's right there, he's so clear, can't you see him?" I squinted and strained to see something, but clearly, this vision wasn't meant for me. I'll never forget the radiant smile on her face as she watched. This type of facial expression and demeanor were completely out of character for her. I asked what he was saying, and with great assurance, she replied, *"I'm waiting for you, I'm waiting for you."* Whatever emotions transpired in that vision, it gave my mother unbelievable peace, preparing her for what was to come. Weeks later she passed away on the operating table from a blood clot to her brain.

I didn't talk about my first vision for a long time. Ten years passed before I had the courage to write this down for a teacher I trusted, Jack Miller, who was guiding me through my doctoral work at the University of Toronto, and teaching courses on meditation. When I think back on the experience, it felt completely natural and seamless. It was an intense feeling of being loved, of enormous healing and energy, but most of all, peace. Because these emotions were so strong, there was no reason to prove or discuss what I experienced with anyone. There is sacredness to these experiences that you just don't want anyone to spoil or dishonor. It happened in December 23, 1985, when I had been seriously burned in a house fire. My injuries were severe, second and third degree burns to 45 percent of my body. The survival rate for this type of injury is not high. I was told afterwards that most patients burned this badly usually slip in and out of a coma, and die within the first two weeks, and ironically they don't die directly from the burns, but from infection. Because of this risk of infection, anyone who came into my room had to be completely covered wearing slippers, a gown, and face mask. All I saw for the first few weeks were people's eyes; it seemed I was looking at windows to their souls, and I would marvel at how beautiful the skin on their faces appeared.

That first evening I was in intensive care hooked up to life support systems. My immediate family had all come to see me. However, the risk of my dying from infection was so great I needed to be isolated. The vision took place just after everyone had left. Several nurses made sure the IV, respirator, morphine drip, and all the life support systems were operating. The double doors leading into my room were closed, and I was left for the night, perhaps to die. However, when everyone left, the excruciating pain seemed to subside. I don't remember feeling anything. Then, directly in front of me at the top of the ceiling I began to see white, swirling clouds. This didn't seem strange or out of the ordinary, just peaceful and intriguing. Amidst the clouds were many faces, but they weren't clear. They seemed to half materialize, then fade away. I watched this for perhaps a minute. Then to my right in midair I became aware of the presence of my mother who had died four years earlier. This vision or hologram of my mother was incredibly clear and she looked more beautiful than I could have imagined. She was glowing, radiating a love and peace that is difficult to describe with mere words. She was smiling down at me. I didn't hear words, but felt her saying, *"Everything is going to be all right.*" Those words were as clear and distinct as her image. Simultaneously, I felt an intense energetic transmission. It was like waves of warmth and love enveloping me, like being covered in a soft blanket. There was a knowingness that everything would be okay. I watched in complete tranquility, like a baby receiving reassurance from its mother, and then fell peacefully asleep.

For the longest time I didn't understand this vision. I had no idea who these beings in the clouds were, or why they appeared. I thought my mother had somehow given me a miraculous healing, because I did survive. From the beginning, my experience as a burn patient wasn't normal; my doctors couldn't explain why I didn't fall into a coma. I was conscious and aware of everything the first two weeks. I was told I'd have to have surgery several times because skin grafting normally doesn't take the first time. Your body usually rejects the grafts, so it needs to be repeated over and over. All my grafting took the first time. I was told that I would probably need numerous operations for years afterwards to release my skin, particularly in the joints, because it would become tight and inflexible. I needed the initial skin grafting and nothing further. I was prepared for the fact that my face might be permanently scarred and I might never look the same. My face healed miraculously and looked completely normal after two years. I was told I would be in the hospital for one full year, possibly longer. I was in the hospital for one month. I was told that all physical exercise would be extremely difficult and painful because I would have limited mobility in all my joints and this would be permanent. A year later I was back at work, and teaching fitness classes in the gym, and there has never been any lack of mobility in my joints—over twenty-five years later they are often tight and at times painful, but I have a full range of movement.

My recovery was not easy, but it was definitely a miracle. I was in terrible, unrelenting pain for five years. That was one thing the doctors were right about. For two years I needed to wear a special skin tight Jobst suit which covered my entire body and provided the natural tension of the skin I had lost. But I survived. I've realize now that being burned was a karmic debt from several previous lives that needed to be paid, and this was definitely not something inflicted on me. I will be eternally grateful for the strength that vision with my mother gave me. Without that vision, I'm sure I would have given up. The physical and emotional pain was just too overwhelming.

So what was that vision all about? I now understand that we are always given choices. I could have chosen to die that night. My mind and body were screaming out, "What were you thinking when you agreed to this? It's far too painful! I don't want to go through with this!" But it had been written into my soul's contract; of that I am sure; my soul believed this was the best way I could work through sectors of karma and wipe the slate clean. Meanwhile my mind was reeling in disbelief. My mother knew this. It was far better to just get it over with. I had already come this far. I needed enormous reserves of support to stick with my original contract because it was going to be brutally painful physically and emotionally. I understand now that the faces in the clouds were the many souls who had gone through similar experiences. Perhaps they had been burned in previous lives and were telling me the same thing as my mother. "Don't turn back now." My soul understood this, although my rational mind didn't. A few years later at the Art Gallery of Ontario, I saw a painting that looked *exactly* like this vision. It was called Concert of Angels, painted in 1672 by Giovanni Battista Gauli. When I first saw it I was riveted—I knew instinctively that many others had received similar visions, and had been able to translate this into sacred art. If I had artistic talent I would have tried to paint something similar. My mother appeared to give me that final convincing push of love, strength, and warmth, so I could complete my spiritual contract. She knew how difficult this would be and was granted permission to visit and let me know that "everything would be all right."

For the longest time my ego tried to convince me that I had survived this fire because I was somehow special. Being a burn survivor gave me almost a celebrity status for several years, because I had survived something that was almost physically impossible. Unfortunately this inflated my ego even more. Finally, I understood that I survived this fire because it was something I needed to do. I needed the experience of this fire to understand many things. But my most humble revelation was that I survived this fire because I still had enormous amounts of karma to work through and understand. I needed to survive to repay all my karmic debts, and hopefully carry out my dharma or destiny. There was still lots of work to do. Life was not over, it was just beginning.

Ten years after the fire, I was still struggling emotionally with what had happened. Part of me felt like a victim, and emotionally, I hadn't healed. I had great difficulty accepting the scarring on my body. I felt like an alien, a monster, and my mind convinced me that if anyone saw how ugly my scars were, they would run away in terror. I was afraid if I exposed myself, no one would like or love me, because these scars were so hideous they made me completely unlovable. Throughout the whole ordeal of recovering from the fire I always felt I had to be stoic, but inside I was angry and bitter that this horrible thing had happened to me, and never felt it was socially appropriate to express the rage inside me. I pretended to be okay, immersing myself in academics, completing my

Masters degree, then a doctoral degree in applied psychology, and hiding behind long clothing even in the hottest summer weather—until I had this dream.

Cremation
I am in an unfamiliar church-like place. There is a woman at the front of the church in front of a white casket. There are four or five people behind her waiting to say good bye to the person in the casket. This woman is lingering a long time over her husband, clasping his hands and stroking his face lovingly. Then I realize he's not dead. He's speaking to her.

Finally the priest comes up and separates them. The people behind quickly pay their last respects. The man in the casket doesn't speak to these other people. I remain at the front, the last person who goes to the casket. I can see intense fear, regret, and apprehension in the man's face. He does not speak to me, but I know he's alive. Then the priest slides a panel over the casket, sprinkles something, then sets the casket on fire. With horror I realize the man is being cremated alive! I cannot understand why anyone would allow this. I am enraged and cannot control my anger towards these people. I decide I must tell them how I feel. I begin yelling and telling them I was burned and how horrible it was. I'm screaming that this ritual is something I will never forget or forgive, it will always leave a horrible impression on me. What they're doing is barbaric. I cannot understand why this man would just submit to being burned. I feel quite self-righteous in telling everyone off as if they don't know any better and it is somehow my duty. I feel terrible, like a victim at the same time because I could not prevent this death. But, there were absolutely no screams or protests coming from the coffin which amazes me.

It took me a while to understand this dream completely. At first I was just totally caught up in the emotional intensity of it. Then I realized that symbolically, I am the man in the coffin, at peace with this decision to be set on fire. Perhaps this man represented my soul, the wiser, calmer, all knowing part of me, understanding this fire was a karmic debt I needed to pay, and I would survive. The part of me that goes ballistic, screaming at everyone, is my mind or left brain. My mind or ego, with its limited vision, simply didn't have the ability to foresee that perhaps this could be purification by fire, like the archetypal phoenix that is consumed by fire, and always rises up again. My mind desperately wanted to act like a child and take a temper tantrum.

The whole feeling in this dream (until I started yelling) was peaceful and loving. It was obvious the friends, the wife, and priest, loved this man. It was even more obvious that this man who was being cremated was completely content with his decision. Somehow this dream was telling me I needed to make peace with what had happened. I could rant, rave, scream, and appear self-righteous, but it wasn't going to change anything. I needed to express all those bottled up emotions, and find that place of peace and resolution this dream was trying to show me. This is the wisdom, genius and miracle of dreams. Nightly self-therapy, free of charge. One dream, can alter a lifetime, turning bitter despair into contentment and peace.

This dream was an opportunity for me to express all the anger, rage, and bitterness bottled inside me for ten painful years. I needed to move on because ten years of living in long, hot clothes was enough. After the dream I felt quite different, as if I could face issues I hadn't faced before. Something clicked inside me with this dream, and for the first time I had the courage to wear short sleeved T-shirts, without feeling total humiliation—a major emotional breakthrough. What is amazing is that shortly after being burned, I went to a husband and wife team of psychiatrists, specialists in burn therapy, but I was completely frustrated with these visits. I felt they had absolutely no understanding of the emotions that a burn survivor experiences. These visits made me feel angrier, more insignificant, and lonelier. But this one dream accomplished what they were unable to do—emotional healing. This is the sacred and astounding power of dreams. I'd be lying if I told you I'm completely okay with all my body scarring. It's a constant challenge, especially when I meet someone and they look at my skin with horror, and ask what happened. Before the dream, I hid from the world and felt like a monster. After the dream I had the courage to expose myself to the world, and deal with people's reactions.

The fire took place in 1985, and I'm still healing. My left arm, burned the deepest almost to the bone, is still contorting, changing, tightening, and I'm constantly stretching it to keep it mobile. But I've never needed surgery. Thanks to my vision and dream I survived. Everything has been all right, just as my mother promised. That vision gave me tremendous faith. Although I have great respect for doctors, nurses, physiotherapists, and occupational therapists, and believe they are often guided, that one experience went far beyond any therapy I received in the physical world. Spirit heals—of that I am absolutely sure.

CHAPTER ELEVEN
Meditation the Portal to Peace

Meditation and action:
He who knows these two together
Through action leaves death behind
And through meditation gains immortality.

The Upanishads

If You Can Breathe You Can Meditate

MEDITATION IS OFTEN PERCEIVED AS a mysterious or highly religious ritual, best left to a saint, mystic, martyr, Buddhist monk, or Hindu holy man. There's a perception we have to sit cross-legged for hours, inhaling incense, chanting OM until your back aches, your butt hurts, your joints stiffen, or you've received mystical messages of nirvana and bliss. Most of us believe we're incapable of receiving spiritual guidance; it was probably better suited to the mystics of the middle ages. Besides, we're used to receiving messages via e-mail, cell phone, or blackberry. But the truth is even babies meditate, and they've never been to an ashram or monastery. As children we meditated for hours, although we had different names for it, like watching clouds, lying on the grass, swinging, or slowly licking an ice cream cone. As long as you can breathe you can meditate, and if done in a fashion authentic for you, meditation is relaxing and enjoyable.

Many never try it because some priests or monks tell us the purpose of meditation is only reach God. Twentieth-century Trappist monk Thomas Merton wrote that meditation "aims at bringing you to a state of almost constant loving attention to God, and dependence on Him," or to "enter into a conscious and loving contact with God." But in this century, the real experts and advocates of meditation are Buddhist monks, who seldom mention God in their writings or teachings. So why do Buddhist monks spend their entire days in meditation if they don't believe in the God of Christian religions? Perhaps because it feels good, is rejuvenating, enjoyable, and it's one of the best ways to acquire enlightenment, wisdom and compassion. Meditation, like life, was never meant to be hard, bitter, and devoid of peaceful or pleasant emotions.

One of the most widely read Buddhist monks of this century is Thich Nhat Hanh, who now lives at the Plum Village monastery in France. Originally from Vietnam, he has authored more than 100 books of poetry, fiction and philosophy. Thich Nhat Hanh encourages hugging as a meditation practice. He says if we're distracted and thinking of other things, our hugs will be distracted too, and we won't enjoy them as much. He tells us, "When you hug your child, your friend, your spouse, I recommend that you first breathe in and out consciously and return to the present moment. Then, when you hold him or her in your arms, breathe three more times consciously, and you will enjoy your hugging more than ever before."

Meditation is simple, yet powerful. It's not a form of mind control, in fact, quite the opposite. Since we're constantly controlled by our minds, what we want to achieve with meditation is quieting the mind and allowing our spirit, inner truths, or internal genius to come forth. We don't meditate to control, but we can focus on our breath, positive energy, love, grace, or peace, and understand that the genius of spirit will channel these attributes in a dharmic fashion. An example of this was a two month meditation experiment in 1993, aimed at preventing violent crime in Washington, DC. The National Demonstration Project to Reduce Violent Crime brought together 4,000 meditators from 60 countries to see if group meditation could reduce crimes including homicide, rape, assault, and robbery. This was an experiment based on research from 41 previous studies. Twice a day, from June 7 until July 30, participants meditated in large groups hoping to reduce stress and crime, and during this time violent crime dropped 25 percent!

The health benefits of meditation are enormous, and so the earlier in life we can start a regular practice the better. The Medical College of Georgia screened 5,000 high school students and found that 156 had stress and high blood pressure issues putting them at risk for developing hypertension. With just two 15-minute meditation sessions every day, one at home and one at school, they were able to lower their blood pressure during the four months of the study. Researchers also discovered that their blood pressure continued to drop four months after the sessions ended. The students who meditated also had lower rates of absenteeism, less suspensions and fewer violations of school rules.

In 2013 researchers in Wisconsin, Spain and France reported the first joint study showing that meditation actually produces molecular changes in the body that reduce inflammation. The study examined the effects of meditation with a group of experienced meditators compared to a group of control subjects who engaged in quiet non-meditative activities.

With the experienced meditators eight hours of mindfulness meditative practices began to affect the genes that are targeted in anti-inflammatory and analgesic drugs. Meditation actually down-regulated those genes known to cause inflammation.

In addition to the many health benefits meditation is important because we're constantly bombarded by information, ideas, trends, and technology, and told how and what to think by parents, schools, religions, television, radio, magazines, books, business, and workplaces. With all this information it's possible to follow the crowd and take paths that don't support us, becoming entangled in a forest of false beliefs. We may become robotic without realizing it, devoid of the joy of never having an original or creative thought, and losing the ability to access our internal blueprints, dharma or path, those inner truths which give us purpose and peace. Our parents may convince us to follow in the family business, when our destiny and place of real joy may be something entirely different.

As we've learned, there is no ultimate authority on earth. No parent, religion, school, or country has the edge on insight, truth, or genius and this can be discombobulating because our mind desperately wants to cling to something external. Even though there is justice and truth on earth, we're immersed in karma since earth is the place we come to clear this karma away. Every parent, religion, business, and government is a mixture of both karma and dharma. When institutions or leaders claim infallibility, which is really a form of control, they are operating from their egos and minds rather than the wisdom of spirit. Genius and truth come from inside us. This is why consulting our dreams and finding a meditative practice we enjoy is so important. The Buddha achieved enlightenment, the highest form of wisdom, by sitting under a Bodhi tree. We can't and probably wouldn't want to go back to those simpler times of Buddha or the early mystics, but we can meditate and still use our computers and cell phones when needed. When we meditate, we stay on course, and our soul is not in constant chaos. When we stop a meditation we enjoy, like running, painting, sailing, or hiking in the woods, we become bombarded by all the noise, ideas, and everything physical around us. We would all be raving lunatics if we had never, ever, meditated. Most of us have been meditating at some point in our lives, only we call it something different, and we're often not aware just how sustaining this time was. Except if we stop, we became more anxious, short tempered, scattered, and confused. Sometimes we don't make the connection—no one really teaches us that focused, solitary activities like slowly taking time to sip your cup of coffee in the morning as you watch the trees, and settle your mind for the day, is a form of meditation. Many musicians, performers, public speakers, and athletes will take a few moments by themselves before they face the crowds, breathing slowly and centering themselves to prepare. Walking your dog, watching nature, painting, drawing, playing a musical instrument, petting your cat, nursing your baby, riding a bike, listening to classical music, or walking alone, are valuable ways to meditate. And your home provides endless meditative activities. This is why Buddhist monks are assigned many of these duties in monasteries: washing clothes, ironing, cooking, baking, dusting, vacuuming, sweeping, tending to indoor plants, raking leaves, maintaining the lawn, gardening. Even taking time to quietly sit on the toilet without distractions can be meditative. Is this not a form of focused attention? I've had some of my best insights while sitting on the john.

Staying in a world of constant noise and busyness is like having a slow spiritual or emotional leak—eventually it depletes us. It doesn't fuel our energy level or spirit, it's not in our best interests, and never brings us feelings of harmony, insight, or peace. It seeps into our psyche like an insidious virus, and we're often not consciously aware of how it wreaks havoc with our wellbeing. Think about how annoying it is trying to listen to a radio all day long with constant static; this is life without any meditative practice or connection to spirit. When we're focused and tuned into spirit it's like having the clear, powerful, often calming frequency of our favorite music or radio station. But for most of us, daily stresses cause our internal dials to shift into static and we lose that clear reception. To turn our dial back to the right frequency, we need only to center themselves, slow down, and take a few deep breaths. Then it's as if our spiritual antenna goes back up, and our focus is stronger and more relaxed. When we allow ourselves time each day at something we take pleasure in, like taking a walk, nature photography, rocking a baby, or watching a sunset, our natural gifts are brought to the forefront, and they become our source of inner intelligence and guidance. This is how we stay on course and prevent our souls from being in constant chaos. Meditative activities comfort, soothe, inspire, and guide us. They're an internal compass preventing us from getting lost. They may become our refuge during the darkest times, our best friend, just as our soul, spirit, God, the universe, the force, or whatever you wish to call it, becomes guidance, a lighthouse in the storms of life. Meditation has the power to restore us—if only we give it a chance.

Combining Meditation with Dreams

I know that if we meditate on a dream sufficiently long and
thoroughly—if we take it about with us and turn it over and
over—something almost always comes of it.

C. G. Jung

Sleeping and dreaming are incredibly important. Depending on body weight, the average person can live between four to six weeks without food; but if we are completely prevented from sleeping for just two to three weeks—we won't survive. The breakdown begins with exhaustion, forgetfulness, confusion, anxiety, disorientation, and then paranoia. Severely sleep deprived individuals actually start hallucinating because their spirit is desperately trying to take them into the dimensions of sleep where they can be guided and restored. Lab rats chronically sleep deprived die after two or three weeks. They lose weight, their body temperatures fall, and they develop body sores that don't heal. The reason? A complete breakdown of their immune systems. Trying to navigate through life without sleeping and dreaming is like trying to walk without a backbone or spine—we collapse without this much needed support. We dream to keep us vitally alive. Our dreams are constantly helping us sort out emotional issues and preparing us for future challenges. Bringing dreams into conscious awareness is the stuff of genius. This free wisdom is always inside us; all that's required is setting aside quiet, focused time, to journal our dreams and meditate on their meaning.

Since dreamwork and meditation are meant to work together as partners, one of the best ways to begin a meditation practice is to journal your dreams. This is great single pointed focus every morning as we lie in bed for a few minutes and just allow the dream to drift back into conscious awareness. Over the years I've found even if I don't remember a dream, those first few minutes after waking up are golden. It's during that time I always get insights about what I'm writing, make connections, or something important might drift into awareness. Much of this book is the result of those golden moments. After we've written down the dream, if the meaning isn't obvious, we may decide to meditate or reflect on it. We can always ask for clarity and guidance around the dream. Once we clear our minds, it's surprising what surfaces. The answer may not come right away, especially if we've gone forward in time in the dream, but with faith, a little patience, and continued focus, it will. Meditation is one of our greatest ways to achieve insight and peace. The more we meditate the more insight filters through, even when we're not meditating. Meditation is like reconnecting our telephone lines to the spirit world, and this dimension is always eager to calm, soothe, and inform.

When I taught grade one, we meditated just about every day. It's certainly not true that children can't focus. We kept it short and sweet, they saw its value, and they loved this time of the day. Hopefully, it prepared them to become meditators later in life. I used to tell my students that God can't talk to us if our telephone lines are busy. Later, when I taught grade six, we started with five minutes of meditation or guided imagery every day, then after two or three weeks we would increase this another five minutes. Our five minutes of meditation grew to 45 minutes, and these eleven-year-old children were loving it, and wanting to do it longer. When I taught secondary school, after I introduced meditation or guided imagery, many students would beg me to begin the class this way. I realized that in their stressful, chaotic, busy lives, these moments provided a needed time of rest and sanctuary. As Ricky Martin said, "When you're surrounded by noise all the time, how can you hear God?"

Just as it's impossible not to dream, it's equally as impossible not to meditate sometime in our lives. But there's a critical difference; we all dream for an hour or two every night, but meditation is usually a conscious choice. Sitting in the bathroom can be meditative, but we can choose to sit on the john with the radio blaring, reading a magazine, or using a cell phone! Most of us choose to spend very little time in meditation, so we wonder why we're stressed, forgetful, or scatterbrained, what gave people like Einstein that cutting edge, and why depression and suicide rates are constantly rising. Have you ever heard of a Buddhist monk who didn't meditate? Have you ever heard of a stressed, depressed, scatter-brained, or suicidal Buddhist monk?

The Myth of Multitasking

To do two things at once is to do neither.
Roman philosopher

The world only whispers her secrets to those who stand still and listen.
That's the reason the only difference between 'now'
and 'know' is one very silent letter.
Kate Nowak

We live in a world with two villains, *noise and busyness*, both are unnatural and unhealthy but we've become so accustomed to these vices, it's hard for most people to survive even a few minutes without them. We get nervous and jittery when there is silence, the same way a drug addict gets jittery without a fix. Although one of the oldest proverbs tells us "speech is silver, but silence is golden," we're not sure anymore that this is the case. To complicate this further, the ego or mind has convinced us it's cool and desirable to be constantly busy, to work overtime, double time, skip lunch, miss vacations (valuable reflection time), to have most days and nights on your calendar full, and to plan every weekend. Our society has been brainwashed into believing that having a Blackberry, iPod, cell phone, tablet, and computer means we're important, indispensable, on the cutting edge, popular and trendy. It's absolutely fine to use all these devices, in fact many jobs and schools require them, but it's not fine to become dominated by our devices—it's always about balance. The truth is we've devolved into a society that has lost the ability to simply stop, reflect, relax, and breathe. Einstein, Nobel, Jesus, the Buddha, Gandhi, and Mother Theresa didn't have any electronic gadgets, and they managed to get their messages out just fine. To survive this insanity, we do the polar opposite of meditating to become focused and more aware. We multitask, believing this saves time, making us more efficient. But rather than making us smarter, we're morphing into an era of digital dummies addicted to a digital world that dumbs us down. This has created what doctors now refer to as a treatable disease, Digital Attention Deficit Disorder or DADD, and one could argue that these 3 Ds represent disrespect, disconnection, and depression.

Dave Crenshaw has written an entire book about this, *The Myth of Multi-tasking: How "Doing it All" Gets Nothing Done.* Since it's impossible to be present, and really listen to someone, while attempting to do something else, he defines multitasking as "a polite way to say I have not heard a thing you said." Neuroscientist Michael Merzenich discovered that multi-tasking impedes our brain's ability to make positive changes in brain mapping, changes that are converted into long term memory. In numerous experiments Merzenich found that changes in our brain's circuitry *only* occur when we pay attention, or focus closely on *one* task at a time.

Dr. Edward Hallowell, a psychiatrist, and expert in the field of attention deficit disorders, human connection, and managing excessive busyness, agrees that multitasking makes us less efficient. He explains, "No one really multitasks. You must spend less time on any one thing. When it looks like you're multitasking—you're looking at one TV screen and other TV screen and you're talking on the telephone—your attention has to shift from one to the other. Your brain literally can't multitask. You can't pay attention to two things simultaneously. You're switching back and forth between the two. So you're paying less concerted attention to either one." This switching back and forth actually reduces our productivity and increases mistakes by up to 50 percent. In short, multitasking makes us dumber. It's ineffective mind clutter. How focused, peaceful, or truly aware are we, as we drive our cars, polish our nails, talk on a cell phone, and eat our breakfast? Or make supper as we talk on the phone, iron a shirt, check our e-mails, and watch television? Do we *really* need to talk on a cell phone in the middle of a gym, spinning class, while we're driving, or in the bank while a teller is doing our transactions? With all this information overload, we forget important anniversaries and birthdays, we mix up dates and times, arrive at our child's concert two hours late, and leave babies in cars, forgetting they're even there. Dr. Hallowell had so many technically crazed individuals showing up at his office believing they had Attention Deficit Disorder, or ADD, it led him to the discovery of a different disorder he calls ADT or Attention Deficit Trait. When hyper-stressed ADT individuals went on a holiday, or switched to a relaxing setting, the symptoms went away. With true ADD sufferers, the symptoms never completely go away, no matter where they go. While Attention Deficit Disorder, or ADD, is something an individual is born with, a neurological disorder with a genetic component, ADT is a creation of our technological times. Hallowell says it's like a "traffic jam in the mind," and traffic jams don't have to last forever.

The symptoms of Attention Deficit Trait are distractibility, restlessness, irritability, impulsive decision making because you have so many things to do, and a constant sense of needing to go, rush, run around. Its victims seem crazed with an inner frenzy and impatience, leading to difficulty focusing, staying organized, setting priorities, and managing time. They're underachieving and not working to their full potential. They produce less, answer questions in a superficial manner, their wellspring of new ideas runs dry, they start working longer hours and sleeping less, exercise less, spend little time with family and friends, and generally despite the long hours, their accomplishment is disappointing. Dr. Hallowell explains, "They're all running around, working their tails off. But they're really at the whim of the market. They think they're working hard, and they think they're being productive, but they're not. They're busy, but they're not thoughtful." Attention Deficit Trait is another slow insidious virus that takes away the best of an individual. If left untreated, Hallowell says a sufferer "is robbed of his flexibility, his sense of humor, his ability to deal with the unknown. He forgets the big picture and the goals and values he stands for. He loses his creativity and his ability to change plans...he is prone to melting down, to throwing a tantrum, to blaming others, and to sabotaging himself. Or he may go in the opposite direction, falling into denial and total avoidance of the problems attacking him, only to be devoured. This is ADT at its worst."

Hallowell believes the reason for under accomplishment, stress, and mania is our technocentric way of life, where it has become normal to talk on the phone while reading e-mails and eating pizza. Computers, e-mail, voice mail, instant messaging, cell phones, and social networking have made the world one huge distracting circus, creating a multitasking stress our minds were never designed to handle. In the past, we've been able to overload our bodies with manual labor, but with all the technical gadgets now available, we have never been able to overload our brain circuitry in the same manner. An overloaded brain is like a computer hard drive that's filled to capacity with no memory left—it's slow, inefficient, and prone to crashing completely. When our brain circuits become overloaded, we create the illusion of working and being productive, when we're not; we're just treading water. Hallowell explains that as our minds fill with noise, the brain gradually loses its ability to fully attend, or focus on anything. If we don't allow ourselves time to stop and think, we're under utilizing our brain. Our brains are best equipped to think, analyze, dissect, (left brain functions) and then to innovate and create (right brain functions). When people simply respond to bits of information, they lose the ability to go deep. He estimates that in the corporate world ADT has reached epidemic proportions affecting 30 to 40 percent of the workforce. "Organizations are sacrificing their most valuable asset, he says, "namely the imagination and creativity of the brains they employ, by allowing ADT to infest the organization. It's not hard to deal with, once you identify it. You need to set limits and preserve time to think. Warren Buffet sits in a little office in the middle of nowhere and spends a lot of his time just thinking. We are not giving ourselves that opportunity." He believes anyone can be hit with the ADT bug, from CEO's to doctors and lawyers who survive in a sea of paperwork, and, even moms, who can drown in the constant activity of taking children from one activity to another, supervising homework, doing laundry, shopping and cooking. Just as there isn't a sedative to stop a traffic jam, there is no magic medication to address ADT—except slowing down. There are employees at high tech companies who *do* escape the burn out effects of ADT because they haven't forgotten how to play. Play is a powerful antidote. Hallowell says, "The best treatment is to take time to slow down and think and connect with the outside world. And to stop being a total slave to your electronics...Properly used, they are wonderful. Improperly used, they are destructive...it's a matter of our learning how to use our technology properly, instead of letting it use us."

One tragic example was the 2008 Los Angeles commuter train crash, where 25 people were killed and 135 injured. The engineer, Robert Martin Sanchez, who died in the crash, was texting a teenager while driving the train. Earlier, while driving the morning train, he received 21 text messages and sent 24! In the hour before the crash he sent out seven text messages and received five. Cell phone records showed he sent a message at 4:22:01, received one at 4:22:03, and the accident occurred at 4:22:23. Little wonder he failed to stop at a red light, and passed through four warning lights, before crashing into a Union Pacific freight train. Another tragedy was the 2011 crash of a medical helicopter in Missouri, where four people were killed; the pilot James Freudenbert, his patient, a flight nurse, and a paramedic. After the accident, the U.S. National Transportation Safety Board determined the crash occurred because the pilot was texting on his cell phone. Freudenbert sent and received at least 240 texts during his shift, 20 of which occurred just before the crash. He was so distracted by his texting, he took off without checking the fuel, thinking he had enough for the 45-minute flight, but crashed after 30 minutes when the fuel tank went dry.

Texting, it seems, is often the prerequisite for insanity. An argument in a Tampa, Florida, movie theatre in January 2014, between two men, one who was texting his 3-year-old daughter's baby sitter during movie previews, and a disgruntled retired police captain, ended in cold-blooded murder. Curtis Reeves, 71, asked Chad Oulsen, 43, who was sitting in front of him, to stop texting before the movie started. Chad, clearly upset at this request, made the fatal mistake of throwing popcorn at Reeves. Heated words were exchanged and Reeves fired his gun hitting Chad in the chest, and wounding his wife Nicole who put her hand on her husband's chest as the .380 semi-automatic hand gun was discharged. Mission accomplished; Reeves calmly sat down as Curtis fell to the ground with blood spewing from his mouth. He died later in hospital. Adding further to the insanity, Reeves' lawyer tried to convince the judge that his client was the victim of an aggressive attack of popcorn and was afraid for his safety. The judge didn't buy the argument and Reeves was charged with second-degree murder. After the incident the movie theatre issued a list of prohibited items on its website; no cell phone use, no texting, and no weapons in the theatre auditorium.

In our technically bent world, the need to slow down to gain sanity and awareness has never been more important. When we don't carve out moments of quiet, we fail to get those whispers from spirit, those golden insights about checking our gas tanks or tires, problems in a relationship, how we can ace that deal at work, start that essay or proposal, settle an argument, or solve a child's behavioral problems. Instead, we have road rage, fatal accidents, nervous depression, panic attacks, insomnia, sleep disorders, suicide attempts, confusion, even murder, because globally we've simply lost the ability to stop, think clearly, or listen.

Consider the dynamics of having a conversation with your best friend; we're usually talking, then listening. Imagine if we *never* listened to our boss at work, teachers, lovers or significant others, friends, relatives, children, or pets. We'd be in serious trouble. It's probably even more disastrous to never listen to our soul, spirit, angels, and the legions of enlightened beings waiting to whisper guidance. Angels never shout over the noise; that's a human quality. Spirit won't scream over a hockey game, television show, dinner party, or iPod, no matter how important the message. Instead it waits patiently until we're ready—only sometimes we never are.

I haven't become aware of this, because meditation has been a constant force in my life. I became aware of this in my early forties when it felt like I lived in a bottomless pit of pain and depression. I desperately needed to meditate. For most of my life I had been incessantly talking and doing. Sylvia Boorstein wrote a book about this, a manual for novice meditators, aptly named, *Don't Just Do Something, Sit There.* There's a famous Buddhist saying, "We're *not* human doings, we're human beings." We rarely give ourselves permission to shut down our minds, rest, and just be ourselves. The mind is like a highly sophisticated computer, and like any sophisticated machine, if you run it non-stop without periods of rest, inspection, or maintenance, malfunctions, blows up, or breaks down. If I don't carve out quiet, reflective times each day I have trouble sleeping, I'm forgetful, I spend hours walking around underground parking lots because I can't remember where I parked my car, I lock myself out of my home, I attempt to make coffee in the morning but forget to grind the coffee beans, then freak because I'm late and don't have caffeine to start the day. I need to meditate because it gives me precious moments of peace you can't buy with all the money in the world. I meditate because it enables the ordinary things in life to become extraordinary—morning mist, watching a bird in flight, truly seeing the beauty of trees, or steam dancing off your coffee cup. Life takes on a whole different quality when you begin to meditate earnestly—you finally experience the meaning of the word peace. You begin to cross those dimensions and experience more moments of heaven on earth, and at times life seems enchanted. It's like that warm glow or slight buzz you feel after having a glass or two of wine—only it happens spontaneously, often when you least expect it. In *Everyday*

Grace, Marianne Williamson tells us "The mind of someone who regularly practices prayer and meditation is *literally a different mind."* When she meditates she is, "more serene, which affects all my interactions as I move through the day. Also, I think I'm *smarter.* I have greater insight, I view situations with greater depth, and my mind is not so cluttered with meaningless preoccupations that bombard us each moment in this increasingly frantic world. My spiritual practice doesn't just make me *feel* better; I think it makes me a different woman than I am when I choose not to do it. Everything I'm involved with becomes infused with a peace I do not otherwise carry. It affects the reactions of people I meet and the outcome of situations I might not even know exist. We don't need to push life so much as we need to experience it more elegantly, to be motivated more by inspiration than ambition."

When we're able to do this, we *do* live more elegantly, and we're able to release our incessant mind chatter more often. This chatter can bring us to the brink of insanity—a mind that won't shut up, repeating things over and over, telling us we're a loser, not smart enough, good enough, or that there is always something we should do or fear. Buddhists refer to this busy place of constant chatter as "monkey mind," "small mind" or *sem.* When we meditate it's like we dive through the dirty, murky, often turbulent waters of *sem* at the top of a lake, to the calmer, cleaner, waters below. Here we access our deepest core, spring fed internal wisdom, the realm of genius, or what Buddhists refer to as Big Mind, spacious mind, or *rikpa,* meaning "intelligence" or "brightness." Buddhist nun, Pema Chödrön, tells us, "Behind all the planning and worrying, behind all the wishing and wanting, picking and choosing, the unfabricated wisdom mind of rikpa is always here. Whenever we stop talking to ourselves, rikpa is continually here." She compares our thoughts to wild dogs that need taming, and says that rather than beating them or throwing stones, we can tame them more effectively with compassion, precision, and kindness. Reaching this calmer place of focused attention is what enabled Einstein to create his theory of relativity. It's how all great painters achieved masterpieces, it's how any genius has ever been able to bring anything of beauty, wonder, or lasting value into our chaotic world. Meditation activates the inner genius that lies deep within our core. However, we can never get rid of those barking dogs completely, just as we are never completely free from our thoughts. But once we're connected to ripka it does begin to permeate everything, just as a few drops of blue dye completely transforms a glass of water. Chödrön explains, "It expands into our resentments. It expands into our fear. It expands into our concepts and opinions about things and into who we think we are. We might sometimes even get the feeling that life is like a dream."

Getting rid of this incessant chatter and creating a quiet mind is one of the best ways to ward off hopelessness, depression, and anxiety. Sometimes this incessant chatter can seem like we're two people—like Gollum from *The Hobbit* and the *Lord of the Rings* trilogy, as the ego vies for attention. An active ego is the source of all of our criticism, judgment and self-loathing—nothing or no one is good enough. The voice of the ego is always the voice that undermines us or holds us back. Meditation can be an antidote for all the vices of the mind, the things that drive us crazy—anger, resentment, jealousy, self-pity, self-loathing, guilt, and fear. When we're fearful our mind is like a recording that's never turned off, playing the same tracks over and over. If we can clear our minds or erase these tracks we feel greater peace, and we're connected to deeper truths rather than the muddle of the mind. When we shut down our ego in meditation we bypass the ego and its illusions and allow greater insight and truth to come through. We may not always receive huge flashes of insight when we meditate, but we do feel calmer, peaceful and focused, and we're better equipped to take on the world, or just get through the day!

As children we were all natural meditators. We spent hours observing animals, gazing at the stars, laying on our backs and watching the clouds, rocking back and forth on a swing, twirling, dancing, focusing on lady bugs crawling up our arm, and shut out the world as we gazed at our ice cream savoring every lick. We built snowmen, went up and down hills on our toboggans, and sat watching snowflakes falling. As we grew into adolescents many of our activities were meditative; skipping, swinging, riding our bike, holding or petting an animal, watching an aquarium, birds, sunset or fire, picking flowers, fishing, playing with sand, painting, drawing, watching an ocean, lake, river, or stream, rowing or paddling a boat, observing the wind blowing, looking at trees, listening to the sounds of nature, running, walking around the block with our dog. Anything we do alone, or with other quiet people, where we *suspend our ego, rational mind and judgment and simply focus on one thing at a time,* is meditation. As children we were all geniuses; it didn't matter that we weren't really going anywhere as we went up and down the hill, that it was cold, that we weren't doing anything productive or making money—all the mattered was enjoying the activity, being in the moment, and communing with nature.

As busy, productive adults most of our thoughts won't really help us evolve or find peace. We want to get rid of all of the mundane day-to-day chatter when we meditate, things like, "I wonder how much I have left in my bank account," "I need to make an appointment to get my haircut," or, " I have to check my e-mails again before I go to bed." With meditation, we suspend our mind, become quiet, and listen so that we can hear spirit's gentle voice. Insights from spirit never shout, bark, judge, demand, or repeat; they float down like a feather from the sky or whisper gently like a lover. And if we're never, ever quiet, we completely miss these wisps of wisdom and whispers of affection. We don't need to be alone in a dark room, sitting cross legged, with incense, chanting strange foreign words. As we became responsible, productive, time-efficient adults, we started believing that being smart meant *only* using your mind. But in balance, spirit and mind always work together as partners. The insights that may emerge in ten minutes of meditation could take ten weeks of mental gymnastics, and save you ten months of frustration.

In one of the final scenes of the movie *Oh God,* George Burns as God is dressed in casual or safari clothes because he's going away. He says he hasn't spent enough time with His animals lately. Watching or being with animals is a perfect meditative activity. Their whole life seems to consist of only sleeping, dreaming, meditating, playing, and eating. Dogs actually sleep for 9 hours a day and cats for 15. That's a whole lot of time in REM sleep or the dream state. If we observe most dogs or cats they just lie there perfectly content for an hour or two; they're meditating all the time, yet our egos tell us we're much smarter. Perhaps we could all spend more time just being with the animals.

Blocks to Meditation

Many of us find it hard to meditate because our mind is going at a furious pace. It's not easy to quiet our thoughts; we have so much to say...This takes practice. We can't just sit down and command silence; our mind is too accustomed to doing as it pleases. Our first step in meditation, therefore, is to be patient. Our mind will gradually quiet down as we wait, praying for silence...Focusing on that we give God an opening. Guidance will follow.

Karen Casey

Meditation doesn't hurt us. It doesn't cost money, and we don't need any equipment. It often leaves us refreshed, grounded, and relaxed. It can give us insights and awareness that can be life altering. It strengthens our immune system, improves our memory and mental functioning, and helps us become more empathetic and compassionate. So why don't we all meditate every day? First, *we don't believe it will help us.* We're so immersed in the physical world that our mind has convinced us only physical things are important, doing things; working extra hours, making more money, taking courses to improve ourselves, making phone calls, or shopping. We live in a fast paced, ego-driven society, that doesn't honor quiet and meditation, or understand its inherent value. When it comes to meditation we've all been brainwashed; instead, we're immersed in activities that don't focus, refresh, or fuel us. The second reason is that *we're out of practice.* As with everything else, learning to meditate does require practice and discipline. But it's natural, like getting back on your bike after a couple of years. The third reason, and perhaps the most popular, is that people feel they don't have the time—there is a perception that we have to meditate for a long time every day for it to be effective—but we can start with just five minutes a day. The fourth reason is that we think there's only one way to meditate, sitting cross legged for hours chanting Sanskrit words. But this is one of many, many ways to begin a meditative practice, and once you read the list provided in the next section, hopefully you'll find a few methods you enjoy. The trick is to make it a regular part of your life. And finally, many people don't meditate because they're *afraid*. On a deep level, we all know we're here to clean up karma, and that meditation may bring up issues we're uncomfortable with or don't want to face. We can easily block out or suppress dreams, but it's different with meditation. Unconsciously we're sitting down and saying, "Spirit, I know my life isn't perfect, speak to me, give me guidance." Initially it can take a lot of courage. But for most people, meditation is a relaxing, pleasurable experience. We're not being told horrible things, and there are no lightning bolts from hell. The spirit that soothes and nurtures us in meditation is gentle, non-invasive, and non-judgmental. It doesn't evoke fear, guilt, self-loathing, or shoulds. It never tells you what to do; these are products of the ego or mind—not spirit. The energy or spirit we connect to when meditating is a gentle, nurturing presence that removes us from all the insanity and illusions.

Getting Started

It may be hard to meditate, but it is even harder not to.

Anonymous

A happy life must be to a great extent a quiet life, for it is only in an atmosphere of true quiet that joy can live.

Bertrand Russell

Meditation is a natural process—it's not something most of us have to learn, since we've been doing it all of our lives. When we're awake our brain waves are in beta rhythms, 12 to 20 cycles per second or cps. When we meditate or dream these rhythms slow down to the alpha state, between 8 to 12 cps. Many people reach a meditative state of perhaps 12 cycles per second sitting in the bathtub or taking a long shower. At 8-0 cps cycles per second we may actually fall into a light sleep. So meditation is that unique place when we're not asleep, we're alert and conscious, but relaxed. In *Freedom From the Known,* Indian mystic Krishnamurti says "Meditation is a state of mind which looks at everything with complete attention, totally, not just parts of it...Meditation is one of the greatest arts in life—perhaps *the* greatest, and one cannot possibly learn it from anybody, that is the beauty of it. It has no technique and therefore no authority. When you learn about yourself, watch yourself, watch the way you walk, how you eat, what you say, the gossip, the hate, the jealousy—if you are aware of all that in yourself, without any choice, that is part of meditation. So, meditation can take place when you are sitting in a bus, or walking in the woods full of light and shadows, or listening to the singing of birds or looking at the face of your wife or child."

If you want to try meditation, it's important to have no expectations, not to judge yourself, and to ease into it slowly. Most of us will not have conversations with angels, or redesign the theory of relativity, but we may rediscover the joy of solitude and peace. Meditation is not about having earth-shattering insights; it's about calming the mind, learning to focus on one thing at a time. It's also about enjoyment. If we can teach our mind to shut down, to be quiet, this helps tremendously during stressful or difficult times. If we've never made an attempt to relax or meditate, when we find out our grandmother has just had a heart attack our mind will race, panic, and throw out a million distress signals. If we've learned to meditate, or calm our mind, when we discover our grandmother is ill we can quietly sit, breathe, relax, and gain a whole lot of peace and insight.

One of my favorite books on meditation is written for teenagers, *Just Say Om!* by Soren Gordhamer. He says when we meditate there aren't "big flashes of light" or "tremendous mind-blowing insights" but we do deepen our ability to concentrate and learn more about ourselves. "There are no great fireworks or huge revelations; it is simply a gradual sensitizing and awakening. It may seem like nothing is happening, but if we look back over several months of working with these techniques, we will notice changes. We will see that we are a little more patient with a difficult friend or a little less likely to react in anger when we are upset."

To start a meditation, pick a time when it's relatively quiet and you won't be disturbed. If you can close your eyes and shut out the external world this is always best. Eventually you won't just see darkness; instead swirling or constantly changing colors, changing forms, and perhaps insightful visions. But some people are uncomfortable closing their eyes, so experiment to see what works best for you. *There is no one correct way, only many options.* At first, meditating for two, three or five minutes a day is fine. As a beginner it's exceedingly hard to jump into a long meditation. It's like running or working out. If you've never run before, you're not going to try running for a full hour your first time. Try beginning with short intervals—then if you have the time and the inclination build yourself up. This is a practice—a mental and spiritual discipline—and like all disciplines you become more and more comfortable with it over time. After experimenting with two or three minutes, you might want to increase this to five minutes, then ten. And you probably only want to increase the time *if* you're enjoying the peace and solitude it brings you—no use prolonging something you don't enjoy. Over time most people find they want to meditate longer, because it feels good. This happens naturally, because you enter a dimension where time slips away and you go with the flow. But the amount of time spent meditating is *not* what is most important, the *intent* is. It's self-defeating to believe someone is better or more spiritual if they spend hours every day in meditation. If you have lots of responsibilities and young children, you may be able to fit in five minutes a day to start, and that's fine. Five minutes every morning and night equals more than an hour a week, and that may give you tremendous peace and awareness.

You may decide to include a few minutes of meditation every day with prayer. Or you may quietly read sacred or inspirational books to start. I like using music, so it may be helpful to use music to help you relax by selecting classical, instrumental, relaxing music, or sounds of nature that you enjoy. Music can also help in the beginning to gauge your time; if you only have five minutes, select two of your favorite tracks that last about five minutes. But it's important that the music has no lyrics, since words engage the mind and shift your focus back to the external world. Often the music helps to keep us focused so our mind doesn't wander—music has that wonderful ability to calm and slow down our brain waves. Just follow the music and relax. Experiment; be a scientist. You may discover you like to begin by reading a page from a book on daily meditations, doing five minutes of focused breathing while listening to music, saying a prayer, and ending with five minutes of gentle stretching or yoga. The possibilities are endless. Eventually you'll find what works. After you've meditated for a while you may begin hearing a distinct vibration or humming sound which is easiest to pick up early in the morning or late at night when the world is quieter. This is the "universal hum" and you are beginning to hear or tune into all things of a higher vibration—the music or sounds of the universe—God, spirit, angels. It's a wonderfully soothing frequency to tune into–there's absolutely nothing wrong with your ears, it's actually there all the time, but in our busy lives it is difficult to discern until we learn to become quiet and listen.

There are many people who simply can't sit, who have massive stores of energy. If you're one of these people, it may be better for you to try a silent walking meditation. Walking meditation is highly under-rated. It helps us focus, gets us outside to enjoy the fresh air, and is one of the best forms of exercise. If it's hard for you to sit, try walking or hiking. If you own a dog, take it for a walk—remember dog is god spelled backwards. Focus on each footstep, become aware of everything around you, and allow your mind to become a blank slate. If you walk for thirty minutes, you may find in the first fifteen or twenty minutes your mind is calculating, planning, sorting things out—then it arrives at a place of rest, where there is greater peace. In the beginning, your mind may become upset because you're no longer allowing it to be the boss telling you what to do, so it will try to convince you that nothing is happening, you're not doing it right, this is a waste of valuable time, it's boring, and you have more important things to do. In dream symbolism, a car represents the physical body, so consider that meditation is like filling an empty car with gas—it's the much needed fuel we need to run efficiently and smoothly. We're not wasting time, only gaining a valuable resource. If we forget to fill our tanks it may become more time consuming, costly—even dangerous. Imagine your mind is like a radio talk station and that you can switch the channel or turn it off. Every time your mind intrudes, breathe, smile, and switch it off. Even when you're not meditating, if you're have disturbing, depressing, or distressing thoughts, switch channels; we can control our minds rather than having our minds control us. It only takes seconds from feeling on top of the world, to being totally distressed by upsetting news. Recognize in these situations your thoughts have taken control and they're just thoughts—like passing storm clouds they will change. Your thoughts have tipped your balance—despite what's happened it always feels better to breathe, relax and tap into the calmness of spirit.

Breaking it Down

There is no need to go to India to find peace. You will find that deep place of silence right in your room, your garden, or even your bathtub.
Elisabeth Kübler-Ross

We can break down all meditative practices into two approaches, meditation with or without a focus. If you're new to meditation, using a point of focus may be the best way to start. In focused meditation, we use something to anchor or narrow our focus to the present moment so our mind doesn't wander. There are many ways to do this; working with breath, repeating words or phrases, listening to music, movement, gazing at something like a candle, aquarium, fountain, flowers, water, trees, mountains, or performing repetitive tasks. Breath work is something we can do with formal training or with little training at all. One of the easiest ways to start is simply placing one hand on your belly and observing how your stomach rises as you inhale, and how it falls as you exhale. All focus is on your stomach and breath. Focused breathing is one of the most relaxing practices on earth. The Sanskrit word for breath is *prana* which also means "life force" or "vital energy," and most of us are completely unaware of this vital life force that animates and relaxes us. In the Taoist and Hindu traditions, breath is extremely important because it's a metaphor for spirit or soul. So breath and breathing is more than just a lot of hot air! When you meditate it's important to remember to breathe in and out through the nose, which has a filtering system that cleans and warms the air before it enters the lungs. The ancient yogis used to say that the mouth is for eating, while the nose is for breathing. There's also an important physiological reason for breathing in and out through the nose. Nasal breathing calms you and removes toxins by getting lymph moving. It brings oxygen deeper into your lungs, and also increases the release of nitric oxide to the lungs. Since nitric oxide also widens blood vessels, it opens up sluggish arteries, and gets your blood moving, helping your blood vessels and lungs to work better. It's also believed that nitric oxide may lower anxiety levels, and keep the brain in balance.

But, our meditation and breathing becomes even more effective if we are understand the difference between regular breathing and deep breathing, and in meditation we definitely want to be breathing deeply to derive all its health benefits: lowering our blood pressure, slowing the heart rate, relaxing muscles, reducing insomnia, decreasing pain, increasing energy, and reducing anxiety and stress. Most of the time, we're engaged in regular breathing or shallow breathing, which originates from the lungs and uses the chest muscles. It's believed that as our lives have become busier, more shallow, and superficial, so has our breathing. To understand this better start doing several sharp quick breaths, as you would in a rush or panic, and watch how your chest or upper body rapidly rises and falls. Now, inhaling through your nose, take a long, deep breath, and you'll see your chest expand slowly this time. To make the progression to deep breathing or diaphragm breathing, it may help to understand exactly where our focus needs to be. The diaphragm is a dome-shaped sheet of skeletal muscle that extends across the bottom of the rib cage and underneath the lungs. The diaphragm, also called the thoracic diaphragm, actually separates the chest from the abdomen and is the main muscle of breathing and respiration. The Native American Indians considered the diaphragm the separation between heaven and earth, since our heart, brain, and lungs rest above the diaphragm and our liver, spleen, stomach, intestines, reproductive organs, and bladder are below. With deep breathing these organs are massaged and bathed in fresh blood and oxygen. The organs are squeezed and released like giant sponges. Deep breathing signals all of the body to work better, which is why it is so beneficial for our health and well-being. However, in many cases this muscle is never utilized properly or enough. To begin diaphragm breathing, we want to take several long deep breaths, perhaps placing our hands just below the belly button and focus on having the breath originate from deep in the belly. This time you will feel your belly rise *first* as you inhale, followed by your chest, then you'll feel both your belly and chest fall as you exhale. The beauty of deep breathing is that it takes very little practice to achieve, while its health benefits are tremendous.

While meditating and breathing deeply we can also use mantras or sacred thoughts, words or prayers. The word mantra comes from two Sanskrit words, *"manas"* or mind, and *"trai"* which means to protect or free from. So a mantra or short prayer is used to protect and free the mind from distractions and insane thoughts. Another translation is using the root *"man,"* meaning to think, and the root *"tra"* meaning tool—so we're creating a tool for focused thought. We can add a mantra to our breathing by repeating phrases such as, "I am breathing in," and "I am breathing out," or "I am breathing in peace, I am breathing out tension." We can slow down our breathing by counting to two as we inhale, then exhaling to a count of three. As we get better at this, we can inhale, then exhale to a count of four, five, six, or seven. Try playing with your breath. Experiment and see what feels best. You may enjoy taking a longer inhalation, by counting to three as you inhale, then two as you exhale. Or you may find it more relaxing by inhaling to a count of one, then exhaling to a count of three. A breathing exercise by Buddhist monk, Thich Nhat Hanh, is "Breathing in, I calm my body, breathing out I smile." You can keep it very simple by breathing and silently saying one word such as peace, calm, quiet, or stillness. As you breathe out, you can repeat the same word or combine two words together such as "peaceful" as you inhale, and "mind" as you exhale. After a while you may want to make up your own mantras or prayers. It can be any phrase like "quiet mind," "peaceful smile," "I align with the light," the name of your God or higher power, or any saint, archangel, or enlightened being, that brings you comfort and peace.

Listening to the sounds of nature can be a calming, meditative practice. We can also pick anything we enjoy looking at, an aquarium, a fireplace, or a sunset. We simply watch, and if thoughts enter, refocus by shifting our attention back to this object. Dance, tai chi, qi gong, and yoga can all become meditation in motion, as long as we are not talking or thinking during our practice, and our attention is focused on the movement and what is happening in our bodies. Focused body awareness can be a wonderful gift. Any repetitive task we enjoy can become meditative, as long as we perform this task in solitude focused completely on our actions.

Objectless awareness is a more difficult or advanced meditative practice. With eyes open or closed we simply become aware of whatever enters our consciousness; changing colors, thoughts, insights, memories, fantasies, temptations, sounds, physical sensations. We merely stay with it, observing what comes and goes with a detached awareness. When I started meditating I used to think if I didn't block out every single thought, I was a failure, or if I didn't make my mind a complete blank slate, I wasn't doing it right. But there are always thoughts, insights, impressions, and ideas floating around in our minds—if there weren't, we'd be dead! Sometimes, I get a great poem or ideas for something I'm writing while meditating, so I actually switch from objectless awareness to a more focused meditation where I'm writing these insights down before I lose them. The trick is to be aware, without letting thoughts rule or control your life. So if you start to meditate and your mind says you really should check your e-mails, the challenge is to know that those e-mails will always be there, and that it is more important to honor this sacred time, and learn to relax.

There is no *one* right way to meditate. It's important to find a way you enjoy so that you stick with it. But you don't have to always stay with the same type of meditation your entire life. Variety is fine. However, if you find something that works, it's always good to stay with it to reap its benefits. When you read this list, you may realize you enjoyed one of these activities, but stopped, and when you did, you didn't feel as calm and centered. Or you may realize you've been meditating but giving it a different name. Here are some meditative methods you may want to experiment with:

In Nature or Outdoors

- lying on the beach
- watching the sunset
- sitting at or watching a campfire
- watching the stars at night or the moon
- watching water, an ocean, lake, river, pond, or fountain
- fishing
- watching animals
- nature photography

Meditation in Motion—indoors and outdoors

- riding a bike or motorcycle
- walking or hiking in the woods
- picking wild flowers
- walking a dog alone
- swinging
- jogging or running
- swimming
- canoeing, kayaking, windsurfing, sailing, paddle boarding
- cross country skiing
- snow shoeing
- skating
- rollerblading
- golf
- tai chi, yoga, qi gong

At Home

- rocking a baby asleep in a quiet room
- watching a sleeping child
- gazing into a fireplace
- petting a cat or dog,
- dancing alone
- watching birds at a bird feeder or animals
- watching an aquarium or fountain
- playing a musical instrument
- crafts such as; quilting, rug hooking, knitting, crocheting, needlepoint, batik, weaving, jewelry making
- watching a candle
- taking a bath or shower and focusing on the water or your breath
- gardening, cutting grass, or watering the flowers or lawn,
- solitary housework such as washing floors, dusting, washing dishes, ironing
- cooking, preparing food, or baking
- journaling dreams or insights
- writing, including writing poetry
- painting, drawing, sketching, sculpting, pottery
- looking at art
- hugging
- sitting on the toilet

When we consider something like painting or drawing, these activities may or may not be meditative. If we're painting and our best friend is with us, we're talking about our favorite restaurant, and the television is on–this is not meditation. If we're alone, the phone is turned off, light classical or instrumental music is playing, and we relax as we paint, this is meditation. If we're writing a list of all the things we need to do, this is not mediation, because in most cases we're completely using our mind. If we sit down and go into a meditation, then after five or ten minutes begin to quietly record our insights or write poetry, this can be meditative.

If nothing on the previous list of meditative techniques really jumped out at you–perhaps you might begin with solitary, focused, eating or drinking. In our fast-paced society, we're so busy, we've developed the habit of gulping down food on the run, never really tasting it, savoring each bite, or appreciating the joys of eating. I used to work with an English teacher, Chris Urso, who would describe eating as "a party in your mouth." We have 9,000 taste buds on our tongues, a whole lot of sensory pleasure to stimulate. There is a Buddhist practice for beginning meditators where you're given one raisin. You put the raisin in your mouth, but don't swallow it. Instead, savor the raisin—allowing it to move around your mouth, becoming acutely aware of its texture, form, and taste. Staying with this for even a few minutes allows you to experience how incredibly sweet one tiny raisin can be.

Most of us don't eat consciously. If you're one of those people, you may want to try the raisin exercise first. If raisins don't appeal to you perhaps chocolate, wine, grape juice, grapes or cheesecake. Perhaps you'd rather try a truly healthy food that appeals to you; cutting an apple in several pieces, eating a bowl of cherries, carrot sticks, or popcorn. Try to do this exercise in slow motion, becoming conscious of everything. To begin, you'll need a glass of wine or grape juice, one chocolate bar (preferably already divided in small squares) or a piece of cheesecake (if you must, the entire cake so you'll have a meditative tool for every day of the week). If anyone gives you a hard time, explain it's a meditative technique to activate genius and heightened awareness. If you've chosen wine or grape juice, this is similar to the raisin exercise. Make sure you're alone and it's quiet. Even though wine is said to be the nectar of the gods, it's advisable to do any wine meditation in the evening rather than first thing in the morning! Pour yourself a small or medium size glass, and spend 10 to 20 focused minutes taking very small sips. Focus all your attention on the wine, becoming aware of its color, taste, texture, how it feels moving down your throat. Swirl it around in your glass and observe how it moves. Smell it. Sip it again and try to determine different bouquets of taste: woody, fruity, dry, sweet. If your mind begins to intrude with other matters, simply refocus on the wine. Hopefully this won't be too hard.

If you enjoy chocolate, try to find a dark organic chocolate bar divided into squares, and if you wish, further divide each square into halves or quarters. Then sit down comfortably, and eat each square, slowly, mindfully, consciously enjoying and tasting every morsel. If you've chosen cheesecake, with your fork or spoon take very tiny bites, again savoring each mouthful and really appreciating and enjoying all the flavors. If you normally woof down a piece of cheesecake in three or four minutes, see if you can stretch this out to 10 or 15 minutes, pausing and taking three or four breaths between every bite. Bon appétit.

INSTEAD

I wanted to be smart, so the world would think me wise,
I wanted recognition, and approval in everyone's eyes.
I wanted to be rich, with oh so many degrees,
I wanted to travel, and cross the seven seas.
I wanted to be physically strong, so I lived at the local gym,
Fitness classes to rocking tunes became my daily hymn,
I even took up yoga, to be flexible with a flair,
But then I got arthritis, and couldn't even sit in a chair.
I've had relentless pain, migraines in my head,
Wiping out my memory, making me brain dead.
I wanted so desperately to work and give back in some way,
Instead my days were spent alone, in pain, most every day.
Perhaps if there is a part of your life in these emotions that I feel,
You'll know that even broken lives can still be very real.
When everything crashes in, and your mind takes a massive blow,
If you learn faith, and connection, then you will truly know.
If you don't have a lot of money, it may be a blessing in disguise,
Because you learn compassion, and what really makes us wise.
No one's life is easy, there's war, death, and disease,
But there are things we can learn, to give us greater ease.
Connection to our spirit, is what allows us to endure,
It gets us through the darkest times, of that you can be sure.
When we connect to spirit, and meditate each day,
When we carve out quiet time, and make sure that we pray,
When we ask to be guided, in everything we do,
Then our thoughts and actions, always will be true.
We'll have spiritual wealth, making us rich indeed,
Surpassing anything physical of want, desire, or greed,
And if we learn to truly love, from deep within our heart,
Then we'll have wealth immeasurable, and we will stand apart.

Marina 2009

Inspired by the poem "God's Answer" by an American Confederate Soldier

303

ACKNOWLEDGEMENTS

IT HAS TAKEN 13 EVENTFUL years to write this book, and in that time, countless people enter your life, so I have many to thank. If I start at the beginning, it was my mother who introduced me to dreams. My mom had possibly the worst dream dictionary at her bedside–every entry entailed gloom and doom. Most mornings she would recount her dreams, whether we wanted to listen or not–Italian mothers can be quite forceful. But, I'm grateful to my mother, because she was the first person who helped me understand we're all time travelers. She frequently went into the future, and was able to foretell events ten years away. Once I hit my twenties and these dream forecasts began coming true, I knew she was onto something. When my mother passed away, I carried on her tradition of having that dream dictionary at my bedside and meditating on its meaning each morning–except I didn't have just one—more like a library.

Dreams helped me make every major decision in my life, so when I began teaching secondary school I was determined to pass this knowledge on to my students. A huge thank you to all the students at St. Augustine's secondary school in Brampton, who taught me so much about dreams, and agreed to let me use their dreams in workshops or classes. These dreams and their insights were so impressive; I've included many in this book. It was impossible to track these students down after 20 years, so if I've used your dream again thank you–and please get in touch with me so that I may acknowledge you in some way.

Meditation was always something I did secretly, but the teacher who really validated meditation for me was Jack Miller at the University of Toronto. When I did my doctoral thesis on dreamwork, Jack thankfully was my advisor, and since that time he has continually supported my work. For almost 20 years he's invited me to his classes to teach dreamwork, and has believed in me during some of the roughest and darkest times in my life. I'm so incredibly grateful for your friendship.

This book has been my own personal journey through pain, and what I've found has sustained me. At times, I desperately needed help. In 2008 I had pretty much given up hope, until I found the Headache and Pain Relief Centre in Toronto and had my first appointment with Dr. Michael Zitney. He was different from the legions of doctors I'd visited—my first appointment lasted two hours so that he really got to

306 | *The Genius of Spirit*

know me. He was incredibly knowledgeable, caring, and empathetic, so every week for six years I've driven to that clinic. When Dr. Zitney learned I had started a book, but was so pain ridden I couldn't finish it, he encouraged me to start small, no expectations, maybe an hour a day when the migraines weren't too severe, and just see what would happen. What happened was 650 pages—much of which I hope will become my next book. To Dr. Zitney I'm extremely grateful—without his support, this book might not have happened.

Dr. Zitney encouraged me to see an osteopath, Dan Palma who was part of his team at the pain clinic. I really didn't want to see Dan—except I was desperate. I'd never been to an osteopath–didn't understand what they did—but decided to give it a try. It turned out to be one of the best decisions I've made. Dan's gentle manipulations helped tremendously, but he helped me in many other ways. His sense of humor always had me laughing, and he taught me so many strategies for pain relief, exercise, diet, and well-being. He worked magic when I had the worst migraines. After two years of seeing Dan, I was able to join a gym again, and after five years I went back to yoga. I am incredibly grateful Dan, for your patience, skill, advice, and support. Your warm professional approach was a godsend. Thanks also to the other doctors at the pain clinic who treated me, Dr. Jack Park, Dr. Harry Sandhu, and Dr. Jeremy Sloan, and to the administrative assistants Lisa Gallaugher and Stephanie Fernandes, who always made me feel welcome. Thanks also to Dr. Brian Kirsh, specialist in chronic pain, whose wise and gentle counsel made a huge impact in my life.

A huge thanks to Igor Jakovljevic and Kim Smith, massage therapists, whose treatments relieved my pain and helped me keep going. Your hands also work magic. I would be remiss if I didn't thank Diane Blackburn, the most amazing Pilates teacher, whose classes were like physiotherapy for my back.

In 2000 this book started as a workshop manual of just over 100 pages which grew as I added the dreams, stories, and anecdotes of workshop participants. Those first students were invaluable sources of information and many of their dreams, visions and stories grace these pages. To the students who attended this Part 2 workshop a huge thanks; Grace Baldasarra, Lucy Bianchi, Cathy Clarke, Sabrina Delgobbo, Eddie and Djanka Gadjel, Donna and David Jones, Lisa, Sarah, Amanda and Larissa Holmes, Sabrina Iacobelli, Linn Kingston, Donna Kiernander, Bernadette Levesque, Joanne Mackie, Lucy Parmigiano, Angela Personnet, Davileen Radigan, Melinda Rapallo, Mark Reno, Patricia Sestini, Maria Watts, and Nancy Wilson. Mimi Grandinetti deserves special mention for her inspiration and help in editing a section of the manuscript.

I've been fortunate to have a family that always supports me—my brother Frank, sister Chris, brother-in-law Doug, niece Lisa, nephew Frank, his wife Debby, and their children Laena and Mason who have given me so much joy! To all my cousins who supported my first book–there are over 50 of you, too many to mention, but I love you all. A very special thanks to my cousin Carole Sisto who edited the first draft of this book many years ago, my Aunt Fran, cousins Frank Cutrara, and Chris and Ernie Collins. Thanks to my neighbors the Stange's who have become like my second family, Angela, Dean, Caitlin and Tyler.

I've been blessed with wonderful friends who encouraged me constantly, bought books for my library, recommended movies, television shows, anything they felt would help. Thanks to my vivacious blood sister Laurie in France, my closest friends Shelley Paul, Jacquie Lewin, Cecilia Song, Maria Watts (who lent me her home to teach workshops), Melinda Rapallo who was a constant sounding board, Susan Skaith, Marilyn Cornwell, Carolyn Esvelt, Valia Zorzini, Janet Correa, Susan Woods, Jeanette Hamilton, Dianne Muisiner, Ruth Brady, Mary Ferlisi, Judy Knighton, Madeline Mont, Deborah MacDougall, Marian and Ian Martin, and Gary Simon. A special thanks to my longtime friend Don Speller for providing his genius insights on Mensa.

An enormous thanks to copy editor Joan Read, who spent many hours editing my final manuscript and gently recommended so many needed changes.

A final thanks to the yoga community that has nurtured my body, soul and spirit for over 13 years, and for the support I received for my first book *Dreamwork Uncovered*. Special thanks to Maureen Rae, yoga teacher extraordinaire whose classes challenge, inspire and nurture. Thanks also to fellow yoga teachers Janet Turcet, Briar Boake, Christine Ling, and Jasmin Chandler.

And finally to you the reader, if you have bought or borrowed this book, I am incredibly grateful.

In yoga, to end each class we bow and say *Namaste*. There are numerous translations for this word, but the one I like best is, "The light within me honors and respects the light within you. When you are in that place in you, and I am in that place in me, we are one." Since this book is about Einstein's quest to find a universal theory of everything–one unifying force or spirit uniting the world, it seems fitting to end with these words. One day I dream we will all be united in the genius of spirit.

PERMISSIONS

The author gratefully acknowledges the following individuals for permission to use their written material: Carole Sisto, Sabrina Delgobbo, Mimi Grandinetti, and Don Speller.

Grateful acknowledgement is made to the following for permission to reprint previously published material:

Craig Kilburger, Marc Kilburger. and Roxanne Joyal for reviewing the chapter on Twenty-First Century Genius on their lives and for permission to use exerpts from their column "Children in China Pay Price for our Cheap Toys," from the *Toronto Star*, December 17, 2007, and information from their books *Me to We: Finding Meaning in a Material World*, John Wiley & Sons, and *The World Needs Your Kid*, Greystone Books.

Exerpts from *Einstein: A Biography* by Jürgen Neffe, Farrar, Straus and Giroux, New York. Originally published in Jürgen Neffe, EINSTEIN. Eine Biographie © by 2005 Rowohlt Verlag GmbH, Reinbek bei Hamburg Translation copyright © by Shelly Frisch

For quotations from "The Collected Papers of Albert Einstein": © 1987–2004 Hebrew University and Princeton University Press; Reprinted by permission of Princeton University Press.

Ultimate Journey by Robert A. Monroe, Broadway Books, a division of Random House, 1994.

"Wake up to Your Life," by Andrea Ferretti, from *Yoga Journal,* April, 2005.

"Overloaded Circuits: Why Smart People Underperform," by Edward Hallowell, from the January 2005 issue of Harvard Business Review (volume 83, no.1, pages 54-63).

Bird by Bird: Some Instructions on Writing and Life by Anne Lamott, Anchor Books, a division of Random House, 1994.

Care of the Soul: A Guide for Cultivating Depth and Sacredness in Everyday Life by Thomas Moore, Harper Perennial, a division of Harper Collins Publishers, 1992.

Me by Ricky Martin, Celebra, a division of Penguin Group, New York, 2011.

The Tao of Joy Everyday: 365 Days of Tao Living, by Derek Lin, Jeremy P. Tarcher, a division of Penguin Group, New York, 2011.

My Stroke of Insight: A Brain Scientist's Personal Journey, by Jill Bolte Taylor, Viking, a division of Penguin Group, New York, 2006.

Everyday Grace: Having Hope, Finding Forgiveness, and Making Miracles, by Marianne Williamson, Riverhead Books, a division of Penguin Group, 2002.

How God Changes Your Brain, by Andrew Newberg and Mark Robert Waldman, Ballantine Books, a division of Random House, New York, 2009.

The Genius Factory: The Curious History Of The Nobel Prize Sperm Bank, by David Plotz, Random House, New York, 2005.

Reprinted with permission of Simon & Shuster Publishing Group from *Einstein: His Life and Universe* by Walter Isaacson. Copyright © 2007 by Walter Isaacson.

Every attempt has been made to obtain permission for works used in this book. If your work has been overlooked, please contact the author and you will be acknowledged in future editions.

REFERENCES

Abrams, Michael. "Einstein Inc." *Discover.* March 2008.

Abraham, Carolyn. "Dissecting Genius." *Macleans The New Brain.* 2013, 6–9.

Adams, Missy. Sliced: "Einstein's Brain." *Discover.* March 2008.

Alexander, Eben. *Proof of Heaven: A Neurosurgeon's Journey into the Afterlife.* New York: Simon & Schuster, 2012.

Alcoholics Anonymous Comes of Age: A Brief History of A.A. Alcoholics Anonymous World Service Inc. June 1957.

Armstrong, Thomas, "The Natural Genius of Children," accessed May 30, 2010, http://www.institute4learning.com/natural_genius.

Arthus-Bertrand, Yann. *Earth From Above: 365 Days.* New York: Harry N. Abrams, 2001.

Arthus-Bertrand, Yann. *The New Earth From Above: 365 Days.* New York: Abrams, 2008.

Bach, Richard. *One.* New York: Dell Publishing, 1988.

Bain, Jennifer. "Waste land." *Toronto Star*, January 15, 2011, L1+ L9.

Balkissoon, Denise. "What to do with a huge fortune? Give it away." *Toronto Star,* August 5, 2010, A1+ A14.

Ban Breathnach, Sarah. *Simple Abundance: A Daybook of Comfort and Joy.* New York: Warner Books, 1995.

Bazanova, Olga. "Comments for Current Interpretation EEG Alpha Activity: A Review and Analysis." *Journal of Behavioral and Brain Science* 2, no. 2 (May 2012): 239–248.

Bickel, Bruce and Stan Jantz. *God Is In The Small Stuff.* Uhrichsville: Barbour Publishing, 2002.

Barmak, Sarah. "A Bear Market for Prosperity Theology." *Toronto Star,* October 11, 2008, ID 1+ 6.

Barmak, Sarah. Beware The Urge to Overstuff Your Life. *Toronto Star,* March 28, 2010, IN 1-2.

Belson, Ken and Karen Zraick. "Mourning A Good Friend, and Trying to Make Sense of a Stampede." *New York Times.* November 29, 2008. www.nytimes.com.

Benedict Raffa, Jean. *Dream Theatres of the Soul.* Philadelphia: Innisfree Press, 1994.

Billy Elliot, DVD. Directed by Stephen Daldry. Performed by Jamie Bell, Julie Walters, Jean Heywood. Screenplay by Lee Hall. 2000; Universal Studios Home Entertainment, 2003.

Black, Debra. "Former Justice Honored at Ceremony." *Toronto Star*, April 12, 2008, A22.

Black, Robert. (editor) *Chiron Newsletter of the C.G. Jung Foundation.* 28, no. 2 (April 2009).

Bloom, Jonathan. *American Wasteland: How America Throws Away Nearly Half of Its Food.* Cambridge: DaCapo Lifelong Books, 2010.

Bolte Taylor, Jill. *Stroke of Insight.* February 27, 2008. www.ted.com.

Bolte Taylor, Jill. *My Stroke of Insight: A Brain Scientist's Personal Journey.* New York: Viking Penguin, 2008.

Booth, Phil. "Insight Is On the Way, Taurus." *Toronto Star,* April 7, 2008, L3.

Booth, Phil. "Thought for the Day." June 8, 2013. www.boothstars.com.

Bown, Stephen R. *A Most Damnable Invention: Dynamite, Nitrates, and the Making of the Modern World.* Toronto: Viking Canada, 2005.

Boyle, Alan. "Einstein and Darwin: A tale of Two Theories." April 25, 2005. www.msnb.com.

Boyle, Alan. "Einstein's Revolution Enters Second Century." April 25, 2005. www.msnb.com.

Boyle, Rebecca. "Researchers Achieve Quantum Teleportation Over 10 Miles of Empty Space." (May 2010). www.popsci.com.

Boyle, Theresa. "Illicit Stimulant Use Risky For College Students, Journal Warns." *Toronto Star,* September 7, 2011, GT3.

Braybrooke, Marcus. (editor) *365 Inspirations: Prayers & Blessings.* London: Duncan Baird Publishers, 2007.

Braybrooke, Marcus. *365 Meditations For a Peaceful Heart and a Peaceful World.* New York: Barron's Educational Series, 2004.

Braybrooke, Marcus. *Learn to Pray: A Practical Guide to Faith and Inspiration.* San Francisco: Chronicle Books, 2001.

Buckley, Adele. "Einstein Activist For World Peace." *Toronto Star,* January 13, 2005.

Buettner, Dan. *Blue Zones.* Washington: National Geographic Society, 2008.

Buffett, Warren E. "Stop Coddling the Super-Rich." *New York Times.* August 14, 2011. www.nytimes.com.

Burman, Tony. "Ghosts of Reagan, Thatcher Haunt Today's Economy." *Toronto Star,* November 5, 2011, WD3.

Cain, Susan. *Quiet: The Power of Introverts in a World That Can't Stop Talking.* New York: Broadway Paperbacks, 2012.

CBC News. Plane Fire At Pearson Airport. November 16, 2005. www.cbc.ca.

CBC-TV. *"Are We Digital Dummies?"* The Doc Zone. cbc.ca. November 18, 2010.

Canadian Press. "Mexican Telecom Magnate Becomes 1ˢᵗ Person From Developing World to be Named 'World's Richest.*"* *Toronto Star*, March 10, 2010.

CBS 60 Minutes. *Boosting Brain Power. Wael Ghonim and Egypt's New Age Revolution.* February 13, 2011. April 25, 2010.

CBS 60 Minutes Overtime. *Bill Gates on Steve Jobs: We Grew Up Together.* May 12, 2013.

CBS 60 Minutes. *Bill Gates 2.0.* May 12, 2013.

CBS 60 Minutes Web Extra. *The Giving Pledge: A New Club for Billionaires.* November 17, 2013. www.cbsnews.com/2102-18560_162-57612677

Calamai, Peter. "Building Einstein's Universe." *Toronto Star*, October 2, 2005, D9.

Cannato, Judy. *Radical Amazement Contemplative Lessons from Black Holes, Supernovas, and Other Wonders of the Universe.* Notre Dame: Sorin Books, 2006.

Casey, Karen. *A Woman's Spirit.* Center City: Hazelden Foundation, 1994.

Casey, Karen. *In God's Care.* Hazelden Foundation, 1991.

Chapman, Jamie. *Forbes Report: Billionaires' Wealth Grew by 36 Percent in Last Year.* March 9, 2004. www.wsws.org.

Chilton, David. *The Wealthy Barber Returns.* Kitchener: Financial Awareness Corp., 2011.

Chödrön, Pema. *When Things Fall Apart.* Boston: Shambhala, 1997.

Chopra, Deepak. *Ageless Body, Timeless Mind.* New York: Harmony Books, 1993.

Chown Oved, Marco. "Exploring the Persuasive Power of Meditation." *Toronto Star*, June 7, 2013, E2.

Clifford, Stephanie and Christopher Maag. "For Black Friday First-Timers, Not a Night of Conversion." *New York Times*, November 25, 2011. www.nytimes.com.

Collier, Sandra. *Wake Up To Your Dreams.* Richmond Hill: Scholastic Canada, 1996.

Collodi, Carol. *Pinocchio.* San Francisco: Chronicle Books. 2001.

Corak, Miles. "Promise to World's Children Remains Unkept After 20 Years. *Toronto Star*, November 18, 2009, A27.

Cotroneo, Christian. *Madame Ovary of Bovines. Toronto Star*, August 12, 2005, A2.

Cotterell, Maurice. *The Tutankhamun Prophecies.* London: Headline Book Publishing, 1999.

Crenshaw, Dave. *The Myth of Multitasking: How Doing It All Gets Nothing Done.* New York: John Wiley & Sons, 2008.

Csillag, Ron. "Math + Religion=Trouble." *Toronto Star,* January, 26, 2008.

CTV News. "Women Overtake Men in IQ Tests for the First Time." July 16, 2012. www.ctvnews.ca.

Dale, Daniel. "Youth Rally with Stars, Politicians, Urges Change." *Toronto Star,* October 18, 2008, A6.

David, Ariel and Tom Maliti. "Hunger Stalks a Record 1 Billion People. *Toronto Star,* October 15, 2009, A13.

Davidson, Richard J., and Sharon Begley. *The Emotional Life of Your Brain.* New York: Penguin, 2013.

Davidson, Richard J., Jon Kabat-Zinn, Jessica Schumacher, et al. "Alterations in Brain and Immune Function Produced by Mindfulness Meditation." *Psychosomatic Medicine.* American Psychosomatic Society. 65, (2003): 564-570.

Das, Lama Surya. *Awakening the Buddha Within.* New York: Broadway Books, 1997.

Das, Lama Surya. *Awakening To the Sacred.* New York: Broadway Books, 1999.

Dean, Amy E. *Morning Light.* Center City: Hazelton, 2011.

Deloitte Center for Financial Services. *The Next Decade in Global Wealth Among Millionaire Households.* May 2011.

Dement, William C. *The Promise of Sleep.* New York: Dell Publishing, 1999.

Dickinson, Terence. How Do You Count the Stars in the Sky? *Toronto Star,* May 24, 2005, B5.

Dillow, Clay. *Can Our DNA Electromagnetically 'Teleport Itself?' One Researcher Thinks So.* (January 2011). www.popsci.com.

Doidge, Norman. *The Brain That Changes Itself.* New York: Penguin Books, 2007.

Doolittle, Robyn. Kielburgers to Help Schools in Toronto. *Toronto Star,* April 15, 2009, GT1.

Dolmetsch, Chris and Crayton Harrison. "Mexico's Slim Now Wealthiest Person on Planet: Forbes." *Toronto Star,* March 11, 2010, B8.

Dossey, Larry. *Be Careful What You Pray For.* New York: HarperCollins, 1997.

Duffin, Jacalyn. *Medical Miracles: Doctors, Saints and Healing in the Modern World.* New York: Oxford University Press, 2008.

Dugger, Celia W. "Religious Riots Loom Over Indian Politics." *New York Times,* July 27, 2002.

Edgar Cayce: The Man and His Philosophy. Virginia Beach: Association for Research and Enlightenment. 2013.

Espe Brown, Edward. "Thoughts on Thinking." *Yoga Journal,* November 2001.

Einstein, Albert. *Ideas and Opinions.* New York: Three Rivers Press, 1982.

Farhi, Donna. *The Breathing Book: Good Health and Vitality Through Essential Breath Work.* New York: Henry Holt and Company, 1996.

Fatah, Sonya. "Hindu Mobs Hit Christians." *Toronto Star,* September 22, 2008, AA3.

Fatah, Sonya. "Suicide Rate Growing as Debts Cripples India's Farms." *Toronto Star*, March 24, 2008, AA1.

Ferretti, Andrea. "Wake Up To Your Life." *Yoga Journal,* April 2005.

Fishel, Ruth. *Peace in Our Hearts Peace in the World.* New York: Sterling, 2008.

Flavelle, Dana. "Buying Peak Comes Today.*"* Toronto Star*, December 23, 2005, F1.

Flavelle, Dana. "Top 100 CEOs' Pay Booming Report Finds." January 2, 2014, S10.

Folger, Tim. "One Great Mistake." *Discover Presents Genius,* Winter 2011.

Folger, Tim. "Patently Absurd." *Discover*, March 2008.

Forbes. "The World's Billionaires 2011: Inside the List." March 9, 2011. www.forbes.com.

Forty U.S. Families Take Giving Pledge. Press Release. 4 August 2010. www.givingpledge.org.

Free the Children. *Annual Report 2009.* Special 15th Anniversary Edition, June 2010.

Free the Mind: Can You Rewire The Brain Just By Taking a Breath? Directed by Phie Ambo. Performed by Travis Leanna, Richard Davidson. Written by Phie Ambo. 2012.

Freud, Sigmund. *The Interpretation of Dreams.* New York: Penguin Books, 1991.

Friedman, Harold S. and Leslie R. Martin. *The Longevity Project.* New York: Penguin Group, 2012.

Fromm, Erich. *Psychoanalysis and Religion.* New Haven: Yale University Press, 1967.

Gabaldon, Diana. *Voyageur.* New York: Random House, 1994.

Gaiman, Neil. *Stardust.* New York: Harper Collins, 1999.

Gardner, Howard. *Frames of Mind:The Theory of Multiple Intelligences.* New York: Basic Books, 1983.

Geirland, John. "Buddha on the Brain." February, 2006. www.wired.com.

Gerstel, Judy. "The Genius of Sex Appeal." *Toronto Star,* July 14, 2006, E2.

Gersten, Dennis. *Are You Getting Enlightened or Losing Your Mind?* New York: Three Rivers Press, 1997.

Gibson, Stacey. "Witness to War." *University of Toronto Magazine.* Fall, 2007.

Gilbert, Adrian. *Signs in the Sky Prophecies for the Birth of a New Age.* London: Transworld Publishers, 2000.

Gilles, Charlie. "Nature's Little Secret." *Macleans The New Brain.* 2013, 6-9.

Gilles Wendy, Laura Stone and Josh Tapper. "'Blood everywhere' Tragedy on Train 92 VIA Derailment in Burlington Kills Three, Injures 46." *Toronto Star.* February 27, 2012.

Gladwell, Malcolm. *Blink: The Power of Thinking Without Thinking.* New York: Little Brown, 2005.

Gladwell, Malcolm. *Outliers: The Story of Success.* New York: Little Brown, 2008.

Goldberg Alison, Chuck Collins, Sam Pizzigati, and Scott Klinger. "Unnecessary Austerity Unnecessary Shutdown" *Institute for Policy Studies.* Washington DC. April 2011. www.ips-dc-org/reports.

Golden, Daniel. Building a Better Brain. *Life.* July 1994.

Goodman, Peter S. "A Shopping Guernica Captures a Moment." *New York Times.* November 30, 2008. www.nytimes.com.

Gordhamer, Soren. *Just Say Om!* Avon: Adams Media Corporation, 2001.

Gordon, Andrea. "Blucprint for Living." *Toronto Star,* July 2, 2005, L1-2.

Gorman, Steve. "Text Messaging Figures in L.A. Train Wreck Probe." September 15, 2008. www.reuters.com.

Grannis, Kathy."After Spooky 2009, Halloween Spending Bounces Back to 08 Levels." *National Retail Federation.* September, 2010. www.nrf.com.

Greenfield, Susan, A. ed., *The Human Mind Explained.* Westmount: The Reader's Digest Association (Canada) Ltd. 1996.

Grewal, San. "Ontario Lands Hawking...Finally." *Toronto Star,* June 6, 2010.

Groundhog Day, DVD. Directed by Harold Ramis. Performed by Bill Murray, Andie MacDowell, Chris Elliott. Screenplay by Danny Rubin and Harold Ramis.1993; Sony Home Pictures Ent. 2004.

Gyatso, Tenzin The Dalai Lama. *My Spiritual Journey.* New York: Harper Collins, 2010.

Hallowell, Edward. "Overloaded Circuits: Why Smart People Underperform." *HBR's 10 Must Reads On Managing Yourself.* Harvard Business Press. 2011. www.hbr.org.

Hall, Joseph. "Some Cures Truly are 'Miracles:' Atheist Doctor." *Toronto Star,* October 13, 2010.

Hammond, Corydon D. "Neurofeedback for the Enhancement of Athletic Performance and Physical Balance." *The Journal of the American Board of Sport Psychology.*1, no. 1 (2007): 1-9.

Hanh, Thich Nhat, *Living Buddha, Living Christ.* New York: Riverhead Books, 1995.

Hanh, Thich Nhat. *Peace is Every Step.* New York: Bantam Books, 1991.

Hanh, Thich Nhat. *No Death, No fear.* New York: Riverhead Books, 2002.

Hannaford, Carla. "The Importance of Movement for the Brain." *International Energy Currents.* SpringSummer 2007.

Harbers, Malena. "Protecting Water Draws T.O. Walkers." *Toronto Star,* April 23, 2009, L2.

Harpur, Tom. "Behind the Atheist Upsurge." *Toronto Star*, June 23, 2007, ID6.

Hartigan, Francis. *Bill W.: A Biography of Alcoholic Anonymous Cofounder Bill Wilson.* NewYork: St. Martin's Press, 2000.

Hauck, Dennis William. *The Emerald Tablet.* New York: Penguin, 1999.

Heller, Michelle. *Bathroom Meditations.* Gloucester: Fair Winds Press, 2003.

Henry, Michele. "They shopped Till they Dropped-$1.1B." *Toronto Star,* December 27, 2006. A1.

Hewitt, Katie. "The Art of Necessity." *Toronto Star*, September 26, 2011. U1,U2.

Hilton, James. *Lost Horizon.* The Reader's Digest Association. 1990.

Hinkson, Kamila. "Toronto a Millionaire Magnet, Study Finds." *Toronto Star,* May 19, 2013. A4.

Hluchy, Patricia. "How the 'Master of Death' Spawned a Peace Prize." *Toronto Star.* October 14, 2007, ID 12.

Hoag, Hannah. "No Brawn, No Brains. *Macleans The New Brain*, 2013, 66-68.

Hune-Brown, Nicholas. "Timing is Everything." *Toronto Star.* November 4, 2007, ID1, ID9.

Hutchison, Courtney & Brownstein, Joseph. Girl's 15 Days in Haiti Rubble Raises Survival. January 29, 2010. www.abcnews.com.

Idliby Ranya, Suzanne Oliver, and Priscilla Warner. *The Faith Club.* New York: Free Press, 2006.

Infantry, Ashante. "Singer, Dancer, Humanitarian." *Toronto Star*, May 1, 2007, E6.

Ingpen, Robert & Wilkinson, Philip. *Encyclopedia of Events That Changed the World: Eighty turning points in history.* Surrey: Dragon's World, 1991.

Isaacson, Walter. Chain Reaction. *Discover*, March 2008.

Iaacson, Walter. *Einstein: His Life and Universe.* New York: Simon & Schuster, 2008.

Jackson, Emily. "At Last, Proof Women are Smarter than Men." *Toronto Star,* July 17, 2012.

Javed, Noor. Guru Worries we Won't Win War on Poverty. *Toronto Star,* September 9, 2008, A12.

Johnson, Alex. *The culture of Einstein.* April 25, 2005. www.msnbc.com

Johnson, Alex. *Nutty Professor or One Cool Dude?* April 19, 2005. www.msnbc.com.

Johnson, Robert A. *Balancing Heaven and Earth.* New York: Harper Collins, 1998.

Johnson, Robert A. *Inner Work.* New York: Harper & Row, 1986.

Jumper, DVD. Directed by Doug Liman. Performed by Hayden Christensen, Samuel L. Jackson, Jamie Bell, Rachel Bison, Diane Lane. Screenplay by David S. Goyer, Jim Uhls, Simon Kinberg based on novel by Steven Gould. 2008.

Jung, C. G. *Dreams.* Princeton: Princeton University Press, 1974.

Jung, C. G. *Man and His Symbols.* New York: Doubleday, 1964.

Jung. C. G. *Memories, Dreams, Reflections.* New York: Vintage Books, 1965.

Jung. C. G. *Modern Man in Search of a Soul.* New York: Harcourt Brace Jovanovich, 1933.

Jung. C. G. *Psychology and Religion.* New Haven: Yale University Press, 1970.

Jung. C. G. *Synchronicity An Acausal Connecting Principal.* Princeton University Press, 1973.

Jung. C. G. *The Undiscovered Self with Symbols and the Interpretation of Dreams.* Princeton: Princeton University Press, 1957.

Kaku, Michio. *Parallel Worlds: A Journey Through Creation, Higher Dimensions, and the Future of the Cosmos.* New York: Anchor Books, 2005.

Kaku, Michio. "Through the Wormhole." *Discover*, March 2008.

Kaufman Marc. "Meditation Gives Brain a Charge, Study Finds." *Washington Post.* January, 3, 2005, A05.

Kaye, Danny. Encyclopedia of World Biography. 2005, www.encyclopedia.com.

Kearns, Alan. *The Myth of Multi-tasking.* January, 8, 2009, www.workopolis.com.

Kelly, Cathal. "How Did a Child Survive Libyan Jet Plunge?" *Toronto Star,* May 14, 2010, A19.

Kempermann, Gerd and Fred H. Gage. "New Nerve Cells for the Adult Brain." *Scientific American,* May 1999, 38-44.

Kidd, Kenneth. "Lady's Man A Picture and A Thousand Words on Why Einstein was Such a Babe Magnet." *Toronto Star,* October 23, 2005.

Kielburger, Craig, and Marc Kielburger. "How the Iraq War's $2 Trillion Cost to U.S. Could Have Been Spent." *Toronto Star.* 21 January 21, 2008, AA2.

Keilburger, Craig, and Marc Kielburger. "Children in China Pay Price for our Cheap Toys." *Toronto Star.* December 17, 2007, AA2.

Kielburger, Craig, and Marc Kielburger. "Invest in People Not Weapons." *Toronto Star,* March 24, 2008, AA2.

Kielburger, Craig, and Marc Kielburger. *Me to We :Finding Meaning in a Material World.* Mississauga: John Wiley & Sons Canada, 2006.

Kielburger, Craig, and Marc Kielburger. *The World Needs Your Kid.* Vancouver: Greystone Books, 2009.

Kimen, Shel. *The Power of Genius.* Spring 2003. www.klever.org.

Kirk, Harvey. "Stars Believe Truth is Out There." *Toronto Star,* August 25, 2011.

Kirkpatrick, Sidney D. *Edgar Cayce: An American Prophet.* New York: Riverhead Books, 2000.

Kirkpatrick, Sidney D. "Edgar Cayce: Missing in Action." *The Open Road.* Spring 2013.

Kirkpatrick, Sidney D. "Ghostly Visitations." *The Open Road.* Fall 2013.

Klinger, Scott. "The Cavernous Divide: More Billionaires, More Poverty." March 19, 2005. www.commondreams.org.

Kocieniewski, David. "A Closer Look at Taxes on the Rich." *New York Times.* August 15, 2011, www.nytimes.com.

Krishnamurti. *Freedom From the Known.* New York: Harper & Rowe, 1969.

Kroll, Luisa, and Allison Fass. (editors) "The World's Richest People. " March 2008, www.forbes.com.

Kroll, Luisa. "The World's Billionaires 2011: Inside the List." March 2011. www.forbes.com.

Laidlaw, Stuart. "Embracing Goodness, Without God." *Toronto Star*, August 2, 2008. L1+ L4.

Lamott, Anne. *Bird by Bird: Some Instructions on Writing and Life.* New York: Anchor Books, 1994.

Lang, Becky, ed., Einstein's Universe Collector's Edition. *Discover Magazine.* Summer 2013.

Lazar, Sara W., Catherine EKerr, Rachel H Wasserman, et al. "Meditation Experience is Associated with Increased Cortical Thickness." *NeuroReport* 16. no. 17 (November 28, 2005): 1893-1897.

Lawless, Jill. "Einstein Thought Religion 'Childish.'" *Toronto Star,* May 13, 2008.

Lee, Harper. *To Kill A Mockingbird.* New York: Warner Books, 1960.

Legge, David. Sermon. "Is Heaven a Physical Place. Glimpses of Glory Part 2." Belfast: Ireland. 2007, www.preachtheword.com.

Levenson, Thomas. "Albert the Icon." *Discover,* March 2008.

Levin, Alan. "Pilot James Freudenbert Crashes Medical Helicopter Because of Texting." April 9, 2013. www.bloomberg.com.

Lightman, Alan. *Einstein's Dreams.* New York: Vintage Books, 2004.

Lindbergh, Anne Morrow. *Gift from the Sea.* New York: Pantheon Books, 1955.

Lin, Derek. *The Tao of Joy Every Day: 365 Days of Tao Living.* New York: Jeremy P. Tarcher, 2011.

Lu Vanessa. "Ranks of Rich Set to Swell." *Toronto Star.* May 6, 2011, B1+ B5.

Luo, Michael. "Preaching a Gospel of Wealth in a Glittery Market." *New York Times*, January 15, 2006. www.nytimes.com.

Lutz, Antoine, Lawrence L. Greischar, Nancy B. Rawlings, et al. "Long-Term Meditators Self-Induce High-Amplitude Gamma Synchrony During Mental Practice." Proceedings of the National Academy of Sciences. October 6, 2004.

Macfarquhar, Neil. "Ruthless Despot Kept Unflinching Hold on Iraq." *Toronto Star*, December 30, 2006, A3.

MacLaine, Shirley. *The Camino.* New York. Pocket Books, 2000.

Mackenzie, Norman. *Dreams and Dreaming.* London: Bloomsbury Books, 1965.

Martin, Ricky. *Me.* New York: Penguin Group, 2011.

Mcfadden, Robert D. and Angela Macropoulos. "Wal-Mart Worker Trampled." *Toronto Star,*November, 29, 2008, A3.

McGowan, Kathleen. *The Poet Prince.* New York: Touchstone, 2010.

Mehra, Natalie. Ontario Common Front. *Falling Behind: Ontario's Backslide into Widening Inequality, Growing Poverty and Cuts to Social Programs.* August 29, 2012.

Merton, Thomas. *New Seeds of Contemplation.* New York: New Directions,1961.

Merton, Thomas. *The Seven Storey Mountain.* Orlando: Harcourt, 1998.

Miller, Matthew G. and Peter Newcomb. "World's Richest Add $524 Billion To Net Worth." *Toronto Star,* January 3, 2014, S10.

Million Dollar Baby, DVD. Directed by Clint Eastwood. Performed by Clint Eastwood, Hilary Swank, Morgan Freeman. Screenplay by Paul Haggis, F.X Toole. 2005; Warner Home Video, 2010.

Millman, Dan. *Everyday Enlightenment: The Twelve Gateways to Personal Growth.* New York: Warner Books, 1998.

Mishra, Sandeep. "One Killed in Fresh Flare-up in Kandhamal." *Toronto Star,* October 1, 2008.

Monroe, Robert, A. *Journeys Out of the Body.* New York: Doubleday, 1973.

Monroe, Robert. A. *Far Journeys.* New York: Broadway Books, 1986.

Monroe, Robert, A. *Ultimate Journey.* New York: Broadway Books, 1994.

Monsebraaten, Laurie. "Canada Urged to Invest in Poor." *Toronto Star,* September 28, 2011.

Montagnier L., Aissa J., Del Giudice E., Lavalle C., Tedeschi A., and Vitiello G. *DNA Waves and Water.* December 23, 2010. www.arxiv.org.

Moore Thomas. *Care of the Soul: A Guide for Cultivating Depth and Sacredness in Everyday Life.* New York: Harper Collins, 1992.

Moorjani, Anita. *Dying to Be Me: My Journey from Cancer, To Near Death to True Healing.* New York: Hay House, 2012.

Mueller, Charles. "Wealth Distribution Statistics–1999." United Nations Development Program. www.cooperativeindividualism.org/wealth_distribution1999.

Myer, Stephanie. *The Host.* New York: Little, Brown and Company, 2008.

Myss, Carolyn. *Invisible Acts of Power: Channeling Grace in Your Everyday Life.* New York: Free Press, 2004.

Myss, Carolyn. *Sacred Contracts Awakening Your Divine Potential.* New York: Harmony Books, 2001.

Myss, Carolyn. "January Salon: What To Do While Waiting Under Your Bodhi Tree." January 2007. www.myss.com.

Myss, Carolyn. "December Salon: A Message of Hope and Inspiration. " December. 2008. www.myss.com.

Myss, Carolyn and Norman Shealy. *The Creation of Health.* New York: Three Rivers Press, 1988.

Mystic Places. Time-Life Books. Alexandria: Virginia, 1987.

Mystical Brain Scientists Meet Spirituality Head-On. DVD. Directed by Isabelle Raynauld. National Film Board of Canada. 2006.

National Council of Welfare. *The Dollars and Sense of Solving Poverty.* Volume #130, Autumn 2011.

Ndikubwayezu, Gilbert. "No Room for Improvement Here." *Toronto Star.* July 11, 2011, A3.

Neffe, Jürgen. *Einstein: A Biography.* New York: Farrar, Straus and Giroux, 2007.

Nelson, Kevin. *The Spiritual Doorway in the Brain: A Neurologist's Search for the God Experience.* New York: Dutton, 2011.

Nepo, Mark. *The Book of Awakening.* San Francisco: Conart Press, 2000.

Nhat Hanh, Thich. *Peace is Every Step: The Path of Mindfulness in Everyday Life.* New York: Bantam Books, 1992.

Nichols John. "Michael Moore on Leno: "Capitalism is Legalized Greed.'" September 17, 2009.
www.michaelmoore.com/words/mike-in-the-news/michael-moore-on-leno-capitalism.

Niffenegger, Audrey. *The Time Traveler's Wife.* Toronto: Random House, 2004.

Newberg, Andrew and Mark Robert Waldman. *How God Changes Your Brain.* New York: Ballantine Books, 2009.

Newton, Michael. *Destiny of Souls.* Llewellyn: St. Paul, 1994.

Newton, Michael. *Journey of Souls.* Llewellyn: St. Paul, 2001.

Nutt, Samantha. *Namned Nations Greed Guns Armies and Aid.* McClelland & Stewart Ltd: Toronto, 2011.

Nutt, Samantha. Warchild newsletter. May 16, 2012.

Ody, Elizabeth. "Carlos Slim Tops Forbes List of Billionaires for Second Year." *Bloomberg News.* March 10, 2011. www.bloomberg.com.

Oh, God!, DVD. Directed by Carl Reiner. Performed by John Denver, George Burns, Teri Garr. Screenplay by Larry Gelbart, based on the novel by Avery Corman. 1977; Warner Home Video, 2002.

Olive, Dave. "Benign Builder of Family Empire." *Toronto Star.* June 13, 2006, D1 + D18.

Ouzounian, Richard. "Devoted To a Cause." *Toronto Star.* September 14, 2009, E1+ E5.

Overbye, Dennis. "Einstein Letter on God Sells for $404,000." *New York Times.* May 17, 2008. www.nytimes.com.

Panek, Richard. "The E Factor." *Discover*, March 2008.

Paterniti, Michael. *Driving Mr. Albert*. New York: Dell Publishing, 2000.

Penrose, Chris. "Science has Seen the Future. And It Is Invisible." *Toronto Star*. April, 12, 2008, 1D7.

Petrou, Michael. "New World Order." *Macleans*, February 28, 2011.

Pevere, Geoff. "To Kill a Finch." *Toronto Star*, August 7, 2010, E4.

Phillips, Joseph. "The World of Albert Einstein*." Great Lives Great Deeds*. London: Reader's Digest Association, 1965.

Pickover, Clifford. A. *Strange Brains and Genius The Secret Lives of Eccentric Scientists and Madmen*. New York: William Morrow and Company, 1998.

Plotz, David. *The Genius Factory: The Curious History of the Nobel Prize Sperm Bank*. New York: Random House, 2005.

Plotz, David. *The Genius Generation*. April 15, 2004. www.guardian.co.uk

Plotz, David. *The Nobel Sperm Bank Celebrity*. March 16, 2001. www.slate.com.

Poor No More, DVD. Directed by Bert Deveaux. Hosted by Mary Walsh. A film by Deveauz Babin, producer Susan Babin, executive producer David Langille. 2010 Deveaux Babin Productions.

Porter, Catherine. "Yes, that Sean Penn Is Helping in Haiti." *Toronto Star*, April 18, 2010, A1.

Porter, Catherine. Who Will Care for the Miracle Named Jonatha? *Toronto Star*, January 25, 2010, A1.

Powell, Anita. Actor Using Star Power to Highlight Congo Crisis. *Toronto Star*, November 21, 2008, AA1.

Prayers for Healing. Berkeley: Conari Press, 1997.

Pullman, Philip. *The Golden Compass*. New York: Random House, 1995.

Pullman, Philip. *The Subtle Knife*. New York: Random House, 1997.

Pullman, Philip. *The Amber Spyglass*. New York: Random House, 2000.

Rakaff, Todd D. *A Time for Every Purpose Law and the Balance of Life*. Cambridge: Harvard University Press, 2002.

Redfield, James. *The Celestine Prophecy*. New York: Time Warner, 1993.

Redfield, James. *The Celestine Vision*. New York: Time Warner, 1997.

Regis. Ed. Genius at Work. *Discover*, March 2008.

Reuters News Agency. "More billionaires Sign Pledge To Donate Wealth." December 10, 2010, www.reuters.com.

Reuters News Agency. "Train engineer Was Texting Just Before California Crash." October 2, 2008. www.reuters.com.

Ricky Martin Foundation. www.rickymartinfoundation.org.

Rinpoche, Sogyal. *The Tibetan Book of Living and Dying.* New York: Harper Collins, 1993.

Ritter, Arl. "Betting on a Nobel Prize." *Toronto Star*, October 3, 2005.

Roland, Paul. *Revelations Wisdom of the Ages.* Berkley: Ulysses Press, 1995.

Rogers, Paul. Candy Industry. Annual R&D Survey. 2004. www.candyindustry.com.

Roisen, Mike and Mehmet Oz. "Here's How To Help Your Child Avoid Digital Deficit." *Toronto Star,* August, 14, 2012, E8.

Roisen, Mike and Mehmet Oz. "Meditation, Strange Cravings and the DASH Diet." *Toronto Star,* November 4, 2010, L2.

Rosenfield Daniel, Paul Hebert, Matthew Stanbrook, Ken Flegel, and Noni MacDonald. "Time to Address Stimulant Abuse on Our Campuses." *Canadian Medical Association Journal.* 183, no.12 (September 6, 2011): 1345.

Ross, Oakland. "Nobel Prize 'Sends a Message.'" *Toronto Star,* October 8, 1995.

Ross, Oakland. "The Mystery of all Mysteries." *Toronto Star,* August 11, 2012. IN1, IN4, IN5.

Rowling, J.K. *Harry Potter and the Philosopher's Stone.* London: Bloomsbury Publishing, 1997.

Ruvinsky, Jessica. "Keeping Up With the Picards." *Discover,* March 2008.

Sachs, Jeffrey. *The End of Poverty.* New York: Penguin. 2005.

Sakai, Jill. "Study Reveals Gene Expression Changes With Meditation." December 4, 2013. www.news.wisc.edu/22370.

Samsara, DVD. Directed by Pan Nalin. Performed by Shawn Ku, Christy Chung, Neelesha Bavora. Screenplay by Pan Nalin and Tim Baker. 2001. DVD release 2003.

Sanford, John. A. *Dreams: God's Forgotten Language.* New York: Harper Collins, 1968.

Sattler. Jerome M. *Assessment of Children.* San Diego: Jerome M Sattler, 1988.

Savery, Louis M., Patricia H Berne, and Strephon Kaplan Williams. *Dreams and Spiritual Growth.* Ramsay: Paulist Press, 1984.

Scrivener, Leslie. "Being Smart Isn't Always a Good Thing." *Toronto Star,* January 27, 2008, ID4.

Scrivener, Leslie. "How To Be a 100 percent   Student." *Toronto Star.* July 18, 2010, IN 1+ 4-5.

Scrivener, Leslie. "Fight over God Splits GTA Alcoholics." *Toronto Star*, June 4, 2011.

Scrivener, Leslie. "The Hollywood Halo." *Toronto Star,* October 3, 2010.

Scanlon, Lawrence. "Shaking the Foundations of Charity." *Toronto Star,* November 19, 2006. D1+10.

Segaller, Stephen and Merrill Berger. *Jung The Wisdom of the Dream.* London: George Weidenfeld & Nicolson Limited, 1989.

Seuss. Dr. *Bartholomew and the Oobleck.* New York: Random House, 1977.

Seuss. Dr. *Green Eggs and Ham.* New York: Random House, 1968.

Seuss. Dr. *Horton Hears a Who!* New York: Random House, 1954.

Seuss. Dr. *The Lorax.* New York: Random House, Reprinted 1999.

Seuss. Dr. *The Sneetches and Other Stories.* New York: Random House, 1961.

Seuss. Dr. *The Tough Coughs As He Ploughs the Dough.* New York: William Morrow, 1987.

Sequera, Vivian. "Columbian Jet Crash 'Miracle.'"*Toronto Star,* August 17, 2010.

Shah, Anup. Povery Facts and Stats. September 20, 2010. www.globalissues.org.

Shearer, Ann. *Athene Image and Energy.* New York: Penguin Books, 1996.

Shipp, E.R. "By Sitting She Stood for Millions. *Toronto Star,* October 25, 2005.

Siegel, Alan B. *Dreams That Can Change Your Life.* Los Angeles: Jeremy Tarcher, 1990.

Siegel, Dr. Bernie S. *365 Prescriptions for the Soul.* Novato: New World Library, 2004.

Simonton, Dean. "Spark Genius." *Discover Presents Genius,* Winter 2011.

Starkman, Randy. "From Paralympian to Pro Cyclist." *Toronto Star,* November 26, 2011.

Steed, Judy. "Yes, You Can." *Toronto Star,* November 13, 2008, L1+ L4.

Steptoe, Sonja. *Defining a New Deficit Disorder.* January, 8, 2006. www.time.com.

Stern, Jared Paul. "How Many Millionaires Are There In the World?" February 2011. www.luxist.com.

Sugrue, Thomas. *The Story of Edgar Cayce: There Is a River.* Virginia Beach: Association for Research and Enlightenment, 1989.

Talbot, Michael. *The Holographic Universe.* New York: Harper Collins, 1991.

Taylor, Kylea. *The Ethics of Caring.* Santa Cruz: Hanford Mead Publishers, 1995.

The Body Machine. Written, co-produced, and directed by Robin Bicknell, hosted by Laine Drewery, Discovery Channel, November 30, 2008.

Thomas, Ken. "Thank you, Rosa Parks." *Toronto Star,* October 31, 2005.

Thomson, Sandra A. *Cloud Nine A Dreamer's Dictionary.* New York: Avon Books, 1994.

Thurlow, Ann. "How to Live to be 100 or More." *The Old Farmer's 2009 Almanac.* Canadian Edition. Dublin. Yankee Publishing, 2008.

Tissier, Adrian. (editor) *Poems from Other Centuries.* Essex: Longman Group Limited, 1994.

Tresidder, Jack. *Dictionary of Symbols.* San Francisco: Chronicle Books, 1997.

Turnbull, Barbara. "A Love Built on Helping Others." *Toronto Star,* March 9, 2009, L5.

Turnbull, Barbara. "Emergency Aid is Not a Cure." *Toronto Star,* December 6, 2011.

Turnbull, Barbara. "New Documentary Highlights Meditation's Healing Power." *Toronto Star,* June 5, 2013, E6.

Van Auken, John. *From Karma to Grace.* Virginia Beach: A.R.E Press. 2010.

Valtorta, Maria. *The Poem of the Man-God.* Volume One. Centro Editoriale Valtortiano, 1989.

Van de Castle, Robert. *Our Dreaming Mind.* New York: Ballantine Books, 1994.

VanZant, Ilyana. *One Day My Soul Just Opened Up.* New York: Fireside, 1998.

Veropedia. Albert Einstein. http://en.veropedia.com/vero/article.php?title=Albert+Einstein.

Ward, Olivia. "How to Feed a Hungry Billion." *Toronto Star*, November 16, 2009, A4.

Ward, Olivia. "Our Physicist Popstar." *Toronto Star*, January 9, 2005, A3.

Ward, Olivia. "Gates Pledges $1.5 Billion to Aid Women." *Toronto Star.* June 8, 2010, A12.

Warren, Jeff. *The Head Trip: Adventures on the Wheel of Consciousness.* Toronto: Vintage Canada, 2008.

White, Nancy J. "This is Your Brain on God." *Toronto Star,* April 21, 2009, L1+7.

Wilkinson, Philip & Ingpen, Robert. *Encyclopedia of Events that Changed the World: Eighty Turning Points in History.* Surrey: Dragon's World, 1991.

Will, Clifford. "Was Einstein Right?" *Toronto Star,* October 2, 2005. D1+4.

Williamson, Marianne. *A Return to Love*: *Reflections on the Principles of A Course in Miracles.* New York: Harper Collins, 1994.

Williamson, Marianne. *Everyday Grace: Having Hope, Finding Forgiveness, and Making Miracles.* New York: Riverhead Books, 2002.

Williamson, Marianne. *The Gift of Change: Spiritual Guidance for Living Your Best Life.* New York: Harper Collins, 2004.

Women for Women International. *Democratic Republic of the Congo Factsheet.* Washington, 2008.

World Health Organization. "Obesity and Overweight." Fact Sheet N311, September 2006, March 2013.

Yogananda, Paramahansa. *Autobiography of a Yogi.* Los Angeles: Self-Realization Fellowship, 1999.

Zackheim, Michele. "Children of a Lesser God." *Discover*, March 2008.

Zerbisias, Antonia. "Can Unions Save Middle Class?" *Toronto Star,* September 1, 2012, IN 1, 4, 5.

Zimmerman Jones, Andrew, and Daniel Robbins. "String Theory for Dummies." Accessed July 27, 2013.
Http://www.dummies.com/hot-to/content/string-theory-for-dummies-cheat-sheet.html.

INDEX

CPSIA information can be obtained at www.ICGtesting.com
Printed in the USA
LVOW08s0602300514

387808LV00003B/26/P